THE
ENERGY
PEOPLE

THE ENERGY PEOPLE

A History of PSE&G

by James C. G. Conniff
and
Richard Conniff

PUBLISHED BY
PUBLIC SERVICE ELECTRIC AND GAS COMPANY
NEWARK, NEW JERSEY

ISBN: 0-9602014-1-6

Library of Congress Catalog Card Number: 78-6693

Manufactured in the United States of America by Rae Publishing Co., Inc., Cedar Grove,
New Jersey.

This book is dedicated to the many thousands of men and women of the Public Service Electric and Gas Company, its subsidiaries and its predecessor corporations—and the families of those men and women—who materially, and in certain ways dramatically, improved the quality of life and the economic well-being of their fellow citizens of New Jersey.

CONTENTS

AUTHORS' PREFACE 1
THE GAS ERA BEGINS 23
GAS MAKING MOVES AHEAD 29
ELECTRICITY COMES TO NEWARK 39
FROM HORSECARS TO ELECTRIC CARS 57
McCARTER TAKES OVER 67
McCARTER THROUGH THE EYES OF A
    GRANDSON 71
P.S. TRANSPORT'S ROCKY START 79
THE TROLLEY AND FERRY BUSINESS BOOMS 93
GAS SYSTEM EXPANDS 105
INTERCONNECTION: THE FIRST
    ELECTRIC TIES 123
RUMSONHILL 139
POWER AND CONTROL 151
THE SQUIRE AT HOME AND AT WORK 165
TRANSPORT AND POLITICS .187
COMPETITION ARRIVES IN THE JITNEY 213
THE METER MAN 237
GAS USE GROWS 247
PIPELINE GAS ARRIVES 267
POST WORLD WAR I POWER 281
THE BOOM TWENTIES 293
THE THIRTIES 319
THE FORTIES 335
THE LAST QUARTER-CENTURY AND THE
    FUTURE 343
SUMMING UP 363
INDEX 382

A gaslight glow with a shadow of irony; the building in the background in West Orange is Rosemont, the home of Thomas Alva Edison, whose success with the electric light bulb gradually dimmed gas as a source of street lighting.

AUTHORS' PREFACE

"Keep the reader constantly in mind."
—Samuel Eliot Morison
History as a Literary Art

The great American naval historian Samuel Eliot Morison—who was with us until just recently, spinning salty prose into his nineties—would have enjoyed knowing the man behind this book. Morison rejoiced that "professional historians ... like Allan Nevins" had been "trained in some juicier profession like journalism." He felt that helped them to avoid doing what too many academic historians seem unable to steer clear of: Writing "dull, solid, valuable monographs" that nobody else will ever read except, possibly, other professors. Morison was a crusty old expert writer-mariner who made seafaring live on paper from Viking days to Okinawa and beyond. For him, writers like Nevins broke what Morison called "the chain reaction of dullness," a force which he contended had vaporized the imaginative powers of an entire generation. Morison himself was bringing the past to life, until the day he died, with an imagination of his own that was almost big enough to fill the historian's generation gap. Part of his secret was having made the most of a keen eye and ear for the telling anecdote, all his days.

Arthur F. Lenehan, general manager of information
services for Public Service Electric and Gas Company
(PSE&G), trained in that "juicier profession" of journalism,
shares that equipment. This book, which was his idea and
reflects his kind of experience, will therefore undertake to
demonstrate, to the extent it can, what Morison had in mind.

For instance, Lenehan tells a story about how he came to
PSE&G. As a former newsman, Lenehan likes to tell stories.
Like most newsmen, he has a fund of them. This particular
yarn, though, has a special meaning for the pages you are
about to take your chances reading.

When the opportunity arose, well over a decade ago, for
Art to handle the communication chores of New Jersey's
biggest public utility—the third largest combination gas and
electric company in America—he had some qualms. First, he
no longer would be asking the questions, he would be
answering them. What was more important to him, however,
was the manner in which he would be allowed to answer. He
expressed his queasiness to Donald C. Luce, who was then
PSE&G's president. Luce, an open and direct man, told him
what he wanted to hear.

"Just tell the truth," said Luce.

That assurance meant a lot to Lenehan. He figured that, as
a magazine writer and a newsman, he had been doing his
best to dig out the truth and tell it for years. It was a habit he
did not care to lose. Not, after all, when his commitment to
the facts was at that rarefied level which denizens of city
rooms everywhere like to think is peculiarly theirs.

Yet here he was going to the corporate side, a step your
veteran newsperson does not lightly take, and never did. In
Art's case, however, it was his complete confidence that he
would *still* be able to level with his former colleagues that
helped him make up his mind. It was a nice feeling.

It continues to sustain him, or you would not be reading
this book—a history that was commissioned with no strings
attached and no sacred cows fenced off.

As any man with a taste for history knows, the company's
early years were intriguingly rough-and-tumble. Anyone

who sifts the old annual reports and combs yellowing newspaper files at times too fragile to handle except with utmost care, or has the unforgettable opportunity to interview pensioners with a gleam in their eye and a yen to help recreate the way things were "back then," cannot help but observe a pattern of seemingly endless battle for survival.

Large corporations were not popular then—as they are not now. As the founder of Public Service—Thomas N. McCarter—put it: "The fad of the day is to imprint upon the brow of success the scarlet letter of sin."

While there are similarities between the early days and today, there is also one big difference. Public Service could make many more things happen in its early days than it can now. Today the embattled utility finds itself stymied at virtually every turn.

Robert I. Smith, PSE&G's current chairman of the board and chief executive officer, made note of that recently in a talk to middle management.

"Mr. McCarter," Smith said, "seems to have had more success in influencing the legislature and the governor than John McDonald (senior vice president of governmental affairs) and I have had. An article in *Fortune* during the 1930s reports that 'on the whole, Public Service is pretty successful in having legislation either killed or enacted, according to its wishes.' How times have changed!" Smith remarked.

In passing, it seems only fair to single out for special mention the way the echoes of that battle for survival seem to have haunted the lives of two recently deceased children of the individual who founded the company, Tom McCarter's daughters, Ellen McCarter Doubleday and Madeleine McCarter Kelly, both of whom survived long enough to be interviewed while this book was being written. The fires of the father still burned bright in these remarkable women during interviews, as did other human propensities of his, so that they were able to reveal intimate details of the reverse side of the tapestry during the 45 years their parent worked with, then dominated, and finally fought with many of his associates. The elder daughter Ellen, traces of the beautiful woman she once was still present in her features well past 70, will be hard to forget—maneuvering her angled black cane, a box of Ritz crackers under one arm, serving at the same time a tray of Bloody Marys during her fascinating narrative of what it was like to live in a mansion with McCarter, and what the effect on him was of his daily battles for, and at, Public Service. And the spirited younger daughter, Madeleine, asking an interviewer to make the drinks— "a *very* dry Martini for me, please, straight up"—and, inspecting the result, suggesting that he "float a touch of dry sherry on top, would you? We may as well go to hell in a handbasket," all the while pouring out story after story about her father, interspersed with merry cries of "I'll sue you if you print that!" Tom McCarter must have been quite a man to have begotten such offspring, and to have been able to evoke, so long after his death, a river of recollection on whose surface glinted and flashed anew the blinding coruscations of fireworks long extinguished.

Survival. A word with ominous overtones for anyone caught up, as we all are now willy-nilly, in Isaiah's "day of trouble, and of treading down, and of perplexity" for the energy industry everywhere. But, as we said, there were problems of survival back then too, different yet every bit as real.

It isn't necessary for the historian to know a Deion grid from a pothead, for example, to appreciate the kind of survival the work crews knew as they built the electric distribution systems and laid the gas mains. Even without technical knowledge, the ever-shifting challenge of their milieu comes across in crisp, clear images as the oldsters spin their yarns with voices still sure and powerful. For the historian lucky enough to be on the receiving end of such gut material, the story of PSE&G seems to home in less and less on feisty maneuverings of acquisition or how you wring the water out of stock or make epic descents into the money markets to finance the endless upbuilding of plant and service. Neither does it dwell to excess on any of the other vital but dry-as-furnace-dust details of an industry where, most outsiders persist in believing, imagination is about as much of an asset as a two-day beard on a bishop. Those areas are obviously important. But the kind of thing which brightens that picture for the reader is the way oldtimers interweave their knowledge of technical information with interesting tidbits. Trolley car legends. Flywheels as things of great beauty and awful hazard. Paul Bunyan-type feats in building the Interconnection. Trolleys painted in full color and from every angle on precious silk, works of art that were, incredibly, thrown out. The company's platoon of hall girls. The secret elevator door. Submarine squadrons in Trenton. And much more.

In ways more subtle and shifting than any of the physical challenges involved in making the company become what it is, there was the early struggle with self-appointed, politically ambitious champions of a public that the new and expanding utility was doing its best to serve. The record in this area is juicier, at times, than all but the best of the oldtimers' tidbits.

Read environmentalists and regulators for old-line politicians and you might say that things haven't changed all that much in this 75th anniversary year.

Tom McCarter put his brand deep into the hide of New Jersey. He did it in ways that no longer hold as an acceptable approach in utility circles or, for that matter, in many other circles this side of the Iron Curtain. For well over a half-century, he played in the day-to-day affairs of the commonwealth he loved almost fanatically, a role of naked power-wielding which was perhaps unexampled outside the State House and the legislatures. On not a few occasions his endeavors took him inside. "Far on the ringing plains" that triangulate the northern and central counties, during years when work crews often struggled through howling winds and snowdrifts *on foot* to restore power to storm-isolated communities served by an industry which was then just aborning, Tom McCarter "drunk delight of battle with his peers" to make of his fledgling enterprise the condor of power technology it was to become. Almost invariably, he won. His influence persists visibly throughout New Jersey to this day.

He came close to reaching 90, and was a living legend for most of the decades of his prime, and beyond. He exercised directly over the lives of thousands of employees, and indirectly over many aspects of daily existence for better than three-quarters of the State's population, what was possibly the nearest thing to autocratic control over large territory since Britain's pre-Arthurian kings. The life-style to which he accustomed himself with the practiced ease of a man whose upbringing had prepared him rather well for it may have played a part, the story goes, in stoking the imaginative fires of F. Scott Fitzgerald. The good life he and his family shared when day was done survives now, to the extent that it survives at all, in such vestigial enclaves as Hyannis Port and The Pocantico Hills.

Tom McCarter's admirers are an arcane fraternity. The members draw deep on any recollection of those good old days as if it were an expensive cigar. They still think of the fiery, chronically overweight redhead who in 1903 put together Public Service, as "a man cut from the same cloth as Harvey Firestone and Thomas Alva Edison." Possibly so. By the time he was 35 McCarter had been the youngest attorney general in the State's history, and a senator and judge as well. He hammered and wrestled hundreds of ailing (and some not so ailing, but vulnerable) little local gas and electric companies from the Hudson to the Delaware into what PSE&G is today. But he was neither an inventor nor a trailblazer in quite the same sense as those two milestone figures of American industrial expansion, although he undeniably energized his share of it.

What McCarter was, among other things, was a shrewd, give-no-quarter, advantage-seeking but, in the end, always honorable scrapper. He was a sawed-off, tough-minded, hard-voiced, articulate, Princeton-educated and Columbia-trained lawyer of old New Jersey stock who had a vision very much in the tradition of that freebooting era, and the vitality, staying-power, skill and sense of opportunity to make the most of that vision. On those counts, with interesting variations of a kind you would expect in an age of rugged individuals, there is some reason to draw the parallel his admirers still draw.

Old Tom McCarter's more numerous critics, on the other hand, take a less exalted view. They keep in perspective his considerable accomplishment, it's true, and are grateful to him—when they bother to make the connection—for all things which, up to now, they could plug in and switch on without thinking twice, along with the gas they cook and heat with. But they also delight, humanly, in cutting him and his memory, if not into tiny pieces, at least down to size. God knows he was human enough himself, and gave them plenty to work with. Because more often than not McCarter's critics simply lack insight into both the man and the mores of his time, however, they tend to admire him not at all. In the granite mausoleum at the far corner of a little graveyard on Rumson Road in Rumson, N.J., Tom McCarter thus becomes not the only man to have the good he did interred with his bones. Perhaps these stereopticon dissolves may reveal something of what made him tick, and help restore the balance a little.

Admittedly, the man's incandescent approach to people and situations he regarded as even slightly threatening to his interests, which he always identified with those of his company, makes it difficult, even in retrospect, to take a temperate view of him. In the end, he himself is the reason why critics impugn with flailing vigor his—for them—still white-hot memory, and even his rather impeccable origins. Ask the dignified old-timers still around who knew Tom McCarter if they will share an anecdote or two, for instance, and more often than not they fly off the handle as if you'd stung them with a cattle-prod or raised their electric bill again. *"What!"* one old lawyer bellowed. "You want me to talk about *that* old '@#!!%#!!!&?%#!!!?" The spry irascibility with which they resort to such language is little short of amazing. They don't talk that way about PSE&G. Just about its founder. One such vituperative commentator said, in

addition, that his mother—"an otherwise good and upstand-
ing Presbyterian lady"—used to shoo him under the turnstile
on PS trolleys long after he was 12 because, she told him, "It's
all right to cheat Tom McCarter."

Thomas Nesbit McCarter nurtured a lifelong conviction
that, since he had founded a company and begotten a family,
they were therefore his. He was not the first man to suffer
from that delusion, but in his case there were certain critical
differences. For one thing, he called the company Public
Service—a name he took literally as meaning just that:
service to the public. For the 36 years he was its president, he
felt under no mandate to consider, at the personal level, any
life or lives but his own when it came to a contest of interests.
It was a suzerainty-type operation that expanded so inexora-
bly and at such speed that, had a time-lapse movie of the
uncoiling tentacles of gas mains and power lines into county
after county been possible, it would have looked more like
the too-fast action in an early Pearl White episode at the
nickelodeon. The enterprise, moreover, had to depend
during that evolutionary phase on strong hands and
foresight. In McCarter they were concentrated in a single
entrepreneur, capable of changing course rapidly, with
chess-player skill, in anticipation of coming events, and
capitalizing on those changes. He sometimes went wide of
the target. For example, betting on the electric railway and
public transport to the extent he did as the likeliest avenues
of expansion for Public Service was an early misinterpreta-
tion of future trends in which he had company . Otherwise,
in words and action at every turn McCarter left no one in
doubt that he considered himself to be the repository of that
foresight. This was especially true as the regulatory structure
tightened around him. Though he fought it tooth and nail,
he made clear his position that in hands less able than his
own, the whole undertaking might on one occasion or
another have bucked out of control—his control.

For nearly half a century, McCarter ran Public Service
Electric and Gas Company with a brassy know-how and
unflagging self-confidence that brooked no nonsense from

anyone. That meant every conceivable obstacle to Tom McCarter's forward drive for PS, up to and including Franklin D. Roosevelt and his philosophy of government competition for stockholder-owned public utilities via TVA-type installations. McCarter did not limit his warwhooping assaults to FDR and what McCarter saw as "that man's" anti-free enterprise machinations, however. In addition, smiting hip and thigh in every direction that looked even remotely menacing, he struck out manfully at State and local-level encroachment maneuvers also. Like an early flamethrower that had somehow learned to aim and take evasive action at the same time, he drew effective beads on such targets nearer to home as Woodrow Wilson, vocally opposing with every well-nourished fiber of his being Wilson's anti-utility Seven Sisters Act and Seven Brothers Act. They eventually died by repeal, in large measure thanks to the skill with which Tom McCarter threw his weight around. He further tore up the pea patch, whenever he could seize or manufacture the opportunity, by tilting at such disparate but equally determined, power-oriented personalities as Hudson County's empire-building Frank Hague and earlier, at the other end of the stick, reformer George L. Record. In season and out, Tom McCarter ran Public Service completely as its president. When the season did not particularly suit his purposes—as, for example, during the several winter months he spent each year in Florida—no board meetings took place. To the increasing dismay of a rising new breed of managers, as board chairman he kept on trying to run the show much longer.

Tom McCarter went about what he not altogether unreasonably regarded as *his* business with a degree of ferocious energy that won him, in the press and in the minds of fellow citizens, the taunting sobriquet "Czar of New Jersey." In a way, he was. There is little question that for a period of some 30-odd years he and his two similarly strong-willed brothers—Uzal as board chairman of Fidelity Union Trust Company, which he had founded, and Robert as powerful corporation lawyer and director on many a gold-plated board—did for all practical purposes come close to running the State in a kind of ducal troika. At one point for the 13-year stretch from January of 1933 to December of 1946, Tom McCarter combined in his single person the board chairmanships of both Public Service Electric and Gas Company *and* Fidelity Union Trust (he had been director of the latter since 1900). It was all quite legal, but at the same time a hardly unenviable position to find oneself in. Apart from the interesting speculation about possible political leverage which such relationships engender, however, these and related facts are stuff calculated to arouse excitement only in balance-sheet addicts—and inquisitive newsmen with a flair for needling. People who were close to Tom McCarter say that whenever this walking storm-center heard or read in the papers any reference to himself as the "Czar of New Jersey," it made his jaws work horribly, his eyes bulge, his jowls quiver, his slightly pointy ears seem to vibrate, and his complexion go from a normal ripe-tomato red to deep, pulsing magenta. At least once that we know of, it reduced this iron man to tears.

"How he lived to be 88 without popping off much sooner from high blood pressure, eating the way he did and all, I'll never know," said one medically-astute observer. "Maybe it was those months in Florida every winter."

In the company, there were those who worked for him who worshipped him. One such was his long-time secretary, Miss Luke. When the first minimum-wage law went into effect, McCarter earned her undying gratitude by approving without a struggle (since it was, after all, mandatory under the law) an increase in her salary from $7 to $9 a week. It was probably one of the few times the man who spent his life whirling to counter any move that he felt might deplete the resources of his company, gave in with something like the gallantry of the Princeton-bred gentleman he was. Miss Luke never forgot it. The occasion was among a lean handful when "the roaring redhead" had failed to operate in an area that one commentator has described as "somewhere to the right of Genghis Khan."

An oil portrait of Tom McCarter hangs at one end of the board room on the eighth floor of PSE&G's headquarters building. Under beetling brows that are somehow reminiscent of those worn by the late United Mineworkers Union president John J. Lewis, and a sedately brushed pompadour, Tom McCarter transfixes all comers, from the beyond as he did in life, with the piercing, almost angry gaze of the unreconstructed tycoon he was. That leveling experience would have to include, presumably, any current board members who, arguing in these harsh times present policy and future planning for Old Tom's fief, are foolhardy enough to glance up at the portrait for reassurance.

Take, purely as a conjectural example, McCarter's incumbent successor, Bob Smith, a friendly soul cut from the more naturally cheerful and outgoing cloth of the professional engineer. Bob, although PSE&G's chairman in a period of hard going for any utility's head man, will not only smile at you. He may even wink. It is all but impossible to resist winking back. But if Bob Smith ever forgets himself at a board meeting and winks at that portrait, you can take it as a foregone conclusion that McCarter will resist.

According to the family, Tom McCarter was not the humorless man that others saw as the "Czar of New Jersey." In fact he was extremely witty, they maintain, and depending on his mood could be marvelous company at the table with jokes and wisecracks and stories that convulsed his guests, more often than his wife and children, with laughter. Unfortunately, to date, nobody has been able to recall a single one of those alleged jokes and stories, although there was, as we shall see, one deadpan line his wife used on him more than once that nearly made him choke with suppressed fury. One incident that was reinforced in some memories throws indirect light on the McCarter aura at 80 Park Place. It has to do with an anonymous messenger boy who unintentionally achieved one kind of immortality and risked achieving another kind.

It was an up elevator just before nine, and onto it strode the president, known heart-thumpingly to everyone aboard except the messenger boy. Never one to waste a minute, McCarter was talking a blue streak to his companion. As the companion got off at his floor, McCarter held the door open with his foot to complete the conversation. Conscious that he too had obligations and an armload of things to deliver, the messenger boy at first fidgeted inwardly. Then outwardly. McCarter went on talking. Nobody else dared do more than breathe quietly, but the messenger boy had had it. "Okay, Mac," he chirped, "on or off!" There is no record of what happened next. But whether McCarter ignored him or let the door slide shut, one thing is certain: Tom McCarter was "on"—in spades—all his working hours.

And he was not modest about what he had to say. The widely variegated McCarter processes of thought and articulation are in three volumes which, as he says with Victorian solemnity in his foreword, he had "caused to be printed and privately distributed" in 1933 and again in 1939 and 1945. The first blue-bound book is a 589-page collection of 74 addresses and statements by McCarter published under the umbrella title *One Phase of a Jerseyman's Activities.* Its successor six years later, under the same title but labeled supplemental, is another 563-page doorstop crammed with 52 more pronunciamentoes from on high, plus 20 "friendly editorials" from New Jersey papers that note the changing of the guard at the end of what McCarter in his preface calls his "long period of stewardship in one particular office." McCarter at the height of his powers was not an outwardly religious man, but he did have a lifelong sense of steward- ship which, if not exactly biblical, was certainly patriarchal. A number of the editorials give indirect attention to the limited manner in which the guard changed, but all freely hail the man's genuine contributions to the prosperity of his well- loved New Jersey, and the improved quality of life for its citizens that McCarter's years of toil had helped generate.

It would be a mistake to pretend that these collections of McCarter's sometimes pile driving but always carefully reasoned and richly documented addresses are the kind of reading you would take along for a month at the shore. They are not exactly leaden. McCarter fulminating in print against his enemies is something to conjure with. But they are often, at best, overblown demonstrations of the way an old-fashioned expert could take rhetoric by the tail and make it bellow.

McCarter was not ashamed to employ phrasing which even back then was hackneyed. He actually reveled in it. He is always "taking command of the ship" or "taking time by the forelock" —feats he was undeniably good at. Reading his speeches, you start overlooking the addiction to cliches and bombast. You begin to feel the mesmeric power and you almost revel too.

As this generation of parents knows, anyone who expects reverential awe of offspring is in the wrong business. The rites-of-passage custom of clobbering parental performance is not confined to the current social ferment, however. McCarter's own two daughters dismissed out of hand, as if they were still teenagers, their father's basically heavy copy. And, as we shall see, it *is* his. "Dull stuff," they called it. "Who could read it? You'd be bored stiff." McCarter himself, in his preface to the first book, shows considerable uncharacteristic sensitivity on this point. "It is not my thought," he writes, "to burden the recipients of this work with any obligation to read it thoroughly."

Perhaps so. But the fact remains that as a personal record of some pretty exciting history, Tom McCarter's neglected and needlessly downgraded accounts of just one aspect of a Jerseyman's activities—his role in building Public Service— are all but unbeatable.

One thing that strikes anyone who thumbs through these books is the enormous range of his interests. Those interests, powered by his strong sense of civic duty, were not only the gas and electric industry and electric railways and rate cases. With his usual sharp eye for pinpointing among esoterica the minutest detail, he also moved vigorously into such civic-responsibility areas as what it takes to run schools—right down to phys-ed facilities, nursing services and the cost variations in janitorial-engineering work load "per janitor per square foot cleaned." That was when he reported to Governor A. Harry Moore as Chairman of the New Jersey

Governor's School Survey Commission, to which Moore had appointed him. The survey took a year to complete, from autumn 1932 to early winter 1933. The report itself, in two volumes, fills more than 200 pages of McCarter's first book. In a footnote he says that while the man the Commission engaged to manage the survey, Professor Paul R. Mort of Teachers College, Columbia University, was the principal author of the report, he wrote it "in collaboration and consultation with Mr. McCarter, and it is therefore included herein." Even cursory reading of material McCarter put together on his own is enough to convince the skeptical that unmistakable signs of the heavy but meticulous McCarter hand are all over the Mort report, and that he is not just putting in a claim for what isn't honestly his. One such sign, a natural spinoff from his disciplined instinct to see things first in terms of outlay, is his view that increase in class size in the schools of New Jersey involves "little reason to believe such an increase would significantly impair efficiency." The reduction of the learning process to terms where efficiency at the expense of learning becomes paramount is, of course, a battle that is being waged without resolution to this day.

McCarter's devotion to the lush way of saying something if he had any choice, crops up time and again in such oatmeal prose as "I had no conception of this suggestion which has now fructified into result." It's lawyer-talk with a rich lacing of rodomontade, obviously. But even McCarter's strange habit of reading William Makepeace Thackeray's *Vanity Fair* once a year for most of his life shouldn't have done that to a man's sense of language. (Nobody knows why he had such a fixation on that one book. Possibly its satirical treatment of upper-class snobbism titillated his own sense of involvement in upper-class life the way radical chic captivated some well-to-do people in the recent Sixties. In any case McCarter never discussed it with the family. Apart from being hooked on a single milestone in Victorian fiction, according to his elder daughter Ellen, he looked down his nose at novels.)

Another revealing example of his wide-ranging interest in public affairs crops up in the way he went head over heels into the work of the 1933 New Jersey Alcoholic Beverage

Commission, of which once again, he was chairman. There was some additional reason for this particular dedication, although it was in no way and at no time a discreditable reason. McCarter himself loved a modest but regular before-dinner tipple of whiskey-and-soda or a cocktail—but never of scotch, which he inexplicably despised. In his later years he liked to come up from Rumson for lunch, and would almost without variation ritually introduce among his ample fibers, at a slow but rhythmic pace, three robust bourbon Manhattans. It apparently never got beyond control of his remarkable metabolism, though, as one headwaiter found out the hard way. He touched—subtly, as he thought—on Mr. McCarter's reported largesse in having bestowed on an earlier headwaiter who had served the utility chief well, a token of appreciation in the form of an automobile. Old Tom swirled his second Manhattan and, without even looking up, informed the man bluntly to the contrary.

McCarter was as rock-ribbed a Republican as they make them, all his life. He also held a deep conviction— "less a personal thing than a reflection of the spirit of his time," his daughter Ellen believes—that the only fit role in society for Irish Catholics was as maids, of whom he consistently employed over the years as unending supply at Rumsonhill. But at the same time he felt so strongly about the evils of Prohibition and a man's right to drink that in 1928, in early September, McCarter issued a calmly reasoned statement titled "Why I Shall Vote for Governor Al Smith" that shook the paneling in country clubs all over New Jersey.

"I have voted in 10 Presidential elections, always for the Republican candidate. I believe generally in the principles and policies of the Republican party, and am a strong supporter of President Coolidge," said Tom McCarter with his usual lawyerlike deliberateness. "Nevertheless, I have reached the conclusion after long reflection that I should vote for Governor Smith this year." In view of the foregoing background, this was quite a wrench.

He went on to rank the 18th Amendment as one of the four leading problems facing the electorate over the preceding 75 years—right up there with slavery, the preservation of the Union, and free silver. Right after World War I, he said, "the money and zeal of the Anti-Saloon League put (it) over—attempting by fiat to overcome the habits of humanity from the beginning of the world." He blasted its unenforceability as part of "federal organic law" and the rich contribution it had made to the moral decay of America. With the hammering logic of the law-trained Ulsterman that rode in his genes, McCarter said bitterly, "The day of the bootlegger, of the speakeasy, of the night club, of the hip flask, and of poisoned rum is here. In this section of the country, at least, the Volstead Act is flouted very generally. Through the locker system or otherwise, liquor is available in practically every city, country or golf club. Almost without exception, liquor is freely served in the homes of those within my social environment. Included in this galaxy of potential lawbreakers are cabinet officers, governors, senators and congressmen (many of whom vote dry), politicians of both parties, judges of our courts, lawyers, doctors, merchants, bankers, corporation officers like myself, college presidents and professors, and even ministers ... It is time to call a spade a spade. The thing is a sham and a farce."

To head off the question of what Smith would do if elected and confronted with a hostile Congress, McCarter the skilled rebuttalist said, "Well, if there is an evil to be corrected, a beginning must be made some time ... I think Congress would quickly respond to an expression of public sentiment manifested through the ballot ... I believe that Governor Smith, if elected and armed with the prestige and influence of the Presidency, would with characteristic force and candor take the issue to the people ... It certainly will not help, in the correction of the evil, to support one who believes one hundred per cent in its continuance! At least I shall have registered my protest." Smith would lose in spite of Tom McCarter's vote. It would take almost another seven years for another New Yorker—McCarter would go to the mat with him on other matters—to ride the groundswell of anti-Prohibition sentiment to Repeal.

Those other matters included a small problem which McCarter also dragged into the open in declaring he would back Al Smith. "I have been asked how I can support Governor Smith in view of his stand upon public utilities, with which my life work has been and is intimately connected," he said. "I do not agree with certain of Governor Smith's expressed views upon utilities, but I see nothing to get excited about over them. If it be thought best, I have no objection to governmental agencies retaining control of water-power sites. Mr. Hoover seems to hold somewhat similar views to those of Governor Smith, if I correctly understand his Boulder Dam attitude." But there McCarter drew the line. "I think it would be better," he said, "if governmental activity stopped with the ownership of the sites rather than the construction of generating plants and the sale of the project to private companies for distribution, as recommended by the Governor. I do not agree with his views . . . to the effect that there is no harm in municipalities having the right by vote of the people thereof to embark upon municipal ownership and operation, although this has been substantially the law in New Jersey for a good many years." There echoes in this McCarter prose a sigh of relief as distinct as the needle for illicitly imbibing legislators who voted dry: "Happily," he added, "both officials and people are too wise to make use of any such power in any large way." And, perhaps with an inner chuckle: "A large number of such municipal enterprises have quit after unsuccessful efforts of this character."

McCarter had a natural sense of dignity that served as a bristling backstop to his normally formidable posture before the world. Together they precluded such familiarity as calling him "Tom"—for anyone, that is, except those whom Franklin D. Roosevelt would come to call "malefactors of great wealth." McCarter, despite his addiction to sometimes volcanic discourse, seldom went in for profanity.

It is therefore interesting to note that his flexibility in the light of his own convictions permitted him to back Repeal and turn in some sound recommendations to the 157th New

Jersey legislature about how the State should deal with the coming tide of booze, and at the same time harbor severe reservations about Repeal's sponsor, Franklin D. Roosevelt. One of the most vivid anecdotes to underscore this entered the picture after the nation had its right to drink restored and New Jersey had an emerging structure with which to handle the results. McCarter went to Washington to go into one or another aspect of the endless struggle to keep the government out of his hair and that of other utility people in the private sector. On returning home he told his daughter Ellen that he had met and had a good long talk with the President about their mutual problem.

Ellen Doubleday recalled that her father told her. "I have to say he is about one of the most attractive men I have ever met, but he said 'Tom' without knowing me and I don't like being called by my first name by people I have never met before. But I have to admit he *is* attractive, and I thought I had gotten somewhere. But then on the train coming back from Washington I bought *The Philadelphia Bulletin.* I opened it and read that the President had done exactly the opposite of what he told me he was going to do. The man is a goddam liar."

When McCarter, having stubbornly decided to live to be 88, died three days after his October 20th birthday in 1955, his anti-Roosevelt track record and reputation as "an unrelenting foe of New Deal policies" were still much to the fore. *The New York Times* gave five of the 19 paragraphs in his obituary to another anecdote involving him and the squire of Hyde Park.

"At a convention of the Edison Electric Institute in 1939," the *Times* man wrote, "when he was 71 years old and still called the 'firebrand' of the public utility industry, Mr. McCarter made a speech typical of the man.

"Franklin Roosevelt, he told 2,500 delegates and their guests, had promised him in 1934 that as soon as he balanced the budget he, the President, wanted Mr. McCarter to come down to Washington and fix up the utility situation.

" 'When I get that thing (the budget) off my hands,' Mr. McCarter said the President told him, 'I want you to come down here, come down here a lot, and you and I will settle this thing all right.'

"A roar of laughter rose from the gathering when Mr. McCarter declared, 'Well, I never heard anything more about it but the reason is perfectly apparent. He hasn't balanced the budget yet!'"

The *Times* went on to recall that McCarter had "characterized a Public Service Commission one time as a group of 'political horse thieves,'" and in 1934 had "audaciously handed to President Roosevelt a formal memorandum urging him to cooperate with the utility interests in facilitating a Supreme Court decision on the validity of the Tennessee Valley Authority.

" 'Like you, sir,'" he said, " 'I am lawyer-bred.'" Then and later, that mutuality of their training cut no ice with FDR.

These reminiscences lay far in the future, though, and at the time of transition from the desert of Prohibition to the oasis of Repeal, McCarter was showing his form as always in the detailed report and recommendations he made to New Jersey's lawmakers as Chairman of the Alcoholic Beverage Commission. Whatever he put his muscular hand to, he overlooked no bets.

"The underlying purpose of the Commission," he wrote, "has been to recognize that within a short time some form of the liquor industry would be legal, and it has been the aim of the members of the Commission to so harmonize their various views upon this most difficult subject as to enable the Commission to recommend some kind of legislation that would be in the interest of true temperance. To that end we have set up a plan which if enacted into law and carried out according to its true intent by the officials entrusted with the operation thereof will make relatively easy the sale and consumption of beer, ale and natural light or fermented wines; and make relatively difficult the sale and consumption of liquors and fortified or treated wines." He went on to spell out licensing arrangements which he and his seven fellow commissioners—three of them doctors—had structured for the financial benefit of both the State and the municipalities. He also noted how they had kept in mind the interests of the consumer, so that the fees they were recommending "would not result in prohibitive prices ... and thus encourage the continuation of bootlegging and speakeasies. We are not unmindful," McCarter intoned, his sense of trade-offs and what have come to be known as cost-benefit ratios always smoothly in gear, "of the undesirability of bootlegging, racketeering and speakeasies." Thoughtfully, and typical of his skill at leaving no loopholes, he added, "We have also provided for the licensing of dining-cars and boats."

For those who may think that the sight of women engineers and women in hard hats out in the field climbing poles or descending into personholes as employees of PSE&G today would have sent Tom McCarter up the wall or into shock—well, maybe not. He noted the care his Commission had taken to see to it that the "local boards of alcoholic beverage control, entrusted with the power to grant retail licenses of any kind (should) consist of three persons, not more than two of whom shall belong to the same political party, *and at least one of whom shall be a woman."*

Researching and writing about the developments which have produced this now generally well-regarded New Jersey utility has seemed, on occasion, like threading one's way through a mine-field on a pogo stick. Among those who helped make the trip easier, if not safer, and to whom a debt of thanks is owing, were John Allen, Ed Anderson, Bill Blake, Jack Richards, Dot Conniff, Lois Dean, Ellen McCarter Doubleday, Natalie Fitch, Ed Francis, William Grigat, Owen Grundy, Morris Hooven, David Leitch, Madeleine McCarter Kelly, Jim Killgore, Art Lenehan, John Loftus, Don Luce, Tom McCarter III, Frank McMenimen, Gene Murphy, Mrs. Evan Myles, Henry Nicolson, Don Quick, Darrow Sage, Bob Smith, and Debbie Suta—with apologies to anyone who also helped but, regrettably, somehow got left out. Special thanks go to Florine Hunt and her PSE&G library staff, who went out of their way to provide often esoteric information, and also Charles F. Cummings and his staff in the New Jersey Room of the Newark Public Library, who were particularly generous in answering a variety of questions and tracking down obscure but useful material.

At every hop of the pogo stick it was comforting to know that the only requirement governing the writing of this 75th anniversary history—strengthened by Samuel Eliot Morison's dictum about the need to keep the reader constantly in mind—was the same one Art Lenehan ran into when he signed on: "Just tell the truth." To the degree that conscientious effort and the gleanings of sound but fallible human memories can make it so, then, let the PSE&G story, to date, unfold. Here's how it all began.

—James C.G. Conniff and Richard Conniff
Upper Montclair
April 23, 1978

The meter room of the Newark Gas Light Company in 1895, its valve housing combining the functional with the ornate and, below, part of the gas-house gang for the utility.

The Gas Era Begins

"There is a madman proposing to light London with—what do you think? Why, with smoke!"
—Sir Walter Scott

Until recent years, the corporate symbol of Public Service Electric and Gas Company was a triangle which represented the principal interests of the firm—gas, transportation, and electricity.

Before Thomas N. McCarter founded the company in 1903, literally hundreds of little firms were providing one or another of these three services, often duplicating each other's efforts at prices that reflected the resultant inefficiency.

Gas was the first to begin providing the lifeblood that was to nurture a growing New Jersey, a state that was to become the most densely populated in the nation.

The first gas company in the state, Paterson Gas Light, was organized on September 2, 1825. For no discoverable reason, it remained for years a paper corporation. It did not build its gas works and begin business until 1847, the same year the Newark Gas Light Company, which had incorporated in 1845, opened its Market Street works. Newark generally gets credit for being the 13th city in the nation and the first in

The Newark Gas Light Company made the first gas in New Jersey in 1847, piping it from a plant more modest than the one it grew into, above.

New Jersey to have an operating gas company. Its citizens first purchased gas on January 5, 1847. This was 12 years before the state would get its first street-car company and 35 years before Newark Electric Light and Power would advertise its readiness to do business.

James P. Dusenberry, who was treasurer and a director of Public Service, described the founding of Newark Gas Light, with its tiny works and only four miles of street mains, this way:

"The manufacture and distribution of gas in cities was in its infancy when the Newark Gas Light Company was started in 1845. Subscriptions to the stock were in the same category as subscriptions to the Newark Public Library and considered of civic virtue only so that Newark might be placed alongside of other progressive cities. Joseph Battin, of Newark, a promoter, inventor, and mechanic, in company with several

Philadelphians, was the builder of the plant and, doubtless, had much to do with soliciting subscriptions to the stock, which was $100,000. A number of the prominent people of Newark, including Beach Vanderpool and Marcus L. Ward, were directors of the company. The consumption of gas in 1847, which was about the first whole year of business, yielded an income of approximately $7,600. This increased to more than $12,000 the second year and $14,000 the third year. The original price of gas was $4.00 per thousand cubic feet, which in 1852 was reduced to $3.50; in 1859 to $3.00 ..."

The *Sentinel of Freedom,* a Newark newspaper, remarked following the successful start of Newark Gas Light, that the company had at first been "looked upon by many amongst us as a chimerical scheme, and they not only stood aloof from the enterprise, but dissuaded others from embarking on it." But the steady construction of the new works encouraged others and the stock was then "not only all taken, but sought after." The company began business with "an unusually large number of consumers," including "public-spirited citizens" who placed gas lamps on their sidewalks as well as in their houses. Thereafter, business grew rapidly.

Other gas companies organized in Trenton in 1847, in Camden in 1848, in Jersey City in 1849, in New Brunswick in 1851, in Hackensack in 1861, and in dozens of smaller communities. As these companies grew and their territories overlapped, consolidation occurred. Competition came to Newark in 1873, when the Citizens' Gas Light Company was chartered, and it began immediately to lay its mains parallel to those of the old company, a duplication of investment that proved profitable for neither company. Leaders of the two utilities met in 1875 and divided the city at the Morris Canal bridge. From then on, they coexisted harmoniously in their separate territories until 1895, when they merged to form the Newark Gas Company. In 1898, through the efforts of Randal Morgan of the United Gas Improvement Company of Philadelphia, and of such Newark capitalists as John F. Dryden, Bernard M. Shanley, and Uzal McCarter, Newark Gas and several smaller, suburban concerns were merged into the Newark Consolidated Gas Company. Similar consol-

idations, often involving Morgan and UGI, took place in
Hudson and other counties throughout the last decade of
the century.

The mounting popularity of gas for street lighting, and a
matching propensity for citizens to lament its at times
sporadic availability once they had tasted its benefits, became
apparent early on, as the following editorial from the *Jersey
City Daily Times* for December 1, 1865, demonstrates:

> It is really a disgrace to the city and an outrage upon its
> citizens that our streets are not better lighted. The system of
> lighting the street lights when there is no moon is a farce
> which should be well-nigh played out. By this plan, no matter
> whether the moon gives light or not, so long as the almanac
> says that it might be expected, the street lights are not lighted.
> Consequently, many nights when the moon should shine and
> does not, the people are compelled to grope their way in
> darkness.
>
> The question arises as to who is responsible for such a state of
> affairs. Is it the city authorities or the Jersey City and
> Hoboken Gas Light Co.? Clearly it is the city authorities. If
> the gas light company will not furnish light for which it is
> allegedly paid, it is the duty of the authorities to compel them
> to do so, or have no more of their gas and bring in oil lamps
> from which we could get a continual glimmer of light.

Until 1893, gas companies in New Jersey sold only coal gas,
manufactured in large ovens called retorts. You can
manufacture coal gas in a miniature retort in your own
kitchen, and in that way see firsthand how the 19th century
gas works operated—minus the inevitable sweat and dirt of
the full-scale process in real life. Fill a small cocoa or tea tin
with soft coal and press the lid on tightly. With a nail, punch
a hole in the lid to let the gas out. Place the can on the front
burner of the kitchen range and heat it. When smoky vapors
pour from the hole in the lid—make sure you're doing this in
a well-ventilated room—allow the vapors to escape for two or
three minutes to drive all the air from the can. Then apply a
lighted match to set the vapors, which are true coal gas, afire.
This same gas was the first manufactured gas, and its sooty
appearance caused Sir Walter Scott to remark sarcastically,

"There is a madman proposing to light London with—what do you think? Why, with smoke!" Industry pioneers would soon learn to purify gas of its smokiness, and so it would become evident that a carbon gas, rather than smoke, produced the light.

The manufacture of coal gas left behind several by-products, as anyone who attempts the above "child scientist's" experiment will discover. After the gas has burned off, the tin "retort" will be seen to contain—if you open it when it cools—a dark, gummy liquid called coal tar, and a hard, porous solid called coke. Coke would later be of sufficient value to the steel industry that the Koppers Company would maintain a large coke plant in Kearny and sell the gas to Public Service as a by-product of coke manufacture. But before 1900, most gas companies simply got rid of coke by selling it, usually at a loss, for use as a fuel in the home. One gas veteran recalled to *Public Service News* that "coke was sold to customers at practically the cost of the hauling, and many inducements were given to the purchaser of gas appliances to induce the consumer to try coke." The Citizens' Gas Light Company offered coke as the "cheapest of fuels, broken and screened and delivered, in any part of the city" for $2.50 per truckload. Having had its volatile components burned off, coke, unlike its parent coal, also burned clean in home furnaces and generated intense heat.

Though the by-products business was not to become an important money-maker for Public Service until after World War I, the gas companies of the state practiced "recycling," and not just of coke, long before that. The Paterson Gas Works, for instance, at first used lime to purify the coal gas. It had four iron purifying boxes, 15 feet square and six feet deep, and each containing four trays, filled to a depth of five or six inches with lime. The gas men found it necessary to replace this lime, as it became spent, every two days. In a brief history of the Paterson Works, John G. Whitcomb, a cadet engineer, wrote:

> "In connection with this lime it might be interesting to note that the gas works had a man going around to all the restaurants in town collecting all the old oyster shells which

were then dumped into a small kiln ... and the lime from
these oyster shells was taken out at the bottom slightly slacked
("slaked," actually, meaning to cause lime to heat and crumble
by treating it with water) and stored in the lime shed. The
spent lime was dumped on a pile by the river bank ... Every
spring the farmers from miles around would come and cart
off this lime for their fields. Right here would be a good place
to point out that even back in those days the Gas Company
did a flourishing business in by-products. During the time
when that good old family remedy, which passed under the
name of Rattlesnake Oil, was to be found on every kitchen
shelf, the Gas Works was selling drip oil at the rate of one
dollar a gallon to enterprising patent medicine people who
would mix up some oil of wintergreen, cloves, etc., with it to
cover up the smell, and retail it for about fifty cents per four-
ounce bottle, as the rheumatism cure of the century. Light tar
was in great demand by farmers to help them get rid of
crows; they would soak the corn in it before planting and then
sow it, and woe to any crow that ate any of that corn. At this
period the use of tar for road work was still a very new idea.
In order to overcome any hesitation, the company maintained a fleet of 12 horse-drawn spray wagons, and would sell
tar sprayed on the road for seven cents a gallon. This was the
beginning of the road tar business which today is so
important to the gas industry ... Except for local road
purposes there was no market for the by-product tar and the
surplus was burned under the plant boilers, though much of
it found its way into the Passaic River."

Gas Making Moves Ahead

"It is not necessary to invite attention to the gas light by which my salon of painting is now illuminated; those who have seen the ring beset with gems of light are sufficiently disposed to spread their reputation ..."
—Rembrandt Peale

By 1893, the Paterson works began manufacturing a new type of fuel called water gas. Professor Thaddeus S. C. Lowe, a balloonist and the inventor of the so-called carbureted water gas process, himself replaced the retorts at Paterson with water-gas "sets." These were the first commercial water-gas machines in the state. From Paterson, the process spread throughout the industry and was still used, in modified form, in those Public Service gas works that survived the coming of natural gas.

The water-gas set consisted of three parts, combined in a single tall machine or connected, side by side, in separate towers: The generator, carburetor, and superheater. Water-gas making proceeded, as *Fortune* put it in its 1934 article on Public Service, "with a huff and puff, called the blow and run." Using shovels in the beginning and a crane later on, the gas men loaded the generator with a huge "charge" of coke, which they then brought up almost to white heat by blasting air through it at hurricane force. Shutting off the air with a hand lever, the gas-maker opened a steam inlet from the boilers. The steam—H_2O—reacted, on being similarly blasted through the generator, with the hot carbon of the coke to produce water gas, composed of hydrogen and carbon monoxide. This was a lean gas; that is, it produced only 320 to 350 BTU (British Thermal Units, the quantity of heat required to raise the temperature of one pound of water one degree Fahrenheit) per cubic foot. From the generator, the water gas passed to the carburetor for enriching with oil gas, which had a much higher heating capacity. Here, in the carburetor, a kerosene-like oil was sprayed on bricks heated by the coke from the generator. The oil vaporized and mixed with the water gas, and the combination passed to the superheater, a huge cylinder filled with fire brick laid in a checker pattern. The combined product from the carburetor ascended through the brick checkerwork, which was heated to 1,500 degrees, and in the process it was "cracked"—that is, the oil vapor became oil gas. The combination—carbureted water gas, a hot brown substance—was then cleaned of tar and other impurities (the by-products) and passed to the gas-holders.

The gas could not go directly to the customer because of the intermittency with which it was produced. The "blow and run," alternated at three-and four-minute intervals and the normal stoppages of production—had they not been contained at the plant—would have shut off every pilot light in the territory, causing, as *Fortune* commented, "asphyxia (to) pour from the flameless burners when the flow resumed." Unlike the natural gas you cook with today, the old type manufactured gas could knock you out or worse. The gas-holder, storing enough gas to last the system from run to run, kept the flow to the customer continuous, and therefore safe. It also allowed the gas men to shut a set down as the charge of coke spent itself, after 12 to 24 hours, for cleaning and re-charging. The gas man prided himself on "keeping gas on the town" and planned all maintenance construction with the aim of preventing interruption of service. Finally, the holder enabled the works to manufacture gas at capacity even at night, when demand was low, and store it for use during hours of peak demand. Cornelius Schoonejongen, who went to work as a gas-maker at Paterson in 1893, later described the installation of the first water gas set there:

"Dr. Lowe was then specializing in gases to send balloons up. Dr. Lowe went to the directors of the Paterson Gas Light Company and explained his idea and asked permission to try it out. The request was granted. Where the storeroom is today was then a coal shed. There a machine was put in under his supervision."

The first set had an eight-by-14-foot generator connected to an eight-by-14-foot carburetor and an eight-by-22-foot superheater. It used lump hard coal in the generator and 15 gallons of crude oil, just as it came from the well, on each run. Schoonejongen and his co-workers had to clean the set five times a day, recovering the clinker, or unburned coal, and re-using it, and removing the checker brick that had become fouled with carbon in the carburetor. This was hot, filthy work even later when machines took over much of the burden.

"You got this terrific heat in there," recalls Jack V. Richards, a gas man who rose to the rank of vice president before he retired. "You've got this big coke fire going. Always dirt lying around. Dust. You couldn't help it."

During Richards' time in the gas works, two men knocked down and dragged out the clinker using a four-inch-thick metal bar suspended from a pully. One man stood over the fire and guided the bar, protecting his hands with a piece of canvas, while the other raised and lowered it. "Many a fellow has been cracked on the head with that bar," Richards says. At Paterson, in the early years, workers removed the fouled bricks from the carburetors with a pair of long-handled tongs. Working from the top, they lifted the bricks out one at a time, cleaned, and replaced them. Mr. Schoonejongen has left no record of what the operator of the tongs said when, from time to time, he ran across a batch of 10 or 15 bricks fused solid to the walls.

Of Dr. Lowe's first water-gas set, he continues:

"The idea was tried and was successful. They could make water gas. The Paterson Gas Light Company then proposed to make gas for the City of Paterson. The blower and engine they already had. They needed a boiler. So a boiler operating at 75 pounds steam pressure at highest capacity was installed. They were now ready to make gas. That boiler looked so big at the time they thought it didn't need a stack to carry the steam load. When operations started it was found that the boiler wouldn't carry the steam and that they needed a stack. They had no stack. A lot of barrels were gotten, the heads knocked out and they were set on top of one another. That was the first boiler stack. If you could see that first stack and the present one, you would see the improvment made ... No one around here has seen that machine, but I operated it a few years before it was scrapped."

The business of the gas industry in 1903, when Public Service was born, was lighting. Some gas men had considered gas for home heating, the major use of the fuel today, but none had tried it. Gas cooking was only beginning to replace the coal and wood stoves. Industrial use of gas was almost unknown. Lighting had been the business since the industry's first day in this country, June 13, 1816, when this advertisement appeared in a Baltimore paper:

Oyez! Oyez! Oyez!
"GAS LIGHTS"
Without Oil, Tallow, Wick, or Smoke
It is not necessary to invite attention to the gas light by which my salon of painting is now illuminated; those who have seen the ring beset with gems of light are sufficiently disposed to spread their reputation; the purpose of this notice is merely to say that the Museum will be illuminated every evening until the public curiosity will be satisfied.

Rembrandt Peale

Peale, a shrewd businessman as well as a respected painter—he did one of the great life portraits of George Washington—hoped public curiosity would never be satisfied. He had an interest in a local gas works, and wanted to sell gas street light to the city. He succeeded in doing so, and from this start the gas lighting business spread around the country, appearing, as we mentioned, in New Jersey in 1847.

Gas lighting grew slowly but steadily then in competition with whale oil, which sold for from 80 cents to $1.77 a gallon, and with tallow candles, which cost 15 cents per pound, six candles to the pound. Kerosene, from petroleum discovered in commercial quantities at Titusville, Pennsylvania, on August 27, 1859, replaced both whale oil and candles after the Civil War. It then cost about 22 cents a gallon against a gas price in New Jersey of from $2 to $4 per thousand cubic feet. These prices were evidently competitive, for both forms of lighting remained popular—until an entirely new source of light, one that would replace both gas and kerosene, appeared in New Jersey.

The gas illuminating business in the State faced competition from electricity for the first time in 1881, when arc lamps began to appear on the streets of Newark. This was the beginning of the struggle for the lighting business in the State that would last for the next 40 years. Though advertised in Newark as "the matchless light," electricity at first shared many of the inconveniences of gas as an illuminant. The gas man had to light each street lamp by hand at dusk and douse it at midnight, or when the moon rose. But, while the electric company could light an entire circuit of several hundred arc lamps from the power plant, its employees also had to visit each lamp daily, to trim the carbon burning points. Gas was cheaper and more dependable than electricity then. The power plants shut down so often, one Public Service executive later recalled, that the electric company in Newark routinely supplied its customers with kerosene lanterns. The wise customer kept his gas fixtures in place when he switched to electricity.

In the early years, the electric utilities lacked meters, and this also put them at a disadvantage in competing with gas. You could by then burn gas lamps 24 hours a day, if you could afford the fuel, but electric lighting was limited to the few hours set by contract. The power plant shut down and your lights went out on the electric company's schedule. One unfortunate Union County party-giver encountered this problem in 1886. He dazzled his guests with a brilliant display of electric light, only to have the ballroom cast into sudden and total darkness at the sober hour of 11 p.m. He had, it turned out, neglected to arrange for the power plant crew to stay on late that night. The gas companies had for a time, much earlier, also gone meterless and had sold lighting by the hour. They hired inspectors to keep customers honest. These men greeted those burning lamps beyond the contracted hour with a loud rapping on the front sidewalk and the cry, "Gas lights out!" If you were midway through a spellbinding novel or perhaps a piano concerto, you finished up by kerosene or candlelight. But the development of the gas meter ended this practice well before the arrival of electric competition.

Electric lighting had two important advantages over gas in the beginning. It was, as the "matchless" slogan indicated, less cumbersome to operate—you had only to turn on the switch—and it was also extremely bright, while gas was softer and mellower. When Edward Weston, the Newark inventor and manufacturer, demonstrated an experimental arc lamp to city residents in 1878, local newspapers enthusiastically reported that its light almost excelled that of the morning sun. The city council was soon substituting arc lamps for gas in Newark's seedier districts, particularly at a burying ground between Broad and Halsey Streets, in the hope "that the civilizing effects of the brilliant electric light will compel vice to seek other and darker quarters." But the gas men, who were to prove their adaptability often in competition with electricity, soon found a way to match the brightness of the electric lamp.

Until about 1890, most home lighting fixtures used the gas tip, a device invented by William Murdock, the Scotsman who first employed gas for illumination. One day, wanting to shut off the flow of gas from the end of an open tube, Murdock had capped it with a thimble which happened to be handy. When gas continued to escape through tiny perforations in the thimble, Murdock applied a match to it and found that the gas burned much more intensely than when it flowed from the open tube. Still, the "gas tip," as the commercial version of this discovery of Murdock's was called, produced only three candlepower. But then, soon after the electric incandescent lamp made its first appearance in Newark, the "gas mantle" came to New Jersey. This mantle was a sort of stocking made of cotton webbing containing oxides of cerium and thorium. The gas flame consumed the cotton, leaving only a fragile mesh of ashes— the oxides—which glowed brilliantly with the gas heat. This was a real gain for illumination over the gas tip. Installed by the Welsbach Street Illuminating Company, which still maintains the few remaining gas street lamps for Public Service, the mantle used less fuel than the gas tip while giving off more than six times the light. This invention, and the general reliability of gas lighting compared with the still experimental electric service, saved the gas business. The mantle made obsolete the kerosene lamp, which until then had continued to be an important competitor with gas for the lighting business. Gas soon became the most popular form of lighting in the home and on the street.

Later, gas companies fighting the inroads of electricity would make less of gas light's brilliance and more of its softness and lack of glare, its "amber glow." Advertisements compared gas light to the light of the setting sun. Judging by contemporary accounts and by firsthand experience with gas street lamps in PSE&G territory that are only now being shut down, this was not merely some advertising copywriter's exaggeration. On seeing electric street lighting for the first time, Robert Louis Stevenson wrote:

"A new sort of urban star now shines out nightly, horrible, unearthly, obnoxious to the human eye; a lamp for a nightmare! Such a light as this should shine forth only on murders and public crimes, or along the corridors of lunatic asylums, a horror to heighten horror. To look at it only once is to fall in love with gas, which gives a warm domestic radiance fit to eat by. That ugly blinding glare may not improperly advertise the home of slanderous Figaro, which is a back-shop to the infernal regions; but where soft joys prevail, where people are convoked to pleasure and the philosopher looks on, smiling and silent, where love and laughter and deifying wine abound, there, at least, let the old mild lustre shine upon the eyes of man."

That electric light could be brilliant, even garish, is evident from an 1886 plan of the Common Council of Orange to replace gas lamps on that community's shady streets with four electric light towers, each 85 feet high and carrying five arc lights. The would-be builder of the towers guaranteed "that each (tower) will light an area of half a mile in every direction, so that anyone can see the time by their watches anywhere within that limit." By contrast, the gas lamp's soft refulgence made it ideal for the home and for churches, which remained important customers of the gas utility through the Public Service Corporation's first decade. Certain Baptist churches also used large amounts of gas back then, one company executive later recalled, to heat the water for baptismal immersions.

The gas and electric companies competed fiercely and sometimes to their own detriment for the lighting business. Each offered to install pipes or wiring at the smallest possible cost to the homeowner, or even free. Each also maintained the equipment and fixtures within the home. The gas men sometimes used mild threats to maintain the lighting business that they saw as their sole source of livelihood. At one point, the Newark Gas Company refused to further extend its mains to private customers in Irvington unless that municipality granted it the local street-lighting contract, which the electric utility had taken away in competitive bidding. When the electric company, Peoples Light and Power, organized a gas company of its own, Newark Gas backed down and resumed normal operations. In Newark, the Citizens' Gas Light Company caused a furor by attempting to remove its meters from the homes and businesses of customers who had switched to electric light. The customers balked. One typical store-owner said he wanted the gas light to back up his electric arc light, together with several oil lamps in winter and in emergencies. Still, gas lighting flourished.

In reviewing the history of the gas business in New Jersey, McCarter later said:

"The latter half of that decade (1890-1900) was a period of unexampled prosperity the country over, in all kinds of business, and the people, flushed with commercial and economic success, and inspired by the wonders of the new inventions, entered upon an era of development and of exploitation which, however much accompanied by evils, has on the whole added greatly to the comfort of living and the convenience of the public. Even the gas business, with its half-century of previous life, but theretofore a sleepy kind of business, caught the infection. New uses for gas, never before considered, quickly made their appearance. The Welsbach (mantle) burner, extending the efficiency of gas as an illuminant and cheapening its use, helped it to compete with electric light. New and vigorous methods were adopted by all the companies, enormous sums were spent in extending and developing the plants, the public pulse quickly responded, and the output multiplied by leaps and bounds."

A work crew, its jackets neatly hung on a utility pole, begins the hand operation of excavating for a new engine room for the Peoples Light & Power Company's City Dock station in Newark in April, 1900.

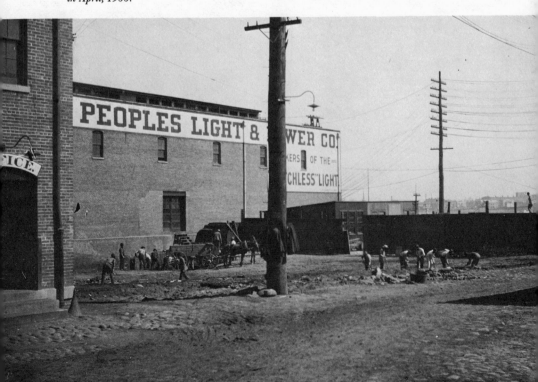

Electricity Comes to Newark

*" ... we provided both gas lamps and lanterns to be used when electricity
failed. Both were often used."*
—Dudley Farrand

The electric business in New Jersey got its small but
auspicious start from an act of the Common Council of the
City of Newark approved on May 9, 1881, authorizing an
expenditure "not exceeding three hundred dollars for the
purpose of erecting five suitable posts in Military Park and
running a wire upon the same, provided the Weston Electric
Lighting Company (an arc light manufacturer located on
Washington Street) will burn five lights thereon until twelve
o'clock each night for two months without charge for
lighting, furnishing attendance, electricity, etc., at their own
expense—on consultation with the Committee on Public
Grounds."

Actually, Newark had seen electric lighting earlier that
same Spring, when Edward Weston, of the company that
bore his name, had established a circuit of 40 arc lights in
and in front of stores at Newark's Four Corners, the
intersection of Broad and Market Streets. Local businessmen
had paid Weston a dollar a day per light for illumination
from sunset to 11 p.m., six days a week. Even earlier, Weston

*A submarine cable stretches 2500 feet beneath Upper New York Bay, sending
PSE&G power to light the Statue of Liberty. She became a Public Service customer
on December 2, 1916.*

and others had "entered the lists against darkness" with
sporadic demonstrations of the powerful arc light. But it was
only after the success of the Military Park experiment that
leading capitalists from Newark and New York organized a
company to develop and carry on the business of illumination. The Newark Electric Light and Power Company, New
Jersey's first electric utility, was incorporated on February 18,
1882, and soon began advertising its willingness "to furnish
electric light for stores, factories, and public buildings on the
most favorable terms." In addition to arc lighting, the
company offered power for motors of one-half to five
horsepower at any point within a mile of its generators,
which occupied a portion of several Newark factories until
the utility built its first power plant on Mechanic Street.

An investment in the electric business was then highly
speculative. Electricity was, at best, incompletely understood,
and its potential was unknown.

"The calibre of the men interested in the new enterprise is
apt to give it, in the minds of present-day readers, a prestige
which in reality it did not possess," wrote Harlow C. Clark,
editor of *Public Service News,* in his brief history of the electric
pioneers. "As a matter of fact, it was an experimental
undertaking, the future of which was for years uncertain and
the path of which was beset with many obstacles."

Dudley Farrand, who joined Newark Electric in 1887 and
later became general manager of the electric department at
Public Service, put it more bluntly: "I have yet to discover a
more hazardous business than was the business of producing
and distributing electricity at its beginning. It was hazardous
from the standpoint of life and limb, and it was hazardous
from the financial standpoint. Knowing as I do the
uncertainty and crudeness of our early methods, I wonder,
as I look back, how anyone was ever induced to risk good
money in an enterprise that was then so speculative."

Farrand spoke of "numerous expensive and tedious
experiments" made by Newark Electric before it was able to
secure its first street lighting contract with the City of
Newark, authorizing the company to replace the dim gas
lamps on Market and Broad Streets with arc lamps. By 1885,

Newark was paying a flat rate of 55 cents per lamp per night for all-night lighting by 100 street lamps, with the rate to drop to 50 cents upon installation of the 150th lamp. Newarkers also purchased power on a flat rate for incandescent light, after the first such bulbs were installed at the Essex Club on Park Place in 1886. There were no meters then to measure how much current a customer used, so even businesses paid for electricity according to a contract that set how many lights they could burn and for how long. Chiselers sometimes hooked up more lights and burned them longer than their contracts allowed; thus Newark Electric and other utilities that had sprung up around New Jersey adopted metering after about 1887. They first employed Thomas Edison's chemical meter, which measured current by the amount of zinc it transferred from positive to a negative plate.

The Newark Electric power plant on Mechanic Street, opened in the early 1880s, was New Jersey's first "central station." Originally built on two lots and soon expanded to cover five, this plant had a capacity more readily measured in lights served than in kilowatts.

"I would not say that the station was designed," the blunt Farrand later declared of the Mechanic Street plant as he found it in 1887. "As far as I am willing to go is to say that it covered the entire lot upon which it was built. The machines consisted mostly of one and two-light machines with a few 10-lighters and one 20-lighter, which was an experiment.

"We had no switches or switch-boards. In most cases the wires leading from the machines were caught over hooks in the ceiling and brought down in 'pigtail' coils to the dynamo terminal. When a machine went out of business, as it often did, we simply detached the wires therefrom and connected them with any available machine. Our business consisted in providing and maintaining 150 arc lamps and 365 incandescent lamps, which latter figure includes those used in lighting the station itself. Our own confidence in the dependability of the service we furnished is indicated by the fact that we provided both gas lamps and lanterns to be used when electricity failed. Both were often used."

Almost all of the company's lights were located in buildings on Broad and Market Streets, within a thousand feet of the Four Corners. The incandescent lighting circuits operated from dusk to 10 p.m. at first, and later throughout the night. Daytime lighting by incandescent lamps began in late summer of 1887, with a small dynamo or generator driven by a 30-horsepower engine carrying the entire load. This same generator also supplied Newark Electric's first industrial power customer, turning a motor at a printing plant a few doors down Mechanic Street. In Trenton, at about the same time, one utility's generator was actually located in a carpentry shop, where it ran woodworking machines during the day and from which, at night, it supplied a circuit of arc lamps. Though sales of daytime lighting were at first disappointing, industrial use of power proved so successful that Newark Electric soon began supplying another, 10-horsepower motor at a coffee-roasting establishment on Mechanic Street. Unfortunately, the utility's generators sometimes slowed down or stopped entirely under the heavy load, with the result that on one occasion a hundred bags of slow-roasting coffee beans were burned to a crisp. A damage suit naturally ensued. By 1889, the Mechanic Street station was nonetheless furnishing electricity for 750 arc lights, 4,000 incandescent lamps, and about 100 horsepower worth of small electric motors.

Newark Electric distributed the electricity from its Mechanic Street station at 70 volts direct current, with one large theater installation at 110 volts. The use of direct current at such low voltages made for great losses in distribution. "Only by the use of copper wire of prohibitive weight and size could current be carried for any distance," wrote Harlow Clark. "In consequence, the area that it was possible to serve from a single generation station was comparatively small, and extension of business beyond this area involved the construction of a new station."

The business of Newark Electric Light and Power grew "steadily, but very slowly" in its small territory, according to *Electrical World*, especially after 1887. In 1891 increasing demand forced the company to build a second power station, this time on the Passaic River. Within five years, the River Station had a load of 2,400 arc lights, 14,000 incandescent lamps, and 300 horsepower in electric motors. Meanwhile, other electric companies opened small power plants in communities around the State. In the Newark area alone, Essex County Electric was incorporated to do business in Orange in 1888, Excelsior Electric in Harrison in 1889, Kearny Electric Light and Power in 1895, Montclair Light and Power in 1895, Suburban Electric Light and Power in East Orange in 1895, and Nichols Light and Power in Nutley in 1895. Within Newark itself, two competitors, the Newark Schuyler Electric Light Company and the Thomson-Houston Electric Light, Power and Heating Company, appeared in 1886.

As these companies grew and their territories coincided, competition, followed by consolidation or financial collapse, was inevitable. Of Schuyler Electric and Thomson-Houston, *Electrical World* later wrote:

> "The two newer companies immediately started in to secure business at any price. Competition was strenuous and at one time prices were reduced so that arc lights were supplied at $1.50 a month on yearly contracts, a rate never since equalled under any condition of power in the electric lighting business. Such ruinously low prices during a period of over six months forced both of the smaller companies out of existence, and they were subsequently bought out by the Newark (Electric) Company (in) September, 1889, and ... June, 1890"

In Hudson County, similarly, the Peoples Light and Power Company was able to weaken and then purchase the Jersey City Electric Light and Hudson County Electric Companies simply by underbidding them for the right to operate Jersey City's 163 street lights. The interests behind Newark Electric, including Thomas and Uzal McCarter and many of the businessmen who would later direct Public Service, eventually took over Peoples Light, adopting the new name and doing business under it. Through Peoples Light, they began gradually to take over most of the small, suburban lighting companies in Essex, Hudson, Morris and Union Counties.

The Peoples Light and Power Company, above, on the Passaic River in Newark, soon after a fire crippled it in December, 1897. It later became Public Service's City Dock Station. Below, the interior engine room of the adjacent Coal Street generating station—two steam engines at rest, the rear one spinning, looked like this in 1916.

Power stations were often built of wood then and used electrical switchboards backed with maple, so fires were common. One of the worst struck Peoples Light on Tuesday, December 29, 1896. It was, says Edward Francis, the unofficial but well-informed historian at Public Service, "the night the lights went out in Newark." The fire gutted the engine and generator room of the River Station, Francis says, "leaving city streets, homes and commercial establishments in darkness. The fire was still smoldering when Philip N. Jackson, the company's president, got on the telephone to the Brush Electric Company in Cleveland."

Electrical World for January 16, 1897, told what happened next:

"The Brush shops were closed and the men had gone for the night and only the night watchman and foreman were around. The telephone operators then called up the residence of the general manager, S. M. Hamill. Mr. Hamill was in Boston. They called the assistant manager, Mr. Prentiss, in East Cleveland, who replied that he would look into the matter at once and telephone them. Mr. Prentiss then telephoned to Mr. Hamill at his hotel in Boston, 681 miles away. Mr. Hamill gave instructions to start the work at once, get out the men, secure cars from the railway and have them switched into the Brush shops and to load every available piece of electric apparatus and also to make arrangements with the Pennsylvania Railroad Company for a special train to run through direct from Cleveland to Newark. By midnight, and before the fire was out, this had been accomplished.

"The dynamos weigh from 8,000 to 10,000 pounds each. They were all loaded by an electric crane in the stock room on shop flat cars and transferred about 400 feet to another 10-ton electric crane, by which they were lifted into the freight cars. By daylight on Wednesday morning (Dec. 30) one half the cars were loaded, and at 3 o'clock in the afternoon 158,000 pounds of apparatus had been loaded in seven freight cars and started for Newark."

Ed Francis says that the freight cars reached Newark "in a little under 20 hours and, right behind them, incandescent generators Jackson had ordered from the Stanley Company in Pittsfield, Massachusetts.

"The ruins of the power station were cleared and the engines found in shape for use. New belting, shafting, and bearings were ordered, and a temporary roof erected. Two Brush arc machines were set up in the Central Power Company station (site of the Branford theater) and 48 hours after the fire started some 250 arc lights were in service in downtown Newark. Four more arc machines were set up in the idle Boyd Street railway power station of Consolidated Traction Company and 600 street lights in Newark and as far away as Bloomfield were lit. A Stanley alternator was set up in the idle Mechanic Street station of the Peoples Company and 4,000 incandescent lamps in Newark, Irvington, and South Orange were lit. On Saturday six of the 13 new arc machines at River Station were in service. On Sunday, five days after the fire, the last machine was reconnected and complete service reestablished—all of it accomplished without the aid of interconnections, and with rail and horse-drawn transportation.

"River Station was completely rebuilt in 1902," Ed Francis concludes, "and after 1903 was known as City Dock Generating Station of Public Service."

One Public Service engineer has joked, no doubt unfairly, that the company's vast physical plant as it exists today was built by men with "weak minds and strong backs." They *had* strong backs, and they needed them, especially during those early years of expansion, experimentation, and consolidation. William Redshaw, who went to work as a wireman's helper for the Edison Electric Illuminating Company in New Brunswick in 1886 and retired with Public Service, later wrote:

"A lineman in those days received a top rate of 25 cents an hour. He worked ten hours a day, 7 to 12 and 1 to 6, six days a week. He furnished his own tools (what there were of them) and carried them stuck through the only belt he wore, the one which held up his pants. If he used a safety belt, it was made of rope while many a lineman used none at all, simply standing on one climber and hooking his 'Democrat leg' around the pole. Today, the line truck carries the man. In 1885, the man carried the truck. He walked from job to job.

He carried his crossarms, wire and other materials on his
back, at first, later acquiring a push cart. He raised poles by
hand (using a pike to tip the pole up and step it), cut his own
gains and lagged his crossarms to the pole. Through-bolts
and crossarm braces were sissy refinements which came along
only after horses and wagons were made standard equipment. A lineman's helper was one part mechanic and one part
pack horse. It is small wonder that the day was called the era
of wooden poles and iron men."

In addition to muscles, electric workers then needed a
combination of ingenuity and daring to get by. Almost all
overhead lines were uninsulated in those day, and Redshaw,
who had advanced to the position of trouble-shooter and was
on his way to becoming a district superintendent, told one
story of the hazards that could result:

"Electricity was as new and exciting to the public as were gas
buggies to horses at a later date. Willie (Redshaw) was sent to
investigate, among others, the Case of the Disappearing
Dishpan. A lady had placed a dishpan in an old-fashioned
kitchen sink and had pushed the rim of the pan so that it
touched the water pipe. Presto! A fine flash, and a piece of
dishpan magically disappeared. Investigation showed that a
guy wire, without benefit of strain insulators, was in contact
both with a live wire and the tin roof of the lady's house. The
roof, in turn, made contact through the roof leader to the
water pipe in the kitchen sink."

A no doubt similar connection "lit up" a tree in front of
Edison Electric's Roselle station each night when the electric
lighting generators started up. This "created lots of amusement" for local boys, according to one newspaper account.
They had driven a nail into the bark of the "hot" tree and
enjoyed "the fun of getting some unsuspecting passerby to
moisten his finger and touch the head of the nail." The
resulting shock was not severe, the newspaper account
concluded, "but it surprises those who are not prepared to
receive it."

Redshaw and his colleagues of course faced more serious
problems, too. The electric system at first had no lightning

protection of any kind, with the result that "Willie was a very busy young man after every storm, renewing numerous fuses for individual fixtures and repairing much damage to interior wiring, cut-outs and key sockets." When lightning struck a line it also often damaged generator coils back at the power station. This happened twice during Redshaw's first summer, crippling both generators at the same time and "resulting in station shutdowns both lengthy and complete." Clearly, some kind of lightning arrester was needed:

> "Ingenuity soon came to the fore, resulting in a home-made gap arrester consisting of a hairpin of fuse wire set in a renewable block. These blocks were then installed on the lines, and those which had operated were renewed by a lineman after each storm. These fuse wire points were next replaced by a miniature sphere gap consisting of BB shot which were, in turn, followed by carbonized lignum vitae between brass plates, a forerunner of the auto valve arresters. These not proving too successful, a swinging ball was suspended over a grounded point, thus combining a spark gap with a reactive blowout mechanism. The station bus (a conductor between different circuits) was protected by Thomson magnetic blow-outs."

As the lighting and power industry gradually overcame such problems, gaining public confidence and with it new customers, electrical development in New Jersey was proceeding more rapidly on another, new front. Leo Daft, an electrical pioneer in the State, had been attempting to operate electric streetcars on horse-car railway routes in and around Newark since 1883. He succeeded in August, 1889, using power from the Newark Schuyler Electric Light Company to drive four streetcars on Bloomfield Avenue between Aqueduct Street, Newark, and Bloomfield. This service continued, though with frequent interruptions, until February, 1891. The craze that was then sweeping the country for this new use of power caught up investors in New Jersey, too, and they enthusiastically undertook not just electrification, but a general expansion of the railway business. The railway companies sometimes bought power from existing electric plants, but more often they built their

The emergence of the electric railway system came to New Jersey in the form of this carrier, produced by Leo Daft in the late 1880s after years of experimentation. four cars of the Daft Electric Railway System ran between Bloomfield and Newark from 1889 to 1891.

own power stations and developed their own technology. Wrote Harlow: "In the ten years between 1890 and 1900, the development of the electric railway outdistanced that of electric light and power. It was largely in the power stations of the railways that the important improvements and betterments took place. These carriers required energy in large amounts, and the railway power stations exceeded both in size and efficiency those of the lighting and power companies. It was in these railway stations that the lesson of economy and efficiency through wholesale power production was taught, a lesson not lost with the men interested in the lighting business, who soon came to realize the advantage of consolidation of resources, both physical and financial."

Both the railway and the lighting and power industries in New Jersey experienced a spate of corporate marriages as the century ended, but the two ends of the electric business remained separate. The many light and power companies of Morris, Union, Essex and Hudson Counties were soon under the control of five large corporations, Peoples Electric prominent among them. In February, 1901, United Electric Company, backed again by many of the individuals and institutions that would make up Public Service, absorbed all five lighting companies. But it was not until June, 1903, that railway, lighting and power in the four counties were finally joined together. The new Public Service Corporation immediately placed its 20 power stations and 24 substations, acquired from Passaic Gas and Electric and South Jersey Gas, Electric and Traction as well as from United Electric, under the single management of its electric department.

When Public Service took over the electric system concentrated around Newark and Jersey City in June, 1903, so James T. Lawson of the electric department later wrote, "there was no Generation Department, no Distribution Department, no chief this and assistant that, specialists were few and far between, no transmission circuits in the same sense that we have them today and no load dispatchers and not a turbo-generator on the system. Each power station was a unit in itself, feeding its own local territory and 13,200 volts (transmission) was considered high enough, too high from some viewpoints.

"We walked or rode to work on trolley cars or on bicycles, and instead of autos we were lucky to have a horse and buggy to cover our territory."

Reciprocating engines, not turbines, still drove the generators in the new utility's power plants. In contrast to the hidden workings of the neatly-enclosed turbine, these huge engines, with their every movement revealed, were a delight to the engineer's eye. They consisted of a single large piston moving within a cylinder at one end and attached, via connecting rods, to a great flywheel at the other. The principle on which they operated may be familiar to readers who have seen steam pistons turning the wheels of a

Engines in the Hoboken Generating Station in this 1895 photo drove generators with the help of leather belts 48 inches wide.

locomotive. Steam, under about 150 pounds pressure per square inch, entered the cylinder through a valve and, expanding, drove the piston back. This force traveled through the connecting rods and a drive belt to the generator and turned it. In the early years, the connection between engine and generator was a long belt, leather, or sometimes rope, running on pulleys, like the fanbelt in an automobile. The two machines were usually set as much as 40 feet apart, requiring an 80-foot belt between them to accommodate the flywheel, which could range for 12 to 25 feet in diameter. This great, spoked wheel—its handsome metal presence dominates most early power plant photographs—was needed, not to transmit the power from engine to generator, but simply to drive the piston back into the cylinder on each revolution.

"I had two beautiful Ball and Wood reciprocating engines when I was in Paterson," recalls Darrow Sage, a 97-year-old pensioner who came to Public Service in 1920. He supervised the last such machines operated by the utility. "I was there when the chief engineer was sick for about eight or nine months. I liked them because they brought me back to my young days when I was raised on reciprocating engines first at General Electric in Schenectady and then at the power plant of the Hudson and Manhattan Railway. It was there I was taught how to indicate them, and taught how to oil and grease them, polish them, keep them shining so they glistened. And when the sun set at night, the light shining on the moving parts would throw flashes of sunlight all over the ceiling. They were beautiful machines. More handsome than turbines. A turbine sits absolutely still, with its buckets (the propeller-like blades driven by the steam) running inside. On the reciprocating engines, you could see the connecting rods and the crosshead crank pin pumping. You had the flywheel as big as 25 or 26 feet in diameter and the rims were two or three feet wide and thick, with big spokes."

"It is something to remember, as many of us do," wrote James Lawson on the company's fiftieth anniversary, "the whirling shafting, belts singing, rows of sparkling commutators, the clank of the engine valves, and flywheels spinning. There was action and glamour as well as a certain amount of danger on every side."

The power station crews seem to have lived in easy intimacy with these machines, ignoring the danger or becoming accustomed to them in ways that would give a modern safety engineer ulcers. They hand-fed coal to the boilers that produced the steam, just as the railroad fireman stoked his steam engine's boilers. The oiler, usually a beginner, spent much of his day filling the lubricators and oil cups, oiling parts, and wiping up oil thrown about by the whirling machines. And when a worker at the generator wanted to pass a tool along to a co-worker at the reciprocating engine, he simply set it on the drive belt and let it ride the distance. Municipal street lighting and the electric railway were still the main customers of the electric department then. As late as 1905, street lighting was using more than 40 per cent of the utility's generating capacity.

Because one demanded power mostly in the evenings, and
the other mostly at rush hours, the workday at a power
station had both hectic peaks and idle periods. Workers
occasionally snoozed when demand was low, Sage recalls,
using the broad leather drive belt on a shut-down machine as
a hammock. This sometimes proved a fatal habit, he says:
"The belts were 42 inches wide and three-quarters of an inch
thick, and fairly long. They used to be the greatest thing for
killing men. The belts were just like a hammock, and the men
would throw themselves down and take a nap. Somebody
would need more power, and they would rush around and
open up the throttle on the machine. The first thing you'd
know, the man on the belt would be running toward the
pulley and he'd come out and you could bury him between
two barn doors."

The belts, which were inefficient as well as occasionally
dangerous, gave way under Public Service to more direct
systems that wasted less energy in the trip between engine
and generator. The reciprocating engines were also inefficient, and they too gradually disappeared from the Public
Service electric system. Wrote Harlow Clark:

> "When electricity made its first demand upon steam, the
> reciprocating engine had been developed to a state where it
> was able to perform the work then exacted of it. But neither
> in capacity nor in dependability did it meet the requirements
> put upon it by the electric central station. It was, however,
> improved in step with electric generating machinery, and
> from (the) thirty to three hundred horsepower reciprocating
> engines of rather uncertain performance that were available
> in the '80s, when central station work was first begun, we (the
> industry) had, by the end of the century, reciprocating
> engines capable of developing 6,000 horsepower, driving
> generators producing 4,000 kilowatts, that worked smoothly
> and with few interruptions. But with these engines the limits
> of the reciprocating engine had been reached; the parts were
> as large as could be shipped from the place of manufacture to
> the place of use. But the demands of electricity for capacity in
> prime movers was just beginning. Fortunately, there ap-
> peared at this juncture the steam turbine, quickly adapted to
> generation purposes by means of the turbo-generator."

"The turbines were more efficient than the reciprocating engines. The principal reason is pretty complicated," says Sage, who operated turbines as superintendent at Essex and Kearny generating stations in the 1920s and 1930s. His hands form an imaginary engine. "You have the piston moving back and forth like this. When it's right here (in), the steam is red hot. When it's here (out), the steam is cold because it has expanded. Now this piston has got to come back again on the next stroke. It will come back and push that cold steam out, and in doing that it chills the iron on the piston head—I mean it chills it a few degrees. When the new steam comes in, the first thing it has to do is heat that iron back the way it was before. And that heat (energy) is all lost."

This loss was reflected in a power plant's heat rate—the amount of fuel, measured in BTU, that it took to produce a single kilowatt hour of electricity. A pound of coal contains about 13,000 BTU, while oil averages 150,000 BTU per gallon. Thus a plant with a heat rate of 13,000 BTU used a pound of coal, or a fraction of a gallon of oil, to produce one kilowatt hour. The lower the heat rate, the more efficient the plant.

"A darn good reciprocating engine would do 16,000 BTU or 18,000 BTU per kilowatt hour," Sage recalls, "against the first turbines, which did 14,000 or 15,000, and the high-pressure turbines today that do less than 9,000."

Public Service installed its first turbine at the Coal Street generating station in Newark in 1905, and added three more vertical turbines in 1905 and early 1906 at the new Marion Generating Station. Marion was constructed not through the PS electric department, but through the North Jersey Street Railway Company, its main trolley subsidiary. The electric department, which was to operate Marion, was then little more than an auxiliary to the railway business. Most new turbines at both Coal Street and Marion generating stations were to power streetcars in North Jersey, rather than light bulbs or run industrial motors, for most of their lives. Though tiny by modern standards, two 6,000-kilowatt turbines at Marion were then "the last word in generator construction," according to a company newsletter, "and engineers from all over the country came to New Jersey to see them. It was impossible to believe that units as large as 6,000 kilowatts could be built, transported and installed."

Load dispatchers later depended on these machines for their quick start-up time, often under ten minutes, but turning on the power that first time was evidently not as easy as the engineers had figured. It was Christmas Eve, 1905, and Dudley Farrand, James Lawson and other prominent men in the electric department were on the spot, as McCarter waited in the comfort of Rumsonhill for news of his first big station.

"The starting up of the first turbine at Marion Station and the various difficulties and details involved in connection with its operation are firmly fixed in my mind," one young engineer later recalled, "as we spent the entire day and most of the night in getting ready to carry load so that a telegram might be sent to Mr. McCarter advising him that Marion was on the line."

After much delay, having operated the turbine barely long enough to justify the telegram to McCarter, the exhausted crew retired for the night—to a nearby saloon, where, so the story goes, they saw in Christmas morning.

Like all later turbines, the originals consisted of huge, rotating shafts from which thin, closely-spaced buckets or vanes stuck out like spokes from a wheel hub. The originals were unlike subsequent turbines, however, in that their shafts were vertical, standing on end, rather than horizontal. The steam here did not merely expand, as in the reciprocating engine; it moved in hot, pressurized jets that continuously struck and drove the buckets within the turbine, thus turning the shaft. Because of the intense steam conditions within the turbine, the buckets and other parts had obviously to be of tough metal, or they would become brittle and shear off. The search for ever stronger alloys, able to withstand the increasing heat and pressure levels needed to produce power economically, was to occupy Public Service through the present. It has come a long way.

Then as now, the mechanical energy of the spinning turbine's shaft became electrical energy in the generator.

Even today, all generators are merely elaborations of the discovery made by Michael Faraday, an English physicist, in 1831. He found that rotating a copper disc edgewise between the poles of a horseshoe magnet produced a current in the disc. This current he collected via brush contacts on the periphery of the disc and on its shaft. By 1903, the generator had advanced well beyond this primitive start, both in size and sophistication. In place of the horseshoe magnet, most generators had a huge, hollow cylinder, called the field, with alternate north and south magnetic poles set in its interior surface. In the center of the cylinder, replacing the copper disc, was a concentric armature built of laminated steel and carrying a two or three-part system of electric conductors on its surface. As in Faraday's original machine, the armature on most early generators rotated within the field. But because of difficulty in collecting current from an armature turning as fast as 1,800 revolutions per minute, most generators by 1903 used a rotating field and a stationary armature. The spinning turbine shaft thus turned the "horseshoe magnet" rather than the "copper disc." The effect was the same: An induced current in the copper wiring of the armature.

From the generator the electricity passed to transformers, which boosted it to a maximum in 1903 of 13,200 volts for "long distance" transmissions of more than a few miles. This "high" voltage, like today's PS maximum of 500,000 volts, helped reduce the power losses associated with longer transmissions. Most of the larger generating stations had by then substituted alternating for direct current and this, too, helped cut losses. The Coal Street station in Newark, for instance, was by then able to send its power on 13,200 volt lines, supported by 70-foot wooden poles, to substations at Irvington and Montclair, respectively four and seven miles away. But most Public Service lines then carried much less voltage over far shorter distances. Then as now, transformers at substations throughout the Public Service territory stepped this power down to still lower voltages for distributions to power and lighting customers.

From Horsecars to Electric Trolleys

"Where the hell's the trolley?"
—Irate Public Service customers

There had been streetcars in the Garden State long before angry customers of Public Service took to calling Tom McCarter in the middle of the night to demand, "Where the hell's the trolley?"

But by 1903, the electric trolley had been in regular service on New Jersey thoroughfares for less than 15 years. For nearly 30 years before that, streetcars had moved along the rails behind struggling teams of horses. One reason for the teams was that a single horse could not haul a car up a hill, so the early companies arranged to hitch on one or two additional horses. When the team got the car to the top of the hill, the idea was to unhitch the other horse or horses without having the car lose momentum, because once a horse stopped unnecessarily it was hard for the driver to start him up again. Most of these were one-man cars, so the way they got around that problem was to enlist help. The help came in the form of "tow boys." These were youngsters who, for the then munificent sum of 75 cents a day, took on what must have looked like work that was both exciting and hectic.

A former West Hoboken tow boy, Louis Straub, who went on to spend more than half a century in street cars and trolleys, told in retirement how it was with the tow boys when he became one at age 15. "I recall the first time I had to take out a team," he wrote. "I had to work on the Big Hill, Bulls Ferry Road, now Park Avenue, from 4:30 p.m. to midnight. I knew little about the team I had, for when I got down to the bottom of the hill with them I had all I could do to hook on to the car. When I got to the top of the hill, my trouble started. It was necessary to keep the car in motion while unhooking your chain or receive a call from the driver because it was so difficult for the horses to start again. I felt lonesome on that big hill that night, for it was the first time I had ever been out after nine o'clock, and I assure you those horses knew when their time was up. When I brought the last car up, they got troublesome, and not knowing their nature I unhooked them. Without waiting for me to get on their backs they started on to run. When I walked down to the barn, I found the horses, Barney and Pat, waiting for me."

As he became more familiar with his teams, Louis Straub said, he pestered the foremen to promote him from general utility man to actually handling a street car. It was a lifetime ago, but he tells the story with genuine feeling. The first responsibility of a conscientious driver was to put his harness in the shop "and have it painted and cleaned up," said Straub. "I felt proud to hook that gray team to the car to make the dinner trip over Union Hill. I tell you I loved good horses. In the summer, the half-night men (those who worked split shifts) got the jobs with all chartered cars to Eldorado Park (a big amusement park on the Palisades), but you wouldn't mind it when you could hook up four good horses."

The horse-car company, too, apparently took more than just a proprietary interest in its horses, for it assigned them, according to Louis Straub, on the basis of which drivers showed they cared about the animals. In a period when it meant 12 hours a day, seven days a week, he observed that "a driver was supposed to work full-time. They did not like to see him lay off, on account of his horses. They did not like to see other men handle them. If you could not work steady, they would give you the poor horses in the stable, and that was hell, to make time with a poor team and a road-dragger. What I mean by a road-dragger is a conductor that would hang on the bell."

Straub reveals the born horse-lover's bias favoring horse-flesh over all other sources of power when he recalls with obvious relish the somewhat lame beginnings of the electric-powered trolleys. "The first powerhouse was located at the reservoir in Weehawken. It was two small generators which supplied the power for the cars. The trolley service was rather poor, because frequently the power would give out, resulting in the cars being stalled along the road. When this happened we had to get four horses from the stable and tow the cars back to the station."

The transition to electric trolleys was inevitable, of course, but that didn't mean Louis Straub and the other horse-car drivers had to like it. He wrote that service was "very poor" until power came from the 14th street powerhouse, but that then the first electric trolleys— "18-foot Brill cars, single-truck, open front, hand-braked, operated by a rheostat"— rapidly made inroads on the horses. "When we left," Straub said, "the superintendent said to us that if the (electric) trolley cars are not a success, 'none of you expect to return.' Our first trip was made from Eldorado Station, Highwood Park, to 18th Street, Weehawken. We made two trips, 20 minutes to a trip. The superintendent and an electrician broke us in. After we had made the trips with them, we were told we were all right, although none of us knew how to run a car and knew less of a hood switch, motor brush, and motors. All that we did know was how to use a hand brake, and that during the trip the car had to be run at full speed. Otherwise the rheostat got hot and smoked."

The transition from horse to electric power was no overnight proposition, however, and the harsh, grinding life of the horse-car operators remained vivid in Louis Straub's memory all his days. "In case you had an accident on the road, it was up to you (to pay for it). If you broke a window, it was one dollar; if you put a hole in a funnel of the car, it was five dollars. If you did not want to pay it, quit.

"In case the boss wanted to see you, he would give you a call, but there was no going on the carpet to get what was coming to you. No matter where he met you, oh my how he would lace into you! He thought more of his horses than of his men. One special thing was for having lame horses, or if he caught you whipping or yanking a horse, he would not speak gentle to you. He would say, 'Horses cost money, and I can get men for nothing.' A starter, too, had lots of power in former days. He could take you off the board for refusing to take a run out, and if you went to see the superintendent, all he would say was, 'We hire men to do as they are told. Our cars is got to run.'"

Straub called the run during the Blizzard of '88 "the hardest trip I ever made in my life." He said he left the depot at 3:35 p.m. to go over Union Hill to the Hoboken Ferry "double up," which meant four horses to the car. When on the return trip he got as far as Washington and Eighth, "my horses turned their backs to the storm—and it was a *storm:* Hail, rain, snow, and the wind was blowing. We had to turn back to the Hoboken Ferry, and then to the Hoboken stables, where we laid up. At about 9:30 p.m. there was a call came from the Hoboken office asking if the men from the Hill was there yet, and would they hitch their horses to the coach and take this old gentleman home. But what a time it was! Raining, hailing, snowing, and a good gale blowing. I was riding the lead team. We got as far as 19th Street, Weehawken, and run into a snow bank. We had to give up. We unhooked our horses and started for the stable. I was riding one horse and leading the other. I thought I would never get home. The poor horses was one sheet of ice. I reached the stables, but I tell you it was a ride for life, it was, in 1888."

There were 15 million horses in America at that time. Under the impact of electric power for the street and overland haulage, their number had dwindled, by the time Public Service began in 1903, to nine million. That precipitous drop pales before the slide to a horse population today of only about two million nationwide. In that time of transition, a sharp-eyed observer named Thorne, who kept a log on one of the pioneer trolley firms, Consolidated Traction, was making such entries as the demand from "Kearny for better horse-car service," the death by fire of 65 street-car horses at Lyons Farms, and the wretched condition of the horses used on the Harrison Line cars.

A particularly intriguing entry, for April 15, 1894, puts in amusing perspective the outlook of one whose lawyer son was soon to found Public Service. "T.N. McCarter got an injunction against Consolidated putting a pole in front of his residence, 1044 Broad St."

In the decade before the electric trolley, there had been more than 100,000 horses pulling 18,000 street-railway cars along some 3,000 miles of track in cities across America, and before that an untold number of cars being pulled along streets with no tracks or with tracks just plunked on plain dirt and completely unballasted. This golden decade of the horse car represented a phenomenal upsurge in available horse-flesh in the wake of "the great epizootic" of 1872, a kind of equine influenza which laid low so many horses that in some cities men had banded together out of sheer desperation to pull the horse cars themselves.

Horses had a working life of about nine years; they were in those days a valuable commodity that cost about $150 each. Since horse-car operators' wages ranged from $1.25 to a high of $2.00 a week after long service, with absolutely no fringe benefits, it is easy to see how bosses in an age when a social conscience had yet to be born prized the animal in preference to the man. Combined with the $750 price-tag on a trolley, a lack of horse-sense could play havoc with trolley line economics. One way to put good horses at risk, observer Thorne noted, was to stable them head-to-head so that they could spread airborne infections by breathing into one another's faces. Another way was to confine them in stalls too small for them to move around. Yet a third way was to buy a horse and put him right to work without letting him have a day to rest up after his trip in from the country, and then fail to give him a half-pint of linseed oil so that he would end up constipated. Even though horses on the old trolleys worked, usually, not much more than a six or eight-hour day, spending most of their time in the stables, they did work hard, so that a constipated horse was a horse asking for trouble for his owners. This was particularly true if the conditions of the stable where he lived and the grooming and care that he received were not all that they should have been, as was the case in many of the small, competing horse-car companies of that era.

Street cars got their start in the United States from the inspiration of John Mason, a New York Chemical Bank president, in 1832. Under the thrust of his entrepreneurial genius, Manhattan soon had a one-mile stretch of track between Canal and 14th Streets, and not long after, New Orleans, too, had horse cars. It took another 18 years, however, for the next American city to catch the fever. That was in 1850, when Boston imported second-hand cars from New York with the destination "Car to Greenwood Cemetery" still emblazoned on their sides. In the New England capital there had been sharp-elbowed rivalry to be first between two new traction firms, Metropolitan Railway (forerunner of today's MBTA) and Cambridge Railroad. Cambridge won out, and at first let people ride free to sell them on the superiority of travel by horsecar. Inside of a week, Cambridge Railroad was hauling more than 2,000 passengers a day. When Cambridge figured it had people sold, it started to collect fares. That was when all hell broke loose. Reactions ranged from demands that Boston withdraw the Cambridge Railroad franchise, to suggestions that those in charge of the new "rapid" transit system be strung up on Boston Common.

The neck-and-neck situation between horses and other sources of power that developed with the coming of electricity had its harbingers even during the interregnum of the steam locomotive. In New York City, for example, these chuffing, cinders-spitting monsters, called "steam dummies," had to have boxlike structures built around them so that they wouldn't frighten horses plying the streets below.

Electricity brought with it the need for somewhat more agile activity to accommodate its advent. The way people accepted the boon of electric power echoed, in its way, the reaction of horses to steam locomotives. The horses were only scared. But the humans went them one better—not being able to make up their minds whether they did or didn't want the blessings of electricity.

The Thorne log for January 1, 1893, for instance, identifies the alacrity with which Newark and South Orange Railway acted upon receiving a traction franchise before the townsfolk beneficiaries of same could wake up and get the local politicians to rescind it: "South Orange Line secured franchise previous week, and poles and suspender wires are in place. Line first operated Feb. 13, 1893." Speed in getting the cars rolling, if not at first in delivering dependable service, was the ticket.

Consolidated Traction's revenues on its three divisions for 1893 of $420,557.60 dropped off the following year to $301,595.44. Even though it was now serving seven divisions, the dimension of the downhill change from the heyday of the horse cars less than 10 years before was becoming painfully apparent.

While the handwriting was on the wall for the splintered traction companies that were by then running their tracks every which-way across New Jersey, the trolley had proved itself an unequalled convenience and was fast becoming a necessity, in most of the State's cities—except for one defect. The street railway system, whether powered by horse or, latterly, by electricity, required a huge investment of capital, backed up by still more capital to keep abreast of the never-ending need for improvements and extensions.

Mergers began almost as soon as the necessary minimum of two companies appeared in the field.

In his book, *Fares, Please*, John A. Miller outlines the complicated but typical genealogy of a single, six-mile line from Newark to Bloomfield and Montclair: Built in 1867 by the Newark, Bloomfield & Montclair Horse Car Company, it was sold nine years later to the Newark and Bloomfield Street Railway, which, after nine more years, became part of the Essex Passenger Railway. After five years, the Essex Passenger Railway became part of the Newark Passenger Railway. Two years later, the New Jersey Traction Company

leased the Newark Passenger Railway for 999 years. But
after only a single year, the New Jersey Traction Company
became part of Consolidated Traction, which, after five more
years, was leased to the huge, new North Jersey Street
Railway Company. Five years later, in 1903, the North Jersey
Street Railway Company—and with it the six-mile line—
became a subsidiary of the Public Service Corporation. In
just 36 years, the little line had traveled its unchanging route
under nine different names—averaging a new one every
four years.

By 1903, the repeated consolidations throughout New
Jersey had yielded 12 large, independent traction companies.
These dozen firms represented the amalgamation of 96
smaller, separate trolley corporations, few of which had
sufficient capital to maintain their costly equipment properly. There were other problems, too. The railway companies had burdened their properties with heavily-watered
stock and neglectful management, allowing scores of miles of
tracks, expensive cars, powerlines and generating systems to
deteriorate scandalously. ("Watered stock" was a Wall Street
term derived from the larcenous practice of a cattle baron
who, in the 1880s, beefed up his livestock temporarily with
generous quantities of salt and then water before sending
them to market. It came to mean the stock, now in the form
of securities, was priced above its actual worth.) In some
cases these companies had also expanded too quickly into
sparsely-populated and therefore unprofitable districts.
Toward the end of the 1890s, for example, one Passaic
traction magnate, reflecting on a final decision against a new
line from Main and Bloomfield Avenues to Bloomfield and
Montclair, which had been on-again-off-again since 1892,
summed up the fiscal realities of expansion this way: "To
make a trolley road profitable, you need a house every 25
feet."

As late as February, 1903, the *New York Tribune* reported:

"The power of the Newark Trolley Trust in political and
financial circles was the reason given yesterday by a
prominent businessman of Newark for the miserable street-

car service of that city. The railroad company, secure as to its franchises, had ridden roughshod over the protests of the citizens, he said, certain that it would never be called to account by the city officials."

The unnamed businessman listed "corporate greed, over-capitalization and consequent watering of stock" as among the evils of Newark's (and, as it turned out, much of New Jersey's) traction business.

A horrible accident and the revelations made in its aftermath precipitated the final great consolidation of trolley, gas, and electric companies in New Jersey.

Founding of the Public Service Corporation was recalled in a comprehensive, 19-page article in the November, 1934, issue of *Fortune Magazine*.

"It began with a tragedy in Newark," the magazine said. Then, in dramatic detail, it described the accident.

"The morning of Thursday, February 19, 1903, was an icy morning and there was no sand on the tracks ahead of Motorman Pete Brady, operating a northbound Clifton Avenue trolley of the North Jersey Street Railway Co. His car was jammed so tightly with over 100 children on their way to the Barringer High School that he could scarcely contort himself enough to turn the long brass handle that tightened his brake chain. As he started on the down grade at Orange Street he saw the safety gates go down along the tracks of the Delaware, Lackawanna & Western Railroad. But without sand to get a grip and without chance to brake his car there was very little he could do about it. In the absence of a derail switch, which should have been there but wasn't, Pete Brady's car and the engine of the Lackawanna train reached the crossing at just about the same time. The crash split the trolley in two. The bottom half stayed on the tracks; the top half was crushed into a powder of wood and glass.

"They laid the children out side by side in the snow. Eight girls and one boy were either killed outright or died later, and more than twenty children were desperately injured. Newark's Mayor Doremus proclaimed the coming Sunday a day of public mourning..."

In the investigations that followed, it became evident that the North Jersey Street Railway Company was foundering financially. Other transportation companies had the same problem, as did many new, struggling electric and gas companies.

"Patently," said *Fortune*, "the times called for a Man of Vision...The man of vision turned up in Trenton. His name was Thomas Nesbitt McCarter..."

McCarter Takes Over

"The apple does not fall far from the tree."
—Proverb

McCarter had only recently been named New Jersey's attorney general by Governor Franklin Murphy. At 34 he was the youngest attorney general in the state's history.

When the street railway accident occurred in Newark and an investigation was called for, McCarter, by virtue of his office and his interests, was right in the middle of the probe. He had acquired a sound knowledge of the shaky financial condition of some of the state's street railway companies. He had a mounting conviction that there was a crying need for somebody with vision to do something about it. He also felt there was a potential for profit for anybody equipped to take the necessary steps.

He was certainly equipped—in know-how, brain power, inside information, personal and financial resources, and brass—to recognize a good thing when he saw it.

McCarter followed his conviction like a riverboat gambler drawing to an inside straight. Events followed in staccato succession.

He resigned as attorney general. From his own reserves and those of colleagues, he put together an initial $10-million capitalization with which to launch the acquisition program that was to continue for almost a decade.

Out of the first traction, gas and electric companies they brought into the fold, McCarter formed the Public Service Corporation of New Jersey. He became its first president and its only one for the next 36 years, after which he doggedly dug in his spurs as board chairman for another six. When he checked the books for the year after he took that giant step, he saw a gross income of $17 million. By the time he stepped down for good in 1945, gross revenues had risen to $750 million.

His achievement is understandable when one considers that the apple does not fall far from the tree.

Tom McCarter was born on October 20, 1867, two years after the end of the Civil War, at Newton, New Jersey. He was the youngest boy of six children born to Thomas Nesbitt and Mary Louise (Haggerty) McCarter: Uzal Haggerty, Robert Harris, Thomas Nesbitt, Fanny A., Jane E. and Eliza Nesbitt. Their father, a Princeton graduate, Class of 1842, was founder of one of the oldest and most lucrative law firms in the state. He was a senior trustee of Princeton University, served as the chairman of the Ways and Means Committee of the New Jersey Assembly, and—by appointment of Democratic Governor Joseph D. Bedle—was the New Jersey Commissioner for determining the boundary between New York and New Jersey.

While the youngsters were still not fully grown, the family came from Newton by horse-drawn wagon to Newark and settled at 59 Lincoln Park. Both in Newton and Newark, the man who was to found Public Service enjoyed an upbringing that made his world of kerosene lamps for light and coal-fired furnaces for heat not the world of deprivation it might appear to be by today's standards. It was a world of mellow comfort, unquestioned security, and gracious between-wars living. In this rose-colored environment Tom went to Dr. Pingry's School in Elizabeth and readied himself for Princeton. He had a natural self-discipline, his elder daughter speculated recently, but there to steady it further was the stern, dominant figure of his mother. Her iron control, interestingly enough, made all her children adore her, according to Ellen McCarter Doubleday's view of her grandmother—although, Ellen added, "the boys' wives didn't." Of the three girls, only Tom's favorite sister, Eliza Nesbitt, never married.

The original McCarter brought with him the fund of discipline it took for anyone, in those days, to emigrate westward from Europe. That McCarter, an Ulsterman named John, was of Scotch-Irish descent and a covenanter to the core. He came from a deeply committed and uninterruptedly Presbyterian clan. When John McCarter came from Ireland to settle in Philadelphia in 1774, he brought with him a piece of paper signed by his minister attesting that "John McCarter leaves this parish in good standing to seek his fortune in the New World." The founder of PSE&G cherished that historic parchment all his days, even though the only reverence it got from his own children was to have them refer to their ancestor as "Honest John"—a nickname they also applied to founder Tom behind his back. Tom's grandson, John Pierson McCarter has the document now.

All four children begotten by PSE&G's founder are deceased. The eldest, Ellen McCarter Doubleday (widow of publisher Nelson Doubleday) died in 1978 shortly before this book was published. The youngest, Madeleine Barker McCarter Kelly (widow of Fidelity Union Bank and Trust Company vice president and supersalesman Carlos Kelly), died in 1976. Both sons—Thomas Nesbitt, Jr., who became an executive vice president and director of Public Service, and Uzal Haggerty II—are also deceased.

To have sprung from a family like that of John McCarter, which in three generations made it from Philadelphia immigrant to senior trustee of Princeton and a distinguished law practice, says a lot about the McCarters' genes. Tom McCarter was not short-changed. In rapid succession, he pyramided responsibility upon responsibility in a career that moved swiftly into bigger and bigger stakes.

The pattern was markedly parallel to that of "Honest John" McCarter's progress. After serving as an officer during the Revolution, founder Tom's ancestor had moved to Morris County, become surrogate by appointment of Governor Bloomfield, and gone on to serve his adopted

Garden State as master in chancery and clerk of Morris County until in 1807 he turned over the family reins to the first Robert H. McCarter, father of the first Tom McCarter, and went to his reward.

The man who would found Public Service, carrying on the upwardly mobile tradition, left the family law firm to pursue public utility law, and Governor John W. Griggs appointed him judge of Newark's First District Court. Two years later— Tom McCarter was elected vice president and general counsel of the Essex and Hudson Gas Company, and went right on serving on the bench. Private practice and judicial practice, at the time, were not judged to be in conflict of interest. He shucked his judge's robes for good in 1899, though, when the people of Essex County sent him to Trenton as state senator.

He shucked his robes, but not his restless ambition. With Adrian and Chandler W. Riker he formed a real estate firm to put up the Lawyers Building in Newark, and in 1900 he found himself elected to the board of directors of his older brother Uzal's Fidelity Union Trust Company. In 1901 he became majority leader of the Republican-controlled Senate and chairman of the Republican State Executive Committee. By 1902 he was so deeply involved in Fidelity's business activities that the board named him vice president and general counsel. Three months after he took on that double-barreled assignment and put aside his law practice to devote full time to the bank's affairs, Governor Murphy appointed him attorney general.

McCarter, Through the Eyes of a Grandson

"... no other graduate of Yale or Princeton had McCarter's record of attending 58 consecutive Princeton-Yale football games."
—Walter Camp

To sit and watch the checkered autumn sunlight filter over the sandy hair and patrician features of founder Tom's grandson, Thomas N. McCarter III, as he spins recollections of his famous forebear, is to live for a time vicariously in the presence of the forebear. The grandson has none of the latter's aura of the autocratic harumph, of course, because these are the times that are supposedly "a-changin'" with regard to all that, and even a Princeton education uses more adaptable modes these days. As the fourth Thomas N. McCarter in direct line from Honest John to take his degree at Princeton, the incumbent Thomas Nesbitt McCarter III has therefore about him a frankness that makes him as easy a man to listen to as PSE&G's founder is said to have been when his mood was right. That was a condition the family could never be quite sure about until he opened the door at night and, from the look on his face, learned it had been a good day or a bad day at Public Service

Leaning back comfortably in one of the sun-flooded west rooms on the ground floor of the Ivy Club on Prospect Street in Princeton, Thomas N. McCarter III talks easily about his recollections of comments "made to me by my family on my grandfather, and more importantly by second-generation children of early associates of my grandfather, having to do with the initial $10-million capitalization of Public Service. I distinctly recall that the capitalization was broken down between bonds and common stock. Many of the predecessor companies—an impressive 521 of them went into the making of Public Service, you know—were in financial difficulties, so when it came to the capitalization of the new company the 'water' was squeezed out as far as the bonds were concerned. The bondholders therefore had the true net assets. The common stock—which was not really so common, because in those days people were interested in bonds—represented the hope for the future of the company."

Earlier, he had gone into the antecedents of what was watershed capitalization, in more ways than one. His grandfather wrote about it in a personal recollection of how two established firms—Fidelity Union Trust Company and Prudential Insurance Company—aided a new utility venture. "That was before Prudential became a mutual company," Tom III noted. "Uzal H. McCarter was the largest stockholder in the Fidelity Union Trust Company, and also controlled the largest bloc of stock in the Prudential. Both Uzal H. McCarter and Thomas N. McCarter were on the board of directors of Prudential, not only because of personal friendship with John F. Dryden, but because of their stock interest. Thomas N. McCarter also had a substantial interest in the Fidelity Union Trust Company, and although through the years he gave away some of the stock he owned, at his death he was the third largest stockholder in the bank.

"A partial description my grandfather gave of how the Fidelity Union Trust Company was involved in underwriting the original capitalization of Public Service reveals that Fidelity Union, representing Uzal H. McCarter and other related New Jersey interests, subscribed to 25 per cent of the original capitalization. At the same time, the Kuser-Dryden interests subscribed to 24 per cent. Senator Dryden was President of the Prudential Insurance Company, and his son-in-law, Anthony Kuser, headed the South Jersey traction interests. The United Gas Improvement Company of Philadelphia, encompassing the large Pennsylvania-group interest, purchased an additional 25 per cent.

"In addition to this total of 74 per cent, it is my recollection directly from my grandfather, as well as from references in the record, that a Mr. Waterbury, president of the Bank of Manhattan Company, representing himself and other New York interests, subscribed to 8-1/3 per cent initially, and one of the Philadelphia capitalists took an additional 8-1/3 per cent. That left another 8-1/3 per cent which Thomas N. McCarter subscribed to, and if my figures are correct a final one per cent which fell to I don't remember whose interest. My grandfather took pride in the fact, and often talked about it, that initially well over 50 per cent of the original capitalization of Public Service came from New Jersey residents. As far as the interest belonging to Thomas N. McCarter himself is concerned, he began to reduce his holdings in 1935 and by 1942 it had been reduced substantially to less than one per cent."

How come? Was it diminishing faith in his own ability to weather the economic pressures of the Thirties? Was it a prescient awareness of what the gathering problems of wartime, and their unpredictable aftermath, would bring? Was he tiring? Did having been in on the ground floor now seem to have lost its zest?

Founder Tom's daughter Ellen thought another reason may have been that about that time, with the able young hounds snapping more and more audibly at the heels of the old boar for a place in the sun of management, her father "got mad at them, and they at him," and on that score also began to cut his holdings.

The family seems generally in agreement, moreover, that it was not so much Public Service that provided the money which enabled Tom the founder and his guests to go sledding on the grounds of the family estate, Rumsonhill,

dressed in rich velvet, as if they were characters reincarnated
from some Dickensian vision of upper-class life in England.
Public Service had nothing to do with Rumsonhill, in fact, at
least as far as building it was concerned. Tom McCarter III
says that his grandfather built the palatial showplace, only
coincidentally in the same year Public Service came into
being, for $1,000,000—in cash. Obviously, says Tom III, he'd
done very well in his law practice, and must also have turned
a more than pretty penny on the Lawyers Building project in
Newark. Besides, it was in the days when a dollar was worth
more than a shirt cardboard and there was no income tax to
bleed it further.

Where Tom made his real money, aside from banking, the
family maintains, was not only in the power-and-transport
arena but, with his Midas touch in its usual fine working
order, by investing early in the movie industry. He made the
shrewd choice of Fox Film Corporation as an enterprise that
promised to work out well from the start, Tom III recalls, "at
a time, apparently, when the public utility industry was
under pressure from political reform groups between 1910
and 1915. Uzal H. McCarter and Thomas N. McCarter were
two of the 10 original backers Fox invited to fund his
fledgling enterprise, and," as Tom III remembers it, "each
subscribed $50,000 which was apportioned between com-
mon stock and convertible bonds. The $50,000 unit
amounted to five per cent of the company. Both men became
Fox Film directors, and Uzal sold his interest to his brother
around 1913. Later, Thomas N. McCarter divested himself of
his combined interest in Fox."

That was in the early Twenties. The fallout from it, as far
as the McCarters and those close to them were concerned,
was, to use a word the movie industry itself was already
making its own, sensational. At one point, whether from
dividends or partial disposition of stock, Tom McCarter gave
his wife and daughters strings of pearls, a gesture daughter
Ellen distinctly identified with what she said her father
always disparagingly called his "flyer" in Fox Film. Tom III
remembers that when his grandfather pulled out of Fox
entirely, the city of Newark received "a substantial sum of

money to put to work among various charities. At the same time, my grandfather donated funds to build the McCarter Theatre at Princeton."

Ellen Doubleday remembered that occasion well, too. Ellen said that on her father's sixtieth birthday—which would have made it 1927 rather than the early Twenties—he gave his four children $100,000 each, and their mother $200,000, "mostly in Fox Film stock, which he told us to sell because he had lost faith in Mr. Fox. We all did sell, and got out before it went 'way down. My Aunt Lizzie got $100,000, too, and I think somebody else did also. He parted with a great deal of money at that time, and he was very careful about money. Not stingy, because he was generous, but the value of the dollar was awfully important to him."

It was not unlikely that Tom McCarter, whose sense of humor tended to be on the ponderous side when he attempted it in his speeches, had decided to have a little fun with his silver-spoon offspring at that point by staggering the sequence in which he made his benefactions. As far as the record of events in Ellen's memory was concerned, he had to have given $250,000 to Princeton for the McCarter Theatre before he made the other distributions. In any case, the happening as she reconstructed it takes on the overtones of a scene from *The Great Gatsby*. Legend persists that F. Scott Fitzgerald's knowledge of the McCarters' way of life, coupled with his own inability to penetrate the Princeton clubs the McCarters so easily frequented, may have indirectly contributed to this novel.

"Someone had told my father that Princeton needed a theater," Ellen recalled, "and he wanted to give his cherished alma mater *something*. My first husband, Atwood, and I were staying at the Doubledays in Oyster Bay that weekend, and Atwood had to meet his brother in New York on Monday. We didn't have much money because the weekend had cost us every single cent we had. The station didn't have a newsstand when we got on the train into town, but somebody had left a *Times* on one of the seats. I picked it up—and there we were, knowing we had to go to the dock to meet Atwood's brother in a cab, and that we'd have to stop at the Yale Club to cash a check to pay for the cab because we didn't have anything between us—and on the front page of the *Times* it said 'McCarter Gives $250,000 to Princeton University.' We hadn't known anything about it. I was so mad I threw the paper out the window. I was *so* mad. Me without a penny and Princeton with all that."

Tom McCarter III likes to reminisce about his grandfather's numerous distinctions, from the truly monumental to the entertainingly trivial. He points out, for example, that his forebear was one of the first to suggest tunneling under the Hudson River and was appointed by Governor Walter Edge as a member of the Interstate Bridge and Tunnel Commission, predecessor of The Port Authority of New York and New Jersey. He also suggested the building of the Pennsylvania Railroad Station in Newark, along with the Menlo Park memorial to Thomas A. Edison. As Edison's long-time friend and associate in building the utilities industry in the East, McCarter later became first chairman of the Edison Park Commission.

Edison's Menlo Park laboratory was the world's first industrial research complex. It was headquarters for Edison's operations during the 10 years considered to be his most productive, 1876-1886. Out of this laboratory came perfection of the practical incandescent lamp, the commercially practicable telephone, the phonograph, and systems of electrical generators and distribution. He also discovered a phenomenon known as the "Edison Effect" which covers the fundamental principle on which now rests the modern science of electronics. Edison Memorial State Park is just off the Garden State Parkway in Menlo Park, northern Middlesex County, in New Jersey.

Tom III likewise touches lightly but interestingly on a 1937 statement made by Walter Camp of Yale, to the effect that "no other graduate of Yale *or* Princeton had McCarter's record of attending 58 consecutive Princeton-Yale football games." Earlier, Princeton—which tantalizingly withheld from him all his life the trusteeship he coveted, even after his brother Uzal had declined it and urged Princeton to "go

down the street and give it to my brother Tom"—had
bestowed on him a gold football to commemorate his
attendance at 50 consecutive games. "But only games with
Yale," Ellen pointed out. "Never with Harvard."

The grandson includes among his forebear's achievements
his role as one of the organizers of the Edison Electric
Institute, of which he was second president, and of the
Mountain Lake Club in Lake Wales, in central Florida. "He
built a winter home there about 1920," says Tom III, "and
spent approximately two months a year there for the next 30
years."

Asked if, as an investment banker today, he has any idea
how all those 521 companies his grandfather amalgamated
into Public Service had gotten themselves into such serious
financial difficulties, Tom McCarter III says, "There were a
great many predecessor companies that were known as
traction companies in the early 1890s, and they were
controlled by New York, New Jersey and Philadelphia
traction interests. Some of these companies were spread too
thin financially. By that I mean that the income that was
derived from operations went into the pockets of the
stockholders and bondholders with, in too many cases, very
little attempt made to keep the properties in working order.
As a result, when the accident in 1903 that caused a loss of
life at a rail crossing in Newark occurred, indictments were
handed down against the companies that were directly and
indirectly involved. These particular companies happened to
be owned by the Philadelphia interests. Thomas N. McCarter, Sr.—he was now Senior because his father had died by
then—went to Philadelphia and was chairman of the
committee that eventually resulted in the amalgamation of
many of these companies into what became Public Service
Corporation. Later, other companies joined the initial
group."

Crowds like these—celebrating the 250th anniversary of Newark in Lincoln Park and Military Park on May 1, 1916—used the ubiquitous trolley for outings, in great numbers.

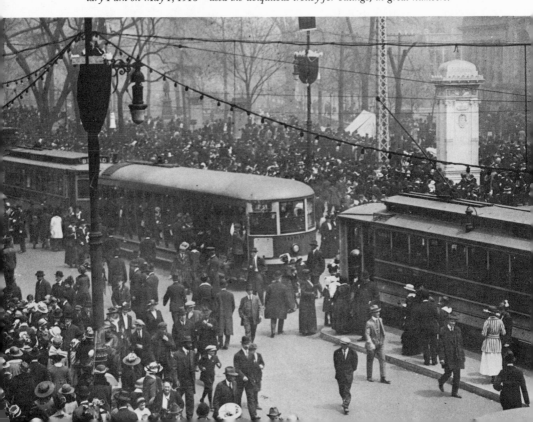

P. S. Transport's Rocky Start

*On Newark's Belleville and Clinton Avenue line alone, 21 of 45
cars spent most of the previous week broken down.*

When McCarter took over, in June of 1903, the new trolley
utility which that consolidation had produced, he found the
property in discouraging condition. Trolley rails had worn
dangerously thin for dozens of miles. The hodgepodge
collection of power plants was antiquated and constantly
overloaded. (One company engineer recalls an old-timer
from a Hoboken plant saying that "at times the load would
be so heavy that they would pull circuits. They'd drop a
circuit for 10 minutes or so, and then put it back, and then
drop another circuit. So cars would be moving in one area
and not in another. That was the situation then." Passengers
on a temporarily shut-down line had little choice but to wait
or walk). There were too few trolley cars and these, in
disrepair to start with, broke down regularly. Moreover, the
scheduled speed on many urban lines was only five to seven
miles an hour, instead of the standard nine. The entire
system was, as one writer put it, in "a state of general
decrepitude that called for renovation."

"Money that might have gone to extensions had to be spent in practically making over the plants of old companies," wrote William E. Sackett in *Modern Battles of Trenton* (1914). "The $4,000,000 (of the new company's original $10-million investment) reserved for betterments fell like a drop in the bucket of need. Larger capitalizations and bond issues of startling magnitude brought many times more millions to the company's aid."

McCarter had promised that the public would be "well served at reasonable rates." But in 1903, the many riders dependent on the trolley lines were not inclined to regard Public Service favorably. At least in the beginning, the new company would suffer the reputation of its unstable predecessors. Indicative of this attitude was a single headline, announcing the founding of Public Service, that ran in the Newark *Sunday Call*. "Now," it deadpanned, "for Another Great Corporation Combination." As Jersey City Mayor Mark Fagan noted, patrons of the railway system had been hearing promises from the old management for years—that new cars were on order, that a new powerhouse was in the works, and so on. Fagan said he was prone to accept the Public Service assurances of better performance in good faith, but added, "I think the present officers of the company should not be surprised that we are all a little skeptical about the new promises which are being made."

Fagan did not note, as he well might have, that the old, prodigal management and the new, abstemious management were practically identical. The faces were the same and so were the companies and institutions they represented. The principal difference was the dominating presence in the new management of Thomas N. McCarter Sr., who had publicly set himself against the old vices of watered stock and mismanagement.

Upon its formation, Public Service moved quickly to meet its promises, ordering 150 new cars, with delivery to begin in November of that year, 1903. While this was more than the old companies had purchased in many years, McCarter realized that this order would "only enable the company to spare the worst of the present equipment for repairs." Thus

The going was rough in the early days of the Public Service Transport division. But there was time for play, too. In this 1909 photo, Public Service Railway employees wait for a trolley to take them to a picnic.

Public Service promptly ordered 150 additional cars. Among other measures it took that first year to improve its properties, the utility hired several of the nation's most respected railway managers, it purchased 1,200 tons of rail "mainly for renewals," it began the streamlining and coordination of many different systems to form one company and, as part of this effort, it undertook the task of "practically remodeling the entire (power-generating) scheme" to obtain more power efficiently. Included in the remodeling was the planned construction of the 13,000-kilowatt Marion Generating Station on the Hackensack River.

These ambitious plans might well have satisfied even the most persistent critics of the utility. It would of course be months before improvements would be evident to trolley riders, but McCarter frankly admitted this and asked for patience. Neither McCarter nor his trolley patrons could then have predicted the havoc that the weather and, to a lesser extent, unionism would play with these plans during those few short months.

The utility's troubles began almost immediately, as motormen threatened to strike over wages, the alleged firing of
union organizers, and the motormen's right to union
representation. Emotions ran high and Public Service felt
compelled to protect its property against "any concerted
attack" by hiring armed guards and constructing 10-foot
fences around depots. In addition, the company prepared a
back-up staff to replace striking trolleymen. These actions
discouraged some of the more conservative workers, and
when the strike came in October, 1903, it quickly failed.
Service was disrupted on many trolley lines, but only partly
and only for a single afternoon.

A more persistent problem during these early months—
and throughout the company's early years—was what Martin
Schreiber, maintenance engineer, called "the endless variety
of both the mechanical and the electrical equipment" it had
inherited through the consolidation of so many independent
roads. This lack of uniformity made the ordering of parts
and the task of maintenance itself more difficult and more
time-consuming than it was for other railway companies, and
was to prove a handicap to the company's efforts to satisfy a
riding public that was both demanding of service and
uninterested in explanations.

The weather that winter brought out all the latent flaws in
the utility's patchwork railway system. Snow covered the
ground through most of December and the mean temperature for the month was the lowest recorded since establishment of the U. S. Climate and Crop Service in 1887. In
Newark, the temperature went as low as five degrees. It
snowed the first week of January; then the temperature
dropped again, to a low of minus-10 degrees in Newark, and
minus-34 degrees in River Vale. Service suffered. By mid-
January, trolley riders were in an uproar against Public
Service. In Elizabeth, city officials, responding to complaints,
threatened to revoke ordinances favorable to the trolley
company. The Law Committee of the Board of Aldermen
sent out health officials and engineers to follow up charges of
infrequent service, overcrowding of cars, and "bad sanitary
conditions." In Newark, one speaker at a North Ward protest

urged the city to impose a $50 fine on any motorman who passed by a person signaling for him to stop. Another speaker charged the new company with "squeezing 100 persons into one car, where there are accommodations for but 45, thus saving the wages of a motorman, a conductor, and the use of a car." He noted that Public Service had started spending money on improvements eight months before, and declared that its railway lines were in more deplorable condition than ever. If it spent any more money, he suggested, the entire system might disappear. Passengers everywhere grumbled about "square wheels"—cast-iron wheels worn flat in places by sudden stops—that caused cars to "limp and hop" up hill and down dale. Some riders blamed square wheels for the racket the cars made, but officials said faulty gears were the cause.

Though unable to solve these problems immediately, McCarter and his company were hardly indifferent to them. In a long letter to the public printed in the *Elizabeth Journal* of January 20, 1904, McCarter responded to "the general complaint" against the company's railway department. He expressed none of the annoyance with the public that his directors were said to feel, but conceded that "the deterioration of the car equipment and the lack of sufficient cars (were) common to the whole system." He noted that earlier railway companies had neither maintained the equipment nor provided for the future. Cars were in such short supply, he said, that the company could not take them out of service for proper repairs. The bad weather had worsened this shortage, causing many cars to "give out in some essential part" after only one or two trips. On Newark's Belleville and Clinton Avenue line alone, McCarter said, 21 of 45 cars had spent most of the previous week broken down. On top of all that, Public Service had begun to speed up schedules to the nine-mile-an-hour standard, inadvertently causing "some confusion and annoyance to the public."

"The company is exerting every effort in its power to improve the street railroad equipment and service," McCarter said, adding that the company had already spent $1.5 million on railway improvements. But he also noted the arrival of only 20 of the 300 new cars ordered, and promised no relief until warm weather, when open cars and new convertible cars would free the worst of the present lot for repairs.

The new cars did, in fact, arrive throughout that spring, and these, along with less apparent improvements, encouraged the riding public. Over the next six years, Public Service was to spend $20 million on such improvements, always with the emphasis on rehabilitation and maintenance. As early as January, 1906, the *Electric Railway Journal* was able to say:

> "The Public Service Corporation now controls, through a long series of purchases and mergers, practically all of the electrical lighting, power, gas and street railway utilities of the larger portion of the State of New Jersey. The benefits to the public in this instance have been many, resulting in lower rates for light and power, better street railway facilities and longer rides, and a far more reliable and dependable service in the supplying of electric light, power, gas and electric railway transportation."

Among the company's major achievements was the renovation of the electric power system, which in 1903 consisted of about 20 plants, many of them small and outdated, employing inefficient reciprocating Corliss engines belted to the generator. Public Service built the Marion Generating Station, with 10,000 kilowatts for street railways and 3,000 for lighting, and started the construction of substations at outlying points. These substations allowed the railway utility to transmit alternating current, which could travel farther than direct current with less loss, and convert it in the hinterlands to direct, 550-volt trolley power. The use of substations and alternating current by the railway business allowed the development of larger, centrally located generating stations.

Public Service Railway Company became a separate, subsidiary corporation in 1907, following passage of a utilities law under which splitting off the railway department from the management holding company effectively removed the books of the holding company from public scrutiny.

By 1911, the utility had purchased or itself constructed 948 new cars, and had a fleet of 2,380 cars, including miscellaneous sprinklers, sand cars, and snow plows. Car and track replacements were to continue through World War I. The company had remodeled and greatly enlarged its huge Plank Road Repair Shop in Newark. It had begun, among other improvements, the replacement of old bridges and the elimination of dangerous railroad crossings.

That it had also begun to improve the lot of the workers is clear from a personal recollection by Robert S. Tomkins which ran in the June 1, 1928, 25th Anniversary Edition of *Public Service News:*

"In the year 1903 I was paymaster for the North Jersey Street Railway Company and recollect the first time I was called to Newark by Mr. P.S. Young and our late Mr. James P. Dusenberry. At that time there were several paymasters and the above gentlemen were desirous of obtaining from them an idea as to how all the different utilities which had been merged could be brought together under one head, so that one paymaster could handle the entire situation.

"After the above plans were submitted and several consultations had been had about the work, the writer was appointed paymaster for the entire corporation. For some time before this the old company had been in financial straits and many times the paymaster had to wait several days before funds could be obtained for the men on their regular pay days.

"I have a vivid recollection of the first time I met our new President, Mr. Thomas N. McCarter, to whom I had to come to obtain his signature on a pay check, and upon reaching Newark and stating my errand to his secretary, I was ushered at once into his presence and asked as to my errand. Mr. McCarter signed the check and then asked me several questions about the paying of the men and the general conditions, both of which seemed to interest him very much.

"There had been much speculation among the clerical force regarding what was about to happen when Public Service took hold of the railway lines and it was with much gratification the writer found not only Mr. McCarter, but also

Mr. P.S. Young, most cordial to all the old employees, and
from that time until now, have found them at all times willing
to give any and all employees their support."

From 1903 to 1916, the peak years for the railway
company, ridership expanded from 215 million to 451
million passengers. What was it like to ride the trolleys then?
That depended on where you were going and when,
according to Ed Francis. Now 60 years of age, and still on the
job as a senior staff engineer, Ed Francis remembers riding
the trolleys to Bloomfield High School and Newark College
of Engineering, to Bear Stadium in Newark, and to the
beach at Atlantic City. He has also studied and written about
the Public Service railway system, and knows its now-
scrapped equipment so well that he speaks of cars by their
serial numbers. On a lightly-traveled line such as the
Elizabeth to Kenilworth or the Orange Crosstown, he says
you would probably ride one of the smallest cars, called
"dinkies" or "Toonervilles," measuring just 18 or 20 feet in
length, plus a platform at either end—the "Toonerville"
being the decidedly dinky trolley in the then famous Fon-
taine Fox comic strip. On a busier line—in Newark, say—
your car might run from 24 to 32 or, later, 36 feet in length.
The smaller car would be centered on a single, four-wheeled
truck. While this was a secure enough arrangement, Ed
Francis recalls that mischievous children sometimes hopped
on the back of such a car and seesawed it scarily. The longer
cars were generally more stable, with a four-wheeled truck at
each end. In winter, your car would be enclosed, and heated
by a centrally located stove which the conductor would
occasionally stoke with coal or wood from a pull-out bin. In
summer, the car would be partly or entirely open. Either way,
you would not have to wait long for its arrival. Headways of a
few minutes were common, except in the dark hours of the
morning. That was when customers out late, freezing and no
doubt at times feeling no pain for other reasons, would take
it into their heads to phone McCarter and ask him where the
hell his trolley was. Otherwise, Public Service trolleys were so
frequent that their patrons were said not to need shelters
even at the system's outermost corners.

The "fender," an elaborate cowcatcher, shown here on the front of this car on the Broad Street, Newark, line, saved the Company and pedestrians much grief.

At least from 1903 to 1928, the exterior of your car would be painted according to the Public Service scheme, cream and chrome yellow, with Tuscan red trim and a black undercarriage. Lettering was also black. In the 1920s, the utility converted cars on its busier lines to so-called deluxe service by reupholstering their interiors and painting them outside in a handsome maroon. Most cars indicated their route name and number in an illuminated clerestory window at either end of the car, or by a painted sign on the side. This was an improvement over the methods of relatively recent horsecar days, when according to Ed Francis, the many cars on Broad Street, Newark, indicated their routes by their body color during the day and with similarly colored lanterns or "signal lights" at night.

In 1895, Broad Street cars had a red signal light, Bloomfield cars a blue, Harrison cars red and yellow, Kearny-Arlington cars white and blue, Mt. Prospect cars blue and green, and South Orange green and red. On Market Street, the Market and Bowery cars had blue and red, the Orange line had green, Rapid Transit (an electric trolley) had yellow and blue, and the Central Avenue (also electric) had green and yellow.

One unusual exterior feature of the railway cars was what trolleymen called the "fender." This was an elaborate cowcatcher, to borrow a railroad term, on the front of the non-reversible cars and at both ends of the double-enders. In the early decades, the Public Service fender consisted of curved strips of steel joined to form a sort of fixed shovel. The fender was as handsome as a good wrought-iron fence, but its purpose was practical. It scooped up any pedestrian accidentally hit and kept him away from the wheels as the car slowed down. Trolley accidents were common then, despite company safety programs, and the fender saved many families, not to mention the company claims department, much grief.

The railway company served what was even then a densely-populated area, urban and suburban. Indeed, it operated on more than 100 miles of track in Newark alone. And, as had the horsecars, its trolleys stopped practically at every corner. You could enter the closed car at either end and—since there were no coin boxes until 1907—head straight for your seat. If it were cold enough and if you were among the first riders aboard, you would probably pick a seat near the stove. People tended "to drift that way," according to Mr. Francis, because the temperature could drop into the fifties at the far ends of the car. On one of the longest closed cars, which seated 54 and stood many more than that, you could choose between cross seats and side seats. Most of the smaller cars, seating just 32 people, had only side (or longitudinal) seats, facing in. Your car would be handsomely decorated inside, with cherry or mahogany paneling in a maple-leaf pattern, and rattan seats with brass fittings. The floors were hardwood, grooved along the length of the car for drainage. As the car started to roll, the conductor would come to your seat, take your fare, and ring it up on the pull-strap register overhead. Most rides cost just a nickel before 1918, with a free transfer to intersecting lines. On the 55-mile Fast Line trip from Newark to Trenton, however, you could pay as much as a dollar, a fare comparable to that of the steam railroads. Running time on that trip was two hours and forty-five minutes, eight miles of it through the streets of Newark and Elizabeth and the rest on private right-of-way. **Most Public Service lines were of course far shorter, ranging**

Broad and Market Streets, Newark, as the evening rush hour begins in 1912, above. Below, the same corner 15 years later, when buses and the auto were competing with trolleys for space.

down to the .72-mile Park Avenue shuttle in Rutherford. According to one company survey, the average rider in 1911 traveled less than two-and-a-half miles per trip.

The trolley cars were seldom very fast inside the cities because of horse-drawn traffic in the early years and general traffic congestion later on. As late as 1925, in fact, the railway company complained that horse-drawn milkwagons, which often stopped directly on its tracks, were slowing down morning traffic on its lines. A more occasional traffic problem was fire and, in particular, the hoses strewn across street and tracks to fight it. The railway company beat this problem with "tower wagons," on emergency call, that could string hoses over the trolley power lines and out of the way, or with a "hose-jumper," a sort of portable trestle that enabled the car to pass over the hoses. But the trolleys themselves also contributed to the congestion. A tally taken on January 11, 1911, a typical day, showed that 562 trolleys crossed the intersection of Broad and Market Streets, Newark, during the single rush hour between 5:15 and 6:15 p.m. (A similar survey 15 years later showed only 172 trolleys during the busiest half-hour of the day at that same intersection, but by then they were joined by 218 buses and 1,072 other types of vehicle.) Such traffic and the frequent stops kept the average scheduled speed on most lines, back then, at under 10 miles an hour. On at least part of one line in 1916, the posted speed limit was just three miles an hour. Given room, though, the trolleys could go faster.

"Now when they got beyond the central city," Ed Francis recalls, "you had to look out for the streetcars because they sailed. The local type street cars could probably get up around 30 miles an hour. If you got on a line like the Trenton Fast Line in 1913, they would hit 60 miles an hour or more on private right-of-way."

The most popular feature of railway travel in the first two decades of this century was undoubtedly the open-air car, which came into service each year on about May 1st. In the beginning, at least, the open car had no sides, windows, or screens, and was, except for its roof, entirely open to the elements. It had no center aisle, either, and the cross

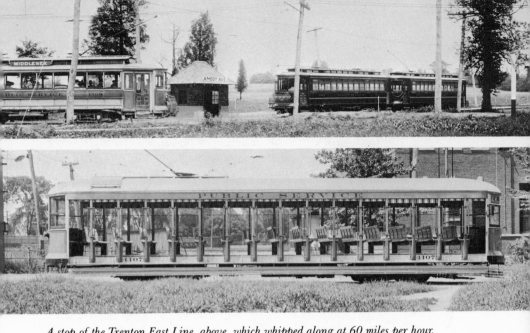

A stop of the Trenton Fast Line, above, which whipped along at 60 miles per hour. Below, striped side curtains are just visible along the top edge of the roof on this open air trolley of 1916, popular before the days of air-conditioning.

benches, of which there were from 8 to 16, depending on the length of the car, seated six abreast. You could board at the bench of your choosing, stepping up via a nine or 10-inch wide hardwood "running board" that ran the length of the car. In addition to the 96 people the longest open cars seated, many more rode the running board, hanging on at the sides. Until the 1920s a conductor collected fares, leaving the motorman free to operate the car.

Public Service usually carried more passengers in hot weather than in cold, with June the best traffic month of the year. Why? Says Ed Francis: "Most people thought it was a joy to go for a ride on the open-air trolley out into the country." The open car, with its gentle breezes, was probably the closest most people came to air-conditioning. It was also certainly the cheapest, easiest way to get out of the hot city for an evening. Even though vacations took many riders from urban lines, other lines easily made up this loss by carrying people on open-air "trolley parties" to reservations such as Eagle Rock or South Mountain, to amusement parks built—sometimes with railway money—along trolley routes, and to such shore points as Boynton Beach in Woodbridge.

The *Evening News* had this to say of the Eagle Rock run, on its closing in 1924:

> "Just how many thousands have been hauled up the long grind to the rock possibly may never be known. In the finer days of the spring and fall, and all summer long, the car is well filled every evening as those who have returned from work finish their evening meals and start out for a breath of the cooler air at the summit of the rock."

There were, of course, some disadvantages to open-air travel. "Sometimes they'd be out kind of early on the open-air cars and the people would be complaining about the chilly weather," says Ed Francis, who rode completely open cars as late as 1940 in Wildwood. "But once they brought 'em out they usually had to keep 'em out because normally they would exchange the motor trucks and controls from the closed cars and put the closed cars in storage for the summer."

Another problem was the infamous Jersey Skeeter, which, along with other insect pests, was far more abundant then. A June, 1903, report tells, for instance, of a car stopped literally in its tracks, halfway between Bound Brook and Dunellen, by a swarm of mosquitoes "nearly as thick as rain drops." The swarm seized the car and held it for 20 minutes, as motorman and passengers watched unhappily from a safe distance. Potato bugs stopped another car between Boynton Beach and Rahway, according to a similar report, simply by covering the tracks so thickly that the trolley wheels spun uselessly. The motorman finally applied sand to the rails, and the car sped over the bugs "without a flinch."

A final problem for the open cars was dust. Until about 1915, many roads outside the city were unpaved, and a trolley car traveling over them in dry weather could stir up something of a storm, to the annoyance of its riders. Bloomfield Avenue beyond Montclair was for a time such a street. The railway company tried to control the dust problem, not always successfully, with sprinkler cars. These ran back and forth on dusty routes, wetting them down every few hours with water or, later, a tar solution.

The Trolley and Ferry Business Booms

"... they ran this Metuchen shuttle back and forth. That was a line where the motormen knew everybody and he'd take grocery orders and pick things up downtown and bring them back to the ladies."
—Ed Francis

Despite all these problems, people flocked to the trolleys come warm weather. One summer, more than half a million people visited Electric Park on the South Orange Avenue line in Newark, where the main attraction, in addition to the usual rides, was an illuminated fountain. Public Service did well by the park, not only supplying it with electricity, but transporting most of its patrons, at a nickel each way. The public also crowded into Grand View Park on the Singac line out of Paterson; Washington Park, with its famous "Shoot the Chutes," on the Camden, Gloucester, and Woodbury line; and Olympic Park in Irvington, where the trolley company actually built the turnaround loop on its Springfield Avenue line into the park entrance. Also popular were Woodlynne Park, Camden, and Riverside Park, New Brunswick, which the railway company owned.

At Palisades Park, according to Ed Francis, Public Service was doubly blessed: "They operated the ferry from 125th

Street, New York, and the trolley cars from the ferry up the face of the Palisades to the park. And on summer nights, and Saturdays and Sundays, the people came over from New York in droves. That was a nickel fare on the ferry boat, and a nickel fare on the shuttle up the hill. Or you could walk if you had the ambition. But they went up the so-called park shuttle by the carload."

Among those who took this route regularly were the hero and heroine of that original of cliffhanger serials (no pun) *The Perils of Pauline*, who came over on the ferry from New York and rode up the Palisades on the trolley to Fort Lee, where the film was being shot.

The close and prosperous relationship between railway companies and the amusements was standard throughout the industry. Nor was it only a summertime thing. The company gained many young customers on its Orange Crosstown line, for instance, by putting up the much-anticipated "red ball" placard on its cars when the skating ponds were open. Public Service carried many skaters to what is now Soverel Field in East Orange. But, while always eager to attract riders, the utility never went so far as did some companies. One predecessor of Public Service had attracted 5,000 people to Knight's Park, Collingswood, in 1897, by staging a head-on trolley crack-up, followed by a fireworks display.

Some Public Service lines were interesting enough on their own to draw pleasure riders. A contemporary trolley guide described the White Line, which began as an elevated railway in Hoboken, this way:

> "The old, original route to Passaic and Paterson, known as the White Line run, is easily reached at its starting point in Hoboken by means of the Christopher or Barclay Street ferries. This still remains one of the best trolley lines about New York, and the dash down into the Hackensack Valley in the first part of the trip is very enjoyable. The car travels for nearly half an hour through uninteresting Hoboken and Jersey City Heights. Suddenly it makes a sharp turn. In an instant there is spread out before the traveler the valley of the Hackensack far below him. The car shoots down the straight,

narrow turnpike on the cliff's side, a mile or more in length.
Here, on the meadows, are Homestead and Secaucus. Then it
moves across the flats, a journey of over four miles."

Another interesting line, also over the Palisades, was the
connection with the ferry at Edgewater. The White Line cars
at Hoboken made their climb up the Palisades on a gently-
rising trestle, at right angles to the cliff face. But at
Edgewater in the early years, the car climbed parallel to the
cliff, directly on the face, by means of a "switchback," a
device that made "hairpin" turns unnecessary. The car
climbed halfway up on a road cut into the rock, and stopped.
The motorman then walked to the far end of the car, which
was a double-ender, swung the trolley pole around, and
resumed the climb to the top in the opposite direction. Later,
a horseshoe curve replaced the switchback and became
popular in its own right. The main point of interest at
Edgewater was that you could look out your window and see
300 feet straight down. Or, if you were queasy about heights,
you could look straight out at Manhattan and the Hudson.
Said the *Electric Railway Journal:*

> "The river at this point is about a mile wide and upon a clear
> day the view extends from Yonkers, 10 miles above, to the
> hills of Staten Island, 18 miles below, and over and across New
> York City to Long Island Sound and the hills of Long Island.
> At night the scene is also a fine one. Myriads of lamps trace
> the streets of the city and the sky and water glow with
> reflection."

'Public Service lines climbed mountains then, and while the
trip up was enough to make you brace yourself with hands
and feet, the trip down could be better than a roller-coaster
ride. Writing again of the Eagle Rock Line, the *Newark
Evening News* said:

> "Away down the hill...is the bottom where one will land if
> the brakes ever fail. Two systems of brakes are used, in
> addition to a sand-drag which permits the wheels a firmer
> hold on the rails. One brake is set before the return trip is
> started, and is kept on until the bottom is reached. Halfway
> down the steepest section of the hill is a "turn-out" which is

kept open so that, should the brakes lose their hold, the car would be turned into a field. This once happened when the car was filled to capacity and broke loose some distance above the switch. One woman suffered a fractured leg and a few others were cut and bruised, constituting the only casualties.

"I have run this car for years," declared the motorman ... "and I never fail to get a kick out of the trip down hill. I always take a look at where I might land if things went wrong, and then I grab hard on the brake handle and hold on like sixty. I was coming up hill once with a good load and she slid back nearly 300 feet, even with the power on. We slid back nearly 300 feet, in spite of brakes, sand and the motors. You never can tell when that is going to happen, although you can't go backward fast against the brakes."

Railway journals made much then of the possibility of traveling from New York to Chicago or Boston by trolley, taking advantage, of course, of the many transfer privileges en route. Within New Jersey, it was likewise possible—if you knew the trolley system well enough—to nearly span the entire state. Such a trip would start, Ed Francis recalls, just over the border in Suffern, New York, and end up in Ocean City, shy of Cape May.

"You could come down to East Paterson on the North Jersey Rapid Transit and go into Paterson on the Public Service Hudson River line. Change at Paterson to the Paterson-Newark line and go to Newark. And, well, you could go from Newark to Trenton by either of two routes. If you wanted to go the fast way, you could take the Fast Line directly. Or you could go by Bound Brook on the Union line, change to the Raritan line to New Brunswick, and then pick up the New Brunswick-Trenton car. At Trenton, change again to the Public Service car running to Camden and then, at Market Street, get the electric train, the West Jersey Seashore Railroad, to Atlantic City. Change at Pleasantville and go into Somers Point. Cross the bay there to Ocean City and change to the Ocean City electric railway line and wind up on the southern end of Ocean City. That would be about the farthest. It would probably take you all day, eight or 10 hours."

The car in center left, its windows boarded up, was Car Number 6000, shown at Penn Station in Newark. It carried paymasters who paid railway employees wages in cash right at the car houses along the line. The murder of a paymaster in a 1926 holdup ended the practice.

You could also string together different lines to get from North Jersey to Long Branch or Sea Girt, or catch a "foreign" line (such as the Morris County Traction Company) to Lake Hopatcong. More important, says Ed Francis, you had a car "every 10 or 15 minutes straight through" from Newark to Paterson or practically any other important city in the State. And you could count on "Owl Service" to keep things moving through the night.

"The most popular car on the Public Service railway system," says Ed Francis, "was a car which the public never rode in. In Newark it was car No. 6000, the pay car. Paymasters paid railway employees in cash at the various car houses, and traveled over the system in their special car. Cash on pay-day ended in 1926 when a paymaster was shot at the Central Avenue Car House in Newark." The *Evening News* for June 15, 1926, gave details of the holdup-murder, which had taken place on June 4th:

"Theodore M. Conway, Public Service paymaster, who was shot and killed June 4 by bandits who entered the railway pay car at Central Avenue car house, Newark, had been with the organization fifteen years, starting as a clerk in the Bloomfield car house . . .

"The high regard in which Mr. Conway was held was shown by the fact that several hundred gathered at the Home for Services ... Among the Public Service delegation was President McCarter and a number of other officers of the various companies.

"Mr. Conway ... (who) would have been 34 years old in August ... was shot down without warning, and although he, Hugo Schwernitz and John Doyle, guards, were armed,they had no chance to draw their weapons. Mr. Schwernitz was also shot ... in the right shoulder ... The bandits got away without any money ...

"Two suspects have been arrested and it is believed identified as members of the gang, of which there were four or five. A reward of $5,000 was offered by the company for the arrest and conviction of the bandits. The company has also announced that hereafter the pay car method will be abandoned and the men paid by check."

Nature provided less gory memories of trolley life. "The most vivid thing I remember is the snowstorm of December, 1947," Ed Francis says. "It was probably the last storm that really shut down transit, and we had some 27 inches of snow. At that time I was working in Public Service Terminal, Newark, and sometime around three o'clock in the afternoon somebody decided maybe everybody ought to go home because the snow was getting deep. Knowing how things were, instead of going on a westbound car (home to Bloomfield) I took an eastbound trolley car to Pennsylvania Station and found an empty car there, which, by the time it got to Broad Street, had a standing, swinging load of 160 people or so. They packed 'em in down the aisles, on the back platform, the front platform and all. I understand from some of the trolleymen they could've picked up a lot more than that, too, if they were coming out of the shipyards.

"The next day we went down to Bloomfield Center to see how things looked. The plow (a railway service car mounted with a nose plow) from Montclair carbarn was just breaking through. He had to back up and hit the packed snow, which the automobiles had packed down. The sweeper behind it

would throw all the stuff off the track. In fact, the plow
would run up on ice and the sweeper would have to pull him
off, because once the plow was on ice it had no circuit to its
motors. In the winter they had a big force of snowplows and
sweepers that cleared the track. Even when the buses started,
Public Service ran a few plows and plowed the streets..."

An earlier snowstorm, the famed Blizzard of '88, evoked
equally vivid memories from Patrick A. Barrington, a trolley
car operator who lived through it. He told about them in a
Newark Evening News interview 50 years ago. Barrington
recalled drifts as high as 20 feet that tied up the horse cars
for three full days:

"Snow? I never saw anything like it before or since. I
remember I couldn't open the front door of my home
because of the snow against it. I had to get out of an upper
window and shovel the snow away. Then it was a matter of
tunneling your way to the sidewalk.

"I worked my way down to the carbarns. They were at
Belleville Avenue, now Broadway, and Arlington Avenue
(Newark). There was no chance to get a car out and running.
But we got out sweepers, drawn by eight horses, and
gradually made headway in clearing the tracks. It was three
days before we could run.

"It wasn't quite so bad on the Mulberry Street line, though,
and some of the other lines. We ran sleighs there in the winter
time, big sleighs holding about twenty people. The passengers liked it, sort of a hayride ...

"Hay isn't so far off ... because all we had in the sleighs and
cars to keep people warm was straw. Passengers would stick
their feet in the straw on the floor and keep warm that way. It
was some time before we got in stoves."

One of the things Ed Francis remembers best was the
friendliness of the motormen, especially on smaller lines:
"Well," he says, "you had a line like the Metuchen shuttle,
which was a little piece of track that was more or less left over
when they joined the line out of Perth Amboy with the line
out of New Brunswick. So they ran this Metuchen shuttle
back and forth. That was a line where the motormen knew
everybody and he'd take grocery orders and pick things up

downtown and bring them back to the ladies. It was the same story in Kenilworth on the Kenilworth line and on the Arlington shuttle up here in Arlington.

"I was on a car in Philadelphia when the motorman stopped in the middle of the block and jingled his bell, waiting for someone to come running out and get on. It was his regular customer, so if he wasn't on the corner, the motorman would stop in front of his house. They did that on the so-called Swamp Line from West Orange to South Orange. The same crews had been there for years. They knew all the passengers and they'd stop at a stop and if someone wasn't there they'd jingle the bell and look and hope he was coming."

The *New York Tribune* described one such motorman, perhaps with some exaggeration, in 1916, when Public Service was seeking permission to abandon its Kenilworth line:

> "Ain't I deservin'?" (Elmer Guy) queried. "I'll keep runnin' her, Public Service or no Public Service. Only them city smart Alecs attending Upsala College in Kenilworth give me a lot of trouble by rockin' the car. But I get even by reportin' 'em to their teachers. Nuther'll I get cigarettes they want me to buy for 'em down to town."

The *Tribune* pictured Guy stopping not just to pick up stray customers, but to talk with "an old lady who used to know his wife's great-grandmother," and to set out cabbage leaves for the rabbits, in atonement for a rabbit he once killed on his daily run:

> "How fast were you going?" asked the other passengers ...
> "'Bout four miles an hour. 'Scuse me—I seen Mrs. Smith, and I better go back for her. I allers like to accommodate folks, I do ..."
> Against the protestations of his two passengers, who said they had only an hour and a half to reach Aldene, two miles away, Elmer Guy got out, reversed the trolley pole and sped back to Mrs. Smith's farm. That lady managed to squeeze into the rear door of the car..

Guy then collected Mrs. Smith's fare, and she asked if the planned shutdown of "his" line bothered him any.

"Wal, I should say it would," said Elmer, when he returned from taking a small stone off the track. "Ain't I been on this trolley line nigh onto half a dozen years? Ain't I carried things for folks and made the passengers wait while I been buyin' things in the village fer 'em? Ain't I allers kept the car warm if the passengers get the wood to make the stove? Ain't I been feedin' the rabbits along the line? Ain't I got the best library in town under this seat, with Ellen Glim's 'Two Weeks' and Shakespeare's 'Silas Marner'? Besides all that, ain't I the only man can run this trolley?" (Elmer may also be the only one to believe Shakespeare, rather than George Elliot, wrote "Silas Marner".)

Conditions were, of course, a good deal more efficient, if less folksy, on the railway company's busier lines.

Even before the coming of the bus, Public Service Railway was more than just a trolley company. In the consolidations of 1903 and thereafter, it had inherited, and now operated, two ferry lines and a pair of inclined elevators. The elevators, both up the face of the Palisades, were a leftover from the horsecar days, when it took four horses more than eight minutes to haul a wagon or railway car up from Hoboken to the Jersey City Heights. By driving the horse and car onto the elevator and letting a steam engine do the work of lifting, the railway man could make the same trip in one minute. When railway electrification deprived the elevators of that share of their business, the elevators survived by carrying horse-drawn wagons and trucks up and down the heights. While the trip up cost a quarter, according to Ed Francis, it took only 15¢, thanks to gravity, to get back down again. The elevators, regarded at the time of their building as being among the mechanical wonders of the world, closed down and were dismantled in the late 1920s, when motor trucking and the opening of the Holland Tunnel made them obsolete.

The Public Service ferry lines, across the Hudson River between Edgewater and 125th Street and across the Kill van Kull between Bayonne and Staten Island, proved more durable. Originally operated for horse-drawn traffic and the occasional herd of cattle, as well as for commuters, the ferries profited in the 1920s from the general move to suburbia and the development of "bedroom" communities. Like electricity in the beginning and the amusement parks, the ferries were at first an adjunct to the railway operation, feeding important Public Service trolley lines. For the same purpose, Public Service worked happily with a number of trans-Hudson ferry lines operated by unaffiliated companies. But for a time, after public acceptance of the automobile but before the building of the major tunnels and bridges between New Jersey and New York City, the ferries were money-makers in their own right. The utility's largest boats were the *Tenafly* and the *Hackensack*, each 185 feet long and 45 feet wide and weighing 1,310 tons, and each loading 50 automobiles via four gangways. Four other boats plied the Manhattan-to-Bergen County route, and two much smaller boats carried a small but profitable traffic across the Kill van Kull. The Kull route covered a distance of only about 1,700 feet, but, said one captain, "you'd be surprised how strong the current sometimes is and what dense fogs we've had to wallow through." Weekends, Public Service ferries were chartered to operate on the Newburgh-Beacon ferry run. But when the commuter business began to fall off, Public Service sold its Bayonne ferry in 1937 and the Edgewater line in 1943. Some Public Service ferries that survived the sale and the eventual shut-down may still be operating. The *Thomas N. McCarter,* for a time, became the *Newport News* on Chesapeake Bay.

Another unusual transit operation was the Bergen Turnpike Company. Chartered by the State Legislature in 1802, this was the oldest company in the Public Service genealogy. The utility acquired it when it took over the Jersey City, Hoboken and Paterson Street Railway Company, which had secured control of the Bergen Turnpike Company to build a trolley line along the turnpike from North Bergen to Hackensack. Legal battles over steam railroad crossings on the route delayed operation of the trolley lines until April, 1903. Even then, there was a break in the line, across which passengers had to walk, at one railroad crossing in Little Ferry. Public Service operated the turnpike as an incidental to its trolley operation, but it is not clear how long the utility actually collected tolls on the road. It began negotiations to transfer the turnpike to Bergen County in 1912, but the road did not become public until late in 1915. A final transit operation was the Yellow Cab Company, through which Public Service for many years operated a large taxi fleet in Newark and in Camden.

Straw hatted against a June sun, observers watch as Miss Ellen McCarter, daughter of Thomas N. McCarter, prepares to christen the ferryboat Fort Lee *in Wilmington, Delaware in 1915. Below, the* Tenafly *makes its way across the Hudson; it was capable of carrying 50 autos, loaded on four gangways.*

"Tell Me What You Eat

And I'll tell you what you are." The author might added, " Tell me

HOW YOU COOK IT

And I'll tell you what you will be." A coal stove, with its dirt, soot and ashes, makes women old before their time. Buy a

GAS RANGE

And keep your youth. **$8.50 to $13.50.** **Connections FREE. $2 down, $2 a month.**

GAS DEPARTMENT
PUBLIC SERVICE

Public Service customers were getting messages like this, on the back of gas bills in 1905. Those who paid within five days of presentation of the bill got a discount, and commercial offices were open from 8 a.m. to 9 p.m.

Gas System Expands

"Good Cooking is not so much the result of a good cookbook as a good
range."
—Public Service slogan

At about the turn of the century, gas companies began to push the gas range and the automatic water heater—the "new uses" for gas. Some gas companies even handed out stoves free to customers who agreed to purchase a certain minimum amount of gas each month. Gas men seemed at first to value the range not so much for its own gas-consuming capability, as for its possible beneficial effect on the lighting business. Said *Progressive Age,* the gas industry journal:

> "A householder who finds that a gas range is cheaper than a coal range and that a gas log is not to be despised as an occasional auxiliary heater, will generally not think it worthwhile to run an additional bill for electric lights; and he is an easily made friend of the gas engine."

Perhaps with that thought in mind gas men at Public Service promoted the range almost from that company's first day in 1903, under the slogan, "good cooking is not so much the result of a good cookbook as a good range." It offered gas ranges from $9.50 to $15, or for $2 down and $2 a month. This business and the water-heating business grew so rapidly for Public Service, which sold 16,400 ranges in 1904 alone, and for other utilities that gas men were soon arguing, successfully as it turned out, that they should measure the cubic foot according to its heating capacity—how many British Thermal Units it contained—rather than in candlepower. The sudden development of the cooking business surprised the gas men, but perhaps it should not have. At about this time, *Ainslee's Magazine* described conditions in the gasless kitchen this way:

> "Cooking would be more of an art and less of a gamble if the heat could be put where it was wanted and nowhere else, and its intensity were under the perfect control of the cook. The oven that will not come up to the right temperature, or that will not bake on the bottom, the chimney that draws the wrong way when the wind is from the northwest, the dampers that refuse to do as they are bid, the kindling that burns out without lighting the coal, all tend to make cooks the most evil-tempered of mortals."

The gas range, in addition to soothing the spirits of troubled cooks around the State, allowed the gas business at Public Service to grow even when, after about 1914, the gas lighting business fell off rapidly. Public Service, which was after all both an electric and gas company, was by then promoting electricity for lighting and gas mainly for cooking. Some gas men evidently resented this usurpation, as they regarded it.

"My uncle, Henry D. Whitcomb (the first general manager of the gas department) went on vacation one time," says Henry W. Nicolson, a retired distribution engineer, "and it was at the time they were changing over the terminal building from gas lighting to electric lighting. The electric department had had electric lighting for quite a while. While my uncle was on his vacation, Mr. McCarter, who was the president, had the gas lights taken out of my uncle's office and electric lights put in. When my uncle got back, he hit the ceiling and he called Mr. McCarter and he told him if he didn't get those blankety-blank electric lights out of his office within two days, he was quitting That night the electric lights went out and the gas lights came back.

To celebrate National Gas Range Week in 1915—the first gas range had been manufactured 51 years before—Public Service offered six makes of cabinet ranges, ranging from the relatively spartan Reliable, at $25.50 to Acorn Baby Grand, at $60.75. You paid $2 down, $1.50 a month for the former, $8 down, $8 a month for the latter.

"My uncle was such a fanatic on the subject of gas. He loved it and he loved the gas business. Out at his home in East Orange, where I used to go spend the weekends when I was in college, he had a gas light over his chair. And my aunt had more and more of the gas lights taken out of the house and electric lights put in, and I heard him say one day, 'Daisy, if you ever take that gas light out over my chair, I'm going out of the house the same day.' And when he died the gas light was still there over his chair. They stayed in his office until after he died, too, and then they all came out."

Unlike the financially-troubled streetcar lines of the State, New Jersey's important gas properties were sound physically and fiscally when Public Service took them over on June 1, 1903. They needed new capital for expansion, which consolidation would enable them to obtain, but not the sort of general rebuilding and reorganization that the railway and electric companies required. This was due partly to the careful management of the United Gas Improvement Company (UGI), which had controlled the major gas companies of Essex, Hudson and Passaic Counties and which now had a large interest in Public Service. Gas was also older and more stable than its sibling utilities, and was hindered neither by the public uneasiness that still slowed electrical development nor by the kind of upheaval that the switch to electricity had caused the railway companies.

The main tasks before the gas department in 1903 were the interconnection of existing gas plants and distribution systems for increased reliability, the concentration of production in the most efficient plants, and the expansion of production and distribution facilities to meet the increasing demand for gas. Public Service immediately built new gas holders at Paterson and Camden, each with a two-million-cubic-foot capacity, and added 50 new ovens to the 100-oven coke plant on the Delaware River in Camden owned by its subsidiary, the South Jersey Gas, Electric and Traction Company. This plant produced coke for the steel industry and for use in Public Service boilers, tar, ammonia, benzol and other by-products, and coal gas for the city distribution system.

The improvements made to the water-gas works at Paterson, one of the new utility's most efficient plants, were typical of those made by Public Service throughout its territory. John G. Whitcomb, the cadet engineer, reported in 1941:

"In 1903 the Public Service (Corporation) succeeded the Paterson Gas and Electric Light Company, and from this point on the plant began to expand rapidly. In 1905 the first section of the present generator and boiler house was built and Number Four water-gas set was installed in the new building. The demand for gas increased so rapidly that at the end of one year it was found necessary to install Number Five gas set. This completely filled the new generator house and any further expansion would require additions to the building. Because of the increased capacity of the new sets, the two fan blowers in the old boiler room, which had been supplying air to the sets ... were unable to handle the load. So in 1908 an addition was built on the exhauster room and Number One blower and Number One Passaic Pusher were installed. The first pipe under the Passaic River was laid in 1910. It was 12 inches in diameter and was made on the bank and floated out to position, where it was filled with water and sunk into its final position. In spite of the fact that this pipe never rested on any prepared foundation, it is still in use today, and the records indicate that it has never given any trouble.

The Paterson Gas Light Company, although the first gas utility organized in New Jersey, in 1825, did not begin operations until 1847, shortly after the Newark Gas Light Company. The Paterson firm's gas works, above, was a producer as part of PSE&G until earlier this year, when gas manufacturing ceased.

"In 1911, the four round purifying towers were added to the square boxes to handle the increasing load. This move, however, was regarded by many with a jaundiced eye, as it involved cutting down a flourishing orchard of pear trees which extended from the back of the purifying house all the way to Rye Street. These trees were tough customers and they used to thrive on adversity; the more spent oxide (from the purifying boxes) that was piled around them, the more and better-flavored pears they produced."

The dusty, red oxides of iron were a hazard, to the eye at least, at all gas works then. The men usually piled them 18 inches deep in the yard, for airing and re-use, and from there they were often tracked throughout the gas works.

Public Service added additional blowers and pushers to Paterson, both to supply air to the gas sets and to push the gas through the purifiers and other new equipment. As demand grew, it expanded the generator house to include the Number Six water-gas set in 1916, and Number Seven in 1921. It also increased the plant's boiler capacity to supply steam to these sets. It introduced the use of compressors, not just at Paterson but throughout its territory, to provide the high pressure—up to 50 pounds per square inch—needed to send gas long distances. Before 1903, Edward Earnshaw, chief engineer of the gas department, later wrote, "the gas works were obliged to depend upon the pressure of the holders to transfer the gas from one district to another." The gas holder worked like a lung, expanding as it filled with gas and collapsing, with some resultant pressure on the gas, as it emptied. Some gas holders had rigid exteriors that hid the rising and falling of their lifts. But with others, the passerby could see the holder rising and falling in telescoped sections, like a collapsible drinking cup turned upside down. (In gas jargon, such a holder "cupped up" and "uncupped.") While these impressive structures were needed to guarantee the continuous flow of gas, they produced too little pressure for long-distance transmission, and so limited the area a gas works could serve.

Public Service installed a compressor at Paterson after it acquired the gas business of Bergen County. The compressor enabled it to supply that territory with gas via a new four-inch main from Paterson to Ridgewood. With the load in Bergen transferred to the Paterson works, Public Service soon shut down an outdated and inefficient coal-gas plant at Ridgewood.

McCarter regularly reported on developments like these in the territory, all in accordance with the company's aim of effecting a single, efficient, coordinated gas system:

> "The Corporation also obtained during 1911 franchises for the distribution of gas in Madison and Morris Plains. This resulted in the construction of a trunk line from Morristown to Newark, the shutting down of the plant of the Morristown Gas and Light Company, and the distribution of gas generated at Newark throughout this entire community. Similarly, South Amboy plant shut down, and gas generated

The hand-pumped, horse-drawn drip-tank truck, used to remove water and light oil condensate from mains, gave way in 1926 to a truck whose motor powers the pump. The "drippage" went back to the gas works, where light oils were drawn off and sold.

at Camden was sent, via the already existing pipeline to New Brunswick, to South Amboy. In this latter locality the mains of the Company have also been extended to Old Bridge, Spotswood and Helmetta in Middlesex County. Other gas extensions made during the year include the Borough of Haworth in the Bergen Division; Little Falls and Totowa in the Passaic Division; and Florham Park in Morris County."

Laying a main was never simple work. The main, usually of cast iron, had to be buried deep enough to prevent the frost from reaching it in winter and to reduce the possibility of shock from heavy traffic. It had to rest on a solid foundation and be evenly supported, even where it ran through swamps and under rivers. It had to slope slightly toward some point so that the water vapor and light oils in the gas would collect at "drips" when they condensed. (Gas workers pumped these "drips" out regularly.) The joint between sections of pipe had to be carefully made. As Henry Nicolson put it, when he was superintendent of distribution, Newark district, "A joint which will hold tight against a hundred pounds of water pressure might leak badly under half a pound of gas."

The "cement joint" common then was a crude affair by today's standards, but it was effective. The gas man set the straight end of one pipe section into the bell-shaped end of another, then packed the bell with twisted yarn or jute. The caulker worked cement mixed to a putty-like consistency in around the jute, then drove in another length of jute, compressing the cement into all the uneven surfaces of the pipe. A final application of cement finished off the joint. Sometimes the caulker used a deeper bell and made the final application with lead. A set of standards surviving from that period calls for three pounds of cement, 12 pounds of lead, and nine ounces of jute on every joint of an eight-inch main—and there was a joint every 12 feet on lines that ranged up to 90 miles in length.

In 1916, Public Service built a 16-inch main from Jersey City to Harrison, thereby connecting its West End Works on the Hackensack River with the Market Street Works, Newark. This line required the digging of a seven-foot-wide tunnel through solid rock, 100 feet below the surface of the Hackensack River. The line ran above ground, on piles, through the marshland between the Hackensack and Passaic Rivers and required the daily attention of an inspector, particularly in the spring and summer mosquito season, to keep away meadow fires set to burn over the insects' breeding grounds. The next year, Public Service again bored under the Hackensack, constructing a 654-foot-long tunnel, to carry mains between the coke plant in Kearny and the West End Works.

It introduced automation into what was a complex operation requiring skilled artisans. In 1903, all water-gas sets had been hand-operated. To begin a single blow and run, the gas-maker opened the air-blast valve by cranking a hand wheel, a task made more laborious and time-consuming by the wheel's being only six inches in diameter. When the coke reached its proper temperature, he closed this valve and introduced the steam by shifting a lever. A pointer was affixed to the shaft of the lever and slid over a brass plate, calibrated to show the position of the steam valve.

Compressed air hoses feed the caulking hammers of workmen caulking a 30-inch main, above. The network was under continous expansion; below, a 30-inch main goes in in Newark, in 1923.

The gas-maker held the lever in place with a set-screw. Finally, he raised the stack valve off its seat by pulling on a swivel-jointed rod.

"The set was shifted from blow to run to standby by the proper manipulation of these three valves," wrote John Whitcomb, "and when we consider the short length of the cycle and the amount of labor required to change the valve positions, it is easy to see that the gas-maker's job was not an easy one."

Public Service replaced these hand methods with a centralized system of automatic, hydraulic controls. With increased efficiency in mind, it replaced muscle with machinery wherever it was economically practical throughout its territory. George W. Curtis of the company's southern division, contrasted the old and the new methods in a 1928 letter to *Public Service News*. Of 1903, he remembered:

> "When collections were made and cash was carried to the bank in a bucket; when the ovens (at Camden) were increased to 150, later being replaced with 37 even more efficient that the 150 old-type ovens.
> "Coke was stored and loaded through the efforts of some 150 yard men and the work was done by hand, quite a contrast to the handling by improved machinery and approximately six yard men. Coke was handled by probably 66 men, who were required to load the cars by way of conveyors ... while today three men and improved machinery do this work in a more efficient manner.
> "In the boiler plant about 45 men were employed; today better results are obtained with six."

Such economies enabled Public Service to cut the price of gas, to $1 and 50¢ per thousand cubic feet, even as fuel and other costs were climbing.

As it improved the gas company's physical and financial set-up, Public Service also moved quickly to better the lot of its workers. On his retirement from Paterson Gas Works in 1943, Cornelius Schoonejongen recalled:

> "When I started work 50 years ago, the plant was operated by the United Gas Improvement Company from Philadelphia,

Pa., who had a lease on the plant for 20 years. In 1900 their lease expired; I had worked seven years for them. The Paterson Gas Light Company then took the plant and I worked for them for three years. That is a total of 10 years. Ten years of hard labor. Nothing was done for our welfare. Many of the old men were out on charity, some taken in by relatives, and others, veterans, went to the Veterans Home and died shortly after from grieving. In 1903, Public Service took over this plant. They immediately started to improve working conditions and began welfare, old-age pension and sick benefits. Hours of work were changed from 12 to eight per day. Then later, work days were changed from seven to six, and yet later from six to five days a week. One-week vacations with pay was given, and later two weeks. Sick benefits were enlarged to full pay. Then The Depression started. Anyone working for Public Service never knew what The Depression was. Public Service wages were increased from time to time. I will tell you of an instance, of a man I knew. He had been a hard and faithful worker for 50 years with a concern. When he reached this anniversary he was called into the office. The management thanked him for his service and gave him a gold watch and chain and told him that he was not needed any more. Pleading for some sort of job, he was refused. He was through and not wanted. Does Public Service do this? No. It carries on even to the grave. Funeral costs are provided. No Potters Field. I myself thank Public Service for all they have done for me.

Henry Nicolson, who joined the gas company after World War I, also testifies to the better working conditions at Public Service. "I was a fighter pilot with Rickenbacker and that group," he recalls, "and I came back. I had been working for Koppers Coke before I got into the Air Force and at that time Koppers was working an 11-hour day shift and a 13-hour night shift. Every two weeks you worked 24 hours on Sunday so you could get the next Sunday off. I went over to see the general manager at Koppers; he wanted me to come back. I said, 'Are you still working 11-hour day shifts and 13-hour nights?' He said 'Yes, we are,' and I said, 'I can't take it.' So I went over to Public Service, where my uncle, Henry Whitcomb, was vice president and general manager, and I said, 'Uncle Henry, will you give me a job?' And he said, 'Sure I'll give you a job,' and so I went in the cadet course. They worked a normal eight-hour day."

Though conditions generally were better at Public Service, they did not work out so well for Nicolson, at least not at first, as they must have for other workers. This was because Nicolson reported to Jim Lane, an autocrat and an insomniac.

"My uncle called in Mr. Lane, who was general superinten-dent of manufacturing, and he said, 'Jim, this is my nephew. During the week I don't know who he is. Over the weekend I may have to lend him five bucks. But take him down to Market Street Gas Works and teach him to make gas.' I showed up the next morning at Market Street at eight, and Jim Lane, the general superintendent, was already there. So I said, 'This is bad.' The next morning I showed up at seven, and Jim Lane was there. The next morning I showed up at five, and Mr. Lane was there. So I said to myself, 'You are not going to beat me in again,' and I got in at 3 a.m. At about a quarter to five, in he drives in his automobile. When I got to know him better after a number of months, he was a great man for getting in early, do your work, and go home. I asked him, 'Jim can't you sleep?' He said, 'No, I can't. When I get home and my wife has dinner at 6 o'clock, I have my dinner and then I get my coon dogs and go out on the Ramapo Mountains and I coon hunt until midnight. At midnight, I come home, get a glass of milk and smoke a cigarette and go to bed. At two o'clock I wake up, go downstairs, get another glass of milk, smoke another couple of cigarettes, and go back to bed. At four o'clock I wake up, go down, get a little breakfast, get in my car and go to work.'"

Small wonder, then, that Lane was, in the words of another pensioner, "a tough old geezer ... who did not believe in any wasted time."

Like everything else in those days, gas work—and even getting to the work site in the first place—took muscle. Cars, trucks, and motorcycles did not become standard equipment until the mid-1920s, so work gangs trundled their picks, hammers, shovels, and pipe through the streets on overloaded hand carts. The meter-reader walked, and the lamplighter, usually a schoolboy, carried a long, cylindrical kerosene torch and pedaled a bicycle from street lamp to street lamp. (Later, the Welsbach Street Illuminating Company replaced the lamplighter with an eight-day clock that turned each lamp on and off automatically.) Even the managers of the gas company made their inspections by bicycle.

"When I was superintendent of distribution, Orange District, comprising what is now Summit, Orange and Montclair offices," John A. Clark later wrote, "I covered the territory from the Summit to the Passaic line on a bicycle most of the time, at that. Gas was used then largely for illumination, and for the running of gas engines. The introduction of gas ranges and automatic water heaters was just getting under way at that time."

Jack V. Richards, retired vice president of gas operations who joined Public Service as an engineering cadet in 1921, recalls the bicycle days under Clark:

"When I started I commuted from Dover. Sometimes I would drive my car in and then I would have to get on a bicycle and go look up services. That means you go to a house of someone who has applied for gas and you have to find out where you are going to put the meter, make a sketch of it, and return to the office. I had to go from Newark to Orange, to Maplewood and different places, and it was all by bicycle. I don't know whether it was discipline, or economy, or just to rub your nose in it. Some of us would make sure the bicycle had an accident once in a while so that we would have to come back on the trolley car, and then we would go out some other way to look up services. One day I was called in to see Mr. Clark (who had by then earned a reputation for bullheadedness) and I said, 'Look, I think you are past the horse-and-buggy day. This riding the bicycle is a lot of damned nonsense, going to Arlington and places like that to look up services. I could do in one day what it takes me a week to do, if I had a car.' Well, even the super only had a Model T Ford then. He said, 'Richards, when I was a cadet I used to ride up there on a bicycle, and it's in the same place

Gas men who went to the homes of customers in the 1920s were still using bicycles. These men were photographed outside the Newark Gas Distribution Shop in 1924.

now as when I rode there.' I said I'd like to transfer, get into the gas works. He said, 'Well, give it a couple of weeks and maybe I'll get you a car.' Two weeks went by and I got a notice to transfer to the works. No car. That's how he got rid of me."

But Clark did not subject only his employees to the rigors of bicycling. He often left the Model T in the parking lot when he wanted to check on his work gangs. "John Clark was a wonderful man and he really knew the business and he loved it," Henry Nicolson recalls. "When I finished my cadet course, I was moved from Paterson to Summit and became the first superintendent of Summit and Morristown Distribution. We were building this low-pressure line that went from Harrison Gas Works and Market Street Gas Works all the way up to Morristown to supply the holder there. Mr. Clark, in charge of the Distribution Department, would get on the train in Newark with his bicycle and ride up to Morristown and would pedal from Morristown all the way down looking at the gangs, all the way back to Newark."

However difficult the young cadets may have found bicycling, it was nothing compared to the work exacted from the street gangs. These gangs began a typical day by breaking pavement. "One man would hold the chisel and the other two or three would strike with eight-pound hammers," reported *Gas Age*. "This was hard work. The progress made by these gangs if they worked continuously, was slow, but they did not work continuously. To estimate that 25 per cent of the time was lost in resting, talking and lighting pipes would be conservative." Each man was expected to dig enough ditch in a day to accommodate four or five lengths of gas main, and each length was 12 feet long. The ditch was 18 inches wide and went down as deep as four feet, so that the cast iron pipe would not buckle and leak when the ground froze in winter. For this, the man received about a dollar a day, which was evidently a good wage then. An old-timer at Public Service recalls how glad one man, who had been tending orchids at a greenhouse in Millburn, was finally getting "a good job." The job consisted of digging a gas main trench halfway across Essex County. The gangs dug year-round, stopping only for storms and when the ground froze to a depth of 18 inches. It may have been hard, dirty work, but even ditchdigging required a certain skill and knowledge, as well as endurance.

"The amazing thing to me," says Nicolson, "is that we could lay in a new four-inch gas main, cast iron, for anywhere from six to eight cents a linear foot." Nicolson remembers one example that revealed artisanship, even in a ditch digger. "At that time we were using the Ames No. 2 shovel, and the salesman came in to see me with a new Wyoming shovel, the Wyoming Red Edge, it was called. I said, 'Our men don't like the Wyoming Red Edge shovel.' He said, 'I don't believe it.' I said, 'All right, I'll show you.' We went out to a gang that had six men in it and I said to the foreman, 'Put your shovels away.' Before we had gone out we had taken the identification marks off both types of shovel so that you couldn't tell from looking at them whether they were an Ames No. 2 or a Wyoming. We then laid out the six Ames and the six Wyomings, alternated them right along on the ground. We called the men over one by one to pick out a new shovel. They would pick the shovel up, feel it, and put it down, pick up another and feel it, and they they would go off with their shovel. When they were finished, there were six Wyoming shovels left on the ground, and the Ames had gone off with the men. I couldn't tell the difference, but the men who were using them all day could tell just the slight difference in heft or balance."

Sometimes the ditch-diggers were required to use rather less subtle skills. The late James N. Killgore, who was born in 1882 and came with Public Service in 1908, remembers distribution as two-fisted work. "That's all it was," he said, "blood, sweat, and tears. Every main was a problem. We'd run into water pipes, electric wires, telephone wires. There was always a battle between me and whoever had charge of that as to who was there first and who had the right to go through. Once we were crossing a spur of the Lackawanna Railroad in Kearny. We couldn't get a permit from the railroad. Mr. Clark, who was in charge of distribution, called me one day and said, 'Now, we're going through there. Tomorrow morning I want you to get every man in the street department out there with a pick handle.' He said, 'We're going under that railroad.' We were going to fight our way across if the railroad tried to stop us. As it turned out, the railroad inspector came out and ordered us to stop, but we went right ahead and dug under and laid the main. We put timbers under the tracks to carry the trains, and we went across without any further incidents."

Despite their subterranean conflicts, the various utilities of the State usually worked somewhat more peaceably together. "We had a street foreman named Salvatore Malanga," Nicolson recalled, "quite an amazing fellow who had been with the company a great many years. In those days, and I'm talking about one of the worst winters we ever had—the winter of 1934—we had well below zero temperatures, and we had a great many broken mains. The frost would push the mains down and break them. It was cast iron pipe. I was super of the Newark Distribution Department and we had about 16 crews out working day and night trying to fix these leaks. Pick-and-shovel crews, each one of them pushing a cart. We didn't have automobiles in those days for the street department. Each man had a two or four-wheel cart he would push from job to job. This particular night it was about 10 o'clock. I was making the last tour around the gang to see how they were making out, and I came to Sal Malanga and he was packing up his tool cart with all his tools. I said, 'How did you make out, Salvatore?' He said, "I found the broken main and I fixed it and I'm just getting ready to go home.'

"Just as he said that, up drives a telephone company car. Now, Sal had a record for driving a leak bar through three telephone cables, which cost us plenty to repair. A leak bar is a steel pipe we drove into the ground to get the smell of a gas leak. We'd drive a hole and put the pipe in and sniff to see where the gas was strongest. The telephone repairman got out of his car and climbed the pole right near where the tool cart was, and we could hear him as he took down the data. He said, 'Measure down the pole 13 inches and then go out from the curb four inches, measure east on the street 32 feet, six inches.' He comes down the pole, we help him measure, and he gets to 32 feet, six inches and there's a bar hole in the street. It amazed us how the telephone company could tell him over the wires where the trouble was. So I said to Sal, 'Okay, Sal, unload your tools and go to work.' We opened up the street and pretty soon we got down and there is this bar hole right through a wooden telephone duct. That job cost us $450 because there were so many wires in that cable that had to be cut and spliced. It was just tough luck."

Making power and keeping it flowing was hard and exacting work, but it produced cama-
raderie in formal terms, like the generating station baseball team, and informal, like this
central division outing to Seidler's Beach in Cliffwood, with what appears to be a heavy catch
of fish in paper bags advertising the resort area.

Interconnection:
The First Electric Ties

*Mr. McCarter heads up this big utility company and he can't even
change a fuse."*
—Mrs. Thomas N. McCarter

Today, the electricity that lights your reading lamp may
come to you via a vast system of high-tension interconnections, from any of 500 generating units located
throughout a triangular, five-state area of 50,000 square
miles. It was not always so. In 1903, each of the 20 Public
Service power plants was independent of the others. There
were few connecting wires between plants and no high-
voltage transmission lines to carry power into outlying
districts or into other states. Each plant served the immediate
surrounding neighborhood, an area often only a few miles—
and sometimes a few blocks—in diameter. The plants, which
were necessarily small and numerous, produced power for
use almost on the spot. There was no "load dispatcher" to
shoot a power station's output off to some unheard-of
location. This suited the power station crews, who liked their
independence and dreaded "interference" from the Newark
office, just fine. Having your own power station back then,
being a plant superintendent, was Darrow Sage recalls, like
being a local king: "You were unknown, and everybody in
that neighborhood was dependent on you for their heat,

Making the grade on the trestle from 15th Street, Hoboken.

their light, power, and comfort. You were the unknown power. You were never reported in the papers as long as your machines were running and the power came on, yet you were absolutely essential. The superintendent had the right to hire and fire, and to do everything else. The coal was bought by the purchasing department, which was in Philadelphia then, and was delivered to you in cars, but from then on, everything was yours."

Donald M. Quick, who retired as assistant to the chief engineer in 1967, tells one story of a neighborhood's dependence on its power station, not just for power and light, but for transportation: "Hoboken substation had originally been a generating station with the old Corliss (reciprocating) engines. It had the feeders supplying the trolley that came down the viaduct from Palisade Avenue, passed right near the Hoboken station, and then went out to the pier. Well, the station was manned by operators who worked four in the afternoon to midnight, midnight to eight in the morning, and eight to four in the afternoon. The frequency of the trolleys left a bit to be desired at midnight;

they came maybe every hour. So the man on duty at the station, on the four-to-midnight shift, would watch for the car coming down the trestle, because his relief would be on that trolley. And as soon as he saw that car stop and his relief, the other operator, get off, he'd go over to the board and take that breaker out so the car wouldn't have any power. It couldn't move once the breaker was tripped. And when the relief came in, he'd wait while the four-to-twelve operator went out to catch the trolley home. Then he'd go and put the breaker in so the trolley could move. Things were less rushed in those days."

If independence and isolation were advantages to the freewheeling power station crews, they were, alas, a hindrance to almost everyone else. When a plant broke down, its customers went without power until crews could repair the damage. Because the plant was not interconnected with its fellows, other plants could not provide emergency power to blacked-out neighborhoods. Moreover, the operation of many small generating stations—in 1903 the largest Public Service generator produced only 1,800 kilowatts—hindered the utility in implementing economies of size. The small stations required more men to operate less efficient machines. Finally, many of the stations were badly located, in terms of both customer demand and coal and water delivery. In January, 1906, *Electrical World* summed up the task before the still new Public Service Corporation this way:

"Consolidations like the one we are here considering nearly always tend to better service by substituting uniformly good methods for a mixture of good and bad, by dealing with operative problems as a whole instead of in dissociated fragments, and by giving the whole system a financial stability and relieving it from the hand-to-mouth existence that has been the fate of many a small company ... Again, through a given territory plants have sprung up responsive to local necessities and have grown with these necessities. Presently their 'sphere of influence' touch and more or less costly competition follows, seldom benefiting the consumer to any extent, but injuring the parties to it. Looking at the area as a whole, it is generally evident that the stations are located in the wrong places, the several (distribution) networks are not so disposed as to help each other, the railway lines do not transfer at the right places, if at all, and the fares are both high and ill-adjusted. Now it is possible as in the case of the Public Service Corporation, for a consolidated company to step in, put the heterogeneous plants into touch with each other, replace the inefficient ones, lay out the feeder system for the whole territory, unify the transportation systems so as to get efficient transfers and through lines, and in general to give better service while itself gaining from lower operating costs and smaller general expense.

"Of the advantage of welding a group of local distributions into a network there is little need to speak. It secures generally a higher efficiency of security against breakdown, both of lights and traction lines. By generating current on a large scale and distributing it efficiently, the cost can be greatly reduced and the price lowered without injuring the system as an investment. The natural tendency in a small and inefficient station is the policy of small sales and high prices, while if a large system is well administered large sales and lower prices are the rule."

The steady development under Public Service of the 13,200-volt transmission system and, in particular, the linking together in a single network of formerly independent stations and substations, greatly increased the area any one generating plant could serve. By January, 1906, all but the Morris, Boonton, and Hoboken plants in the northern area were interconnected, mostly at 6,600 volts. It was thus possible, for the first time, for even the most distant plants in the area, at Paterson and Elizabeth, to serve each other's territories in an emergency. The emergency power would, admittedly, have had to travel a somewhat tortuous route: From Paterson via the Passaic substation, the Secaucus station, the Palisade Avenue and Marion Stations in Jersey City, and the Newark stations at City Dock and Coal Street, before finally reaching Elizabeth. Or the other way around to Paterson.

"The tying in of these stations has proved highly useful," *Electrical World* nonetheless wrote in 1906, "and guarantees practically continuous service by eliminating interferences in service from breakdowns in any of these stations."

The link-ups also made for increased efficiency. Marion Generating Station, then the most modern and economical in the system, could now reach with its power into all the most populous areas of northern, and following further tie-ins, central New Jersey. (The company's South Jersey plants, though also joined by Public Service into a network among themselves, were to operate independently of the northern and central systems until 1929.) PS could thus supply comparatively cheap power to areas formerly served by small, isolated and inefficient power stations. This extended capability was the beginning of the end for the station superintendent as neighborhood king. Public Service, committing itself early on to the large, centrally-located power station, soon began shutting down small stations, at Orange and Plainfield, at Palisade Avenue in Jersey City, at Campbell Street, Newark, and at Hackensack. When the utility encountered difficulty securing a right-of-way for high tension lines to the 315 and 840-kilowatt Boonton and Morristown plants, it simply disposed of them, first by lease to a Morris County company and later, in 1921, by sale—thus losing out on what has since become that area's lucrative business.

At the same time, as part of a general reorganization, Public Service pursued economical development along two paths: It gradually beefed up the capacity of its bigger plants, and it began linking them to new and much-needed substations, either on abandoned power-plant sites or at more productive locations around the State. In 1916, a company committee on transmission policy reported:

> "The first step toward economy was the rebuilding of some of the generating stations, usually replacing belt-driven generators and old boilers with direct-connected generators driven by Corliss engines and modern boilers, which at that time were fairly large, up-to-date and economical.
> "With rebuilding of these plants the idea of centralization was gradually taking root, and with this idea a step was taken which at the time was good engineering, namely the

installation of a few trunk circuits at a potential of 13,200 volts.

"With the advent of the steam turbine, and large generating units, making it possible to centralize large amounts of generating capacity under one roof, it became necessary to raise the transmission potential generally throughout the system to 13,200 volts in order to build the plants in the most favorable locations and still be able to transmit economically.

"Numerous substations were connected to these circuits and as a rule replaced the older steam-driven plants, but in many cases the Company was confronted with such rapid increases in business, that through being unable to finance replacements, the older steam plants could not be abandoned but had to be continued in addition to the substation equipment."

Public Service added 850 kilowatts to the Hoboken Station on the Hudson River and 4,000 to the railway generating plant at Cranford, making the latter a combined light, power and railway generating station. It almost doubled, to 9,600 kilowatts, the generating capacity of the Paterson plant, while halving the number of machines in use there. At Marion, it pushed the generating capacity from 13,000 kilowatts in 1906 to 75,000—11,000 more than originally planned—in 1913.

As in the reciprocating-engine plants that preceded it, the boilers at Marion were originally hand-stoked by "muscle-men" wielding large, scoop-like shovels called "banjos." "They had to be experts," says Ed Francis, "to open the door and fire the coal into the far corners of the firebox, left and right, and to the rear. And they did it eight hours a day." Public Service soon installed steam-powered stokers at Marion, but even these required a watchful and heavily-muscled crew to keep them running.

"It took the continuous attention of the operators." says Francis, "to load the hoppers with coal and feed it and make sure that the coal burned right and that the ashes went over the back and into the ash pit. You'd get wet coal and you'd have to 'poke' as they called it, to get it to feed down right. The coal was pushed forward by rams and any kind of debris—whether it was metal, or stone, or what—would

The coal stoker: "You'd get wet coal and you'd have to poke . . . to get it to feed down right."

cause some kind of breakage to the stoker drive. Most of the rams were equipped with shear pins. Every time you had something in your coal—a railroad spike or a brake shoe—you'd break your shear pin, and you'd have to stop and replace it. There was a joke among the operators that they all carried their own 'specials.' A 'special' was a hard nail. They'd have this hard nail in there in place of the shear pin, and the stoker would run all right but eventually you'd break the stoker casing."

Until World War I, Marion Station hauled the ash away from its boilers by horse and cart, either dumping it on the site that was to become, decades later, Hudson Generating Station, or selling it to a cinder-block company that soon moved in across the street. In addition to stoking their boilers, the crews at Marion also had to keep the ash moving. "They'd have a slagging problem in the firebox," says Francis, "and at night they'd have to open the firebox doors and use a slash bar to get clinkers loose and get rid of them. So depending on the coal they were burning, they'd have either hard work or no work." Later, the utility replaced the horse and cart with a small railroad to remove the ashes.

Public Service established its first parallel operation in 1906, connecting Marion, Coal Street and Secaucus stations at 13,200 volts. Thereafter, generators at the three stations ran as a single unit, with their output pooled to serve a shared load. Parallel operation saved money and made for increased reliability of service, and was to become the rule throughout the Public Service system. Meanwhile, the utility shifted the load of the abandoned Orange station to a new substation on Lincoln Avenue and divided the South Orange load between existing substations in Newark and Irvington. It built a new substation in Belleville to accommodate that community's railway and lighting needs. In central New Jersey, where Public Service obtained control of several electric companies in 1905, a predecessor had already begun the work of streamlining by replacing small generating stations at Rahway, Carteret, Perth Amboy, New Brunswick, and Bound Brook with a central station in Metuchen and a system of substations. Public Service continued this work. It installed two 1,000-kilowatt turbines at Metuchen and, though not so quickly as it had planned, made over a network of five plants and three substations into one of two plants and seven substations. Metuchen was "never destined to become a large station," according to William Redshaw, "because of its fundamental limitation of a small water supply".

He observed:

"Driven wells produced water too hard for boiler use, forcing the station to use city water for make-up. A brook was dammed to provide water for its condensers. The flow proved inadequate, and was augmented by the driven wells. More wells were driven and, finally, a cooling tower was installed. Even so, on warm days the station was operated under difficulties."

When demand threatened to exceed the Metuchen plant's 3,000-kilowatt capacity in 1911, Public Service promptly built a new, 9,000-kilowatt station on a more judiciously chosen site in Perth Amboy. It gradually expanded this plant to take over the ring of substations in Central New Jersey until it was finally able to shut down Metuchen in 1921.

Public Service pursued the same general policy with its South Jersey system, building up the lighting and power plant at Trenton and the light and railway plant on 15th Street in Camden, and extending power lines from them throughout the territory. Again, it gradually closed down smaller generating stations and established new substations in their place. "A new transmission line has been constructed from Trenton to Princeton," McCarter reported in 1911, "thus enabling the Company to shut down the old, decrepit station at Rocky Hill, and for the first time to furnish satisfactory service to the people of that locality." In July, 1912, declaring its intention to do business only in New Jersey, Public Service disposed of its few properties outside the State, including the southern zone's 494-kilowatt lighting plant in Bristol, Pennsylvania.

By the end of its first decade, Public Service had largely staked out its territory as it now exists. It had acquired electric properties in Bergen County in 1905, and, later and on a smaller scale, in Weehawken, Carteret and Perth Amboy. By 1913, it was serving a rich corridor, 120 miles long and 15 miles wide between the nation's first and third cities, containing a majority of the State's residents and virtually all the State's industry. As its business grew, the electric department had—to quote an in-house department history— "attained sufficient importance to warrant its incorporation as a separate operating company." The Public Service Electric Company, wholly owned by its namesake, took over the generation, distribution and sale of current on July 14, 1910. This included the operation of railway generating stations. By the end of 1913, just before a spate of power station abandonments, the new Company was running no fewer than 203 generators at 32 generating stations, with 56 substations. Its long-distance transmission system, which had measured just 47 miles in 1903, now stretched over 576 miles, while its customer distribution system carried more than 14,000 miles of wire, up from 4,200 miles in 1903. Public Service had committed itself to the development of an underground distribution network through crowded areas, apparently in response to universal distaste for the cluttered overhead wiring of early electric days. By 1913, this expensive system measured 119 miles, a jump from only 25 miles in 1903.

"Already twenty-one municipalities have underground construction work in the most congested business centers." wrote Dudley Farrand at about this time, "and it is hoped to start similar work at other points as, and when, finances will permit and the growth of the business will warrant the expenditure. During the last few years our investments in underground construction have approached nearly half a million dollars annually, and it is expected that this amount will be increased in future years. Here again is another illustration of replacement, as overhead lines, though in good operating condition, are abandoned and scrapped when replaced by subways (underground wires) and the loss in investment due to the transaction runs into very large figures."

The electric business had grown steadily, at a rate of about 11 per cent annually, in the previous few years, especially as industry began demanding power. In those days, many businesses still generated their own electricity from small power stations. "I remember," one veteran of the southern territory later said, "when all the newspapers, the State House, and all the hotels in Trenton had their own power plants." But high capital costs, inefficiency, and an inability to take advantage of constant electrical innovation led many companies to Public Service.

"The (business) public is beginning to realize," said McCarter in 1911, "that the wholesale power rates of the Electric Company are more profitable to the consumer than the practice of operating single plants, steam or electric, including all the proper charges in connection therewith." Greatly bolstered by this trend, the company's light and power load for the first time exceeded its railway load in 1913. Significantly, street lighting made up a much smaller share, only 18 per cent, of the company's total electric load than it had formerly—even though the number of street lights served had tripled. Public Service still considered itself a trolley company first, but electricity was moving up fast on the outside. Said McCarter, at about this time, to the company section of the National Electric Light Association:

> "I play no favorites in the three departments of our company but to carry the vernacular of horse racing further, rather play them one, two, three across the board. They are all doing splendid work, and comparisons between them are odious, but I cannot blind myself to the fact—and it is right that you, who are laboring so hard in the Electric Company vineyard, should know—that, taking this year (1916) by itself for example, the net earnings of the Electric Company will for the year be more than double those of the Railway and Gas Companies combined. This gives you an idea of how essential the earnings of your company are to the whole Public Service."

But then he added: "Now this is not always going to be so, nor has it always been so," and went on to emphasize his confidence in the Railway Company, and in the Gas Company. Meanwhile, the electric business continued to grow at an "astonishing" rate.

McCarter always frankly admitted his ignorance of electricity. He was a lawyer, not an engineer. "When our engineers begin to discuss volts, amperes, kilowatts, rheostats, single-phase and three-phase, gasometers, and the like," he later said, "I look wise, say nothing, and ask no questions, lest I appear like a friend of mine who, when the game of golf first made its' appearance in this country, inquired what would happen 'if you put the tee in the caddy.'" Despite his studied silences and his long-standing emphasis on the railway business, though, no one could doubt McCarter's usefulness to the Electric Company during the coming period of rapid, at times headlong, expansion. To meet the booming customer demand for power, his engineers now wanted to build two huge, new power stations, at a cost of millions. It was McCarter's job to get the money. A Public Service pensioner tells a story on the point, about a young engineer in the company's training program who was sent to Rumsonhill on some minor repair work: "Tom McCarter and the engineer were standing there and

Mrs. McCarter said, 'You know, Mr. McCarter heads up this big utility company and he can't even change a fuse.' And Tom (for once having a comeback to his wife's playful twitting) said, 'Yes, but maybe this young fellow would have difficulty going over to Wall Street and borrowing a million dollars.'"

With the potential of the electric business still uncertain, with the wage, fuel and tax burden on the company worsening, and with the rate regulation imposed by the State, obtaining the required funds could hardly have been easy even for McCarter. In a 1915 argument before the State Court of Errors and Appeals, McCarter said:

> "The capital requirements of the three underlying com-
> panies, which the corporation must furnish, aggregate about
> $6,000,000 a year. In the future the sole source of supply of
> this money will be the further sale of Public Service stock or of
> notes convertible into stock at a later date. In order that this
> financing may be more practical, I indulge the hope that
> some day the earnings of the underlying companies will reach
> a point where they will, in turn, justify an eight per cent
> (dividend) by the parent corporation. With all the troubles
> that confront public utility companies, with interest rates the
> world over going up, and with incomes a source of taxation,
> the moneys required for the future development of the
> properties controlled by Public Service will not be attractive to
> investors upon a five or six per cent stock basis."

Public Service nonetheless obtained the needed funds and began construction of Burlington Station, on the Delaware River midway between Camden and Trenton, in 1913, and of Essex Station, on the Passaic River in Newark, in 1915. The utility designed Burlington to serve all South Jersey and particularly its two rapidly expanding main cities. Its power reached both cities via 13,200-volt transmission lines. The big power plants at 15th Street, Camden, and at Trenton continued to operate, supplementing the output of the new power station. But with the opening of Burlington in June, 1914, the Electric Company abandoned five small, obsolete generating stations in the area, replacing them with as many substations. Burlington supplied these substations with power from two 60-cycle vertical turbo-generators, each producing 3,000 kilowatts, that Public Service had removed from Marion to make room for more powerful equipment there. To these, the utility added a new, 11,250 kilowatt turbine in 1915.

Like Burlington, Essex was to stand almost exactly between its two main load centers, Newark and Jersey City, and "as near as possible to the load center as it would (develop) in future years." It began service November 6, 1915, after only eight months and eight days in construction, with a single, 22,500-kilowatt turbine, to which a twin turbine was soon added. The plant earned engineering approval for its efficiency and for its layout, with the boiler room at right angles to the turbine room and with the switch-house detached. Public Service had designed Essex for ready expansion, and company engineers were clamoring to take advantage of that capability almost before the station had produced its first kilowatt. In a speech to Jersey City Rotarians in 1917, McCarter gave a hint of the kind of infighting that was then going on over just how fast Public Service should expand its whole electric plant:

"Last year we had a phenomenal year. This country had a great wave of prosperity, and so our business increased enormously, so that when our general managers came in and said we must have this and that to keep pace with this enormous increase in business, we were faced with a difficulty. Ordinarily these items have aggregated nine million dollars, but we have pared them down to six million. We do not give these boys all they want. When we began to consider our estimates for this year we were up against the demands of the general managers for twenty million dollars for improvements to keep pace with last year's growth and this year's business. It was out of the question to raise this sum. By the most careful pruning we cut it down to nine and a half million dollars. That sum we raised, and we are preparing to go forward with that sum; but as sure as I stand here the time will come when we will not be able to raise such sums of money as that, or even less, to develop this great property throughout the State, unless the people of the State are willing to let the company make, under all the conditions existing, such return as will attract sane, sober businessmen to make the investment."

Even in 1916, a "phenomenal" year by his own retrospective judgment, McCarter was naysaying the rapid expansion his Electric Company wanted. Noting bad conditions in both the Railway and Gas Companies, he told his engineers:

"So, too, with capital expenditures—no improvement will be made that we can get on without making and still maintain proper service, but you must realize that in a large corporation, such as this, there are certain matters which have to go forward if proper service is to be maintained. For example, it is necessary, if we are to take care of the load next fall, that we have in operation the first section of the new Essex Power Station, which is now under construction, and which calls for a large expenditure and is a great undertaking, to most of which we are already committed—I would like to stop if I dared, but it is too great a responsibility to assume, and that work must go forward, and so there are other matters here and there which will of necessity go forward, but, generally speaking, we must stop all expenditure until the clouds break away."

If building Essex was a hardship for Public Service, it was, so time soon proved, a necessary one. The war in Europe began to affect the utility in two ways, greatly increasing industrial demand for power and at the same time hindering the company's efforts to meet that demand. Starting in 1916, the war brought the company industrial contracts for "enormous" (and unprecedented) quantities of power. By 1917, 67 per cent of the utility's commercial power load was going to industrial customers whose work was directly or indirectly connected with the war. In 1918, that figure approached 90 per cent. Said McCarter, in the annual report for that year:

"Demands for power, largely from various war industries, continued to call upon the full capacity of the generating stations throughout the year. The excessive loading of the generating plants and systems as a whole continued up to the time of the signing of the armistice, and while the safe all-day rating of the 60-cycle system in the Northern zone was 100,000 kilowatts, at times the load was as high as 109,000 kilowatts. In the Southern zone, the safe all-day rating was 18,000 kilowatts, but at times the demand was as high as 22,000 kilowatts.

Public Service was, as *Electrical World* later said of war-burdened utilities in general, "operating (its) equipment to the limit, regardless of economy and maintenance expense."

Meanwhile, the Electric Company faced severe shortages of both coal and labor. It had contracted for coal at $3.25 a ton, but when war and increased world demand diverted much of the available supply, its contractors could not all deliver. Public Service had to purchase its coal on the open market, at $6 or $7 per ton, and was even then able to maintain only a day-to-day supply, with no reserve for emergencies. McCarter noted that the company could not pass this emergency cost on to its customers, as would any other industry. He called this "a melancholy illustration of the results from and dangers of rigorous rate regulation." At the same time, labor was scarce and its cost was climbing. In addition, said McCarter in his 1917 report:

"Public Service Electric Company was materially handicapped during the year by the failure of manufacturing contractors, owing to war conditions, to deliver apparatus and supplies as promised. At the Essex Power Station the 35,000 kilowatt unit ordered in 1916 was completed as to installation, but necessary adjustments made it impossible to place it in service in 1917, as was anticipated ... At Perth Amboy a 12,500 kilowatt turbo-generator was installed but as at Essex, and for like reason, the date of delivery was so deferred that it was not possible to get the machine ready for service before the end of the year."

The combination of high demand and helplessness to meet that demand was no doubt trying for Public Service, especially since, as *Electrical World* noted, "applications for power had to be refused in many cases." Applications *not* related to the war effort, that is. But the real crisis for the Electric Company was to come after Armistice Day.

Rumsonhill

"What a place to come home to after a day of rate-hike hearings!"
—Weekend guest at Rumsonhill

The home that Tom McCarter built for his family the year that he founded Public Service in 1903 was a 32-room red brick Georgian mansion. Appropriately, by reason of its perch atop the loftiest rise in Rumson, he named it Rumsonhill.

Tom McCarter had a kind of Adam-in-the-Garden-of-Eden flair for naming things. He had just named Public Service, for instance, and with comparable propriety: he wanted the new company to be of service to the public. For the next 45 stormy years, he gave his every waking hour to accomplishing that. On the record of his brainchild's performance, McCarter was good at naming things—almost prophetic, in fact. On that same record, he was also good at orchestrating storms.

Rumsonhill was a showcase of wealth and power. Successful men of that era built themselves such imposing piles as much to let the neighbors know they'd made it as for their personal comfort. A suitably regal three-story dwelling with a skylighted fourth floor, Rumsonhill had ornate ceilings almost as high as a museum's. Its two-foot thick walls insulated against heat and cold. Heavy canvas secured the plaster against cracking before any decoration went on.

Tom's eldest daughter Ellen says those walls weren't all that great. In parts of the house they were of hollow tile that let the patriarch know more about what was going on than his children always cared to have him know.

Each of Rumsonhill's 12 bedrooms had its own palatial bath. Bulky furniture matched the heavy oak paneling, and there were 10 fireplaces. Apart from the stretches of hollow tile in the walls, though, so far as the only other family to occupy Rumsonhill after Tom and his wife sold it many years later could discover, there were no secret panels or hidden rooms.

A deeply coffer-ceilinged main hall of awesome dimensions led in from the great porte-cochere, where access to the house was via a raised first step to accommodate dismounting from a carriage and, shortly, from the high runningboards of the early cars. This hallway opened into a spacious central foyer. From the floor immediately above there boomed a built-in music roll-playing organ that often filled the big, echoing structure with such favorites of Tom's as *Botany Bay*, *In the Shade of the Old Apple Tree*, *Bunch of Violets* and *Little Annie Rooney*.

McCarter liked these songs so much that when he was in a good mood, as apparently happened more often that the man's fiery temper would lead one to believe, he enjoyed belting them out as solos in his rich baritone.

When he was in a *really* good mood, his younger daughter Madeleine remembers, he would—although not a particularly religious man by nature—have her join him in a duet of "Oh, I love to tell the story/Of Jesus and his glory." As the youngest of the four McCarter children, Madeleine was also the closest to her father, and the memory of those duets, recalled during an interview, made her choke up a little.

Tom McCarter's favorite of favorites, though, was a melody that did not exactly lend itself to either solos or harmonizing. It must therefore have created some interesting atmospherics at Rumsonhill when that (for 1903) up-to-the-minute thing on the second-floor balcony cranked up its mechanical innards and settled down to a moody rendition of the owner's No. 1 preference—Gounod's *Funeral March.*

Above the main-floor hall area the interior walls of the mansion swept up dizzyingly past oaken balconies to the stained glass skylight in the copper-clad roof. Rumsonhill was in many ways a child's paradise to grow up in, and this enormous well at the heart of their existence held a special fascination for the McCarters' two sons, Tom and Uzal, during the boys' earliest years there.

While their father was in Newark energetically talking more and more little gas and electric companies into abandoning their shaky independence to join the much healthier PS fold, the McCarter male heirs whiled away many a rainy afternoon happily risking their necks by launching themselves time and time again, to the accompaniment of maniacal shrieks, off the second-floor balcony onto the overstuffed chairs and sofas in the great hall underneath.

What this may have contributed to the incidence of early heart disease in the servants is a matter for speculation, since governesses are no substitute with boys for a mother whose own often fragile health sealed her off from most such goings-on. So far as anyone knows, *third*-floor-balcony launches were a bit beyond even the McCarter appetite for high-flying adventure.

Regardless, a house guest who witnessed the second-floor dives remarked later, "McCarter could hardly have foreseen the use the boys would put the place to, but as with everything else the old man did, he had equipped it with something worth having—furniture that could take it."

In the basement at Rumsonhill there were kitchens on a scale Henry VIII might have installed if he'd had the technology, a correspondingly oversize dumbwaiter for hauling gargantuan feasts to the baronial dining hall above, a wine cellar like a bank vault, and a regulation squash court. There was also a pioneer version of an appliance that even a modest home today would not willingly be without. It was a gas-fired clothes dryer, but one so huge you could walk in to hang wet garments on rows of racks, then close the door and set automatic shut-off controls for whatever time-span and temperature the load called for.

A swallow's view of Rumsonhill, above, and the front entrance to the McCarter home in Rumson, below.

In multi-chimneyed splendor the new McCarter residence rose angularly against the sky above its better-than-200-foot-elevation building site. Across meticulously kept landscapes near the main house that included eye-pleasing statuary and a classic English rose garden, past the estate's farmed areas and the green fields beyond, the occupants and their guests could enjoy a three-way view of the water of the Atlantic Ocean and the Navesink and Shrewsbury Rivers.

It was a refreshing prospect, in every way superior to the one the McCarters had looked out on at their home at 59 Lincoln Park in Newark, or from grandfather McCarter's house across from it where he'd settled when he trundled his family and all their belongings in from Newton by horse and wagon in the middle 1800s. Friends who were privileged to experience the view from Rumsonhill recall it as having been "simply breathtaking."

The view today is somewhat different. The 12-foot-high brick gateposts with RUMSONHILL cut deep into their massive concrete capitals in eight-inch letters still flank the entry, just as when McCarter ordered them built. When the Queen of England came by on her visit to America as the guest of Franklin Roosevelt, the squire of Rumsonhill put aside his dislike for FDR to erect special bleachers between the gateposts to hail Her Majesty's passage through town. She was, after all, the Queen of *England*.

The name RUMSONHILL, now a bit worn at the edges, is still quite visible to anyone passing in a car, as it must have been to the Queen. Several hundred feet inside McCarter's mighty iron fence, which developers also wisely left standing, the enormous beech tree beneath whose heavy limbs his sheep once safely grazed still flourishes. Since the pivotal moments in 1960 when the wrecker's ball found itself tested to the limit by the mansion's rugged walls, the prized McCarter acreage behind that fence has yielded to the erection of expensive homes better geared to a relatively servantless era. Nearly a dozen such executive and professional residences occupy, at elegant random, the 220 acres that once knew only McCarters, their groundskeeping and farming staffs, and the 14 live-in help who combined their skills and energy in administering Rumsonhill to the master's demanding taste.

In addition to the fence and gateposts, there is one more impressive reminder that even here on the home acres dwelt a man with the kind of imagination it would take to found an enterprise like Public Service. On either side of the paved road McCarter built across his sprawling property, winding majestically up one side of the rise crowned by Rumsonhill and sweeping in a graceful serpentine down the other side to the less imposing rear entrance on Ridge Road, a towering dual colonnade of ancient sycamores continues to delight the eye. Today, at one point where the new layout of the Rumsonhill acres interrupts the original flow of the roadway, the big trees march right up to the front door of one of the larger homes, leapfrog its roof, and take up their course again in the back yard.

These sycamores, more than 200 of them, were a special source of pride to McCarter. They represented a welcome change from his daily routine of balance sheets and all the other complexities that went with managing a rapidly expanding utilities empire, and, as with everything else at Rumsonhill, he took full advantage of it. He enjoyed being chauffeured down between their flickering sunlit columns each morning to catch the 7:37 at the Red Bank railroad station, and back up the leafy aisle with headlights glancing off their scabrous trunks each night.

It would be a mistake to let the changes which have overtaken McCarter's estate inspire gloomy thoughts about "the boast of heraldry, the pomp of power" and how "the paths of glory lead but to the grave." Despite Tom's tastes for the Gounod march, there is not much parallel here for the irony of fate which the poet Shelley wove into his scathing sonnet on the tyrant Ozymandias, the ruins of whose towering monument to himself in the desert gave time's lie to his boast, "Look on me, ye mighty, and despair!" McCarter may have been only selectively aware of life around him, but he was, on balance, no Ozymandias at heart.

He did too many things that were human, things that dyed-in-the-wool tyrants seldom get around to doing.

One hall girl (as they called messengers at P.S. in those days) still remembers with gratitude the way McCarter reacted when, during one of the many occasions on which he was under running attack in the press as "the Czar of New Jersey," she became the accidental instrument of what he may have briefly imagined was an assassination attempt. Her awe at being assigned to deliver important papers directly to Mr. McCarter made her overly nervous, she figures, looking back, and to compensate she must have thrust out her hand with unusual vigor to turn the knob of his office door. Somehow her hand slipped and went right through the frosted glass, sending shards of it crashing inward. McCarter, she recalls, jumped up violently and rushed out from behind his desk exclaiming, "Oh my God! Oh my God!" and then, when he saw it was a hall girl and not an assassin, "Are you hurt? Are you hurt?" She will never forget, she says, how he gently extricated her hand from the peril of the glass still in the frame, stanched with his own handkerchief the few superficial cuts she had miraculously escaped with, and saw to it that she received immediate medical attention. Only then did he think to ask her for the important papers he'd been waiting for. She was still clutching them in her other hand.

"I was a young, impressionable kid, perhaps," says McCarter's secretary for 13 years, Frank McMenimen, "but I thought he was a great guy from start to finish. He could bawl you out if you did the wrong thing, for instance, but never in my life did I hear him say, 'Remember what you did yesterday.' Once it was over and he had told you you were wrong, that was the end of it, which I think was a great trait.

"One thing I learned the first week I went to work for Mr. McCarter was that you'd better not lie, because you had too many things to cover up. Like Nixon. If Nixon had come out the morning after and said, 'It was a bunch of jerks that did this thing, and I'm gonna throw every one of 'em out,' that would've been the end of it. When I made a mistake, I always went in and told Mr. McCarter, 'I goofed.' And it was quite pleasant, y'know, because there isn't too much anybody can do then. Of course, if you goofed too many times, he'd fire you. But if you knew he was going to bawl you out, you could—up to a point—take the wind out of his sails by admitting it."

Frank must have had plenty of opportunity to goof, and a healthy record of avoiding it. With McCarter's other secretary, Frank Davis, McMenimen held power of attorney and co-signed all McCarter's checks. It is interesting to note that the boss evidently trusted the two men implicitly, for they were not bonded. "Oh, he trusted us, all right," say McMenimen. "I have carried over a million dollars in negotiable securities into New York for him on occasion."

McMenimen still feels the presence of Thomas N. McCarter Sr. — "Mr. McCarter," as he invariably calls him— so strongly that he sometimes slips into the present tense in talking about him, as if the man were still alive and in charge at Public Service.

In commenting on the fact that this hardnosed industrialist was extremely sentimental, McMenimen echoes the recollections of McCarter's not-always-sentimental children. The elder daughter, Ellen, said she remembered her father returning to Rumsonhill from Newark one evening during a period when there were parades on Broad Street to denounce him as "the Czar of New Jersey" for his part in allegedly running the State with his brothers Uzal and Robert. The tears were streaming down his face, she recalled.

"The tears would stream down his face at the drop of a hat," said Ellen Doubleday, "as is true of all the McCarters. We have weak tear ducts."

That night, at any rate, her father sobbed to his startled family, "Why do they call me 'the Czar of New Jersey'? All I want is the good of everybody, and to make it a good company."

McMenimen bears this out. "He was very sentimental," he says. "If he gave speeches where he reminisced, the tears would come to his eyes. The last time I was in his office as his secretary, he broke down and cried. Even though *he* had gotten me the new job. He cried because I was leaving. And the very first day on that job, he had a dozen roses sent over

Michael Kahn, producing director of the McCarter Theatre Company since 1974, guides Kathryn Walker, Donald Madden and Patricia Elliott through the American premier production during the 1976-77 season of Per Olov Enquist's "The Night of the Tribades." The Princeton theater was created with a $250,000 grant from Thomas N. McCarter in 1929.

and then came over himself to congratulate me. He didn't send for me. *He* came over to *my* office. Now if you know the layout of the Public Service building, where he was in the front on the eighth floor, and in my new job, I was way in the back, you know that that was a long walk. A *long* walk. Mr. McCarter was that kind of person."

Frank McMenimen says Tom McCarter moved quickly when he made up his mind to do something. McCarter attended a meeting of the board of directors of Fox films one day, resigned, and began disposing of his Fox Movietone stock almost immediately. That night Tom gave his wife $200,000 in Fox stock and $100,000 each to his four children (outright to the girls but in trust to the boys), $250,000 in Fox stock to Princeton for the McCarter Theatre—and the next

day began unloading Fox stock until he had none left. He got
out at the right time, since the stock plummeted soon after in
the 1929 crash.

When Hoover was running for re-election against Roosevelt, Frank remembers, there was a meeting at the old
Mosque Theater on south Broad Street and Hoover was
scheduled to stop off to say a few words there en route to a
pre-Election Day speech in Madison Square Garden. Tom
McCarter was to meet him and escort him to the Mosque,
and since Mrs. McCarter was going to be late arriving from
Rumson, he asked Frank McMenimen if he'd mind taking
her with Vivian McMenimen and himself. He had given
Frank two platform passes earlier. The McMenimens, who
considered Mrs. McCarter "an absolutely lovely person,"
were delighted to oblige.

"She pulled in at the back of the Public Service building,"
Frank tells the story, his face lighting up with pleasure, "and
we tooled out onto Raymond Boulevard. Not a soul in sight.
We swing left on Broad Street. The sidewalks are jammed,
but there isn't another car anywhere. They've cleared Broad
to accommodate President Hoover's entourage, of course,
but without flickering an eyelid Mrs. McCarter says to her
chauffeur, 'Never mind, Peter, just drive right on!' He does,
and so help me, not a policeman steps out to stop us.

"Everything is blocked off in front of the Mosque as we
pull up, but we make a big U-turn and get out. The place by
then is packed to the doors. Mrs. McCarter was such a stately
person that her mere presence inspired awe, and the crowds
parted as we swept in to the ticket-taker. Well, he made the
mistake of telling her there was no more room. She just
looked at him and said, 'Well, I have a *platform* pass.' He
didn't know who she was, but like anyone else meeting her
for the first time he was, shall we say, impressed. 'All right,
ma'am' he said, 'I'll put a chair up there for you.' And she
turned to us and said to him 'And these two children are with
me.' He wound up putting *three* chairs up there."

McMenimen laughs and shakes his head at the memory.
"There I am, up there in front with my wife and Mrs.
McCarter, and all our vice presidents back of *me*, one of the

slaves. And of course when Mr. McCarter comes in he has to sit down there in the audience because there's no more room on the platform, this time for sure. He didn't mind. He just grinned at us and never said a word about it later."

McCarter was apparently an interesting mix of knowing when to refrain from asking questions that could embarrass, and of *not* knowing when he was leaning too hard on people. Public Service worked Saturday mornings back then, and after a whole long Friday when nothing much was happening, McCarter would sometimes get on the phone at four in the afternoon and loudly require of some poor soul legal papers or reports that could only be gotten together and approved or signed over the weekend, since Old Tom wanted them on his desk at nine sharp Monday morning. More than once, such alarms and excursions chewed up an underling's weekend. When what McCarter wanted involved PS finances, as it almost invariably did, it also meant assembling the information and then hauling it out for checking to Long Valley, where Vice President for Finance Lyle McDonald lived peacefully without benefit of telephone. On a Saturday or Sunday back then, by all accounts, Long Valley was pretty much an all-day trip.

Frank McMenimen sees McCarter's having always been accustomed to having things done for him as the explanation for this kind of seemingly inconsiderate behavior. "You see, nobody told him otherwise, or spelled out for him that it would take someone a certain amount of *work* to do those things. I do not think Mr. McCarter would have asked *anybody* for that kind of performance, except on rare occasions, if he'd realized what was involved. But nobody told him." There is a pause and a chuckle. "*I*'d tell him, though."

Which makes McMenimen a rare bird, since even McCarter's daughters agreed completely that that was the man's biggest problem: Nobody had the guts to stand up to him.

Not that it was always necessary, McMenimen recalls. Sometimes common sense would do. Every Saturday morning around 9:30, for example, McCarter would call in to 80 Park Place from Rumson in quest of some information he needed for the work he was always doing, even on weekends, to move the company forward. "He himself *never* came in on Saturday," Frank emphasizes, "but he *always* called up on Saturday. And this is another indication of the kind of man he was, as far as I'm concerned. When he would call up Saturday morning, he would ask his questions of whoever answered the phone, either Frank Davis or myself. So long as he got the answers he required, he would never ask for the other person.

"So Frank and I reached an agreement where we wouldn't both have to come in on Saturday. He would come in one Saturday, and I'd come in the next Saturday. Now, Mr. McCarter wasn't stupid. If I answered the phone this Saturday, and Frank Davis answered the phone the next Saturday, and then I answered the phone the following Saturday, and so on, well, he wasn't that stupid that he didn't know what was going on. But he never embarrassed us by asking for the other fellow."

Dedicated golfers can best assess Thomas N. McCarter's form here, in a place and time and event unknown, but it is perhaps safe to say that he found greener fields in board rooms than on golf courses.

Power and Control

"My father couldn't have been elected in New Jersey if he'd run for
dogcatcher."
—Ellen McCarter Doubleday

The disappointment that Tom McCarter Sr., experienced at being so devoted to Princeton but never making it as a trustee, was compounded when he was offered the chance to fill out the term of U.S. Senator Dwight Morrow, his grandson, Tom III, recalls.

Morrow had died during the Twenties, and at a meeting in Deal, politics as usual making strange bedfellows, Frank Hague had offered the opening to his old foe, Tom McCarter of Public Service. "The stipulation," says Tom III, "was that my grandfather resign his connections with Public Service completely. He declined to do this, and that was the end of the matter. I should point out that at the time when this offer was made, it was common practice throughout the United States, particularly in the West where mining and oil interests wielded enormous power, to have in office on Capital Hill, Senators who were also connected with major industrial conglomerations. As far as my grandfather's having turned down the proferred U. S. Senate seat is concerned, though, in my opinion he could not have been reelected had he, on completion of the vacancy term, had to

A McCarter troika: Brothers Robert, Uzal and Thomas.

run for the seat on his own. People in a position to know have assured me of this. The reason was, primarily, that he represented in the minds of the people of New Jersey the largest financial conglomeration in the State, one which in its earliest days had been politically controversial. His older brother Uzal was, after all, president and controlling stockholder at the time in the largest bank in the State, and his still older brother Robert was perhaps one of the two or three biggest corporate lawyers."

Said Ellen, with her usual succinctness, "My father couldn't have been elected in New Jersey if he'd run for dogcatcher."

This aura of means clung to Tom Sr. from birth, and for him especially, ambitious as he was to serve his country as well as his State, carried with it political penalties that must have been therefore doubly galling. Yet if he chose at any point to take cold comfort from the sour rumination of a far more ruthlessly ambitious predecessor and contemporary, John D. Rockefeller, there is no indication that it did a great deal to soothe his ego, then or later. "Great prejudice exists against all successful business enterprises," Rockefeller had observed when the government, as he saw it, took him to court for successfully building an empire. "The more successful the enterprise, the greater the prejudice." McCarter, though, was surely realistic enough to know in his heart that by doing what he did to help New Jersey achieve industrial prominence and prosperity and a better life for its people, he had in a way brought on himself the prejudice that dogged him all his days.

Like anyone of his drive and resultant stature—not to mention inheritance—he could probably not have done otherwise. The McCarters, of course, took from Old Tom's enterprise nothing like what the Rockefellers have managed to hold together over several astute generations, nor on the other hand have they inherited the accompanying political test-case headaches of that enduring dynasty. Even so, there are interesting parallels.

A minor one lies in something John D.'s elder sister Lucy once said about him that summarized with homely precision his career as the first of the oil-barons. "When it's raining porridge," she remarked, "you'll find John's dish right side up." It mightn't be stretching a point all that much to say the same of Old Tom McCarter. Also, John Rockefeller built Standard Oil into such a gargantuan monopoly as inevitably to have drawn the lightning of antitrust action. He did it by eliminating competition. He did that, in turn, by buying up competitors, one by one. Public Service, too, went along for years buying up lots of little companies, most of which would otherwise have gone to the wall, either from shaky financing or geography-limited distribution facilities. PS was no Standard Oil, of course, but antitrust actions filed against Standard Oil which shook the country in the 1890s and early 1900s were fraught with lessons and warnings, however, that Tom McCarter no doubt carefully filed away, with his lawyer's keen-eyed awareness of possible parallels, for future reference. Judging by his mobile instinct for turning a personal profit amid altruism, it seems doubtful that the lesson of the porridge bowl was lost on him either.

Besides being a stockholder or bondholder in some of the predecessor companies of Public Service, his grandson points out, and over and above the profit he must have turned on the Lawyers Building project, "he was a director, at the time, of a number of local banks—as well as president of Union County Trust Company for one—and president of the Second National Bank of Red Bank, vice president of the Essex and Hudson Gas Company, second vice president of Fidelity Union Trust, and so on. His initial salary with Public Service was $50,000 a year." Tom III noted at another point that in his heyday Tom Sr. reached a peak of $200,000 a year as president and then chairman, (the result of a large bonus one year) and then took successive cuts during the depression. By 1941, the salary of the top post at PSE&G was down to $100,000 and only in recent years has it climbed back over the $150,000 level.

"I believe he also had the first $500,000 life insurance policy ever issued by The Prudential, of which he had been a director," Tom III recalls. "His father left an estate of, I believe, somewhere in the area of $750,000 in 1901. My grandfather was one of six children, three boys and three girls, so I assume he inherited one-sixth of whatever the net of that was—bearing in mind that there were no inheritance taxes in those days.

"If you ask where the money came from that he invested in all his various enterprises, I would presume that, apart from his share of the inheritance from his father's estate in 1901, all of it came from earned income. He was a stockholder in a number of companies, and had been a large earner from the practice of law, going back to the very old days of his involvement with incorporations. He was also instrumental in putting together some of the predecessor companies that he eventually amalgamated into Public Service. Aside from being involved in real estate, it helps to bear in mind also that many of his close friends in the early days were people who later achieved national prominence in the financial and business worlds. Some were sons of families who had already attained national stature."

In later years McCarter became a director of many major U. S. corporations and also served for more than 20 years as a director and member of the executive committee of Chase National Bank of New York.

Perhaps his discernment in using his connections constructively to raise ongoing capital for expanding Public Service had something else going for it that provided as much of the necessary thrust as his personal sense of commitment. That was his capacity to endure. When he was over 84 and not frequenting Newark with his resounding presence so often any more, he surprised everyone who had mistakenly thought the old lion was dozing his life away in Rumson or Lake Wales, Florida, by storming into a board meeting at Fidelity Union and demanding, in a voice that could still make the windows rattle, to know why in the hell they hadn't raised the dividend on the bank's stock lately. Only a few days before he died four years later, a visitor to Rumson who was in a position to do so, noting how gray he looked and how cold his hands were, lectured him sharply on the need to take better care of himself. Although confined to a wheelchair by then, McCarter let fly at his visitor with a bawling-out worthy of his best days at 80 Park Place. Exasperated, the visitor shook an angry finger at him and said, "No wonder nobody comes to see you!" Eyes snapping and nostrils dilating with his old delight in verbal combat, the man his own children had joined others in nicknaming TNT exploded. "Don't you shake your finger in *my* face!" he roared. Far from contributing indirectly to his demise, the incident probably helped energize his circulation enough to let him make it to his targeted age 88. Three days later, the fires which had been part of this fabulous figure's very nature cooled forever. One can hardly say the same of his memory.

The strength of the chemical bond in the McCarter genes alone would not permit that. In clearly admiring tones, Tom the grandson puts at the top of the heap among the things which made his forebear operate the way he did "the inspiration he drew from his father. The father of PSE&G's

founder had an unusual law career throughout the State of
New Jersey and gave his namesake an appetite for the
adversary relationship which never deserted him. Next to
that in making him run, probably, was his tremendous
fondness for his older brother Uzal, who for the first 30
years of this century was considered the leading financier in
the State. Uzal and he were obviously close because they
served on a number of boards together. Remember, Uzal
brought him onto the board of the Prudential, and all the
men who were on the original board of the Pru were among
the leading people of the United States, including Judge
Gary of U.S. Steel, representatives of the Morgan interests,
and so on."

A lighter but related aspect of such heady associations is
Tom III's recollection, that "F. Scott Fitzgerald was Class of
'17 at Princeton, and obviously wrote many of his stories
about classmates and the parents of classmates from
Princeton. There are in the possession of friends of mine
dinner lists showing a good many of the people who came
down to Rumsonhill, and F. Scott Fitzgerald is among them,"
said Tom III. "There is an unproved theory, you know, that
The Great Gatsby and several of his other novels were based on
members, or families of members, of the Ivy Club at
Princeton, which Mr. Fitzgerald did not get into." Sitting in
that storied edifice on Prospect Street, which McCarters *did*
get into, and listening to someone named Thomas N.
McCarter III talk of that storied past creates a not
unpleasantly eerie feeling, like a walk in the streets of
Newport, Rhode Island, on a midnight in summer. Ghosts
move in the warm fragrances and no longer mean anyone
harm, if they ever did. Ghosts, like children and memories
and men with an apocalyptic vision of power for an entire
State, seldom do.

But it is autumn in Princeton in the Seventies of a new
century, with PSE&G coming up on its 75th anniversary, and
The Founder's grandson too, with a mild reshifting of focus,
comes back to the present. "This has always been a matter of
speculation, of course," he emphasizes of the implied
Fitzgerald-Rumsonhill link. "Still, there are some interesting

similarities between the corporate developments and families in control of big corporations in New Jersey, and some of F. Scott Fitzgerald's stories."

High-jinks at Rumsonhill or elsewhere in the Garden State never quite compared with Newport entertainment, of course. Guests at parties of the Rhode Island super-rich sometimes got to dig with little scoops of solid gold or silver for diamonds and rubies and emeralds salted thickly in long, deep troughs of white sand. They took home what they found. Thomas N. McCarter had little use for that kind of excess; when he wanted to show great disdain for the then-popular sport of the very rich—polo—he called its participants "polo-playing dudes." And his son, Thomas Jr., did not endear himself to his father by leaving his father's employ in the 1920s to go into stockbrokering and, via a Long Island home, Syosset society, Thomas McCarter III recalls. "I must admit," said Tom III, "that my father was, as well, a polo-player of note."

Utilities had to have been in the McCarter blood, because Tom III's father left the brokerage business to join the predecessor company of today's Niagara Mohawk Corporation in the insurance department, and subsequently became an operating vice president. It was to prove a path back to a father whose son now merited a place at PS. "At the time," says Tom III, "Niagara Mohawk's predecessor was controlled by the Schoellkopf family from Buffalo. They were the same family that had founded and still controlled most of the utilities in upstate New York. At that point there was also a gentleman in New York City named Floyd Carlyle, chairman of Consolidated Edison Company, who was, of course, known in the utility industry in the State of New York on an equal basis with my grandfather in the State of New Jersey.

"In any event, after my father had been in Watertown and then in Syracuse, and having then risen to vice president and general manager of the main operating company of the old Niagara Mohawk, he wrote a paper giving an analysis, for the benefit of the board of directors, of the way the operating companies were then developing, with a contrasting emphasis on the way *he* thought they ought to develop. Either Mr.

Carlyle or one of the Schoellkopf brothers sent my grandfather a copy of this paper. After he read it, he wrote my
father that he was well pleased that father's bosses were
beginning to think so highly of him. He said, moreover, that
he was personally glad to see my father had apparently taken
hold of himself and was beginning to amount to something.
Last of all, he suggested that in the next few months he
would like him to come down to Newark to discuss the
possibility of his taking a position with Public Service. This
my father eventually did."

Tom McCarter III points out that, while his grandfather
may not have had an aura of inflexibility, he *did* have
adaptability. Tom notes, for example, that when the rising
fireball was in the New Jersey Senate he "was considered
somewhat of a reformer himself, in the early days, specifically in the work where he was instrumental in the passage of
the Meeker Election Law, and also in his work with the
Passaic Valley Sewerage Commission." Tom McCarter, Sr., *a
reformer?* So it seems. "I mention this," Tom III goes on,
"because at a later date, namely between 1910 and 1920,
there came a time when as president of Public Service he
fought the reform group. He was a particular foe of Mr.
George Record, who at that time was a noted liberal
reformer."

The kind of nimble footwork that building a utility called
for, and which Old Tom McCarter was clearly adept at,
spanned decades, as Tom III deftly brings into focus. The
overturning of the Seven Brothers and Seven Sisters Acts,
which Woodrow Wilson had put through and which were
"adverse to corporate conglomerations," for example, was
due "principally to the efforts of Robert H. and Thomas N.
McCarter." Not that Tom Sr. was concerned merely with
insuring a minimum of restraint on the operations· of the
utility industry. He seems to have been just as determined
that at least that portion of it which *he* operated should have
about it a hallmark of integrity. Certainly the way he brought
Public Service through the unsavory backwash from the
Insull debacle of 1930 bears that out—especially since the
clinching testimony to that effect came from one who,

underneath all the cigarette-holdered smiles and deep Dutch
chuckles, probably had as little use for McCarter as McCarter
had for him.

"The Samuel Insull utility empire," says Tom McCarter
III, "was the largest public utility combine in the United
States in private hands, and was controlled by the Middle
West Utilities Company of Chicago. In the aftermath of
its collapse, the Public Utility Holding Company Act went
into effect in 1934 or 1935. Coincidentally, my grandfather
was president of the Edison Electric Institute in the years
1933 and 1934, and was therefore the industry representa-
tive at the time the legislation was enacted. The industry at
the time obviously had a black eye because of the Insull
collapse and that of the underlying companies, which I
believe represented some 2.5 billion dollars in assets. Many
stockholders throughout the midwest lost their savings
because everything they had was tied up in stock with these
companies, so that for the second time in this century—the
first having been what led up to the Seven Brothers and
Seven Sisters Acts—the public utility industry was in
exceedingly bad odor. Actually, in the 1890s and even in 1903
when Public Service was founded, as you will recall, the
industry had something less than a good name, but then it
was simply that the underlying companies which went to
make up Public Service were in such poor financial condition
that their physical condition led to loss of life and a turning-
point. Admittedly, you had a much larger analogy of this in
the Insull affair, one that the Public Utility Holding
Company Act was designed to prevent from happening
again.

"The thing that I find impressive is that when that Act
became law, Franklin D. Roosevelt made the comment—and
this is documented in briefs filed in 1940 and 1942 before the
Securities and Exchange Commission—that an exception to
the so-called 'watered stock' companies was the Public
Service Corporation of New Jersey, which FDR pointed out
was an integrated system in the State of New Jersey. He
remarked that this company's assets were real, and therefore
it should be excluded under the provisions of the Public

Utility Holding Company Act." Tom III adds, almost as an afterthought, "FDR apparently thought the company was entirely in New Jersey, when in fact there were outside connections such as transport, and at a later date there was an electrical pool connection with various other States which is now common procedure in all utility systems."

The accolade from Roosevelt must have warmed Old Tom's heart considerably, not least because the company could cite it in the briefs to which Tom III refers. Public Service was at the time defending itself after having been accused of being a subsidiary of the United Gas Improvement Company of Philadelphia and the United Corporation of New York. McCarter was able to note that the President of the United States himself had declared that Public Service did not come under the Act which the government was trying to apply.

People who were in fairly close touch with the workings of the founder's mind say that when he retired on his 78th birthday and finally severed all executive connections with Public Service, this time for real, he was a man very much discouraged with the public utility business. They say that the reason for his discouragement, perhaps doubly burdensome because of his years, was the amount of State and Federal regulation that had developed, starting with the enactment of the 1935 Public Utility Holding Company Act. He felt that the various forms of government regulation would inhibit the growth of the industry. These same sources, who because of the highly personal nature of their observations wish to remain anonymous, found that during the last six years he headed Public Service as board chairman he was much concerned with "and possibly embittered" by the problems of increasing regulation. His naturally bellicose temperament then, failed to soften with age, as targets of that temperament can testify.

Mention of regulation reminded Tom III of some of the delicate nuances its presence can entail. "I believe it was in the Thirties," Tom III said, "that there was some talk of merging the United Gas Improvement Corporation and Public Service of New Jersey. Thomas N. McCarter was offered the presidency and chief executive officership of the surviving corporation. He turned it down, and he was able to persuade the directors of UGI, who represented approximately a 20 per cent stockholding in Public Service, that this would be extremely dangerous for the following reason: The Public Utility Holding Company Act had already gone through. My grandfather reasoned that, if the two companies were to merge, the survivor could no longer be excluded, as Public Service alone had been, because they would then be operating in New Jersey *and* Pennsylvania."

Had the amalgamation gone through, it would have been the largest public utility operating company in the U.S. Public Service alone had by then grown to be the seventh largest utility in combined gas and electric sales, and is today third in the nation.

If the merger had taken place, moreover, there might have been fallout of a kind having nothing to do with size. Although Tom Sr. would have been the surviving chairman of the board and chief executive officer, it is unlikely that he would have been able to maintain the iron-grasp control of the total resulting organization that he had with Public Service. First of all, it would no longer be a New Jersey company. Then too, the Philadelphia men were an outstanding group of corporate executives. Odds are it would have been a team operation, and McCarter's history shows he was a deep-dyed individualist and not much of a team man. It is, of course, pure conjecture, but possibly he felt this in his bones and let it ever so slightly reinforce his main and persuasive argument about the Public Utility Holding Company Act.

PS, then, would carry the McCarter brand. Tom III says, "I was once told by a man in Boston, whose father had been a founder of the Boston Edison Company, that what Thomas N. McCarter had done in New Jersey could not have been done in any other State because of the fact that in New Jersey there were so many diversified factions that none of them was strong enough to control the whole picture. This is illustrated by the fact that, initially, it was a question of a New Jersey interest, a Philadelphia interest and a New York

interest in this area, whereas in other parts of the country
there were very strong individuals who could just step in and
take over.

"In this instance, until 1903, there was no strong
individual. At a different level, of course, there were strong
individuals who had their own interests, but they could not
get along together. What my grandfather was able to do, the
thing which is at the root of his achievement, was to combine
them effectively into a single cooperating unit which he
christened Public Service. When I was at Princeton, there
was a freshman course in politics that attempted to compare
the concentration of economic and political power in two
different States. As it happened, the States were Ohio and
New Jersey. I mention this as casting another light on what
my grandfather did because it pointed out that while in Ohio
one family apparently controlled everything in the utility
field, in New Jersey it was one *man*—but he did not
personally own all of it, as was the case in Ohio. Although my
grandfather, rivaled distantly by one other man in Philadelphia, was for a time the largest individual stockholder in
Public Service, he never *owned* Public Service, much less
whole utility chains. His control was for that reason all the
more remarkable."

Control. It rolls on the tongue like warm cognac, and is a
word to conjure with, a word bound up—in its etymology
and overtones—more intimately with accounting than with
the profession of law. But for almost all the years between
the moment when the young man dreamed ahead at
Princeton, to the golden hour when his mature image in oil
looked down the the paneled board room in Newark, control
was, for all practical purposes and in every waking moment,
the embodiment of an approach to human as well as
corporate relationships that became Old Tom McCarter's
watchword.

Control. No doubt the money-making instinct he inherited
from his Scotch-Irish ancestors made it essential to his peace
of mind that he *have* an eye at all times on the till—a view he
frankly enjoyed. Unarguably, in order to build Public
Service, control in the hands of a man like this, at that time

and for years after, was indispensable. Control of those dimensions, however, once savored is hard to relinquish. From Tom McCarter's inability to do that there arose in his later years a growing failure to see himself through that all too rare equipment—the eyes of others—which led to curmudgeonly bitterness and disappointment.

Except perhaps when the tension he created at Public Service relaxed a bit, the electric and gas and transport people who on the job felt the grinding power of McCarter control, must have thought that they alone knew its full meaning. Some of the tension disappeared, at least on the surface, during the annual New Year's Day reception at which he distributed flowers to the ladies and candy or cigars to the gentlemen who were his employees. It is more likely, however, that nowhere was the complexity of the stubborn character underlying Thomas Nesbitt McCarter's need and capacity to dominate more interestingly exposed to view than in that universal forum, the privacy of his family's bosom. With no apparent awareness of how cold and remote a figure it must have made him seem, he signed letters to his children, "Your affectionate father," and then, incredibly, as if to insure their knowing who that might be, the full signature, "Thomas N. McCarter."

Writing letters—in overly dignified or hectoring tones, depending on the recipient and nature of the case—is almost as overpowering a compulsion among lawyers as talking well and endlessly, and Tom McCarter, Sr. was no exception. When he extended his paternalistic outlook to Public Service, which he did early on, one way it manifested itself was in a Niagara of letters. Over the years he wrote many thousands of them. The legend around 80 Park Place is that anyone who wrote in to complain about his bill or about any other aspect of service was sure to hear personally from Tom McCarter.

An audience, straw-hatted, almost, to the man, waits for Thomas N. McCarter to tug on a line that will begin ground-breaking operations for the Public Service headquarters—the Terminal Building in Newark—on June 24, 1914.

The Squire at Home and at Work

"He was really a wonderful talker and full of wit when he talked off the cuff, but whenever he wrote anything out he became dull."
—Ellen McCarter Doubleday

The way the squire of Rumsonhill and his brothers Bob and Uzal chose to discuss their personal affairs—at least, said Ellen Doubleday, as far as "each other's houses, and characters, and families" were concerned—went far beyond anything the Joneses or the Smiths of any era were likely to have thought up. For one thing, a consideration that both astonished and delighted the Joneses and Smiths who were privileged to listen in, the brothers' discussions focused exclusively on the three men's own families. Morning after morning on the 7:37 out of Red Bank, they joined their perhaps unconscious histrionic talents to hang out the McCarter wash in a scene that some perceptive exploiter of nostalgia is bound to work into a musical.

Following a Rumsonhill breakfast that a Percheron in his prime might have made do with, McCarter would roll down the sycamore-lined drive on his way to the station, for however brief a stretch at peace with himself and the world. The interlude seldom lasted beyond the station. The breakfast itself had been of a kind to warrant a pause, as the author of Old Tom's favorite novel liked to bedevil his readers by suggesting, for us to take a quick look at it.

"Would you like to hear what breakfast was like at Rumsonhill?" said Ellen Doubleday. "For us children it was some fruit—not fruit juice in those days. And then cereal and milk.

"But for *him* there was a piece of cold apple pie or cold mince pie, a steak and creamed potatoes, or liver and bacon and eggs. And he ate it *all*, including tea (he never drank coffee) and hot rolls and butter, but no marmalade or jam. We had a three-course lunch every day also, whether he was home or not, and a three-course dinner of really heavy food that rose to five courses if there was company—lots of meat and potatoes, but not so many green vegetables in those days even though the farm on the property grew everything you could think of."

Thus happily stoked of a morning and ready for another big day at Public Service, Thomas N. McCarter would, with the conductor's hand respectfully on his elbow, hoist himself up the steps of the 7:37. His sons usually didn't ride to the station with him and that made him angry.

Tom Sr. made no bones about wanting to steer his sons into the same line of work he was in, and he had put both boys on the payroll at a starting salary of five dollars a week—not such a slave-wage as it may seem for those days. Far more painful for the young men, according to their elder sister, was the fact that this meant they had to go up with their father every morning on the 7:37, because they were supposed to be on the job by nine.

For Old Tom this meant that his sons would also travel to the station with him in the one car—a reasonable economy, if not a reasonable expectation, and certainly in keeping with McCarter's pre-energy crisis habit of going around Rumsonhill turning out the lights if he found no one using a room. That kind of economy around the homestead had such a negative effect on the family, according to Ellen Doubleday, that "for the rest of our lives, after we married and left home, Tom and I said the hell with it and left the lights on all over the place wherever we lived. Except when they ask for a blackout, I still do."

To son Uzal, unfortunately, Old Tom's prophetic determination to conserve on irreplaceable resources by using only one of the five or six cars he maintained meant nothing. Disrupting the rigid Rumsonhill ritual—you couldn't go in for breakfast until the clock struck the hour because Tom Sr. kept the doors locked—Uzal would come ripping down the stairs just after the entourage had left for Red Bank, grab a fierce couple of bites, hurl himself into one of the other cars and screech into the depot just as his father was boarding. His brother Tom, knowing what was coming in the car his father would occupy, had prudently gotten on further down the train.

Uzal headed for another car too, his stomach full of mixed emotions knowing his father was at least aware he'd made it. His father, he also knew, was aware that now the chauffeur would have to go back and get another chauffeur, then drive him to Red Bank to return the car Uzal had used. Uzal never missed the train, said Ellen, but neither was he ever on time to ride with his father. He couldn't win either way, actually, since he had to balance the strain of riding with the paterfamilias against the searing experience of starting each day knowing his father was up ahead thinking about the wasted gasoline, and indeed talking out loud about it, and would for that reason alone be in a foul temper with anyone unlucky enough to cross him that day.

The talking out loud would not begin until a fascinating process that never varied had run its course. The three McCarter brothers, occupying three separate seats one immediately in front of the other so that each could have his own window, sat there in solitary splendor ("Nobody ever wanted to sit with them, Ellen recalled) reading their morning paper—"always *The Herald*," said Ellen, "never *The Wall Street Journal*."

At precisely the same instant, as if on a signal that Ellen claimed no one was ever able to figure out, the three men would complete their scan of the news, snap the papers shut with a flourish, fold them, tuck them under their arms, and begin a loud conversation about their families that often lasted all the way to Newark. The other odd thing about the event was they never turned their heads to look at one another, but just kept looking out the window while they talked.

"Everybody fought to get in that car," said Ellen with a woman's appreciation of what the opportunity must have meant to the neighbors. "And the voices of my father and my uncles were just *stentorian*, mind you. You could hear 'em from one end of the car to the other. They discussed their children inside out. The boys were always in trouble. There was nothing those three men left to the imagination. If there was a speck of dust or a lampshade not aligned properly in their homes, there was hell to pay for the wives and on top of that everybody heard about it on the 7:37. All our friends would make it a point to tell us what they'd heard about that morning.

"There were such scenes if there was a bit of dust that my cousin Isobel, Uncle Uzal's daughter, said that when she got married she was going to say, 'Dust, I welcome you!' All three men had terrible tempers, and they let you know flat out if they didn't like something. Which was pretty often. I myself used to say I got married so I could have breakfast in bed, after all that waiting around until Papa came down and the servants opened the doors as the clock struck."

When Ellen did get married, first to Atwood Violett and later to the publisher Nelson Doubleday, her father waited on each occasion until the home ceremony was over and then, as she went out the door of Rumsonhill with her groom, handed her as a wedding present $500 in cash, remarking as he did so that he thought it would be "enough to get home with if I didn't like it."

McCarter's daughters seemed pretty much to agree that, although they loved their father, he tended to give his children a hard time—possibly in part because, as Ellen saw it in retrospect, "I think they gave him a hard time in Newark. I don't know what the feuds were all about, but there were some pretty big ones."

She guessed that after a day of non-cooperation which began with Uzal's exasperating last-minute dash for the train, her father may have thought that "it would be great to have at least his children, grown up though we were, sitting around and saying, 'yes, papa'—but we didn't. We gave up arguing and did as we pleased."

Ellen attributed this to the fact that "we all inherited some of him in us." Old Tom wouldn't argue. He'd just brush aside anything he didn't like or agree with. He even made his own rules at bridge, a game at which Ellen said he was "fair." It was before the new rules, but he would have paid no attention to them anyway, she claimed. "He was a law unto himself. But he was a good card player and, among his cronies, a player for high stakes. He was a good poker player too," she added, "and I think that that showed in the way he ran his business."

He and Ellen, as the eldest child, were often at loggerheads. When she began to take an interest in politics, he called her a "champagne socialist trying to operate on a beer income." As her liberal interests increased he stepped up his penchant for sticking labels on things by calling her a "parlor pink." When she told him she was going to vote for Franklin Roosevelt, he went into a long harangue about her disloyalty to "one whose privilege it has been to stick to you through thick and thin." Even when hectoring his children McCarter couldn't resist the rounded oratorical flourish.

"Of course this was pure tear-jerking," Ellen said later, "but it didn't entirely stop me. I called him up just before the 1936 election and told him I wouldn't vote at all unless I heard differently from him about my decision, because I just couldn't bring myself to vote for Landon. I didn't hear from him, so I didn't vote. He had no qualms at all about appealing to sentiment."

McCarter's idea of the right way to behave was to go into business and make a success, said Ellen, but since her first husband "couldn't have cared less as long as we had enough to eat, I wanted to go into business, because we were a little strapped. It didn't occur to me my father would object. It was just a little dress shop in Red Bank that I wanted to go in on with a friend, but he wrote me a letter saying he'd have to leave the community he had lived in all his life because he

couldn't stand to have a daughter working. So I asked him
why he'd spent all that money on my education and given me
all these so-called semi-intellectual tastes if I had to spend all
my time with the carpet sweeper and washing clothes and
bringing up children. I suppose it was bribery, but he gave
me more money."

Women's Lib, Ellen felt, would have driven her father up
the wall. "However, if he was convinced that a woman
engineer or planner was capable," she hastened to qualify
her statement, "he had the kind of mind that would not go
against her. If he'd been ill and had to go to a woman doctor,
though, I don't think he'd have had any trust in her. He was a
product of his time, but he was able to see change and
sometimes accept it. Not that he'd ever admit he *liked* what he
saw, even after he'd accepted it."

Once Ellen wrote him a letter asking for some further help
in improving her life style. She said he wrote her back: "My
dear Ellen: Your letter is extremely well expressed and
makes me realize that I was wise in spending all that money
on your education, but I do not agree with one word you
said. Your affectionate father, Thomas N. McCarter." That
ended that, she recalled.

In a way, McCarter had made his own bed and the
children were almost inevitably going to see to it that he slept
there. As they came of age he gave them club memberships.
McCarter, although he had sold the Rumson Country Club
the land it stands on to this day and was a lifelong charter
member, remained at best a hard-breathing duffer on the
links. Each of the four McCarter children had enjoyed the
same allowances growing up as did the Rockefeller children—25 cents a week—but on birthdays there was a cake
with a five-dollar gold piece buried in the slice that was
carefully flagged for the child celebrating. When the eldest,
Ellen, made her New York debut at age 18, however, her
allowance—despite Old Tom's displeasure that she couldn't
have "come out" in New Jersey—went to $125 a month. In
1916-1917 she pointed out, that was quite a nice sum.

"I thought it was just for my clothing though," she said,
"and I was wrong. I quickly found out that he'd *given* us the

Thomas N. McCarter officiates as president of the Rumson Country Club during a weekend visit by New York's Governor Alfred E. Smith. At left is New Jersey's Governor George S. Silzer. They're watching a U.S. Army polo team competing against a Rumson team. McCarter later supported Smith in his bid for the presidency.

club memberships, but out of our allowance we had to pay our caddie fees. Father wanted us to learn golf, to use the country club and the beach club, but when you signed those chits and he got them the following month, he took them off your allowance. I gave up playing golf at that point, but that upset him, so he paid my caddie fees for me."

McCarter was the kind of parent who could discipline a grown daughter who refused to break a foursome golf date to join him on his boat by telling her she had to go to bed without supper for being "impudent." When he repented a bit and sent a maid up later with something to eat, Ellen locked her door and said she didn't care for anything. "I," she recalled, her eyes flashing with the old McCarter fire, "could be as stubborn as he was."

The boats played a big part in the lives of those at Rumsonhill, even though only Tom Sr. apparently relished using them. At one point, Ellen remembered, in order to impress Nelson Doubleday— "whom my father admired because he'd accomplished something"—her father and her uncle Bob came to visit her and her second husband by water. The two sailed majestically into Glen Cove one right behind the other, *each on his own yacht.*

"He loved the water," said Ellen. "In his youth he had a
sailboat, but later on he bought power boats. And he gave
them the most peculiar names. He called one the *Relax,* but
of course everybody else called it the Ex-Lax. I think it was
an Elco. Then he had one he named the *Virago.* I don't know
why. He liked the ladies a lot, but when he was in a bad mood
he'd say he had named it after my mother. That wasn't true,
though. He worshipped her, and she was exactly right for
him.

"My father never swam much, but he liked to come over
and watch us. In addition, I regret to say, he liked to have us
go with him on his boats. Just before the war he had a big,
lovely boat that we were kind of glad he had to sell because
Sunday afternoons he'd make us go out with him. We'd go
out around Scotland and Ambrose Lightships, depending on
his mood, and if we were going to the one further out I'd get
out of going because I got seasick. Father always took the
Sunday papers along, and after he had carefully finished
them he would tie them and throw them to the men on the
lightships. He loved doing that."

McCarter's children learned early to outwit their father's
draconian rules about such family basics as what time to be
home from a party. For the Rumson young set in the jazz
age, parties all over North Jersey were big-time affairs, and
when Ellen, Tom and Uzal knew the curfew was midnight or
one in the morning for a bash that wouldn't really come off
the pad until three, they simply went into cahoots with the
servants to let them in, and sneaked up the back stairs. After
such a night it must have been a problem to be on deck fit as
a fiddle for breakfast at Rumsonhill, as was mandatory, but
Ellen says they handled it without father's being any the
wiser. Madeleine, who was younger, got to none of these
affairs.

Ellen used to talk Public Service garage employees in
Newark into letting her park her car there, again without
McCarter's being aware. It would have been too bad if he'd
found out, she says, because he was so strict about even the
most minute detail of company policy. Even after she was
married he'd send her to Public Service to buy her

appliances, for example, but he would never let her get them at a discount because she was an employee's child. That was one paternal restriction she had no luck whatever in talking her way around.

She says that although electricity was his business, her father knew no more about it or where it came from than the old lady who thought her bill was high because the stuff leaked out of her wall sockets if she didn't keep plugs in them. As a businessman McCarter knew enough about where the electricity *went*, though, to encourage people to use more of it by giving them free electric light bulbs in the early days of Public Service. The company abandoned the practice when subscribers went into the millions, but one present-day employee maintains the family began buying its own light bulbs much earlier when it found that Old Tom's free bulbs were steadily going up in wattage.

His concern over waste of the product at Rumsonhill had a runner-up, however, in water. "It was a brick house," Ellen conceded, "but those hollow-tile stretches in the walls were something else. I had the room above Papa's, so that my bathroom was over his bathroom. I would let the water run to brush my teeth, and one morning at breakfast he said, 'Ellen, when you brush your teeth you let the water run.'

"'Yes, Papa,' I said.

"'Well, Ellen,' he said, 'that's very wasteful.'"

As any father will understand, Ellen said she "happily went on letting the water run ever since."

Anything that cost money irked Tom, but his children admitted he ordered a swimming pool at Rumsonhill because he saw one on the Doubleday estate at Glen Cove. He did the same in ordering the planting of flower gardens, they claim. He knew chrysanthemums because of his devotion to Princeton-Yale football games, but they say that otherwise he wouldn't have known a daisy from a dump-truck and wanted lots of flowers just because Doubleday had them. He wouldn't ask what it cost. He'd just say, "Have it done." Actually, Mrs. McCarter had extensive greenhouses on the estate and displayed her flowers at Madison Square Garden's annual show in New York.

Yet telephone bills would drive him frantic. "We were not allowed to call New York," Ellen said. The man some suspect of having moved to Rumson from Newark because irate patrons of Public Service Transport would call him up at all hours to ask where the hell the streetcar was, struggled for years in the trap he had set for himself by installing a telephone that his wife and children talked on by the hour, as wives and children will, with their friends—most of whom, naturally, for quite a while continued to live in and around Newark, which from Rumson is a toll call.

"I remember a discussion between my father and Uncle Uzal," said Ellen. "As usual, my father was complaining about his phone bill. I heard him say, 'Uzal, what are your telephone bills like?' And my uncle said, 'When Jennie calls they are high, astronomical in fact, but I don't care, Tom. She didn't want to come down here to live, and if it gives her some fun to call up her pals in Newark or New York or wherever, let her have it. It doesn't really matter.' That made Papa pipe down for a while. We didn't hear so much about phone bills, at least, although he never did give up on the electric lights."

Ellen McCarter Doubleday may never have quite recovered from discovering that when they lived in Newark, her father would take her as a baby in her carriage to Lincoln Park, on weekends when the maid was off, stash her behind some bushes, and forget her while he read the Sunday papers, a chore to which he gave himself over with total concentration. Whether she howled or napped she was still not sure, but she survived to look back with great warmth and affection, and a touch of filial amusement, on the foibles of an over-achiever whose reputation as "The Roaring Redhead" tended to obscure his all-too-human performance as a husband and father.

One time his unawareness of what was going on around him was hard to believe, but Ellen swore it was true. McCarter was such a loyal, not to say fanatical, Jerseyite—his family having been involved with the life and government of the State since right after the American Revolution—that

Ellen said you could talk in his presence of the Jersey Shore
or the Jersey meadows, or even of Jersey*man* as he liked to
call himself, but "he had a bit of a chip on his shoulder"
about insisting that everyone call the State *New Jersey*.

"He felt so strongly about this that he wouldn't own
anything in New York", Ellen continued. "Of course, we did
have those successive apartments in New York, but they were
always in my mother's name. He loved New Jersey that
much—and besides, at that time in New York there was a
personal property tax which he might have been liable for.
We called the various apartments we had the town dump,
because we all convened there, which he rather enjoyed.
They were nice apartments. Each of us had his or her own
room."

They may have been nice, but there was also something
funny about those apartments, Ellen said. "We always landed
in a place of ill repute—45 Park Avenue, 77 Park Avenue,
277 Park Avenue—but my father never knew it. Or if he did,
he never told us. We found out on our own. And these places
were always glad to get him in, because he was respectable."

As a driver, according to Ellen, her father was a cut or two
below that. "He drove," she said, "but it was a very dangerous
operation. He always drove on the lefthand side of the road
and kept looking around. I took several trips with him and I
tell you it was perilous. I was old enough to drive but the
opportunity just wasn't offered to me. His favorite car was a
specially built Cadillac. It lasted 10 years, and at that point he
gave up driving, which I think was wise. But while he had it
he enjoyed having his Filipino chauffeur sit in the rumble
seat while he himself drove. I don't know what happened to
the chauffeur when it rained, because my father would never
relinquish the wheel. It was a big open two-seater, so I guess
the poor man got wet."

A former mayor of Rumson remembers McCarter roaring
down Ocean Avenue in Sea Bright in that car, but occupying
the rumble seat and with his feet up above the chauffeur's
shoulders, leaning back and enjoying the sunshine and

yelling at the top of his lungs, "Come on, Emil! Come on!
Let's show 'em!"

If even on a weekend that seems faintly uncharacteristic
behavior for one of New Jersey's first citizens and leading
industrialists, in public it may have been. In private it would
have struck those who knew McCarter best as entirely
consistent. One of the refreshing things about the man was
that he never hesitated to be himself or say what was on his
mind.

It is hard to escape the impression that Tom Sr. may have
felt sincerely that he was never in better company than when
he was alone. "For him to be relaxed," his daughter Ellen
said, "he had to be in a group he liked—and he didn't like
many groups." His younger daughter Madeleine, who got to
know her father perhaps better than the three older children
ever did by playing cards with him ("he always cheated") and
taking long walks with him to study the inscriptions in
cemeteries, said toward the end of her life that he especially
liked to shut the doors to the library, spread out company
papers on card tables and work over them for hours, of an
evening when there was no company. "I never knew a
harder-working man," she said. He also liked to practice his
speeches out loud behind those doors, she recalled, "but of
course you could hear him right through them, thick as they
were."

Ellen said her father's sense of propriety tended to get in
the way of his natural instinct to be friendly, so that "he
called every one of my men guests 'Mister.' It scared some of
them so they dropped their coffee. Only if they came around
often enough would he begin to use their first names. I think
now it was deliberate, the 'Mister' thing. It was part of what
made him ask for their ideas about world affairs, and of
course none of them had any ideas at all."

There was always criticism, of a more explicit kind, when
her brother Tom's friends came for the weekend, "which
could be pretty wild affairs," Ellen recalled. "They would do
something wrong, and my father would complain to me
about it. I said to him once, 'Why can't you take them as they
are? After all, you were young once. Now times have

changed, and they like different kinds of things than you do.'
And he said, 'I can't do that. My mother never did that. She
had to speak her mind, and I have to speak my mind. If I
think something's wrong I have to say so.'"

There were times when he didn't even wait for something
to be wrong. Take the subject of bedtime. On evenings when
he closeted himself away to work on Public Service papers or
to practice one of his speeches, he always observed bedtime
punctually. He believed it was important to get in a solid
eight hours of sleep every night, and 10 o'clock saw McCarter
heading for the big bed with the enigmatic pastel portrait
above it of a lady in a long white gown, her soft tresses
tumbling about her shoulders as she sat with the fingers of
one hand entwined in the mane of a contented-looking lion.
Did he see himself as the lion in lifelong happy submission to
his high-born wife Madeleine of the Baltimore Barkers,
whom he described once to her younger daughter as "the
queen of Rumsonhill"? Nobody knows for sure. The portrait
hangs today in the living room of Mary Hemschoot Miles in
Fords, New Jersey. She grew up on the Rumsonhill estate as
one of the children of McCarter's chauffeur and, along with
the portrait, inherited some of the Rumsonhill furniture and
McCarter's own sterling silver-backed hand mirror, comb
and shoe-horn. Despite its owner's enormous girth, the shoe-
horn is only 10 inches long.

For McCarter, the matter of bedtime overrode all other
considerations sacred or profane—or social. Even when
there was company, no matter who the guests at Rumsonhill
might be or how many, when 10 o'clock came McCarter
would pull out his watch, snap it open, look surprised and
exclaim in a loud voice, "Why it's 10 o'clock! Time for bed.
Good night, all"—and, without further ceremony, up to bed
he would go. How he knew it was 10 o'clock *before* he pulled
his watch out, nobody ever discovered. The family still thinks
that after a certain point he just got bored and *hoped* it was 10
o'clock, and from long experience could approximate it
closely enough so that five or 10 minutes either way made no
difference. As regards the company at Rumsonhill, his
daughters suspected that while McCarter enjoyed mingling

Madeleine McCarter and her father.

with his fellow businessmen, it was true only up to a point "because he was unquestionably the intellectual superior of almost everyone he associated with."

For a person with a mind that well-endowed and agile—at least in McCarter's case—boredom was always just pulling up under the porte-cochere to menace him with a visit. Take sermons, for instance. Except when he himself was delivering one to his errant offspring, or to the Edison Electric Institute which he was proud to have headed, or one of the State commissions which a succession of governors gave him charge of, McCarter hated sermons. They bored him glassy-eyed. When, therefore, the family did manage to get him into a church—once a year, at Easter—he would share his displeasure with one and all by sitting up front and loudly jingling a pocketful of coins throughout the sermon. This embarrassed his wife, who knew better than to try anything then and there (she had her own way of evening things up), and amused the children no end. What the minister thought is not on record.

What is on record is an experience which may help to explain such anti-homiletic behavior. McCarter liked to brag to his daughter Madeleine that when he was growing up, in spite of having had "a very stern mother who used to scare us to death," he had been "outrageously attractive, an absolute wild man." This attractiveness seems to have made his four years at Princeton especially memorable because, he told her, in spite of having been brought up in a strict Presbyterian atmosphere he was "quite popular." He balanced the popularity he said, and felt he even enhanced it, by joining other attractive young people in going to the Presbyterian church at Princeton to hear Jonathan Edwards preach.

The good times attendant on being popular that McCarter was having began to overbalance the piety, however, and reached such proportions as to draw the attention of the university's president, Dr. McCosh. "I got this notice at my rooms," Tom told his daughter, who was all ears at the confessional tone in her father's voice, "advising me that Dr. McCosh would expect me to wait upon him at 10 o'clock the next morning. I tell you frankly I was scared. I was ushered into his study and left there, and then Dr. McCosh appeared. He said, 'Well, Mr. McCarter'—McCosh was a Scot and spoke with a very heavy burr, so that it came out 'Mis-terrrr McCarrr-terrr—'you got my note. I'm very glad to see you, Mr. McCarr-terrr. And how is your father? And how is the lady, your mother? McCarr-terrr; let us pray.'

"He got down on his knees right there in the study," Madeleine said her father told her, "and papa, absolutely terrified, got down on his knees too. There wasn't any prayer for his soul or for the McCarters or for Princeton or anything like that, but just a nice prayer to God. Then they stood up, and Dr. McCosh stuck out his hand and said, 'Mr. McCarr-terrrr.' And that was it. I thought it was the smartest reprimand I'd ever heard of. McCosh knew my father was raising hell, and that he had to be reprimanded, but he never said a word to him. He just said a short Presbyterian prayer to God."

The reprimand subtle was not then or later lost on Tom Sr., but while it may be one thing to be gently taken to task by the president of Princeton with an oblique assist from the Almighty, it must have been something else again to be given one's comeuppance, however gently, by a wife, however beloved.

Mrs. McCarter had her own way of handling the redheaded fireball she'd married, a way that had nothing to do with her passion for gambling. That passion was such that she was for years well-known as one of the more astute handicappers at Pimlico, and her husband indulged her in it without complaint. Being married to such an overbearing personality inevitably demanded of her an occasional adjustment of the great man's sense of proportion, though, and one particulary delicious zinger that Madeleine McCarter got away with time and again on him would have done wonders for the morale of Vinnie, the cheerful-doormat wife and mother in the Clarence Day drama, *Life with Father*, if she'd been able to bring it to bear in the genteel guerilla warfare she waged with her macho mate.

McCarter, like most people, wasn't always infallible when it came to remembering names, particularly if he met someone he knew unexpectedly, or whom he hadn't seen for a stretch. Like most people, he hated to admit it. So when he and his wife were at a social affair or attending a Princeton-Yale football game and he ran into a classmate or business acquaintance whose name escaped him, he would mumble something deliberately incoherent and then say loudly to the unrecognized individual, as a cover-up, "And this is my wife Madeleine!"

As a queenly woman conscious of her aristocratic Baltimore antecedents, it was a tradition with Madeleine Barker McCarter, all her life, to turn social amenities into full-scale productions. On such occasions, therefore, she would turn to her husband with an innocent stare and, in tones that were cultured but every bit as audible as his, ask him pleasantly, "And what did you say the name was, Tom?" It was her moment of revenge for the coin jingling during sermons, and she made the most of it.

Thomas and Madeleine Barker McCarter, at the Florida home of McCarter whimsically called "Uncle Tom's Cabin."

Apart from routinely undoing him like that, though, she was devoted to Tom McCarter in a way that today's feminist movement keeps assuring itself went out with highbutton shoes and bombazine. He was, in her eyes if seldom in anyone else's, a man who could not only do no wrong but was sometimes too right for ordinary mortals to comprehend.

Once when the chauffeur was sweeping along the parkways of Long Island at a speed presumably greater than was necessary to get her to a dinner at the Nelson Doubledays on time, for instance, a patrolman flagged them down. Before he could go into his lecture, Mrs. McCarter had leaned forward imperiously to command his attention.

Ellen's daughter Madeleine, who was accompanying her grandmother, told her mother later that Grandma said without preamble to the astonished cop, "Officer, what's the trouble? You say we were going too fast? What's the speed limit?"—and without giving him a chance to answer any of her questions—"Well, we never go over the speed limit. Mr. McCarter doesn't like it and doesn't permit it, you understand."

The dumbstruck cycle cop, who even on Long Island seldom ran into such self-assurance, had of course probably never heard of Mr. McCarter, Ellen figured, but it was too much for him. He just swallowed, saluted and resignedly waved her on to Glen Cove, unticketed.

The McCarters' affinity for the manner royal and things identifiable with it, such as royal entourages, did not always break that neatly for them. One of the more notable debacles, Ellen Doubleday recalled, was when the King and Queen of England were visiting here as the guests of President Roosevelt. Ellen's father was making a speech about some aspect of the utilities industry while they were in this country, and people who heard it didn't realize until he was near the end that in dragging into it at length his plans to invite the royal couple to Rumsonhill and entertain them there, he was only kidding. "He was really a wonderful talker and full of wit when he talked off the cuff," said Ellen, "but whenever he wrote anything out he became dull."

His sense of humor about inviting the King and Queen in for high tea may have been on the heavy side, but as it turned out he wasn't entirely kidding about welcoming them to Rumsonhill. "They had spent the night in a private car on a siding in Red Bank," Ellen said, "and since my father had found out they would be coming past our place quite early in the morning on their way to Sandy Hook, as I recall, my father had had this great big bleacher built in our gateway on Rumson Road. We were up to greet them, and there were quite a number of us out there ready to wave and cheer, but the royal party went by at 75 miles a hour, with the Queen holding onto her hat and nobody bothering to notice us, much less wave. He didn't let on, but I think my father felt it was kind of a fiasco. We didn't dare kid him about it."

That was understandable, since according to all reports Tom Sr. was not a man who dearly loved a rib. Ellen liked to recount with a special poignancy what she considered one of the best ribs anyone ever had the courage to try on him. His own family, by then long since inured to his fulminations, was the perpetrator.

After spending their childhood in luxury counter-balanced by a disciplinary code so rigid it begged for—and got—several kinds of mostly clandestine defiance, the by then grown-up McCarter children joined their mother one evening to hold their collective breath, pile the old man into one of the half-dozen cars he maintained, and conspiratorially bundle him off to Manahattan.

McCarter wasn't the kind of man that even a well-meaning family could manhandle like that with impunity, and all the way up from Rumson he kept demanding to know where the hell they were taking him. He found out soon enough

"We took him to see *Life with Father,*" Ellen said, "and while we were a little nervous about it, we hoped his sense of humor might overcome him and he would see himself as others saw him—especially his nearest and dearest. It didn't quite work out that way. He stomped out in the middle of it."

They were probably lucky he stomped out instead of storming the stage. He wasn't one to swallow his anger, and when he was ticked off he let you know. "What did you take me to see *that* for?" he kept snorting all the way home. Nobody had the heart to ask in return why he'd puffed up the aisle for the exit halfway through one of the funniest and longest-running plays in the history of the American theater.

Two more little stories all but complete the infinitely varied picture of this complex, paradoxical human being. No, *two-and-a-half* little stories.

The first has to do with an actual picture—the one hanging in the board room at 80 Park Place. Ellen thought it was a fine likeness, but her father hated it, she said. "The poor artist had the most terrible time getting my father to hold still for it," she said. Nor was it just a question of getting him to hold still. "He—the artist—would come to our apartment just after we'd finished breakfast, around 8:30 I suppose, and my father would sit at once for exactly one hour, not a second over.

"Well, one morning my father was in a particularly nasty mood. Glowering, he perched on his stepladder. When he felt the hour was up, he snapped open the pocket watch he always wore ready on a chain. The artist thanked him, and he left. When the apartment door slammed, the poor man said to me, as he gathered up his things, 'I'm sorry, I just pretended to paint him. The way he looked today, I could not bring myself to paint his face.' Imagine having to *pretend* to paint for a whole hour! Yet I know my father was flattered that the company wanted to have that portrait of him. Not pleased, mind you: flattered. It took a lot more than flattery to please Thomas N. McCarter."

The second story lights up the loyalty which the human touch this supposedly granitic personality sometimes displayed could generate. "When my daughter's first child was born," Ellen recalled, "she and her husband, a naval officer, were transferred to Miami, and I went down to lend a hand. She was staying in a boarding house run by two wonderful women who were very kind to her. I took down a layette and old-fashioned diapers you had to wash, and I asked if I could use their kitchen to boil the diapers. They came out in the yard to help me hang the diapers to dry, and I said, 'You know, you're awfully nice to do this. Thank you for being so good to my daughter.' And these two women said to me with one voice, '"One for all and all for one," as your father always said to us on New Year's Day.' I practically dropped the load of diapers. Both women had worked for Public Service. They remembered those New Year's receptions at which my father used to shake hands with everyone in the company. When they left they got one of those little medallions or whatever it is you get when you leave, and that was it, but they never forgot that saying of his. I think they believed he meant it. I do too."

And the half-story? One part of it has to do with an occasion on which he exhibited a sense of humor bordering on the droll. In addition to Rumsonhill and the "town dump" apartments in his wife's name in Manhattan, Old Tom maintained a palatial winter residence in Lake Wales, Florida. He got a special kick, at Christmas, out of sending picture postcards of the place to friends up north, each block-lettered in his own bold hand "Uncle Tom's Cabin."

The other part has to do with the kind of moxie that made the man go, a determination to survive that is impossible not to admire. He was in remarkably good health for most of his life except for a chronic arthritis, Ellen said, but because of his immense bulk he had to have his own tailor make his clothes. Stores didn't stock his size. She remembered the last wardrobe he had made—a complete outfit, including tails. He did it in full confidence of getting a lot of wear out of it, the year before he died at age 88.

	Very Well %	Fairly Well %	Not Well at All %	Not Sure %
Sound reliable company	54	40	2	4
Treats their customers fairly	45	45	3	7
Has friendly courteous employees	45	44	3	8
Efficient	43	44	4	9
Monopoly	39	25	12	24
Modern progressive	38	52	3	7
Has enlightened management	19	33	6	42
Genuinely concerned with cleaning up the air and water	16	32	13	39
Dynamic	15	34	14	37
Bureaucracy	14	19	18	49
Only interested in making money	11	28	39	22
A real leader in the community	11	23	13	53
Polluter of the environment	7	21	28	44
Slow to serve public needs	6	13	65	16
Too large to be efficient	6	10	63	21
Old fashioned stuffy	2	8	66	24

Transport and Politics

"The fad of the day is to imprint upon the brow of success the scarlet
letter of sin."
Tom McCarter

In 1972 and 1973, Louis Harris and Associates conducted studies for PSE&G to find out what its customers thought of it. The result was flattering in most respects. It was so flattering, some people didn't believe it.

In both surveys, PSE&G's reputation for overall service was high—90 per cent of those surveyed gave it a positive rating. New Jersey residents were asked to express their opinion of PSE&G in a variety of ways. One of the ways was to give each person a card with a list of favorable and unfavorable words or phrases about the company. They were asked whether the words of phrases described the company "very well," "fairly well," or "not well at all" and an interesting pattern of response occurred as listed on the facing page.

"Once again," said the Harris pollsters after the 1973 survey, "a reputation for courteous employees, for efficiency and reliability, for treating customers fairly, dominates the response. Similarly, the most negative statements are rejected: very few people find the company old-fashioned and stuffy, or slow to serve public needs, or too large to be efficient."

As utility bills rose along with consumer ire, that image may have become somewhat tarnished in the mid and late '70s, but not much. An October, 1977, poll conducted by the Gannett News Service in New Jersey strongly endorsed nuclear power and showed very little negative response when people were asked to grade beleaguered utilities on their efficiency. A total of 14 per cent gave utilities an excellent mark, 24 per cent above average, 45 per cent average, 6 per cent below average and 7 per cent poor. Four per cent did not answer. Another indication of the positive light in which New Jerseyans regard utilities was their response to suggestions that state or local governments take over and operate electric and gas companies. The idea of state government taking over was rejected by a 64 per cent to 22 per cent margin. The notion of local government running utilities was opposed by a 69 to 18 per cent margin. The missing percentages represent people who had no answer. Gannett New Service is part of the Gannett Co. Inc., of Rochester, N.Y., which publishes about 75 newspapers throughout the United States, including two in PSE&G's territory in New Jersey—the *Courier-Post* in Camden and the *Courier-News* in Bridgewater.

To most people, it may seem strange to realize that things were otherwise during the company's first 30 years. Early on, the Public Service Corporation was not given very good ratings by its customers. It was, in fact, cordially hated in many parts of New Jersey. The company honestly worked hard at delivering dependable service. Yet, even as its customers rode its trolleys and buses and enjoyed the comforts and convenience of its electricity and gas, they saw the source of many improvements in the quality of their lives, not as a benefactor, but as a kind of octopus with its tentacles fastened tightly about the State, slowly choking the life out of it.

To the narrowed eyes of this unreasoning hatred, Thomas N. McCarter—who, as one letter-writer put it, "always had the faculty of rubbing the public's fur the wrong way"—had become "the king" by process of self-coronation, and was now the grasping, domination-minded Czar of New Jersey.

Longevity of service is a hallmark of Public Service employees. Thomas N. McCarter, second from right, in his role as president of PS in 1936, is about to present diamond-studded pins for 50-year service to PS and its predecessor companies. The men are, from left, Charles Wort, Louis Straub, Henry Burns, Frank Lawrence and Patrick Connors. With McCarter is Matthew R. Boylan, in charge of operations at the time for Coordinated Transport.

"The Public Service Corporation is what we are after," said a group of Ridgefield Park Republicans in 1905, expressing what was already a common attitude toward the utility. "It has become bigger than the Republican Party in New Jersey and is bigger than the entire State." Not bad—in a sense—one might think, for an outfit only two years old. The only explanation that comes to mind for such a vitriolic reaction to so young a corporate entity is that prior to 1903 there had been only a widely scattered infant industry consisting of independent and often ramshackle little firms. Suddenly, there loomed this unified monolith—a rapidly growing giant which, moreover, had the effrontery, the *hubris*, the sheer gall to call itself Public Service, and then rub salt in that wound by actually charging the public for the services it was now rendering with mounting efficiency.

For such offensive visibility, more than a few men and women "went after" Public Service during those years. At a hearing before the Board of Public Utility Commissioners, for instance, one lawyer happily taunted McCarter:

"Now look here," he admonished the utility president, "you're no king. You're not the State of New Jersey. You're just a citizen being cross-examined on transactions concerning the company."

Others found smaller ways to "get back" at the company, such as jumping fares, and worse. A Hudson County judge encountered this problem head-on in 1920. As he sentenced two conductors convicted of robbing the coin box, he noted solemnly that it was *wrong* to steal —"even from the Public Service Corporation."

What reasons other than resentment of bigness and success might there have been for the all but instantaneous rise of so much animosity between Public Service and the people of the State?

At the practical level, the company's much-complained-of trolley service may have turned some people against the utility. "The flat wheel," an opponent of the company once remarked, "is the only thing 'on the square' about the Public Service Corporation." So perhaps did gas and electric rates, as well as corporation profits, both of which the public inevitably deemed too high. Moreover, as McCarter himself later noted, the company was the most visible business presence, with its power lines and its huge railway system, in a period of public antagonism toward corporations "and quasi-public corporations in particular."

Virtually all early critics of Public Service harped on its immenseness and its omnipresence, its being "bigger than the entire State," as if great size alone were reason enough to condemn the company. After 1903, the utility and its imposing logo, a triangle within a circle, were suddenly everywhere, where there had been no such unifiedly pervasive force before. Though no one put the argument so plainly, people seemed to resent Public Service for implanting that dominating presence in their streets, behind their houses, over their heads, in their basements, almost wherever they turned—and this despite the many benefits which that presence brought them. A trolley scene that for us may seem charming in retrospect was, for more than one critic of the company, a scene of streets encumbered "with heavy rails

and unsightly overhead construction, and (with) huge
juggernauts of danger ... "

Public Service unnecessarily aggravated this resentment,
as early as 1904 and as recently as 1972, by erecting poles and
even high tension transmission towers without first seeking
the permission of municipal and other governing bodies
involved. The first such incident occurred in January, 1904,
when the North Bergen Township Committee adopted an
ordinance directing its road supervisor to cut down poles
and wires of the Public Service Corporation "which had been
put up without the authority of the township officials." The
unauthorized construction was intended to improve trolley
service, about which the same committee was then over-
wrought; but the politicians, in their anger at the utility's
high-handed ways, chose to ignore any apparent contradiction. In North Bergen and other communities, Public Service
was eventually able to prevent the dismantling of its
equipment. But such after-the-fact settlements hurt the
company's image with the public. The *Newark News* commented on a typical incident in 1915:

> "Public utility companies profess not to understand the
> 'unreasoning criticism' sometimes leveled at them by the
> public and the newspapers. A recent incident before the road
> committee of the Board of Freeholders ought to be
> enlightening, at least to the Public Service Railway Company.
> That corporation was sharply censured for what the commit-
> tee regarded as its contemptuous treatment of the county
> board. Not only does the corporation refuse to remove its
> tracks from the sides to the middle of Springfield Avenue, as
> ordered by the road committee, but it proceeds to tear up
> paving and put in switches without waiting for the commit-
> tee's permission or consent. This is a way that public utility
> corporations have, and to such high-handed methods is due
> no small measure of their unpopularity."

But it was not just the corporation's size and the ubiquity
of its equipment—whether authorized or unauthorized—
that turned people against Public Service in the early
decades. The most frequently repeated charge against the
utility then—and one that seems to have gone far with

Labels within image:
FIDELITY TRUST Co.

TROLLEY
PUBLIC SERVICE CORPORATION
CAR

MORRIS COUNTY

STATE
OF
ESSEX

UNION COUNTY

NEWARK

CALDWELL

HUDSON COUNTY

PASSAIC CO.

"THE STATE OF ESSEX."

An editorial cartoon that appeared in the Newark Truth *on June 6, 1903.*

audiences—was that the Public Service Corporation, by means that reputedly bordered on the corrupt, had gained an iron-fisted control over the State and its lawmakers. Politicians, self-seeking and otherwise, regularly denounced the utility for maintaining a "large and influential" (sometimes "large and corrupt") lobby in Trenton. Others called the lobby "a submarine squadron," carefully directed by McCarter himself. And more than one gubernatorial election advertisement promised . . . a clean and honest administration of the State's affairs

FREE
from the sinister
influence of the
PUBLIC SERVICE LOBBY

Over the years, Public Service saw itself and its lobby charged specifically with "hand-picking" some State leaders and politically killing others (including some it had once supposedly hand-picked); with using large sums of money to defeat some candidates and to build up others; with placing money in politically-connected banks, and in banks run by members of the Public Utility Commission; with seeking control of the Public Utility Commission through the Legislature and the Governor's office; with participating in a nationwide pro-utilities propaganda campaign that included editing from textbooks all favorable reference to municipal ownership of utilities; with employing for lobbying purposes the former leaders of both the Democratic and Republican State organizations, as well as some still-active party powers; with owning the State GOP "coat, shoes and breeches," as one Democrat put it, felicitously enough; and, finally, with maintaining such strong control of the State Legislature that it could push through bills it wanted—or had even written itself—and deftly block bills it opposed.

"On the whole it (Public Service) is pretty successful in having legislation either killed or enacted, according to its wishes," *Fortune* magazine reported in 1934. "In the *sui generis* politics of New Jersey, Public Service, to an extraordinary degree, is the State; and the State, to an extraordinary degree, is Public Service . . ."

To such charges and the imputations of government investigators, McCarter replied: "The fad of the day is to imprint upon the brow of success the scarlet letter of sin." Rarely, if ever, in fact, could any accuser prove outright his charge against Public Service.

Occasionally, the lobbying charges had their lighter side. In 1916, the public mind must have boggled as the candidates, practically to a man, smeared one another and, in turn, were smeared as "tools of Public Service," or worse. Of another election, only three years earlier, but entirely different in complexion, the *Newark Evening News* offered this waggish editorial:

> "The Public Service Corporation was once described by President Thomas N. McCarter as being 'the football of politics.' In this campaign it would seem as though this characterization did not apply unless there has been a change in that kind of football rules. Here's one candidate for chairman of the Democratic State Committee making a speech before Congress, telling that the (trolley) company is the most popular institution in New Jersey; another aspirant for the same job is assisting the corporation to secure its desires; legislators who would be returned to Trenton are asking the voters for their votes on the strength of their records in passing trolley bills, and seekers after municipal jobs are boasting that they are all right on the street railway plans. The 'kicker,' who is all by his lonesome trying to continue the old football game, is being avoided by the other party leaders. All of which goes to show that things have changed since the 'limited franchise and equal taxation' (reform movement) days, and that political issues have progressed a whole lot."

Mostly, though, the charges against Public Service were dead serious. Twice in the company's early years, for example, formerly docile legislators rebelled and described in detail their confrontations with McCarter and other powers in the company. At times, embittered local officials also joined in alleging strong-arm tactics by Public Service.

Public Service was hardly the first New Jersey utility to endure such charges, or, if the charges were true, to have maintained potentially compromising relations with politicians and the State government. In the 1903 trolley accident involving the North Jersey Street Railway Company which killed nine schoolchildren, for instance, the New York *Tribune* noted that the prosecutor presenting the negligence case to the grand jury was himself a large stockholder in the defendant company. The *Tribune* later added: "Not only does the North Jersey Street Railway Company control great political and financial interests in Newark, which it uses for its own advantage to the injury of the average citizen, but also, Newark men charge, it has a perceptible influence on legislative affairs."

The men who helped form the Public Service Corporation were also undeniably influential. Among the company's first directors were David Baird, Republican boss of Camden County, and thus of all South Jersey, who was also president of a Camden bank; E.F.C. Young, president of a Jersey City bank and recognized Democratic boss of Hudson County; George R. Gray, associate justice of the State Court of Errors and Appeals, then New Jersey's highest tribunal; Thomas Dolan, president of the United Gas Improvement Company of Philadelphia; John I. Waterbury, president of the Manhattan Trust Company; John F. Dryden, United States Senator from New Jersey and president of the Prudential Insurance Company; Leslie D. Ward, vice-president of Prudential; Thomas N. McCarter, former State Senator and Attorney General; and Uzal McCarter, president of the Fidelity Trust Company in Newark.

Despite this influence, however, it was not long before Public Service found itself facing a growing movement to restrict its powers and regulate its actions.

The first bill to regulate utilities other than railroads came to a vote on the last day of the 40-week legislative session of 1907. In response to public demand, both political parties pledged themselves to some form of regulation; throughout the session they had argued about just which form, particularly whether a regulatory commission should have rate-making powers. Thomas N. McCarter arrived early for the final meeting of that Legislature, bringing with him John

J. Burleigh, a Public Service vice-president and lobbyist, and David Baird. The three men, who opposed regulation and particularly regulation of rates, repaired to the office of the State Treasurer, where, according to the *Newark News* account, "they kept in touch, until an early hour (of the morning) with numerous Senators and Assemblymen, former members who are supposed to know a thing or two, James R. Nugent (Democratic boss of Essex County), who has been accredited with control of the House majority, and everyone supposed to have a voice in the Senate majority except Governor Stokes."

The account said little more about the Public Service presence, except to note that the three men left the State House at 2 a.m., by car, only after the Assembly had "readily and deliberately killed the bill, which had been demanded by both parties in their platforms and (was) evidently so popular before the formal opening of yesterday's session..."

That same day, the *Newark News* editors wrote: "All the forces methods, powers, and influences that could be brought to bear on the Legislature were marshalled at Trenton by the Public Service Corporation and men connected therewith, from the president down to some of the most expert of its lobbyists. They were on hand before the hour fixed for session, and they brazenly stayed at the State House as the guests of State officials to see that their orders were obeyed."

Though the 1907 bill failed, others followed it in the Legislature until a weak regulatory law passed in 1910 and a strong law, the strongest in the country, succeeded it in 1911. Public Service, attempting to protect its interests, fought hard against these bills. In a 1908 speech before a legislative committee, for instance, Frank Bergen, the company's General Counsel, went so far as to declare that one such bill would effect "a mild revival of the French Revolution" with a "Reign of Terror" over industry and commerce—plus a revival of the thumbscrew and rack "in less repulsive form."

The Public Service Corporation seldom replied to the lobbying charges against it. "I have conceived it to be wiser," said McCarter in 1907, "in the performance of my duty as

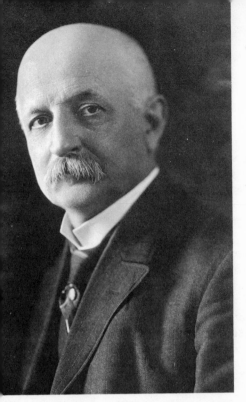

Public Service's general counsel, Frank Bergen, saw initial legislative attempts at gas and electric utility regulations as a "mild revival of the French Revolution," where the "Reign of Terror" had business and industry as its victims.
When Edmund W. Wakelee left state politics for the legal staff of Public Service, one editorialist said, in effect, that he'd still stay in his former field. He proved an effective spokesman for the utility.

president of Public Service, to refrain from speech-making ... The public, rightly or wrongly, has not been in a receptive frame of mind, and anything that I ... have said would have had little, if any, effect."

The familiar charges surfaced again in 1912 and 1913, when State Senator Edmund Wakelee became chairman of the State Republican Committee and then, on resigning political office, a lobbyist for Public Service Corporation. David Baird, Daniel Voorhees, and Franklin Murphy, all of whom had been closely associated with Public Service or McCarter, were prominent among those who selected Wakelee, prompting the *Newark News* to laud the party sardonically for its "freedom from corporate dictation." It told its readers:

"In his long legislative career, Hon. Edmund W. Wakelee, of Bergen, displayed so much zeal on behalf of the people and such determined hostility to corporate aggression that this name became a synonym ... for sturdy independence and hatred of privilege. So dangerous did he appear to corporations that they insisted upon sending him to the Legislature year after year in order that they might keep a close watch upon his actions and checkmate any move that he might make inimical to their interests.

"With the identical purpose of keeping him in the limelight, where he could do them the least harm, these same special interests (McCarter among them), two years ago, selected him as the Republican candidate for Governor, but were thwarted in their philanthropic designs by an ignorant and deluded electorate, which erroneously and stupidly imagined that any candidate favored by the public utility corporations must necessarily be a corporation servant. They failed utterly to see that it was the desire of these corporations to put Mr. Wakelee in the position where he could do them the least harm."

When Wakelee left official politics just 15 months later to join Public Service, the *Newark News* editorialist added:

"The announcement that Edmund W. Wakelee, former Republican State Chairman, will join the legal staff of the Public Service on the first of the year, is not likely to be followed by another announcement that he will retire from active political work ... On the same staff, Mr. Wakelee will find another former State Chairman, but a Democrat, William B. Gourley, who has also gone out of politics officially. But quite naturally these two former chairmen and a number of retired party workers now retained by the utility corporations, are still interested in politics. The science of government has a lot to do with the control of such corporations, and it is good business for them to have in their employ men who are expert in this science..."

Wakelee, a forceful speaker and a shrewd parliamentarian, was to prove useful to Public Service, defending it persuasively in public and, on the evidence, in private as well. A Democrat, speaking of a bill to create an elective utility commission, later testified inadvertently to the ex-Senator's effectiveness as a lobbyist when he said, "Wakelee was there with his smile and held the bill in committee and it never saw the light of day."

Some men may well have been sincere in opposing the Public Service Corporation. However, the big utility was, for many, little more than a political hobbyhorse. Later politicians seem to have attacked the company with no thought more serious than for the votes which that attack would bring them. They advanced their careers—and, in Frank Hague's case, a political dynasty—with election-year bombast aimed at Public Service. The company was a handy target, and public reaction was predictable.

In the 1916 election, such thinking culminated in a barrage of anti-Public Service speeches and advertisements. These included charges that "the Democratic party ... never was more subservient to the control of the great public utility monopolies," while the Republican gubernatorial candidate, Walter E. Edge, was "handpicked" by Public Service. Candidates attacked "Tom McCarter's Submarine Squadron" as well as "the Sinister Influence of the Public Service Lobby." One Republican practically boasted that the "great interests" of the State, presumably including the utilities, had set up a $25,000 fund to beat him in his race for the State Senatorship from Essex County. He could not prove the charge or elaborate on it, but he did not need to. Nor did those who employed the Public Service "smear" always feel obliged to stick by their words.

Otto Wittpenn, the Democratic candidate for governor, remarked on the vagaries of that campaign: "One of the Republican candidates for Governor declared in the primary fight that the people of the State were being overcharged more than a million dollars for gas alone. Now he is coolly seeking to throw sand in the public's eyes by urging the election of the very candidate for Governor whom he was painting only the other day as the creature of the Public Service lobby."

Despite such contradictions—and there were many—the campaign lumbered on, lacking any real issue other than the Public Service Corporation and its lobby. Said the *Newark Sunday Call*:

"The great bugaboo of the campaign in New Jersey this year is the Public Service Corporation. In this city, Mr.

Charles P. Gillen, the independent candidate for Mayor, proclaims that Public Service does not own him and gives out the impression that that corporation does own other candidates for the office of Mayor and is doing some diabolical deeds in this community. Mr. Wittpenn ... has charged lately that Mr. Edge ... has been a tool of Public Service in Trenton.

"The indictments contain no particulars. Much is implied but nothing ... proved. We submit that the gentlemen should be more specific. Let them tell in clear terms what iniquities Public Service has committed. We believe the people want to know. The corporation has given Newark an excellent trolley service and has contributed more than any other agency to the upbuilding of the city in the last 10 years, especially in the outlying wards. But if it is debauching legislators, or controlling Mayors or Aldermen in official acts, the fact should be established. Evidence is wanted, not guesses or hints. Any demagogue can fool some of the people with insinuations..."

The only serious charge to come out of the campaign was one made by Wittpenn that Edmund W. Wakelee, representing Public Service, had planned and directed the meeting at Paterson in May at which Republican leaders made Edge their gubernatorial candidate. Wittpenn charged that the Paterson conferees were "a hand-picked committee carefully selected by former Senator Wakelee" and added that Wakelee had not only "engineered" the Edge campaign, but had authored the resolutions adopted at the Paterson meeting. The *Newark News* quoted Wittpenn as saying:

> "This same Senator Wakelee, who engineered the big Edge meeting of machine leaders in May, is at the head of a group of lobbyists employed by the Public Service Corporation and its business allies that, for cool daring, outrivals anything ever attempted in the palmy days of William J. Sewell. This cheeky band, headed by Wakelee and 'Uncle Dan' Voorhees (the former State Treasurer), has come to be known throughout the State as 'Tom McCarter's Submarine Squadron.'"

Mr. Wittpenn added that the "squadron" contained from six to 10 "expert legislative handlers who boldly assumed personal charge of the work of killing or passing bills" but who saved the Republican legislators a lot of work.

Wittpenn returned to the theme of Public Service influence on Edge late in the campaign, after Frank Bergen presided at one of the Republican candidate's rallies.

Noting that the next Governor would appoint a majority of the members of the Public Utility Commission, Wittpenn said: "Think of it, gentlemen, the general counsel of the Public Service Corporation, the legal advisor of Tom McCarter's submarine squadron which performed so well around the State House lobby, introducing my Republican opponent, who is supposed to be so vitally interested in a plank of his platform that would increase the tax on that company's franchises from two to five per cent!"

But this contradiction was insubstantial, said Wittpenn, for, although Edge pretended to support a higher franchise tax now, he had helped block such a tax as a State Senator, and had otherwise cooperated with the utility lobby. There was another contradiction here. Even as Frank Bergen sat nearby, Edge, the "utility candidate," had counterattacked Wittpenn for being himself a Public Service candidate. And so it went, down to election day, when Edge won the governorship and Charles Gillen, an antagonist of Public Service, became Mayor of Newark. The two most virulently anti-Public Service candidates, Wittpenn for Governor and Edmund B. Osborne for State Senator, were defeated. Thomas N. McCarter, who had remained silent, if seething, throughout the campaign, finally spoke up. Of Gillen Wittpenn, and Osborne, he said:

"They did not confine their malicious attacks to their public speeches, but the newspapers of the State were filled with paid advertisements of the same general character ... One of the chief bases of their attack was the allegation that this corporation maintains at Trenton, during the legislative session, a pernicious lobby, for the purpose of improperly influencing legislation. This corporation does no such thing.

"As long as conditions remain as they have existed in the past and as they are at present, the corporation will, if I can control it, send its officers to Trenton to represent it in a legitimate, straightforward way in the light of day.

"This corporation is seldom interested in any affirmative legislation. When it is so interested it goes about the matter in precisely the same manner that any other company or individual would do under similar conditions, but every year over 10 per cent of the bills introduced in both houses of the Legislature are bills which, intentionally or otherwise, directly affect the property and rights of Public Service. There are tax bills, there are rate bills, there are confiscation bills and there are strike bills, in all more than 100 every year. Those of us chargeable with the responsibility or the management of the affairs of this corporation would, indeed, be recreant to our trust if we did not exercise the American right of free speech in reference thereto. It is a matter of everyday experience for delegations of the public, of all kinds, to go to Trenton to exercise their influence in favor of, or in opposition to, this or that measure pending before the Legislature. It is frequently an act of patriotic service for one thus to participate in legislative councils. According to our traducers, when we seek, in the same manner, to protect ourselves from the character of legislation above referred to, it is not an exercise of right, but an act of scandalous lobbying.

"When the theorists, the demagogues and the fakers cease attacking this corporation in the manner above indicated, we shall be only too glad to be relieved of the vexatious burden of self-protection.

"This corporation is honestly trying to carry on a great work of upbuilding development throughout this State, from which it is seeking a reasonable return commensurate with the risks and effort involved. This, I believe, the people of the State are rapidly realizing to be the truth. At all events, it would not seem as if the making of Public Service the feature of their campaigns had been particularly successful, as two of the three gentlemen above referred to were overwhelmingly defeated for the offices they sought, and the third, while elected, ran many thousand votes behind his ticket. Throughout the campaign this corporation remained altogether silent on the subject..."

But later politicians did not heed the lessons of the 1916 election. They continued to make generalized attacks on the Public Service lobby. One of the more detailed charges against the utility was made in 1919, again an election year, by

Charles V. Finch, a Republican State Committeeman from Hudson County. Finch alleged that Public Service had contributed $5,000 in 1918 to the Hudson County campaign fund of Walter E. Edge, who was then running for the United States Senate. Referring to the Utility Commission's 1918 decision to raise trolley fares from five to seven cents, Finch termed the contribution "a token of appreciation from the Public Service Corporation for Governor Edge's kindness in prevailing upon his Public Utility Commission to hand it a present of several million dollars in increased fares."

Finch's motives in making the charge were undeniably political. He declared the cash had been passed by a lieutenant of David Baird to Hudson County Prosecutor Pierre P. Garven, Edge's campaign manager in Hudson County. And Garven was now opposing Finch in his bid for re-election as a Republican State Committeeman. Garven replied to the charges with a $200 slander suit against Finch, while John L. O'Toole of Public Service called them "the veriest rot." Finch promptly rejoined the fight, with more details and with a promise to tell his story to any grand jury or court. He suggested Garven add United States Senator Edge's denial to his own, saying: "Senator Edge is most facile in that regard. He will deny anything. His entire political career, composed of victories at the polls by steadily diminishing majorities, has been based on 'kidding' everyone with whom he came into contact. He 'kidded' pretty nearly everyone in New Jersey, except 'Tom' McCarter, president of the Public Service Corporation. Foxy old 'Tom' had been 'kidding' the public himself for too many years to be taken in by a mere Atlantic City boardwalk political faker.

"Consequently, when Edge promised to deliver the Public Utility Commission decision in favor of a seven-cent fare, in return for which the Public Service was to fill the Edge campaign chest, McCarter insisted that the decision be rendered the day after the primary. He wouldn't trust (Edge) to deliver the goods after it was certain Edge had been nominated and, as you (Garven) with your keen interest in all that affects the public welfare, will recall, that outrageous decision was in fact handed down the day after Edge was nominated."

Finch added:

"I cannot permit this opportunity to pass without letting it be known that the leaders of the State Committee knew nothing of the Public Service Corporation's contribution until after it had been made and distributed. It was evidently a private transaction. One of the men high in the councils of the party informed me of what had taken place. He had entered an emphatic protest to money being taken from such a source, but as the deal had already been sealed, signed and delivered, his objections were of no avail."

The *Jersey Journal* commented:

"... The $5,000, it is charged, was only part of a big contribution that the Public Service made to the Republican campaign fund in various sections of the State after that decision that so handsomely increased receipts of the company. (In fact, the Railway Company continued to lose money after the fare hike.) It is further charged that no accounting was made of this money and that the Corrupt Practices Act was directly violated in this respect."

The *Journal* called Finch "an insider who ought to know what he is talking about" and said his charges deserved attention, even though Finch's underlying motive was to defeat Garven. When the slander suit went to trial less than three weeks later, Finch produced another state Committeeman and a former county chairman, as well as several Edge campaign workers, to corroborate his story. Garven countered with denials from Newton A. K. Bugbee, the former State Republican Chairman, and from the Baird lieutenant. The presiding district court judge concluded that "there is no evidence to show that Mr. Garven ever got the money and so the justification for the attack fails." Several newspapers called for a fuller investigation of Finch's charge, but nothing came of it. Prosecutor Garven won not only his slander suit and a $200 judgment, but the election as well. As for Public Service its railway company continued to lose money after the decision "that so handsomely increased (its) receipts," showing a deficit of $301,716 in 1918 and $589,999 in 1919.

If Wittpenn, Osborne, and Finch gained little by their attacks on Public Service, the Frank Hague machine in Hudson County easily made up for them. "Next to prohibition," said the *Newark News* in 1930, "the Hague organization probably has made more use of its political attacks on Public Service than any other issue." Hague himself was fond of boasting how he had increased the assessments "on the Public Service Corporation from $3,000,000 to $30,000,000, and on the railroads from $67 million to $160 million."

"These were enormous increases," said Dayton D. McKean in his 1940 book *The Boss*, "which promised to bring in ample funds for the maintenance of the growing organization."

That organization depended on its antagonism toward Public Service at the polls as well. Said the *Newark News:*

"When Edward I. Edwards ran for Governor with Hague's endorsement in 1919, the five-cent fare issue was made to order. The Public Service sought to popularize the zone fare system. In Republican strongholds like Camden there had been rioting when Public Service sought to herd riders into lanes. Edwards fanned the flames.

"Three years later the long strike of Public Service operators gave the Democrats another chance to capitalize on the situation. Hague (who was then closely allied with the independent busmen) flooded Jersey City with independent buses, allowing them many privileges. Edwards' successor (as Governor), George S. Silzer (also a Hague ally), played another master stroke for the Democrats when he directed a court action to rid the streets of Public Service property unless the transportation company resumed service. Service was resumed.

Hague himself belabored Public Service at every opportunity. In 1929, for instance, he borrowed from Edward Osborne the charge that Public Service had set up a fund to defeat him in his bid for re-election as Mayor of Jersey City. Without offering details or indicating his sources, Hague alleged that the utility was backing anti-Hague candidates. Public Service Coordinated Transport was then buying up competing buses around the State, and Hague charged its

aim in attempting to oust him was to break independent
control of the bus business in Hudson County:

> "I charge that all this manipulation of candidates is due to a
> movement headed by Walter Dear (owner) of The Jersey
> Journal with his lawyer, Bob Carey, and the Public Service
> Corporation and some of its officials located in Jersey City to
> try and bring about the defeat of my colleagues and myself so
> that the Public Service Corporation may get control of the bus
> transportation system built up by the present administration,
> which is now valued at $15,000,000. . . .
>
> "The Public Service Corporation has successfully located in
> every city of this state and has control and monopoly of the
> transportation system in every section except Jersey City. This
> company has endeavored for 10 years past to get permits to
> operate buses in Jersey City, so that it may obtain control. Up
> to date the Public Service Corporation has never received
> permission from the City Commission over which I preside
> for any franchises.
>
> "Bus franchises today are held by independent bus owners.
> The plan of the Public Service to obtain these franchises was
> hatched as far back as July of last year when a meeting was
> held in the Public Service offices in Newark at which Judge
> Speer, Judge Carey, Walter Dear, Paul Seglie, David Baird, a
> director in the Public Service, Thomas McDonald and others
> were present."

Boasting that Jersey City's independent bus system, which
Hague said carried 40,000 passengers a year, was "one of the
best transportation systems of any city of its size in America,"
and that it was "largely through this system of adequate and
efficient service" that Jersey City had "grown in leaps and
bounds, increased property values, and developed various
sections of the city," Hague continued his attack:

> "McDonald was then Superintendent of Elections. As noted
> in the newspapers at the time, McDonald was requested to
> appear at this conference because this group wanted him to
> resign as Superintendent of Elections, and said to him on that
> occasion that the reason they wanted him out was to make it
> possible to try and bring about the defeat of Hague and the
> four Commissioners at the Spring Election. Since this
> meeting, this same group that summoned McDonald before

it, and after his refusal to resign had him ousted by the Legislature, has been in frequent conferences, and what do we find?

"We find none other than Walter Dear, his Jersey Journal and others of this combination in opposing the present city commissioners, trying to convince several candidates that it was to their interests to run on his ticket in order to bring about the defeat of myself and colleagues. He painted a beautiful picture that his ticket has the guarantee of $50,000, and that if the candidate would agree to run upon this ticket there would be $50,000 more that would go toward the buying up of the opposition candidates so that only one ticket would be in the field against the so-called Hague ticket.

"It is generally known that Dear is actively engaged at this present moment trying to make good his prediction that he would eliminate all candidates by putting them on the auction block and that only five candidates would be in the field against the present city commissioners. From the names of some of the candidates mentioned I do not think that Walter Dear will be entirely successful in his efforts through the use of money to retire these individuals.

"From my observation and knowledge of Walter Dear, and I can say the same of his brother, Judge Dear, I know I am not alone when I say that neither Walter Dear nor his brother, the judge, would give up $5 toward the election or defeat of any candidate. Knowing the Jersey Journal owners as I do and as thousands of others know them, it can readily be seen that this money is coming, not from the Dears, not from the candidates, but from the Public Service Corporation."

J. Owen Grundy, City Historian for Jersey City, in a letter to assist the writing of this history, provides the following scenario on how it came about that Frank Hague, who had so vigorously opposed Public Service at every turn, overnight seemingly underwent a complete change of heart and became, if not a friend, at least an accessory to the corporation's purposes by letting its buses come in to compete with the privately-owned lines, and in other ways: "The independent bus owners, for whom the noted George L. Record was counsel, launched a movement to change Jersey City's form of government from Commission form to

City Manager form as a means of striking back at Hague for breaking his long-standing arrangement with private bus lines to give them a virtual monopoly by not letting Public Service Transport come into the city in competition with them on certain lines. Record, as you know, was Corporation Counsel of Jersey City in Mayor Mark Fagan's administration, beginning in 1902, and fought Public Service tooth and nail. He had retired from politics and was representing various independent bus lines. Now, he advised them to crusade for City Manager form to bring Hague to terms. (Frank) Schoenfeld had been a Hague Democrat Assemblyman from Hudson County, but 'broke' with Hague on this issue. They brought Walter Millar, field secretary of the National Municipal League, to speak at a big mass meeting for City Manager form of municipal government, and began gathering petitions required to be filed with the City Clerk for a referendum on the change. When they filed the petitions, Hague's City Clerk rejected them, saying the signatures were rife with fraud, errors, signatures in the same handwriting, signatures secured by misrepresentation, etc. Several so-called anti-Hagueites, who had been soliciting signatures, quit the movement, went over to Hague, and were given big jobs on the city payroll. One of these was Robert A. O'Brien, whom Hague made Secretary of the State Racing Commission. This killed the City Manager movement. It disbanded. Schoenfeld went back to Hague and quit the business of being president of the independent bus owners; he was made an investigator in the Hudson County Prosecutor's office.

"It was at this time that rumors were abroad throughout Jersey City that Hague had been in serious trouble over his Federal income taxes, and that he was forced to compromise with Public Service in order to save himself from Federal indictments. The story was that he went to U.S. Senator Walter E. Edge, Republican (with whom Hague had had a working agreement during Edge's first term as governor, 1916-19), and Edge went to General W. W. Atterbury, of Philadelphia, then president of the Pennsylvania Railroad and G.O.P. National Committeeman from Pennsylvania.

General Atterbury was very close to Pennsylvania's Andrew W. Mellon, of Pittsburgh, then Secretary of the Treasury. You must remember that Public Service was largely controlled by United Gas Improvement Company in Philadelphia, which later was, in turn, controlled by United Corporation, a national utility holding company. General Atterbury, before approaching Mellon, got in touch with Tom McCarter, and explained Hague's problem. These corporate masters worked closely in cooperation. McCarter quickly suggested that part of the bargain should be that Hague would relent and permit P.S. bus lines to come into Jersey City. Hague relented, P.S. came in, and Hague made a cash settlement with the U.S. Treasury Department, without any criminal prosecution. Hague's cash was borrowed from Theodore 'Teddy' Brandle, powerful labor leader, head of the Structural Iron Workers, who years later sued Hague for the money, saying it had never been repaid. Former Judge Robert Carey (a Hague foe) represented Brandle," the Jersey City historian concluded.

Earlier in the game, the general public had apparently been more or less content with the company's railway system—once it got on top of the rehabilitation and maintenance challenges—until about 1915, when a new round of protests began. Riders complained that, in the years since it had rebuilt the trolley system, Public Service had done little to extend it, especially in the fast-growing suburbs. The new Public Service Terminal in Newark, with its underground tracks and two levels of railway terminal— "one in the basement and one on the second floor, with the second floor the busier," says Ed Francis—eased that city's traffic problems. But what about the company's other territories? In its 1974 history of Public Service transportation, *Motor Coach Age* put it this way:

> "Many outlying trolley lines were laid with only a single track and were not upgraded as the population grew and the suburbs expanded. At the same time, the absence of alternate routes to and through central business districts hampered the flow of cars at peak hours. In the face of a doubling of the number of revenue passengers between 1904 and

1914... Public Service did little except add more streetcars and several new carbarns...."

Contemporary newspaper reports, which include frequent complaints of inaccessibility in the suburbs and immobility in the city, generally bear out this assessment.

"Although the corporation was formed with broad objects stated," said *Electric Railway Journal* in 1911, "it has conducted its affairs along lines which naturally were not foreseen perfectly at the time of organization. For instance, the railway lines have been extended comparatively little. The principal increases in mileage have resulted from the acquisition of properties. The great development in the railway properties... has been one of rehabilitation. Track and equipment have been reconstructed and modernized. Some of the properties had been extended freely into outlying districts by the earlier companies, and as they reached some lightly-settled territory development has been awaited."

Why did Public Service devote so much attention to maintenance and so little to the development of new lines? One important reason was the nickel fare, which was written into and required by the company's franchise agreements with each of the scores of communities it served. In 1912, McCarter, who was serving as president of the American Electric Railway Association, said of the nickel fare that "no factor... has so contributed to the development of the American city in the last 25 years..." The problem was, he said, that as the city expanded, as the company purchased existing lines, and as free transfers became more important, the rider was able to travel farther and farther for the same fare, causing the company to earn ever less per passenger mile.

In 1907, another railway president in the same situation commented:

"The electric street railway may not increase its fare, yet wages have increased, and the cost of materials has advanced 40 per cent in three years. The public are ever expecting greater facilities, which require heavier track, larger cars,

Maintenance, in car shop, above, and on the road, was a constant headache. Below, reconstruction of roadbed on Frelinghuysen Avenue near Princeton Street, Newark, in 1910.

increased power, more car houses, more efficient and, therefore, higher-priced trainmen, better and more frequent renewal."

As McCarter himself later put it, "A starved horse never yet pulled a heavy load." In these circumstances, the railway company badly needed a rate increase. But local officials threw themselves bodily into the fight against a hike of even a penny, and it was not until 1918 that Public Service obtained the desired change in its franchise agreements, raising the fare to seven cents and providing, for the first time, for a penny charge for transfers. In the meantime, Public Service Railway had little choice but to delay expansion. The situation was further complicated by the successful political movement to limit the duration of new franchises. McCarter often attacked the limited-franchise law, saying it had discouraged expansion of the railway system.

Competition Arrives in the Jitney

"Five Cents or Walk"
—Boycott Slogan of Camden Shipworkers

In this unready state, Public Service Railway Company for the first time encountered competition. The nickel-a-ride jitney originated in California in 1914 and spread quickly eastward, appearing in New Jersey's larger cities by early 1915. At first, Public Service and other trolley companies did not consider the jitney a serious threat. In most cases the jitney was no more than an open touring car, carrying passengers on its running boards, as well as on its seats. Even its name, taken from a then-popular slang word for the five-cent piece, was silly, ephemeral. But this new form of transport rapidly proved itself otherwise.

Because they had no set routes or schedules, no franchise or tax obligations, and no regulation, the jitneys often went only where the money was. In New Jersey, most drivers simply worked the Public Service lines, stealing fares, as *Motor Coach Age* put it, "in the classic fashion." Drivers commonly swooped down in front of a trolley car, grabbing up a full load of passengers and leaving none for the scheduled trolley. Some drivers worked only at rush hours, leaving the unprofitable middle part of the day to the railway company. And when a trolley strike occurred in Brooklyn, many jitneurs—or jitney-bus operators—simply abandoned their normal routes for bigger business across the river.

From the start, the jitneys cut a substantial slice out of the railway company's earnings. McCarter commented on this in the company's 1913 annual report: "In the cities where they are still operating they are doing so in diminished numbers—many operators finding the industry unprofitable. The jitney movement, however, has caused a substantial loss of revenue to the Railway Company."

In fact, many jitney operators *did* get out of the business early on, or later, when they found they had not made enough money to replace their old, worn-out vehicles. There were other problems as well that came between the jitneys and their patrons. The jitneys were frequently involved in accidents, but because the operators had little money and no insurance, injured riders went uncompensated. Beset by such problems, many operators quit. Alas for Public Service, others quickly filled the ranks.

Did Public Service have cause for complaint against the jitney? McCarter thought so, in spades. If his company had to endure regulation, right down to the rates it could charge, because it was a monopoly, it should also enjoy the main privilege of monopoly: Freedom from competition, and especially from "unfair"—that is, unregulated—competition.

"This competition as it is now carried on is an inequitable and unconscionable thing," McCarter once said. " ... I have never been quite able to understand what the great solicitude, public solicitude, for the jitney fellows is. Every street railway in the State is under the control of the Utility Commission ... and every telephone company, every water company, every sewer company, every gas company, every electric company. Why on earth aren't those fellows? What superior star watches over them and says, 'Everybody else shall be regulated, but you shall go scot-free so you can give these other fellows the devil'? It is unreasonable to ask that they should be made a utility and put under the control of the Public Utility Commission, as we are?"

In February, 1915, the company moved to limit the jitney, presenting to the Assembly Committee on Corporations a bill subjecting jitneys to franchise regulations, including set routes, and to the same gross receipts tax the railway company paid. When the effort failed, McCarter remarked: "The public does not seem disposed to put upon this new user of the highway any portion of the innumerable burdens which it imposes upon the Railway Company, with which the jitneys compete. It is believed, however, that within a reasonable time there will be proper regulation of these vehicles."

McCarter was not alone in bitterly protesting the incursions of the jitney. On the street, a West Orange official charged, trolley cars sometimes "deliberately collided" with jitneys "to prejudice the public against buses." In addition, fistfights between jitney and trolley car operators were not uncommon. This did little, however, to discourage a public that was both enthusiastic about the automobile and resentful of Public Service.

A letter-writer to the *Newark Evening News* expressed the latter attitude most clearly in 1923: "The buses are the natural outgrowth of the Public Service action in refusing to make (all but a very few) extensions since the State in its wisdom limited the length of franchises. The buses through private initiative have built up immense expanses of territory which would never have been built up if they had depended on the charity of Public Service."

In 1916, after much lobbying by the utility, the State legislature passed its first law to regulate jitneys, providing a five per cent franchise tax and requiring jitneys to carry liability insurance of at least $5,000 per car. This law, which politicians suggested was written by Public Service, quickly put the touring car out of the transport business. But the box-type bus flourished in its place, especially in 1918, when a trolley strike and a wartime shortage of manpower forced Public Service to curtail its operations. In addition to these problems and charges of poor service and "shameful" crowding on its trolley cars, Public Service in 1919 introduced a cumbersome zone-fare system that drew protests from riders and from some trolleymen around the State. In Camden, shipworkers stoned Public Service cars and

organized a boycott under the slogan "Five Cents or Walk."
In Newark, the Director of Streets and Public Improvements
urged an expansion of jitney service to fight the "outrageously high" fare required under the zone system. Such
pressure soon forced Public Service back to the straight fare
system, but at eight cents a ride.

Nothing seemed to go well for the Railway Company
during those years. Good news was mixed inevitably with
bad. At one point, for instance, the *Newark News* commented: "Even those who have been most bitter in their
criticism of Public Service can hardly help handing a bouquet
to the street railway company for the good work it has done
in battling with the all but overwhelming storm of sleet and
snow." The kicker was that, in clearing its rails, the utility had
opened up the city to "trucks, automobiles, and jitneys ... (so
that) this very advantage offered has been used to the
disadvantage of the street cars."

In each of the five years after 1917, the Railway Company
operated at a dollar loss in the hundreds of thousands. In the
sixth year, it worked its way back to a $525,000 profit—only
to lose $1.5 million in 1922, the seventh year. This miserable
record matched that of railway companies around the
country.

But Public Service did not—could not—back out of the
transit business; it had at the very least to protect an
investment that now totaled more than $100 million. To this
end, the Railway Company in 1921 began replacing the old
two-man car on many lines with the more efficient single-
truck cars operated by the motorman alone. (The Railway
Company called this the "safety car," but its riders nick-
named it the "Toonerville" or the "Kiddie Kar," for its
tendency to "rock, bounce, and sway over rough track.") In
addition, the utility had begun a Statewide campaign to
"thoroughly test out" the legality of the jitney competition. It
filed 36 bills of complaint in State courts charging the
jitneurs with subjecting it to an unlawful competition, and
with hindering it in the performance of its public obligations.
At about the same time, the company released a strongly-
worded attack on the jitney, written by Edmund Wakelee,
then Vice President and General Solicitor:

Snow as a seasonal hazard for trolley operation; here, a new crew clears the rails on Bergenline Avenue and 17th Street in West New York in 1914.

"The (railway) company's powers are limited, its duties set forth. Its organization, its capitalization, its purposes must all be in accordance with the law. On the other hand, anyone who has enough political pull at the city hall may get a 'permit' to operate a jitney. He may not be a citizen; he may not be able to read; his past record may be bad; he may not possess a cent in the world outside of the control of a mortgaged second-hand jitney; and yet there is nothing in the law to prevent his obtaining a permit and assuming to perform a public service for which neither he nor his jitney is fitted. What a peculiar situation is thus presented! The State, in the public interest, takes full control of the organization of the street railway company, but is indifferent to who operates the jitneys."

Wakelee charged that the jitneys were "depriving" the Railway Company of $5 million a year and thus hurting not just the utility but the State and its people. He noted that three out of four of the traveling public used the streetcars, with the fourth riding the jitneys, and said:

"Now, and in the future when the ultimate railway fare is
fixed, no matter what the rate may be, every passenger on the
street railway cars pays and will pay at least one cent more per
ride than would be necessary if there were no jitney
competition. Seventy-five per cent of the public are thus
compelled to pay this extra tax so that 25 per cent may ride in
the favored jitneys..."

According to Wakelee, Public Service wanted not to
eradicate the jitney, but only to make it, like all other forms
of public transit in the State, subject to the Board of Public
Utility Commissioners. In the absence of such regulation,
said Wakelee, Public Service had halted all railway extensions
and improvements, and was preparing to abandon unprofitable lines. The company would return to normal
operation only upon "definite assurance that the capital
invested will be protected..." The Wakelee statement
concluded: "It is either street railways or the jitneys—it
cannot be both."

Critics of the company quickly replied. One letter-writer
described the existing railway system as "pitifully inadequate" and said riders had abandoned the trolleys "because
they charge a higher rate for an inferior service." Another
praised the jitneys as "noiseless" and less cumbersome.
Moreover, he said, they did not encumber the streets with
"heavy rails and unsightly overhead construction, and (with
huge juggernauts of danger.)"

Governor Edward I. Edwards charged the company with
attempting to influence the Legislature and the Board of
Public Utility Commissioners against the jitney, saying. "...it
is perfectly plain that the Public Service Corporation will not
give up the street railway business without a fight. The only
way they can fight is to get rid of the jitney competition, and
the only way they can get rid of it is to control the Legislature
and the Public Utility Commissioners, and impose such
burdensome conditions upon the jitney traffic that it cannot
do business at a profit for any reasonable fare."

In 1921 the Legislature passed the kind of law Wakelee had
demanded, subjecting to the utility board all jitneys in direct

competition with trolley lines. It is doubtful, however, that this gave Public Service the threatened control over the Board members, for the company and the regulatory body were immediately involved in a court battle over just how much competition was legal. The company objected in particular to the Board's policy of allowing existing permit-holders to bring bigger buses into competition with the railway line. On such sometimes niggling grounds the fight continued into 1923.

Until then, Public Service had usually spoken of the jitney as a temporary, albeit serious, problem. Indeed, as late as December 31, 1922, when, by one estimate, as many as 1,700 independent buses were in operation on 179 different New Jersey routes, McCarter was still reporting—at least of-ficially—"indications that the competitive bus business has about reached its peak..." In 1923, the company made an abrupt turnabout. Said *Motor Coach Age*: "Considering the proved appeal that buses had for the public, the fact that many weak car lines were losing money, and the need for expansion and improvement of the Public Service system, management decided that buses were on the scene to stay." On July 1st of that year, rather than extend its track to a new high school, the company replaced trolleys with buses on its Kaighn Avenue route in Camden. Public Service had operated buses temporarily before, during the recent World War, but this conversion and several others at the same time were to be permanent.

What about bus lines in the rest of the State? The utility revealed its intentions in August, three weeks into a strike by trolleymen for a 30 per cent wage hike. Not a wheel had turned on any Public Service line since August 1st, with the company citing its fear "that any attempt to run cars would lead to disorder and the destruction of property." The railway union and others discounted this possibility. They charged Public Service with closing down its railway operation, which was still essential to travel in the State, in order to force the elimination of jitney competition.

"The real reason for the refusal of Thomas N. McCarter, President of the Public Service Corporation, to agree to arbitration, which caused the strike," said one union leader, "is that the company wants to eliminate jitney bus competition either through action of the Public Utility Commission or by a legislative enactment..."

McCarter replied: "The stoppage of the cars ... is due to the action of the men in striking because the company would not accede to the payment to them of an excessive wage which, if it were otherwise fair, the company would have no means to provide. Service cannot be resumed before the men are willing to work for a reasonable wage which the company is enabled to pay."

On August 21st, the utility presented to the public its so-called "Plan of Settlement." Noting the continued presence of "wasteful" and "destructive" jitney competition, and "mindful of the burdens that have been heaped upon it during the past five years," the Railway Company declared it had "never had a desire" to embark on the bus business, but would do so to save the local transportation situation in New Jersey. It offered to buy up and operate, through a subsidiary of the Railway Company, all competing jitneys, to give their operators work, to charge a compromise fare of seven cents on coordinated rail and bus transportation, and to raise wages 20 per cent. In return, the State would agree not to license any new buses in competition with Public Service railway lines.

In saying it desired to save "local transportation," Public Service was of course less than frank about its motives for entering the bus business. It intended, as Percy S. Young, Vice President in charge of Finance, later conceded, to save itself and its substantial railway investment, on which it felt it deserved *some* return. In 1927, the *Newark Evening News* reported this exchange, before the Public Utility Commission, between Young and a lawyer for the municipality opposing an increased bus fare:

> "Now, Mr. Young," counsel continued, "do you think your railway service was adequate in 1923 when you first began to acquire buses?"
>
> "Yes, we considered it adequate."

"Then why did you buy the buses? If the trolleys were giving adequate service, then to operate buses, too, would be to give too much service, more than was needed, wouldn't it?"

"That's right," Mr. Young said.

"Was it not," counsel pressed, "that if you hadn't bought the buses, the trolleys would have been forced into dire financial straits?"

"That's true."

"In other words, it was a case of the first law of nature, self-preservation, wasn't it?"

Mr. Young allowed that was so.

"You buy every bus you can that competes with your trolleys, don't you?"

"Not every bus," Mr. Young corrected.

"Well, nearly every bus?"

"That's true."

At least among the utility commissioners, the railway system's self-preservation through the "plan of settlement" was seen as beneficial to the State. The plan would end needless duplication of services by the jitneys and trolleys, while protecting a large and important investment. Moreover, the consolidation of buses under one management would allow for greater efficiency of operation. The board rejected the notion, then prevalent among critics of the Railway Company, that the trolleys "need never come back." It balked when the jitney operators asked, by way of a counter-offer, for permission to permanently expand bus service to handle the traffic formerly carried by the streetcars.

As the strike dragged on, the board suggested that Public Service operate the proposed bus-trolley service at a flat rate of five cents within the larger cities, with an extra five-cent fare for the trip out to the suburbs. The company adopted the new rates and, when the strike ended by court order on September 20th, after 51 days, found that they "quite largely increased riding" over the old system. Public Service began buying out the independent buses almost immediately. In the next six years it purchased more than 1,300 of them. It paid the old operators well but, unfortunately, got little more for its money than the loss of a competitor and the permit to operate. The decrepit condition of the independent vehicles and the variety among them resulted in "abnormally high" maintenance costs, and soon forced Public Service to replace many of them with new buses. The utility went at this task enthusiastically, pouring millions of dollars into it and building up a fleet, by 1929, of about 2,300 buses on 150 routes, one of the largest such fleets in the world. The improvement in service was quickly evident. In *Fares, Please,* John Miller described the change this way:

> "On a line where the independent buses had been operating on an eight-minute headway and the streetcars had been doing the same thing, the riding public was receiving an eight-minute service—two vehicles together and then an eight-minute wait. After the railway purchased the buses, both cars and buses were operated on a 12-minute headway, arranged so there was one vehicle every six minutes instead of one every eight minutes as formerly. The public received more frequent service, while a savings was made in the number of car miles and bus miles operated.

The public benefited also from the quality of the buses it now rode. The independent buses, run by men "without a great deal of money or bank credit" had, according to *Motor Coach Age*, been "spartan, small and built by a multitude of chassis and body manufacturers." Most of them had manual gearshifts and were known, in Miller's words, for their "grinding gears, the jerking, as the bus was slammed from one speed to another..."

In 1925, Public Service ordered 395 new gas-electric vehicles, on which a smooth electric drive replaced the troublesome gearshift. With this change and others, McCarter was able to boast, in a 1934 article for the *Transit Journal*, of the increase in "safety, convenience, and comfort... Engine power has been increased by 50 per cent to make hill-climbing easy; a dual ignition system cuts down the likelihood of road failures; automatic silencers eliminate engine noises, and the use of deadened ceiling in the body further minimizes noise. Every practicable device to promote safety and comfort of passengers was built into the buses used."

Most Public Service buses were of the "It Happened One Night" movie variety, consisting of a roomy box, sometimes having a "camelback" ridge on top, with the engine jutting out, truck-style, in front. They were handsomely painted outside in cream and yellow—cream and maroon on deluxe lines—and were equipped with tall, adjustable windows that gave the interiors an open, airly feeling. The seats were mostly rattan-covered, though a few luxury buses had wicker armchairs with leather cushions.

Most buses then seated only about 30 people, but did so comfortably. On McCarter's private inspection bus, the flagship known throughout the company as the "Fabulous 5000," eight designer-upholstered easy chairs, four on each side of the carpeted aisle, could revolve to provide a smooth 360-degree scan out the spacious windows for any or all of the eight occupants. While the general ambience was that of a rolling men's club, the imagination finds itself toying with the spectacle of all eight passenger-executives swiveling in unison at a barked calling-of-attention by McCarter to take note of something in need of corporate remedy en route. Each window in this wheeled admiral's barge had somewhat severe tieback drapes that could be drawn for conferences, and set into each panel between windows was a long, discreetly narrow looking-glass for any executive who might want to straighten his tie or pat a cowlick into place before alighting to conduct, without prior notice, the planned tour of inspection. To McCarter's credit, many an old hand who remembers those potentially unnerving visits remembers also the durable Public Service president's habit of plopping his ample posterior on whatever piece of equipment was handy and passing the time of day informally with the men.

The switch to coordinated service did not work so satisfactorily for Public Service as it did for its riders. It was true that the Railway Company's bonds gained added security from the merger of bus and rail businesses, in January of 1928, to form Public Service Coordinated

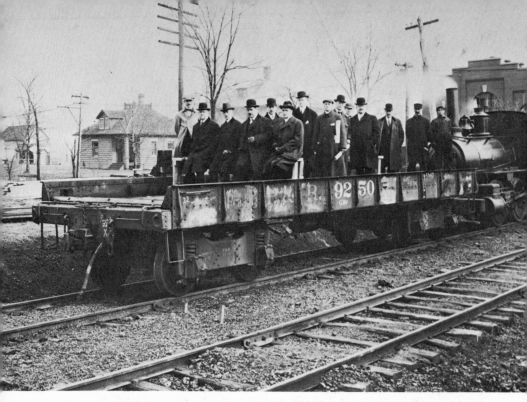

The somewhat spartan accommodations above, as McCarter—second from left—inspected the Fast Line's tracks was the norm in 1912. Times change. Below, the bus he and fellow executives traveled in, in 1930, the "Fabulous 5000".

Transport. But the company soon found that the plan of alternating buses and trolleys on the same route produced too little revenue to pay for the expensive rail and overhead power equipment. The expansion of one-man service throughout the railway system, and the development of efficiencies in the use of power, eased this problem somewhat, but the utility soon began, perforce, to abandon unprofitable railway lines, such as the Elizabeth to Kenilworth, and replace them with all-bus service. Trolley ridership had been declining, despite occasional fluctuations, since 1920. In 1929, for the first time, the buses carried more riders than did the trolley, 343 million against 312 million. The number of trolley cars, which had reached a high of 2,500 in 1921, dropped during the decade that followed to just about 1,400. The railway and bus companies continued to bring in substantial operating revenue—$39 million in 1930—and bus ridership continued to increase, but transportation was now no longer the main Public Service business. That position belonged to the booming electric department, which in 1930 produced more than $67 million in operating revenue.

As had been Public Service practice in the past, the transportation companies sought operating economies not just through technical improvements, but through "improvements" in their relationship with government. Public Service received almost as much attention for its lobbying efforts during this period as it had during its first decade. In 1927, for instance, after years of lobbying, the Railway Company won from the Legislature a law exempting it from almost all its contracted paving obligations. Until then, the company's franchise agreements had required it to pave the street between its tracks and for 18 inches on each side. McCarter had attacked this as a costly leftover "from the days of the horse car," the relief of which would considerably improve the position of the transportation companies.

McCarter's memories of the horse car and its uneconomical performance must have burned themselves into his brain, for he seems to have seldom let needless costs escape his attention—as, for example, when he was laboring to convert the Morris Canal cut for use as a subway. "There is no money in local transportation," he grumped in public, even though he had originally gone in for utility amalgamation because that was precisely where he thought it was going to sprout like the green bay tree for him and his associates. "Raising money for the railroads in the last few years," he added morosely, "has not been a task for a nervous woman."

Small wonder, then, that he had laid about him with his usual vigor when he saw that, at long last, there might be a chance for the company to divest itself of the accursed paving-contract obligations. "When horses furnished the motive power for street cars," he had said in 1925 for the benefit of ears not listening at the time, "there was reason why the car rider should pay for pavement, although it may be pointed out that it was macadam or cobblestone, a much cheaper form of pavement, that he was called upon to furnish, but today he is assessed to provide a much more costly pavement for other vehicles, which in no way contributes to his comfort and convenience, and of which he makes no use."

The new law shifted the paving burden to the municipalities, except where they could show that the trolleys had actually damaged the street. Of this and other lobbying successes that year, one Essex County Democrat pointed at Public Service in an election speech and said, "Never before in the history of New Jersey has there been such complete corporation domination of the State law-making bodies."

That same year, Public Service obtained several laws affecting the bus. In the past, the utility had worked for the regulation and taxation of the bus as its main competitor. Now, as it developed its coordinated bus-rail transportation system, it sought at least partial relief from these same burdens. It persuaded a cooperative Legislature to approve a law exempting buses from the two-cents-a-gallon gasoline tax and pushed through an amendment to an old jitney taxation law, allowing Public Service Coordinated Transport to deduct from the gross receipts tax the the licensing and other fees it paid to the State.

In his 1938 book, *Pressures on the Legislature of New Jersey*, Dayton David McKean, a faculty member at Princeton who had served as a Democrat in the State Assembly, had this to say about lobbying by Public Service:

"Whatever may have been its policy in 1905, the Public Service is no longer indifferent to what goes on at Trenton. The common understanding around the State House is that John L. O'Toole, vice president in charge of public relations, watches from the Hotel Hildebrecht every move the Legislature makes. He has an assistant, Robert Zachary, who spends his time in the corridors of the State House when the Legislature is considering bills affecting the Public Service. The legal department goes through every bill which might conceivably affect the company ...

Many of the legislative successes attributed to the Public Service cannot be proved, and yet legislators generally believe the company to be responsible. In the session of 1935, for example, an attempt was made to remove all exemptions from the gasoline tax, an attempt which would, if successful, have brought into the State treasury two or three million dollars a year at a time when it was badly needed. The gasoline used by the Public Service is ... tax-exempt; but exempt too is the gas used by farmers in their tractors. The word was passed around that the Public Service was ready to finance a campaign by the farmers to maintain the exemptions, and the attempt to tax all gasoline was abandoned ...

In 1927 the Legislature passed an act which relieved the Public Service of any obligation ... to pave between and alongside its street-car tracks. This act cost the cities of New Jersey millions of dollars, and all attempts to repeal it have failed. The officers of the Public Service would probably insist to an investigating committee that the Legislature has granted all these favors on its own initiative, and probably an investigating committee could not prove that pressure was used; but the favors are so valuable that they form strong circumstantial evidence that the company knew what it wanted and got it.

The name of the Public Service Corporation came up repeatedly in newspapers in the summer of 1929, in connection with another costly law that, said critics, its lobbyists had slipped by the Legislature. The Wise Law, so called after Russell S. Wise, its sponsor in the Assembly, empowered the State Highway Commission to regulate and set the terms of railway and bus use of bridges in its control. The bill passed with little comment in April, and though the attack on it which began in July was belated, it was nonetheless fierce, having as its target a little-noticed clause that voided all existing bridge-use contracts between utilities and counties. Critics of the law said Public Service had relied on it "to escape liability for approximately $305,000 charged to it by the Highway Department as the company's share for rebuilding the Hackensack River bridge on the Lincoln Highway," but the utility denied this. J. Ernest Thier, the road supervisor of Bergen County and a lobbyist for Public Service, eventually admitted that he had prepared the bill and that William Speer, the General Attorney of Public Service, "had whipped it into shape." Its purpose, he said, had merely been to meet the relatively new situation of state construction and control of bridges.

Asked by a reporter if he had discontinued his activities for Public Service before giving Assemblyman Wise the bill, Thier said, "I have never ceased aiding Public Service in obtaining legislation in which it was interested." Public Service promised to fight any changes in the Wise Law, but when the Legislature was reconvened in August, it promptly struck down the questionable clause. The episode ended with the *Newark News* scolding the Legislature for its "loose and dangerous" methods and for the casual attention it had originally given the Wise bill.

This law, the paving law, and others like them undoubtedly delayed the eventual dissolution of the Railway Company, but they could not prevent it. From a total of 98 in 1920, the number of trolley lines dropped to just 33 in the next 13 years, much of the loss occurring in 1924 and after 1927.

"Through the Twenties and, oh, by 1930, they knocked out most of the lightly-traveled lines," says Ed Francis. "The Orange Crosstown . . . the Montrose Line from South Orange to West Orange was knocked out by floods in South Orange and they just never rebuilt the track. It was a good opportunity to end the car service. The same thing happened with the Gloucester line (where a boat collided with and badly damaged a drawbridge) and maybe a few others. Something happened and it just didn't pay 'em to resume service. Valley Road in Montclair went out. All the little lines in New Brunswick. The Elmora Line out of Roselle. Almost any branch line that was lightly-traveled was abandoned in favor of buses. And a number of buses died too during the Depression, for lack of business."

And this was the storied enterprise of which, as recently as 1926, Matthew R. Boylan, Vice President in charge of the Railway Company and affiliated companies, had been able to write with pride, "In point of track mileage, Public Service Railway Company is the third largest in the world, and in point of the number of buses operated Public Service Transport Company is the largest in the United States ..."

Odd as it may seem now, most people, and motorists especially, were glad to see the trolleys go. The trolleys slowed traffic, so people complained, not just by their sheer number, but by the presence of their track and wire, along with their safety islands, in the middle of city streets. The

Snow and a parked truck bring a trolley to a halt, tying up traffic behind it on Market Street in Newark in 1923.

suburban, single-track lines, on which cars ran in both directions, passing at turn-outs, were even worse. The trolley car waiting stock-still at a turn-out in the middle of the street could block automotive traffic almost completely. And where the single track was at the side of the road, trolleys ran half the time against the flow of automobiles. Sometimes, where a 36-foot double-ender had to swing wide on tight curve—as on the eastbound track at the corner of Fairmount and Bergen Avenues in Jersey City—the motorist unlucky enough to be squeezing by as the car's ponderous rear end swung to complete the curve found his auto given a nudge to starboard, with resultant fender dimple as a memento. Since by then the trolley was gathering speed to zag into Monticello Avenue two blocks away, the only recourse most surprised motorists had was their own version of the Lebanese curse, "May a streetcar grow in your belly, and the motorman keep ringing the bell!"

The bus, being faster and more flexible, fitted better into the new scheme of traffic. In the 1930s, Public Service substituted buses for trolleys on even its busiest routes, leaving just eight railway lines in operation. Its engineers developed the all-service vehicle, a bus equipped with trolley poles that could use either gasoline or electric power, and this replaced the streetcar on many lines. The trolley-bus, as it was known, enabled the company to preserve costly and not-fully-depreciated electrical equipment, to employ its long experience with the electric motor, and to escape expensive track maintenance. In addition, as *Motor Coach Age* noted, the trolley-bus was legally a streetcar where it ran under wires, and was thus not subject to the complicated law governing changes in service on bus lines. At about the same time it was developing the trolley-bus, Public Service helped introduce the Diesel-powered bus to America and led the industry with many other innovations.

It did so by sending Transport Vice President Matthew Boylan and Chief Engineer Martin Schreiber to England in 1928 to find out what the British were doing with Diesel-electric drive. As John Anderson Miller notes in *Fares, Please!*:

"In England the high cost of gasoline had early resulted in the extensive use of Diesel engines. Enthusiastic Britishers emphasized the advantage of the Diesel to the visitors from the United States. Like most American bus operators, however, Boylan and Schreiber had the feeling that the characteristics of the Diesel engine were not well adapted for driving a bus through mechanical transmission. But Public Service was already operating a large number of buses with electric transmission. If combined with electric transmission, they thought the Diesel engine might become an efficient and economical source of power. So they imported a couple of Mercedes-Benz Diesel buses in 1929, which were equipped with electric drive. These gave very satisfactory service, but the need to send to Europe for replacement parts was a serious drawback. Then came the introduction of the Hercules Diesel engine built in the United States. Immediately, Public Service and Yellow Coach went to work on a new design of Diesel-electric bus, and in 1937 a fleet of 27 units made their appearance on the streets of Newark, the first such fleet in the world."

Though most of its buses followed the old, familiar trolley routes, Coordinated Transport did not confine itself to these routes. It developed a large interstate commuter service, both to Philadelphia in the south and to New York. And where it had served only 150 municipalities with streetcars, it was by 1934 serving some 350 New Jersey communities mostly with buses.

The last streetcar ran on Broad Street, Newark, where 300 cars had once passed each hour, in December, 1937—less than 50 years after the start of electric service. The *Newark News* described the final run of one Newark line in the late 1930s:

"A South Orange trolley car marked 'Maplewood' went westward from Broad and Market Streets at 1:28 o'clock this morning. It was only another trolley car, filled with passengers who sleepily glanced at newspaper headlines, scanned the overhead advertisements of toothpaste and cigarettes, or merely looked at each other. The operator, Walter Way, who has been with the South Orange Line for nearly 30 years, made change and called out streets. Persons got on and off."

"But one passenger was curiously wide awake. For him the westward trip of the 1:28 trolley car to Maplewood was an event. It was not only the last car of the night; it was the last for all time, and David McGregor of ... West Orange, who rode in the first electric trolley to enter South Orange on October 7, 1893, was riding in the last one. The car arrived at the Maplewood terminal at 2 o'clock, started on the return trip at 2:03 o'clock and crossed the Four Corners (Newark) again at 2:35 o'clock. And at 2:35 o'clock, Mr. McGregor left the car, sighed, and waited for a friend to take him home to West Orange in an automobile."

McGregor, a retired chief engineer with Public Service and, before that, chief electrician of the Newark and South Orange Street Railway Company, recalled his first trip for the *Newark News* reporter:

" 'Getting the line into South Orange was something else. There was a court fight that lasted nearly nine months, much of it due to a lawyer who was counsel for both the Lackawanna Railroad and South Orange Village. Eventually, however, the company obtained permission to extend the line. This permission was granted at 9 p.m. on Friday, October 6, 1893, and in order to forestall a threatened injunction the company's officers decided to lose no time erecting the necessary poles and wires. That's when I got on the job.

" 'In less than 10 minutes two carloads of laborers were on the job, digging holes for poles. In spite of a heavy rain the men worked all night and the next morning, with the result that a trolley car reached the center of South Orange Village before noon on Saturday, October 7. Its arrival was marked by the firing of a cannon belonging to the South Orange Republican Club, the ringing of the Village fire bell and the cheers of the crowd that lined both sides of South Orange Avenue... The line was extended along Valley Street to Springfield Avenue, Maplewood, in August, 1896. I supervised the line work on this extension, too. I've seen the old line taken over by Public Service. Now I've taken a ride in the last car.'

"Along came Mr. McGregor's friend, to take him home.

" 'No more South Orange trolleys,' said Mr. McGregor, softly, incredulously."

World War II brought the trolley a return to popularity, but only temporarily. Afterwards, the substitution of bus for trolley, and the development of the bus system—on which ridership reached 630 million in 1936—resumed. Even the hybrid trolley-bus bowed out then, allowing an end to overhead and substation maintenance, as Coordinated Transport built a standardized Diesel fleet. In 1952, Public Service got out of the railway business for good, except to operate Newark's 30-car City Subway, by abandoning its Bloomfield Avenue line to Montclair and Caldwell. Its surviving streetcars, by now well worn out, went to the scrapyard.

Of the once great Public Service railway system, with its 850 miles of track reaching every corner of the State, only vestiges remain, and can be seen today: Some scars on the face of the Palisades; the Fast Line route converted to an electric transmission right-of-way; some worn rails exposed on Montgomery Street in Jersey City, by the library; a few streets made wider than they need to be, even now, to accommodate a long-gone trolley loop.

With the end of the war, Coordinated Transport began to offer express service during rush hours on many lines, a time-saving move that proved popular with riders and profitable for the utility. Public Service also developed some new bus lines during this period, mostly interstate, and in 1945 and 1946 it ordered more than a thousand new buses, in part to make up for wartime delays. With the new buses came a new, drabber Public Service color scheme of two-tone gray with broad, dark-blue striping.

Despite these changes, the automobile soon began drawing people away from the bus, just as the bus had drawn them away from the trolley, and Coordinated Transport went into a slow decline. In July, 1948, with the Utility Commission's approval, the company increased its basic fare from five to seven cents. Bus-rail ridership dropped from 654 million that year to 500 million in 1950 and—as the single-zone fare fluctuated from a court-ordered low of five cents to a high of 10 cents—to just 397 million in 1952. Faced with a large operating deficit, Coordinated Transport started consolidating or abandoning outright lightly-traveled bus lines. It also reduced the frequency of service on many lines. Exceptions to this depressing picture were the interstate and charter businesses. Use of the Garden State Parkway and other new highways improved the company's long-distance bus business, allowing the development of several new express lines. The Route 118 bus from Newark to New York became especially popular with the openings of the New Jersey Turnpike and the midtown Port Authority Bus Terminal, which allowed the substitution of express service for the former slow routing through the streets of Jersey City and Manhattan. During this period, Public Service greatly expanded its promotional work, and, with the purchase of air-conditioned deluxe buses starting in 1956, saw a profitable increase in its charter and tour business. But daily ridership was still declining, even as the basic fare went to 12 and then 14 cents.

Suburban development around New York and Philadelphia continued through the Sixties, to bring riders to interstate lines, while taking them away from shorter, urban routes. The decentralization of business and industry and, in particular, the construction of suburban shopping malls reached by car hurt many city lines. Coordinated Transport responded to these problems, and to rapidly-increasing wages and other expenses, by cutting costs; it attempted to streamline management of the system, and it continued to "stretch" bus headways. Despite its problems, though, Public Service Coordinated Transport, under the presidency of Herbert E. Harper, placed a characteristic emphasis on maintenance of its bus equipment, winning national awards in that category eight years in a row. It also continued to purchase new buses, introducing the so-called "new-look" bus, with its glassy front and its forward-canted side windows, in 1960. This bus gradually replaced the older, boxier buses and predominates in the fleet today.

Transportation continued to take up more of the utility's time than could be justified in dollars. Throughout the 1960s, Public Service found itself forced, with dismaying frequency, to go before the board of Public Utility Commissioners in search of fare hikes. In 1969, when the single-zone fare reached 30 cents and ridership dropped to 207 million, PSE&G spoke publicly of selling its money-losing transportation subsidiary. The idea was not new. "If you know of a buyer," Lyle McDonald had told a stockholder in 1955, "I'll be in my office waiting until midnight." In April, 1970, there was a private purchase offer of $29 million from an investment group headed by John J. Gilhooley, but the offer was withdrawn in early 1971. In 1971, with the old dream of coordinated bus and streetcar service long gone, Public Service Coordinated Transport became Transport of New Jersey. The bus company remains a subsidiary of the electric and gas company, but before the change in name it underwent a change of management. Herb Harper retired after 49 years service, 13 of them as president. John J. Gilhooley, former senior commissioner of the New York City Transit Authority, took over. Soon, Transport got a new "TNJ" logo. Under the new name, the bus company operated its first State-subsidized line. It also began a program of retrenchment, abandoning many money-losing lines, reducing the size of the fleet to bring it in line with decreased ridership, and closing several garages. Today, with daily ridership at about one-half million and annual ridership just under 120 million, Transport operates a fleet of 1,850 buses, about half of them owned by the State through its "Bus Buy Out" program and leased back to the bus company. What is the future of transportation at Public Service? Said the company in its 1975 report: "Unfortunately, despite strenuous cost-cutting measures, the future operation of TNJ is dependent upon the continuation of State and Federal subsidies." This is still true today. In 1976, when it received almost $21 million in State subsidies, TNJ still lost more than $500,000. The basic one-zone fare had meanwhile risen to 40 cents, but, as a spokesman for the company put it, "We'll never make it through the coinbox." The picture improved in 1977, but as the man said, the money that came in through the coinbox wasn't responsible. State and Federal financial help was—along with retrenchment and cost cutting measures.

William Grigat in May, 1974, two months before his death at 82.

The Meter Man

*"I went to a pickle factory and had to walk over the tops of barrels to get
to the meter. I fell through the top of a sauerkraut barrel."*
—A newly-hired meter man

Meter-reading could be chancy work in the early days,
according to the late William Grigat, who read gas meters as
well as electric meters, and supervised meter-readers for 50
years, 39 of them in the Jersey City area, before retiring
from Public Service. Before he died in 1974, Grigat, a blue-
eyed, straight-backed 82-year old, addressed a series of
reminiscent letters to Public Service for use in this history.

Grigat's letters evoke the amusing, at times hilarious,
aspects of the work, as well as the harsher side. He cared
about his customers, especially when they thought they were
being hornswoggled, but even when they tried to outwit the
meters. He liked to leave them feeling—a word he uses
often—"satisfied."

"One day I had a new man out reading meters all by
himself," Grigat recalled. "I asked him, 'How did you like the
day's work?' He said, 'Rotten. I tore my new pants that I
bought to read meters in on a pile of firewood. I stepped in a
hole of a water-meter box full of water—the cover was left
off. I went to a pickle factory and had to walk over the tops of
barrels to get to the meter. I fell through the top of a
sauerkraut barrel. I walked down some cellar steps onto what

looked like a new cellar floor. It was dust, on top of water, and I went into some more water.'"

Grigat did not say whether the man ever showed up for a second day. But he himself took such misadventures in stride. On his first visit to a hospital, he asked where the meters were, and an attendant told him down the hall in a room to the right. Grigat went into the room "and I saw men lying on the floor, and some sitting in corners. It was the dinner hour and I thought they were all sleeping, because no one moved while I looked for the meter." In fact, Grigat found out later, they were all dead. He had been in the morgue.

Another time, he wrote, "my meter reader went through a funeral parlor. To read the meter, which was in the cellar, he had to pass through the embalming room. As he did so he seen a man lying on the table. When he came back to the embalming room after reading the meter, he seen the man sitting up on the table. He got so frightened he ran out of the funeral parlor and could not finish his meter reading. I had to finish the book. The man that was on the table was one of the working men, sleeping on his dinner hour."

Once, in a fish market, Grigat discovered a cellar full of large, vise-jawed turtles, all on their backs, between him and the meter. "I asked the fish market man, 'How do I get to where I can read the meter?' And he said, 'You walk on the turtles; when they are on their backs they can't hurt you.'" So Grigat did, and the turtles didn't.

Funny things happened to meter readers in those days, and maybe still do. One time Grigat was helping out with meter reading on a different route, because the regular meter-reader was sick. "While I am reading the meters on this route," he recalled, "in several buildings that I went in and read the meters I was handed one dollar or two dollars, but was not told what the tips was for.

"So when the meter-reader came back to work, he said to me, 'How did you make out reading my meter route that day?' And I said, 'Fine, but why did these people give me money like that, going in some of the buildings?' He said,

'That was for you not to see anything and keep your mouth shut. They were gambling houses.'"

Not all the perks of a meter-reader had strings attached to them, though. For instance, Grigat told about "a lady on my route where I read the meters and collected the bills. She was a widow. I helped her connect the gas heater for the winter, and disconnect it in summer. I also regulated her gas range and burners. After I finished my route in the afternoon, she made me stop in for a while to keep her company and talk. She gave me cake and coffee.

"One day she asked me if I had a bank account." Grigat, a man of inspiring innocence, apparently saw no ulterior motive in such a question from a widow lady who liked to have him keep her company and talk. "I said to her," he continued, "that on the salary I get I can't afford a bank account. My salary was $17.50 a week.

"So she gave me $5 and said, 'Start a bank account and show me the book.' So every month when I collected the bill, she would have me keep the change to put in the bank account. So when I got transferred to different work, I brought the bill down myself. After six years the lady passed away. I left the account in the bank, and didn't touch the money, so now the book has $1,400.00."

Always an honest man, Grigat added, "In those days when our pay was $70 a month, at least we could have a dinner of breaded pork chop, bowl of soup, cup of coffee and pie for 25¢."

One day he went to read the meters in a basement apartment. "I rang the bell and heard a voice say, 'Come in.' I tried the door, but it was locked, so I knocked again and said, 'I can't open the door.' And the voice said, 'Go to hell.' Later on I came back and the lady of the house let me in. I said, 'I was here before trying to get in. A voice said, 'Come in,' and when I said the door was locked the voice said, 'Go to hell.' The customer told me that it was her polly that had answered me."

Nor was it only parrots that played games with meter readers, Grigat remembered. "While collecting one day I asked the party on the first floor what floor the party I was looking for lived on, and she said, 'Up a stairs.' I go upstairs to the next floor and asked, and she also said, 'Up a stairs.' So I get to the top floor and the lady there said, 'Yes, that party lives in the rear of the house, but on the second floor.' The parties who had sent me 'up a stairs' couldn't speak English, so they sent me upstairs to a party that could."

One house where he was reading meters in the cellar gave Grigat a scare, because when he heard a lot of unusual noise down there in the dark and looked around, he wrote, "I seen cats in the cellar in wire cages. I started counting the cats and counted more than 30. So when I went to the next house, the customer said to me, 'Did you see a cat at the house you just came out of?' I said, 'What cat? I seen over 30 cats in that cellar. I mean *cats*! Why do you ask?' She said her cat was missing. So I went back and asked the customer who had all those cats in the cellar, why she had all those cats. She said, 'The neighbors are terrible. They don't feed the cats.' She fed them, though, and afterwards picked them up and put them in her cellar, so she could go on feeding them."

A little ingenuity sometimes went a long way in solving problems for meter-readers. Grigat had more than his share—of ingenuity, as well as problems. "One day the meter-reader called me at the office and said that he couldn't read several buildings as the cellars were flooded. He asked me to bring the boots. I knew the district, so I looked up the morning newspaper and it said low tide at 1:30 p.m. So I went to these buildings after that time and the cellars were all empty as the river tide lowered. I read the meters and met the meter-reader and gave him the readings. He looked at me and said, 'No boots? How did you read the meters?' So all I said was, 'There was no water in those cellars.' He said, 'When I was at those buildings the water was up to the second steps in the cellars.'" That's how you get to be boss.

Not that he didn't try to keep his men on their toes, flood-tide or no flood-tide. "I always told my men, 'Ask lots of questions,' and I always asked a lot myself." His curiosity sometimes saved the company—and its customers—money, because part of the meter-reader's work then was thwarting the inventive thieves who tampered with their own and their neighbors' meters. Like other readers at than time, Grigat turned on service, tested for leaks, on occasion shut off service for non-payment, and in some cases even carried away the meter itself. One customer complained of high bills despite little use. Grigat, who had a keen eye for such things, discovered that another tenant had switched meters when the complainant went on a three-week holiday and was merrily spinning up the numbers at his vacationing neighbor's expense.

Sometimes the maneuvers a meter-reader got himself involved with went to extremes over which he had no control. "I was sent off to collect a three-month bill in a one-family house. The customer could not pay and would not let any collectors in to shut off the service. I said through the door, 'Lady, it is up to you. I can have your service shut off at the street, and it would not look good to your neighbors to see your service shut off that way. So call up the office and ask them if they could give you more time to pay.' So she called up the office and came out to call me in to answer the phone. I answered, and the boss said, 'Are you in?' I said, 'Yes.' He said, 'Shut it off.'"

A meter-reader was constantly learning, sometimes the hard way. "One day while reading meters in my district at a place that had two tenants to a floor, I knocked on the door and heard a voice say, 'Come in.' I walked in and there I seen the lady standing in a dishpan with no clothes on washing herself. And she hollered at me and said, 'Where do you think you are, in a stable? I am going to report you.' I said, 'I knocked at the door and I heard 'Come in.' So I went next door and said to the other tenant, 'Did you hear me knock on the door and someone say Come in?' She said, 'Yes.' So I said, 'You better come with me to the lady next door and tell her you heard the knock on the door and someone say, Come in.' The lady in the dishpan didn't have her door locked when I opened it to go in. After that l waited until the customer opened the door for me."

In the cellar of a saloon Grigat noticed a wash-boiler on a three-burner gas stove, part of a beer-making process, and

he also noticed a modest gas bill of 48¢ a month. "Being a
gas-fitter, I knew that one large burner would burn 8¢ per
hour and the other two burners 6¢ per hour, so I ordered the
meter changed for not registering properly." The meter
department found the gas diaphragm—a sort of bellows
made of sheepskin—punctured, and then the holes in the
meter itself, through which the punctures in the diaphragm
were made, neatly soldered and painted over. Grigat got a
$20 reward.

Economy often depends on who is defining it. For
example, Grigat recalled that "years ago I used to see the
street department of the gas department dig trenches to lay
gas mains, with the open trenches guarded by a night
watchman in a shanty. Once I saw the gas company lay a
main in an open trench with no watchmen on duty, only
kerosene oil lamps. At night, kids would steal or break the
lamps. I met the foreman and asked him why no night
watchman to watch the trenches and lights. He said, 'The
company thinks it is cheaper to buy a new lamp than to pay
for a night watchman.'"

But at the same time the company was, in its own profit-
motivated way, quite generous with its personnel, as Grigat
attests. Each reader had his own route, he recalled, and on
that route he delivered the bills, collected them on delivery,
and in addition to "working the shut-off notices for non-
payment" collected on the "quarter meters," and took orders
for merchandise, appliances and electric bulbs. "Sometimes
we'd make more commission pay than we did on our
salaries," he wrote, and on top of that might add to weekly
income by making signs for store windows on the route, or
doing repair work for customers on Saturday afternoons.
"The office kept a scoreboard on the wall in the collection
department," Grigat remembered, "and everybody tried to
be on top of the score. The meter reader who had the best
record at the end of the year, with no mistakes in reading, got
an extra week of vacation. The second-best reader got three
days off. And the meter reader with no error in each book
got a quarter. If he had no errors for the month, he made an

extra $5 or $6 for his total meter books. So the readers tried to make no mistakes, and to collect those extra quarters every day."

Grigat was almost as careful of the corporate nickels, dimes and pennies as Tom McCarter was with the company's millions. The barber shop on his route, he recalled, got 25¢ for a haircut and shave in those days—"15¢ for the haircut, 10¢ for the shave." But Grigat reminisced at age 82, "He could buy two pounds of pork chops for a quarter then. Nowadays, what he gets for a haircut and shave won't buy him two pounds of pork chops." Musing in the same vein of economic awareness, he went on, "One customer came to me complaining about the meter reader leaving the light on in the cellar after finishing reading the meters. So I asked him how long was the light bulb burning when you found out. He said, 'Three hours and some.' So I said, 'That would be about 7¢ worth, and here you spent 20¢ carfare to come here to the office and tell me.' So I told him I would tell the meter reader to be careful, and I paid him the 27¢ and left him satisfied."

A half-serious rivalry had developed between the gas and the electric companies, perhaps as a result of their competition for the lighting business. But Grigat, though a gas man, occasionally lent his sharp eye to the sibling utility. At one large store, "I found a coat hanging near the electric meter, and I found a hole drilled through the glass of the electric meter and the hoop of the coat hanger was resting on the disc dial of the meter, to slow it down."

There were tinkerers everywhere. On moving into new rooms in Jersey City, he discovered that the hall lights were hooked up to his apartment's meter. "So I only had the gas meter turned. After a while the landlord said, 'Are you going to have your electric meter turned on?' And I said, 'Yes, after you take over the hall lights and get them off my meter.'

"Once," Grigat continued, "I was sent out to look for missing gas meters where the house had been torn down. I found out the wrecker who tore the house down was a junk dealer. I went to his yard and asked him if he had any gas meters to sell. He said yes, and he brought out two meters. I checked the numbers, and they were the meters I was looking for. So I said, 'I'm from the gas company and those meters are company property,' So he gave me the meters."

Grigat got so good at keeping the connivers from putting one over on him that he on occasion inadvertently put one over on the company. He had shut off the electric meter in one house for non-payment of the bill, he recalled, and "when I shut off the meter I put a piece of paper around the switch blade and closed the switch. Then I put a round disk of cardboard, white with a stamp of gold paint on it so that it looked like the bottom of the fuse box, into the receptacle, and put back the fuses. No current. But when the bill was paid and the man came to turn on the service again, he couldn't get it to work, so he thought maybe it was cut at the pole. When he found it wasn't that, either, he had to call me at the office, and I told him where the paper disk was."

On some routes for domestic service there was a $1 monthly charge that led to occasional hanky-panky. In one house Grigat saw so many lights and appliances that he thought it strange the owner should be paying only $1 a month, so he told the company to put an electric meter on the service pole, to check on how much electricity the house was consuming before the juice went through the meter inside. For finding out, through the meter on the pole, that the actual electricity used came to $18 a month, Grigat picked up a small cash award.

"One day while delivering electric bills at a saloon," he wrote, "I had the owner complain to me about his high electric bills, sometimes as much as $18 to $26 a month, while the saloon four blocks away, which was bigger and had more lights and electric fans, was paying only $1 a month. The other saloon he said, also had an electric player piano.

"Well, I checked the other place and found his electric was being supplied from his house, and the electric bill was therefore only the domestic charge of $1 a month. He had a bypass hooked from his house through the yard to supply the saloon. So I turned that in to the company and they found the bypass. I got $15 for that one."

Grigat recalled with relish an occurrence having to do with

meters that must be about as rare as a hole-in-one in a tornado. He was reading the meters in a firehouse and found that both the gas and electric meters had exactly the same index, or reading. He told the captain that it was the first time in 37 years that he had seen the gas and electric meters in the same place with the same readings. "So if you play the numbers," he told the captain, "try your luck."

Around Christmastime Grigat would routinely try his own luck, and invariably improve it, by telling customers he was hoping to collect from for bills past due, that if he had the most collections in that week he would win a turkey. Clearly not an easy mark himself, he sometimes found customers willing and ready to trip themselves up on their own false suppositions. One woman owed a three-month gas and electric bill, for instance, so the company dispatched Grigat to collect it. When he got to the house he saw a For Sale sign on the front, so he started looking from the house to his bills and back up at the house. He knew the lady was watching him from behind the curtains, and he figured she might begin to think he was interested in buying. Sure enough, she did. When he went to the door and rang the bell, out she popped—for the first time in three months in response to a Public Service ring—and invited him in. When he got inside and told her he was from the gas and electric company to collect her overdue bill, "she was so surprised," he recalled, "that she paid me."

Another time a woman beefing about a "high" electric bill of $1.80, when told the bill was correct, refused to pay Grigat. He said to her, "You have a very nice radio. Do you get much distance on it?" Yes, she told him, she got the Hawaiian Islands, Cuba and South America. "All of which," said Grigat, who knew something about the way time-of-day affects radio signals, "are very far away. You don't get them stations until one or two o'clock in the morning. Surely you don't sit in in the dark?" With his usual deadpan, Grigat concluded, "So she paid me."

Grigat knew the buildings as well as the people. "I met a panhandler who asked me for carfare. He rode on the bus but missed getting off at Academy Street. I said, 'What

number on Academy Street do you have to go to?' He said,
'Number 202.' And I said, 'What are you going to do at 202?
There is no house there, only vacant lots.'"

Another panhandler in the south end of Jersey City asked
Grigat for fare home. "I asked him where he lived, and he
said, '478 Grove Street, Jersey City.' So I asked him what
kind of a house it was and he said a six-family flat. I told him
that 478 was a two-family house, grocery store left side,
butcher shop right."

Decades before social scientists found themselves becoming concerned with the meaning of work, Grigat seems to
have appreciated the subtleties of the problem.

"While reading the meter in a toy factory, I talked to a man
working on an assembly-line table. He was at a machine,
punching parts out for a toy. I asked him, 'Where does that
part that you are punching out go on the toy?' And he said, 'I
don't know,' so I said, 'What do you do with the part you
punch out?' And he said he put it in the box for the next man
to work on. So I went through the assembly line and came
back and showed him the finished toy, and the part he
worked on, where it went."

He practiced the same policy in his own business, visiting
the gas works and learning exactly how they operated. At
one point, he made a detailed cutaway sketch of the water-
gas set, showing exactly how they operated. But it was the
meters he knew best. After 17 years of retirement, he wrote,
"I still read meters in my sleep."

Gas Use Grows

"Mrs. C looked longingly at the cabinet range display every time she came to the office to pay her gas bill. The floor salesman frequently urged her to install one, and she was extremely desirous of doing so; however, there was a drawback. Mr. C was it."
—P. S. Salesman A. J. Fleisch

By the mid-1920s, Public Service was sending out more than 21 billion cubic feet of gas a year, manufactured at nine water-gas plants and two coke plants, one at Camden and the other, not owned by Public Service, at Kearny. The Kearny coke plant and six of the water-gas works—two at Newark, two at Jersey City, one in Hoboken, one in Paterson— supplied the large and important northern territory of Essex, Hudson, Passaic, and Bergen Counties. The gas works at Camden and Trenton, backed up by reserve plants at New Brunswick and Plainfield, served the southern territory. The company's largest plant, on the Passaic River at Market and Jersey Streets, Newark, then had nine water-gas sets, producing 11 million cubic feet of gas daily. At the Camden plant, which had five water-sets in addition to the coke operation, the battery of ovens each day converted 500 tons of coal into seven million cubic feet of gas, 365 tons of coke, and the usual by-products. Each of the 37 ovens took a charge of nine tons of coal once every 15 hours.

For the preceding decade, Public Service had been laying mains of from two to 36 inches in diameter at the rate of 50 to more than 100 miles a year and, from a network of almost 1,500 miles in 1903, that system now extended nearly 3,500 miles. Though small by comparison with today's network of more than 12,000 miles, this was then one of the largest systems of mains in the world. All the Public Service gas plants were interconnected via these mains, so that gas produced at one end of the State could serve customers at the other. This guaranteed continuous service, even if the plant that was a customer's usual source of gas broke down. By extending the range of each gas works statewide, interconnection also enabled the utility to concentrate production in the most efficient plants, without regard for geography. The gas company had 24 holders at its 10 plants, plus 20 "outlying" holders to supplement the distribution of gas and to prevent interruptions of service. Where there had been none in 1903, by the mid-20s Public Service had 600 "district governors" throughout its territory—machinery that reduced gas from transmission pressure, usually about five pounds per square inch, to domestic pressure, about the waft of the human breath.

Domestic use of gas, inside the kitchen and out, had continued to grow, despite competition from electricity and from restaurants. The electric company took business away from the gas range by promoting appliances like the toaster and the electric iron. Restaurants, profiting from the trend to dining out, took away some of the gas company's "big Sunday meal" business. In addition, modern woman, having been freed by gas and electricity from many of her more time-consuming chores, now spent less time in the kitchen. Some gas men, frightened by this development, pondered ways to "drive" her back to the kitchen were she "belonged." Public Service, more subtly, offered a variety of cooking courses in the hope that women—and men—would step up to the stove to cook for pleasure as much as for necessity. At the same time, the introduction of gas appliances such as the dryer, and the increasing use of gas for water-heating and even for central home heating, easily made up for these depredations.

The commercial and industrial gas business had also grown, especially since World War I. There had been some industrial customers as early as 1903. "In those days the hatting industry in the Oranges was in full sway," John A. Clark wrote, "and one of our big tasks was to induce the manufacturers to substitute gas for coal in their factories. This change-over in the hat plants constituted a major portion of our new business in this territory. Instead of the old flatirons which had to be heated on the coal stoves, slugs were attached to the irons and gas connected, adding materially to the comfort and convenience of the workers, as the intense heat and steam from the stoves was eliminated."

Workers blasted through the Watchung Mountains in 1924 to install a 17-inch gas main from Summit to Plainfield, interconnecting the Central and Essex gas divisions supply. The industry began shifting from cast iron to steel about this time, and in addition to the traditional gas welding, PSE&G began the first use of electric welding; that's a Ford Model T engine, driving a generator to power the welder's electrode. While mains range from two to 48 inches in diameter, this is the only 17-inch main in the PSE&G system. See other views of the line on the next two pages.

While such commercial uses of gas became more common during the Public Service Corporation's first decade, it was only after about 1915 that business began to realize the potential of gas. Then, the bread-makers of the State switched from coal to gas in their ovens. The shipbuilders and can companies contracted for large quantities of gas. The newspapers adopted gas to melt down lead bars for conversion into type in their linotype machines. Small commercial enterprises also became a valuable market for gas. Public Service sold gas to delicatessens, barbershops, beauty parlors, cleaners, dyers, hand laundries, tailors, public garages, gasoline stations, and a variety of stores. Such customers used from a few hundred cubic feet of gas per month upwards for heating water, generating steam, hot plates, coffee urns, soup urns, cooking ranges, candy-making machines, hairdressing equipment, pressing machines, sterilizers, Bunsen burners, small industrial furnaces, blowtorches, dryers and other appliances.

Company sales men and women were encouraged to write about their sales in the company house organ. Their writings made interesting reading. Here's a sample:

WHAT THE SACRIFICE OF PART OF MY LUNCH HOUR ACCOMPLISHED.
By Mrs. H.A. Jones,
Floor Saleswoman
Bayonne.

(Mrs. Jones's determination to get at the facts, even at the cost of a little personal inconveninece, helped materially to turn a small sale into a big one. Her good example merits imitation.)

On a hot day in June a consumer called at the office to inquire about a hot plate. Knowing the location and the house in which she resided, I decided to find out why she wanted a hot plate and not a gas range. So I questioned her, and she informed me that they had been using coal for over thirty years and were not particularly in favor of using gas exclusively.

After discussion with her about the advantages of the latter, she was convinced that the argument given was a good one, but, said she, "Oh we haven't the room." On my suggestion she agreed that we take measurements at her home.

On the following day, at my lunch hour, I called and met her with her husband. When we took the measurements we found that by moving the table to another part of the kitchen there was ample room to install a range and water heater. They bought a No. 18-319 Detroit Jewel Cabinet range and a No. 25 Kompak water heater, and also an Iwantu gas iron.

We received word from these people, since the installation was made, that they are very much pleased and cannot imagine how they got along without these appliances for so many years.

In many cases, sales took some doing, as the following example tells us:

OPENING HUBBY'S PORES
—AND EYES.
By A. J. Fleisch,
Hoboken

(Tricks in salesmanship should be avoided, as a rule, but there are exceptions to every rule. Mr. Fleisch tells us interestingly of a sales trick that is not only amusing but absolutely harmless and fully justified. You will note that it met with merited success.)

It may appear unchristianlike to make a fellow being uncomfortable, particularly when a few moments' discomfort meant the changing of a man's habit of several year's standing—but it had to be done in order to sell a cabinet range, and it happened like this:

Mrs. C. looked longingly at the cabinet range display every time she came to the office to pay her gas bill. The floor salesman frequently urged her to install one, and she was extremely desirous of doing so; however, there was a drawback. Mr. C. was it.

Mr. and Mrs. C.'s quarters were limited. The kitchen was the largest room of their old-fashioned apartment, and it contained a very comfortable old couch on which Mr. C. liked to sleep, particularly after dinner on Sundays. There was also a very uncomfortable old coal range, uncomfortable particularly for Mrs. C. in the summer. In order to install a gas range it would be necessary to remove the couch, as the coal range could not be moved, because it was the landlord's, and, besides, it was necessary for heat in the winter.

Mr. C. would not hear of having the couch thrown out, which was what the removal of it meant, because it could not be placed in any other room. So things remained at a standstill until Mrs. C. and the floor salesman developed a little conspiracy against Mr. C. with Mrs. C. as the chief conspirator.

Purposely Mrs. C. remained away from home one Sunday morning, which meant that the usual Sunday dinner was deferred until evening. The cooking, of course, had to be done in the afternoon, during hubby's usual sleeping time. The weatherman evidently joined the conspiracy, for the day was hot. The blazing coal fire within a few feet of the favorite couch made the occupant perspire profusely, and the usual comfortable afternoon's nap was anything but comfortable. When the cooking was done in the morning Mr. C. was always at church, and the heat of the stove was dispelled by afternoon, so that the kitchen was bearable. But trying to sleep in the hot kitchen opened Mr. C.'s eyes, as well as his pores. He realized what it must mean to his wife to be compelled to cook over that hot stove every day, and while this had never come home to him until his own comfort was disturbed, it must be said in his favor that he acknowledged the foolishness of the old-fashioned method of cooking his wife along with the food. The couch was immediately ejected and a cabinet range installed.

N. B.—Mr. C. takes his Sunday afternoon nap on a bed in another room.

Collections were a problem then, as now, and this melodramatic and successful attempt to collect a utility bill was published in a company publication:

CALLING THE BULLY'S BLUFF.

By Mr. Breckenridge.

Mr. W—. owed $287.00 and positively intended to keep on owing it. All reports brought in by men sent to interview him were to the effect that he stood ready, and willing to lick anyone, who cared to call. I called to see him and mentally sized him up as a bluff. At the mention of my business he flew into a rage, called us about everything that he could think of, and offered to throw me out into the middle of the street. All attempts to pacify him, or to turn the subject, met with a fresh outburst. I let him continue until his stock of profanity seemed about exhausted, when I said "Mr. W—, are you through?" His answer was another onslaught, at the close of which, he swore that he would either wipe up the floor with me or put me into the hospital, if I said another word. I calmly took out a cigar, lit it, then, pointing a finger at him, and looking him straight in the eye, said: "Mr. W—, I called to collect this account, and propose to collect it 'Right Now'; when it comes to fight, you will find me not only thoroughly able, but ready as well, and I intend to put you on the floor and step on you, if I hear another word from you." He never said another word, but reached for his check book and paid the account in full. This man only needed someone to call his bluff.

When Public Service opened its new terminal building at 80 Park Place, it allotted valuable space, not just for household appliances "from water heaters and gas ranges to the latest types of room heaters and lighting fixtures," but also for samples of practically every industrial gas appliance when available. The list included laboratory and jeweler's appliances, brazing tables, japanning ovens, bench forges, smoke houses and so on. The utility maintained a large staff to promote such appliances and to help solve industrial fuel problems. This staff regularly devoted showroom and window display space, for a week at a time, to the needs of a single trade, such as plumbing, building and architecture. These efforts apparently succeeded in winning customers, for in 1925 McCarter reported, "The application of gas to industrial processes, which a comparatively few years ago was a negligible quantity, now represents more than 13 per cent of gas consumption, is rapidly developing and has widened extensively the field of service of gas utilities. Combined with the popularity of gas for domestic use, it has largely increased demand and made necessary the extension and improvement of generation and distribution facilities."

The single most important one of these improvements was the completion in 1926 of the Harrison Gas Works, which could then manufacture 30.8 million cubic feet of gas a day, with ample room for expansion. Located on the Passaic River in Harrison, this plant had eight large, hand-clinkered water-gas sets, supplied with steam by four Babcock and Wilcox boilers. The plant also had a battery of waste heat boilers, designed to improve thermal efficiency, which produced 15,000 pounds of steam per hour, per set. Public Service first lighted the fires at Harrison with a small truckload of live coals from the Market Street Gas Works, thus perpetuating the original flame with which the Newark Gas Light Company began manufacturing gas, and which had burned unextinguished since 1847. Harrison embodied all the latest developments in gas plant construction, including the use of the back run process on the water-gas sets (which reduced fuel consumption by about 10 per cent), a liquid purification process, modern coal-and-ash-handling methods, the largest gas-pumping station in the United States, and a number of other labor-saving devices. It was then one of the most efficient and economical gas plants in the nation, extracting 80 per cent of the heating value from the 230,000 pounds of boiler fuel, 730,000 pounds of generator fuel, and 80,000 pounds of gas oil it consumed daily. This naturally made for cheaper gas. At the same time, and with a similar regard for efficiency, Public Service expanded its distribution network, often using welded steel pipe now in place of cast iron.

Another improvement that made for cheaper gas to the consumer was the conversion, at about this time, from gas oil to bunker oil in the company's water-gas sets. Public Service had been "cracking" gas oil—a light, high-grade oil—in its gas carburetors since 1903. The petroleum companies could refine this same oil into automobile gasoline, but for a variety of reasons they had not done so in quantity. Thus, the supply of gas oil had been cheap and plentiful. Then, in the late 1920s, improved refining methods and the increasing popularity of the automobile created a great demand for this oil, driving up its price and making it hard to obtain in large quantities. Public Service met this development by experimenting with a variety of cheaper, heavier oils.

Jack V. Richards, who was then superintendent at Trenton, recalls trying out as many as 35 different types of oil "and when we would come up with something that looked cheaper and usable we would try it in the other plants. We were more or less an experimental plant in the summer time when we were not busy." The experimental bunker oils were so heavy, says Richards, "you had to heat the railroad cars to get it out. In normal weather, you could pretty nearly walk on it." Despite the evident problems in dealing with this new fuel, the gas-makers at Trenton learned to move the bunker oil about (with the help of steam heating lines in the railroad cars and storage tanks), convert it into gas, clean it and dispose of the especially sticky tar residue afterwards. Public Service appears to have been the first utility in the country to adapt this cheap, low-grade oil to gas-making. It substituted bunker oil for gas oil in all its plants, at a substantial saving in fuel costs, in 1930.

Beginning with World War I and continuing through the 1920s, the gas company's industrial by-products business had grown at a surprising and extremely profitable rate. In the old days, most operators had regarded the by-products of gas production as a nuisance, to be burned up or disposed of at little or no return. But by the 1920s, these same operators were carefully collecting and saving tar, ammonia, light oil and other by-products for sale to chemical companies. This lucrative business of course reduced gas production costs for Public Service and, for its customers, gas rates. The war, producing an unprecedented demand for toluol in the manufacture of munitions, had demonstrated the value of these residues. Public Service built plants at Newark, Jersey City, Paterson and Trenton to recover toluol from the gas "drip oil." The toluol, which the utility supplied to the government by the trainload, went to make up trinitrotoluol, the powerful explosive better known at "TNT." After Armistice Day, toluol and hundreds of other coal derivatives were turned to more peaceful purposes, ending up as fertilizer under a South Jersey apple tree, as lacquer in the paint job on that shiny new Ford, as Bakelite in the keys of a typewriter.

Public Service removed the by-products from the gas in several stages. In the condenser, the gas passed through a network of vertical tubes, either inside the tubes with water circulating outside, or outside with water circulating within the tubes. This cooled the gas, causing most of the tar to condense out in the form of a black, molasses-thick liquid. The rest of the tar was removed either electrolytically or by a mechanical tar-extractor. The gas operator recovered the valuable ammonia by either of two methods. He passed the gas through a washer or scrubber consisting of large, revolving plates wetted down with a stream of cold water. In contact with the water, the ammonia gas formed a weak

solution called ammoniacal liquor. Or, he caused the gas to
bubble up through a weak sulphuric acid bath. The
ammonia combined with the acid to form sulphate of
ammonia, which was dried and sold for fertilizer. Finally, the
operator had to remove the hydrogen sulphide from the gas,
to make it fit for general use. If this component were not
removed, the gas would have burned, according to one gas
man, "with a smell like that of burning sulphur, which would,
of course, be intensely disagreeable." For this purpose, the
operator employed the dusty red oxides of iron, mentioned
earlier, in the purifying box. The oxides of iron combined
with the hydrogen sulfide to form sulphide of iron. This
could then be recovered for sale when the red dust was
removed from the purifying box to be revived or reoxyge-
nated, in the open air. The gas industry had also developed a
form of liquid purification, in which a solution of sodium
carbonate absorbed the hydrogen sulphide from the gas.
The gas man could then recover a sulphur sludge of "slurry"
for use in the manufacture of sulphuric acid.

Gas production yielded so many useful by-products that
one gas industry chemist estimated in the late 1920s that 95
per cent of all manufactured articles and chemical products
were derived from, or produced with some compound
originating in, the gas works. Benzol, from the drip oil, was
one of the basic products in all dyes and colors, in paints and
varnishes, in gasoline (to prevent engine "knocking"). Pitch,
from gas-works tar, went into almost all roofs, helped
waterproof highways, and gave trapshooters their "clay"
pigeons. Carbolic acid was the base of all Bakelite products,
and so found its way into fountain-pen barrels, the
mouthpieces of telephones, cigar-holders, and costume
jewelry. Ammonia from the gas plant not only fertilized
South Jersey's apple trees; it also played an important role in
the manufacture of ice.

Working with gas involved a constant danger of asphyxiation. In the plant or on the street, the gas men were always in
close contact with their potentially deadly product. The
repair crewman first located a leak by sniffing at the end of a
metal pipe he had driven into the ground. Then, when he had

Making gas became a wellspring of byproducts. At PSE&G's Camden gas plant coke trucks—the sign on the side says "Orders taken by drivers"—wait to load up in the 1930s. Below, a conveyor piles up ammonium sulphate, for later sale as fertilizer.

dug down to the culprit main, he used his nose again to find the leak's exact source. "He locates his leak," wrote *Public Service News*, "by use of his sense of smell, soap and water (through which the leaking gas bubbled), and good common sense." Common sense would have told most of us to get away from the leak, out of the ditch, and maybe out of the gas business entirely. But the gas men, while respectful of their product, seemed to work around it with little fear or special regard for their own safety. This, though resuscitation methods were primitive and preventive measures downright ridiculous. In an article in *Gas Age* on asphyxiation, one gas man recommended "a nice little bag of juicy apples and a dozen of lemons" as a precaution for men going down into a gas-leak ditch. Each man ate an apple before descending, half a lemon after five minutes of work, and another half when he climbed—or was carried—up for some fresh air. If such witches-scene-from-*Macbeth* type precautions failed, one Public Service rule book recommended the standard resuscitation techniques of the time—plus a nip of brandy as a restorative. Some work crews preferred a particularly sharp German beer for the same purpose and, according to James N. Killgore, a standard first-aid kit in the early years contained iodine, a couple of bandages, and a bottle of Weiss beer.

"The biggest hero in Public Service, as far as I'm concerned, is the man who saved me," said Killgore, who died in April, 1978, at age 95. "I came in one morning and we were right across McCarter Highway from the Front Street gas works. The night men had not left and the day men were coming on and everyone was looking for this terrific gas leak. So I went over to the gas works to see what I could. Our gas mask then was a rubberized bag. You'd fill it with air and pull it over your head and you'd last as long as that air in there lasted. There was an isinglass window to look through. So I had a suspicion where the leak was, and I had them put a rope under my arms, which was not unusual. We did that many times to the men in the gas station. And I put this gas mask on and I kicked the cellar window in at this small building, a valve house. I kicked the cellar window out and turned around and slid down inside. As soon as I got there I saw this plug out of the main, this main was pouring gas out. So I immediately turned to the window, and that's the last I remember. I was really out. And this man pulled me out with the rope. He'd tried to persuade me not to go in there, but I wanted to see. They had to shut off the main valve at the plant to fix it.

"Our method of you might say reviving a man who had been overcome was to give him Weiss beer. That was a German beer. And when I came to, I had Weiss beer coming out of my ears. They poured it down. It was supposed to bring that gas out. I don't know whether it did the trick or whether it was just nature. I couldn't stand the stuff."

What happened, in the absence of resuscitators, when a man overcome by gas went into respiratory failure? "He died," said Killgore.

Explosion and fire were also ever-present dangers. Gas was perfectly safe by itself. Had it been possible to light a match in a holder of gas, the gas itself would have promptly extinguished the flame. The danger occurred when gas mixed with oxygen, with nine parts air to one part gas being the most volatile combination. Then, a spark from a wall switch or a thousand other sources could cause a devastating explosion.

Charles W. Smythe, assistant superintendent of manufacturing, described a typical procedure for avoiding such an occurrence in a 1929 article for *Public Service News:*

"As an example of the elaborate precautions taken, it recently became necessary to take the 15-million-cubic-foot waterless holder in Harrison out of service. With this holder in its lowest position, there remained in it approximately 300,000 cubic feet of gas. In order to make it possible for work to be done, it was necessary to displace this gas under the piston and fill the space with air. Yet at no time could there be a mixture of gas and air. In order to accomplish this transfer of gas to air without getting an explosive mixture, it was necessary to use an inert gas as a medium. An inert gas is one which contains neither oxygen nor combustibles. It will not burn nor will it support combustion. Thus it cannot be

exploded when mixed with gas or air. Such a gas is available in
large quantities at the outlet of a boiler. Boiler waste gases
contain principally carbon dioxide and nitrogen.

In the present instance the inert gas was led in a large pipe
from a boiler outlet through a washer cooler and discharged
to the holder with a compressor. It was fed into the holder
until it had displaced all traces of gas therein. With the space
under the piston full of inert gas, it was then safe to blow air
in, so as to get an atmosphere in which men could work. Four
days and nights were required to complete these operations.

The potential for gas explosions continues to require such
precautions from gas men even today.

"We've gone into many houses and ordered the people out
when the house was full of gas from a leak," says John Allen,
manager of operation in the gas transmission and distribution department. "These things happen every winter. One
recent winter we had three explosions; the winter before
that, one; the winter before that, two. Generally, it is in the
very cold weather, when the windows are shut and for some
reason something breaks and the gas gets into the house.
These situations are very difficult, and it's very difficult to
find the cause.

"Our people are trained to respond where there is a
hazardous situation. They go in, order people out, shut off
the gas, even pull the electricity out to prevent a spark. We
had one a year or so ago. The man ordered everyone out and
everyone went except the owner. He was behind our man
who was standing on the porch, just walking out of the
house, when it exploded. The man behind had flicked one
switch to shut off the lights. There was a spark in the switch
and it ignited the gas in the house. The man was not killed,
but the house was demolished. Our man was injured and so
was the owner. The potential for this kind of situation is
always present, but our people are trained to handle this sort
of thing."

Gas creates what engineers call a "soft explosion." That
means it sort of pushes everything ahead of it, as one Public
Service customer learned the hard way, although he survived
without a scratch. The smell of gas had grown stronger in his

house, he noticed, and after checking to make sure the burners on his kitchen range were off, he called the utility. Before the gas men could get there, though, a neighbor stopped by, caught one whiff of the gas and headed down the cellar. At the foot of the stairs, there being no light switch at their head, he struck a match in order—as he said later—"to locate the source of the leak." He and the owner at once became beneficiaries of the peculiar action of exploding gas. It heaved open the floor over their heads and sent them sailing up through it, as if they had suddenly became lighter-than-air craft, and out through the now rapidly vanishing walls of the house. Again, the building was demolished, but the two men landed unharmed, if a trifle dizzy, in the shrubbery.

From the viewpoint of a Public Service employee, Irwin F. Kreismer's most vivid memory of his years with the gas company also involves an explosion, though not of gas.

"It was Friday, the third week in May, 1950," wrote Kreismer, a service inspector in New Brunswick, in a letter for inclusion in this history. "The time was 7:26 p.m. I was the supervisor starting standby duty in the now defunct South Amboy District of the Gas Distribution Department. The weather was warm and a slight drizzle was falling. It was the night of the Junior Prom for Saint Mary's High School. All signs pointed to a quiet standby. I sat reading my paper completely relaxed. Out in the Raritan Bay, off South Amboy, a freighter was taking on a load of anti-personnel mines. The hands of the clock moved to 7:27 p.m. At that instant a terrific roar, followed by a sharp crack, filled the air. My front door moved in two inches. I ran to the door and looked toward the bay where what looked like a cloud from an atomic explosion was rapidly rising. I knew something big had happened but I did not know what.

"My first thought was, why did it have to happen on my standby. I ran to my car and headed down Bordentown Avenue toward the Gas Shop. As I approached Feltus Street where the shop was located, I saw a crowd of bleeding people coming up Bordentown Avenue heading for the hospital. By this time all hell had broken out. Sirens were screaming, fire

Frederick A. Lydecker, right, vice president in charge of gas operation, turns the valve on a new 42-inch main at the Market Street Gas Works in Newark early in 1954. Henry Whitcomb Nicolson, general superintendent of gas distribution, is at left. The new main brought more gas to the growing Essex and Morris County areas of New Jersey.

engines, police cars and ambulances were racing in all directions. When I reached Feltus Street the police parted the crowd and yelled, 'Here comes Public Service, let him through!' I felt like a hero in spite of, as yet, not having done anything. I reached the shop, unlocked the gate and rode in. Fortunately the shop was in a hollow and had not been touched by what I now knew to have been the explosion of the munitions ship. I rode out through the town and assessed the damage. It was incredible. I don't think there was an unbroken pane of glass in any of the buildings. All the stores along Broadway were smashed and fires were burning at the practically demolished Jersey Central Power and Light generating plant, which was hit hard. All power in the town was out.

"Back at the shop I reported the situation to E. Moke, superintendent of our parent shop, New Brunswick, and told him our men were reporting in without having to be called and at the moment we were in good shape because the explosion had done no damage to the underground facilities. But all pilot lights in town had blown out and calls of leaks were starting to pour in. Jay Oliver, the general foreman in charge of South Amboy, came in, but his home had been wrecked and he was bleeding from a dozen cuts from flying glass. I told him to go home and I would call him if he was needed. As leak calls were coming into City Hall, as well as the Shop, I sent men to work there as well. The men raced around the town like cowboys taking care of the calls almost as fast as they came in. Two men stayed at the shop at the phones. The town was sealed off by the police and it was days before the outside world knew what was happening inside South Amboy. The mayor called in the Army, who patrolled the streets to prevent looting, and it was reported that 22 men vanished in that explosion and several more died later. Our men in the South Amboy Shop at that time were new and in their 20s and did a magnificient job holding the fort. In about two days we had our situation under control, but it was a long time before South Amboy returned to normal. This was one standby I will never forget."

Pipeline Gas Arrives

"The pots are burned ... the canary died–it must have been the natural gas."

—New Natural Gas Customer

Man has known of and—off and on—has employed natural gas since at least 2,000 years ago, when the Chinese piped it through hollow bamboo reeds so they could use the gas flame to evaporate sea water for its salt. Before the Christian era, pilgrims from India were said to have worshipped "eternal fires" in the area around the Caspian Sea. In Delphi, Greece, an oracle became famous for communicating with an unknown substance the Greeks thought to be godlike. Probably it was natural gas. In this country, commercial use of natural gas began in Fredonia, New York, where, in 1821, Willaim A. Hart, a gunsmith, discovered a concentration of natural gas just 17 feet below the surface. Hart transported the gas via hollowed-out logs and, later, lead pipes, and used it to light several local buildings, including Abell House, the Fredonia stop on the stagecoach line between New York City and Buffalo. The inn became famous for its brilliant light. When one visitor, the Marquis de Lafayette, of Revolutionary War fame, wondered how such lighting was possible, he was informed that it came from a mysterious source underground. The Marquis

By the middle of the 1920s Public Service had extended its gas mains to 3,500 miles, one of the largest systems in the world, and continued to build the system, selling such gas appliances as this Kompak hot water heater, offered in 1926.

replied that he had better leave Fredonia in a hurry, as the place was evidently connected with hell itself.

In fact, natural gas, composed mainly of methane or ethane, is somewhat more mundane in origin. According to the most widely accepted theory, primitive animal and plant life, on dying, was gradually covered with sand and soil, which later turned to rock. Under continuous heat and pressure, the organic material became oil and gas. Early drillers often found petroleum and natural gas together, and, not realizing the value of gas, usually let it escape into the air to be wasted. Fredonia, the site of the country's first gas well, was also the home of the first company to employ gas for profit. The Fredonia Natural Gas Light Company began piping gas to customers in the area in 1858. But most gas utilities, including the predecessors of Public Service, continued to depend on manufactured gas. Indeed, it would be almost a century before Public Service would purchase its first natural gas. Why the delay? For one thing, gas men did not then know how to produce the high pressure—normally about 800 pounds, but up to 1,500 pounds per square inch today—needed to transport the gas over the long distances from the drilling field to the customer utility. Besides, the brittle cast-iron and lead pipes then available could not have withstood such high pressures.

The industry began to solve these problems after World War I, and, over the next two decades, more and more utilities made the switch, either mixing natural with manu-factured gas at the gas works, or sending straight natural gas out to their customers. But Public Service continued to find it profitable to manufacture gas in spite of severe, albeit temporary, shortages of new material—first of coal and later of gas oil. Among other considerations that influenced the decision to defer the switch to natural gas, the utility had a large investment in gas-manufacturing equipment. It could not afford to scrap or "mothball" that entire investment, although, in the interests of economy, it had in the late 1930s retired several outdated plants. Moreover, the manufactur-ing plant, which Public Service had steadily expanded through the 1920s and 1930s, had thus far proved adequate to meet demand. The utility did not then need natural gas. The delay had other advantages, for when Public Service finally switched to natural gas, it knew of and could avoid many of the problems that troubled the natural-gas pioneers.

That switch came after World War II, when industrial and domestic demand for gas suddenly mushroomed. Public Service had been promoting gas for home and commercial heating since at least 1925, when it first organized a house-heating department. But that business had grown slowly through the late 1920s and The Depression, with only a few score or, in good years, a few hundred installations annually. By 1937, the gas department had just 5,000 building-heating customers, 84 per cent of them homeowners, the rest industries and businesses. Then came World War II, bringing with it shortages of both coal and heating oil— shortages which, because of the economy and much-advertised "cleanness" of gas (compared with coal), also brought Public Service thousands of home-heating customers. The gas department had not stood still before or during the War. It had completed a costly rebuilding program at its West End Works, and had added a second and then a third battery of 37 ovens to the Camden coke works. It had gradually doubled, to 60 million cubic feet a day, the gas-manufacturing capacity of Harrison. But these improvements were not enough to meet the "tremendous" growth in demand after the War. Public Service then took several other steps toward expansion, including the installation of liquid petroleum facilities at its plant and holder stations around the State. These facilities consisted of large tanks containing liquified butane or propane, which was released, heated and vaporized, and mixed with air to obtain a predetermined BTU value. Public Service used liquid petroleum gas only in extremely cold weather, to supplement the supply of gas for heating. But this added capability also was not enough to meet demand.

Public Service, though it had considered and rejected natural gas only a few years before, now found it advantageous to tap this "outside" source of energy. It contracted with several natural-gas transmission companies for large quantities of natural gas, not only for delivery directly to customers in a pure state but also for mixing with manufactured gas in winter and, in summer when demand plummeted, as a boiler fuel in the Electric and Gas Company's electric generating stations. If "obtained in sufficient quantity and at a reasonable price," the natural gas would, said Public Service, "largely replace enriching oil, which is very difficult to obtain and which is now one of the most costly components of manufactured gas, and it would defer certain capital expenditures for new gas plant facilities." The utility began receiving a daily supply of 4.5 million cubic feet of natural gas on July 12, 1949, from the "Big Inch" pipeline of the Texas Eastern Transmission Corporation. A year later, the 1,840-mile Texas-to-New York pipeline of the Transcontinental Gas Pipe Line Corporation went into service. Public Service had contracted with Transcontinental for 70 million cubic feet of natural gas a day. With this supply, it gradually substituted natural gas for bunker oil in the carburetor stage of its gas-manufacturing process. Natural gas was soon the major raw material in the production of gas. As the heating business grew, Public Service purchased ever larger quantities of natural gas from the two pipeline companies. In 1953, it succeeded in obtaining natural gas for underground storage for use during the winter peak, a move the company considered important to guarantee an adequate and economical supply of gas. It first received gas, 67 million cubic feet of it a day, from the storage pool at Oakford, Pennsylvania, in the winter of 1954-55. Public Service "deposited" natural gas at the storage pool in the summer, when its daily supply of gas far exceeded demand, and "withdrew" it in winter, when demand exceeded supply. The storage pool held far more gas than could any of the Public Service gas holders, the largest of which had a capacity of only 15 million cubic feet. Also in 1953, Public Service contracted with a third pipeline company, the Tennessee Gas Transmission Company, for delivery of 30 million cubic feet of gas a day.

At about this time, Public Service was gradually increasing the heating value of its gas from 525 to 650 BTU. This enabled the utility "to serve present customers more efficiently and to accommodate additional customers and increased loads by materially increasing the effective capacity of Public Service distribution lines ... "Among other important improvements of the early 1950s, Public Service experimented successfully with the cyclic catalytic reforming gas unit, which was to replace the water-gas. The first such unit, installed at Paterson in 1952, produced 11 million cubic feet of gas a day. Because the catalytic reforming set, which cracked a kerosene-like oil, was so much less costly than the standard water-gas set, Public Service in 1954 installed three of the new sets at its plants and converted one water-gas set to catalytic reforming operation. It thus obtained needed production capacity at "a significant saving in capital outlay."

In 1955, Public Service for the first time bypassed its manufacturing plants and sent straight natural gas out to customers in remote locations. Its aim was to avoid the capital expenditure that would otherwise have been required to construct mains from gas plants to outlying load centers and to install added manufacturing and pumping capacity. The utility found it cheaper that first year to convert 38,000 customers to straight natural gas, even though that conversion required the building of five natural gas metering and pressure-reducing stations. This was the start of a 10-year effort that would bring straight natural gas to all Public Service customers and that would reduce the once-essential gas works to a supplementary role.

In making the conversion, Public Service could not simply substitute natural for manufactured gas in its mains. Natural gas was cleaner, drier, and richer than its manufactured counterpart; it yielded 1,040 BTU per cubic foot *versus* the 650 BTU value of manufactured gas of that era. But these were not unmitigated advantages. The greater heating value of natural gas allowed Public Service to send out more energy without increasing the size of its pipes, but it also forced the utility to embark on the herculean task of readjusting every last orifice on every burner owned by each of its approximately 1,300,000 customers.

"You had to go to every single appliance when you

converted," recalls John Allen. "You had to replace all the orifices; every burner on every stove had to be readjusted. Natural gas burns differently. It turned yellow and the flame burned a little higher and we had to turn it down. We had to get into every house. We also had to replace the gas in the pipe that was out in the street."

Public Service introduced natural gas slowly, neighborhood by neighborhood. "Anything that could happen did," says Allen. "You put natural gas in at one end of the main and you waited at the other end for natural gas to come through, and nothing happened. This would be at maybe five in the morning. The next thing, you'd find yourself coming back along the line to see how far the natural gas got and why it didn't get to where it was supposed to. In some cases we would have to go back and find out where natural gas was burning and where manufactured gas was burning, house by house. Sometimes we'd find a blockage under a railroad, where there was a pipe full of water we weren't aware of, or a valve closed someplace. At other times we found that when we brought one section in, the section alongside of it started to come in, too. And we'd find that a piece of pipe had been tied in many years ago and the foreman had forgotten to make a sketch, so we had no record of it. Sometimes it would take weeks to straighten out an industrial customer because their equipment wouldn't burn properly."

Unlike the carbureted water gas from the manufacturing plants, natural gas was dry, and this also caused problems in the mains and in the gas meters. Each meter contained a leather diaphragm that worked like a set of lungs, inhaling gas from the main and exhaling it into pipes that carried it to the kitchen and elsewhere. The diaphragm, which also measured the gas, had to remain pliable to work properly. For this purpose, the gas men carefully selected sheepskins, preferring those from New Zealand, where there were no barbed-wire fences or briars to cut the skins and thus make defects in the finished leather. In the 1920s, Public Service was using 27,272 perfect sheepskins to manufacture 150,000 diaphragms a year. Then came natural gas.

"The manufactured gas was saturated," says Allen. "It had water in it from the steam process, and that kept all our joints in the mains wet and the leather diaphragms in the meters moist. But as natural gas came in, the leather started to dry out and it would crack. The other problem was the joints in the cast-iron mains would dry out, too. The joints were made of jute and cement, and as these joints dried out, we started to get leaks.

"We might have been a little bit behind the industry in going to natural gas, but we had the same problems, and knew the tried solutions. So we started to introduce water into our system to keep the joints and the diaphragms wet..."

Natural gas was also odorless, making it undetectable when it leaked. The problem was solved by chemically odorizing the gas. Asked about other problems, Allen recalls that "people considered natural gas different. It cooked differently; the water wouldn't boil as fast, or it would boil too fast. Pots burned, people said. We had many, many legal claims as we went along: 'The pots are burned, the man dirtied my house, the canary died—it must have been the natural gas.' It was an interesting and difficult time because you got all kinds of complaints. Nuisance claims were tremendous.

"But natural gas permitted us a tremendous amount of growth. There was no way we could manufacture the quantity of gas that was required for the development of house heating and that sort of thing. Plus, it did one other thing. If a cubic foot has 1,000 BTU in it, instead of 600, you are transporting more energy. So it increased the capacity of our pipes and saved us from having to rebuild or expand our system."

By 1960, natural gas amounted to 59 per cent of the utility's total "send-out," with mixed, or manufactured, gas making up only 41 per cent. Natural gas then supplied about 97 per cent of the thermal content of all gas sold by Public Service. The company had continued to build natural gas metering and pressure-reducing stations around the State. These unmanned stations sent out a continuous flow of gas directly to the customer at one of four pressures, depending on the distance of the transmission: 120 pounds per square inch, 60 pounds, 15 pounds, or a quarter-pound—the last being the most common utilization pressure. At the metering station, the gas was also scrubbed of extraneous grit, and it was heated so that the refrigerating effect that occurred when the gas underwent a drastic reduction in pressure would not freeze the ground and water pipes at the station outlet. The temperature of the gas dropped six degrees Fahrenheit for every 100-pound drop in pressure, so a freeze would otherwise have been quite possible. At the metering station, the gas was also humidified with moisture and fogged with an oil or glycol spray to keep it partially saturated. In addition to keeping joints and diaphragms moist, this prevented the carrying of dust into appliances.

Natural gas went system-wide in 1965. Manufactured gas was then no longer essential and was, moreover, comparatively expensive. That year, Public Service terminated its 48-year-old contract for the purchase of coke-oven gas from the Koppers Company. Citing "the virtual disappearance of the market for domestic coke, and the uncertainty of the market for metallurgical coke," as well as the availability of natural gas, Public Service had already scrapped its Camden coke plant. The Market Street Gas Works was also gone. But unlike many other gas utilities, Public Service did not abandon gas manufacturing entirely. As early as the mid-1950s, some gas men had suggested that natural gas would not always be cheap and abundant, and that the manufacturing plants could again become necessary. When regular gas manufacturing ceased at Harrison and the five other gas works, Public Service therefore kept these plants on line, assigning them "peak shaving status." They would manufacture gas to supplement the supply of natural gas on days of peak demand—that is, on the coldest days of winter. On such days, the gas men would add to the natural gas to make a mixture that was 10 to 20 per cent manufactured gas. The mixed and straight natural gases burned identically.

Public Service made other important improvements as it moved to all-natural operation. It had switched from cast

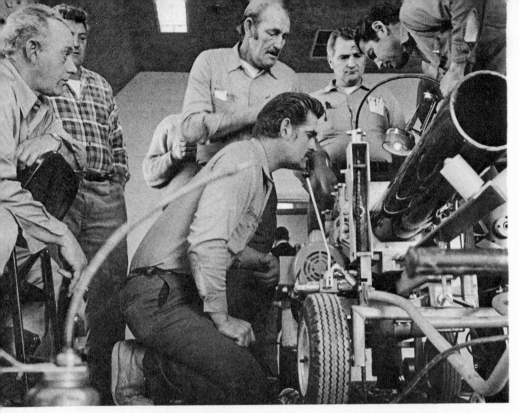

PSE&G work crews learn a new technique for cutting and fusing plastic gas mains, for insertion in existing but aging iron and steel street mains.

iron to all-steel pipe in replacing damaged mains and in laying new mains. The steel was stronger, lighter, and less brittle, allowing the use of high pressure in transmission. In the 1970s, Public Service began using all-plastic piping, which was cheaper and could be installed with less digging by, for instance, running it through existing, but damaged, metal mains. Plastic, however, also presented problems.

"There is a difference between plastics that have water in them and plastics that have gas in them," says Allen. "Many people felt you could use garden-hose type plastic and put gas in it. One company that I know of jumped into plastics right in the very beginning and ended up with serious problems. Up until very recently there was no system we would accept 100 per cent. There were brittle failures, failures of joining, and other failures. We were very careful that we did not use anything but the best plastic for our mains. Another thing is, we still have the manufacturing capability and there are some hydrocarbons in a manufactured gas which will affect plastic if it is not of high quality.

Another important improvement was the development of a liquid natural gas storage facility in the meadowlands of Bergen County. In the 1960s, Public Service contracted with the Transcontinental Gas Pipe Line Corporation, owner of the facility, for as much as 120 million cubic feet of gas a day for winter "peak-shaving." By liquefying natural gas at 259 degrees below zero, Transcontinental could condense and store in five acres gas that would otherwise have filled 67 conventional gas holders, each with a capacity of 15 million cubic feet, occupying 300 acres. This was just one more means of guaranteeing that home heating gas would be available when the temperature dropped.

The predicted, or at least suspected, end to natural gas abundance came in 1969. "The Company has been experiencing increasing difficulty in acquiring the additional natural gas supply needed for future load growth," Public Service reported that year. "It has been, and probably will be for the next few years, necessary to rely to an increasing extent on more expensive sources of supply such as underground storage, liquefied natural gas, and liquid petroleum gas to meet the large estimated peak-day growths."

In 1971, PSE&G charged in a press release that the failure of federal agencies to stimulate exploration for natural gas had created a supply shortage that would ultimately cost New Jersey consumers millions.

"The wellhead price for gas set by the Federal Power Commission is just too low to encourage exploration by gas producers," said Edward R. Eberle, who was then president of PSE&G. "The lack of tax incentives and the reluctance of the Department of the Interior to sell leases on federal lands in areas where gas is known to be has also contributed to the supply shortage. As a result, Public Service and other utilities have had to turn to other means of supply, such as importing liquefied natural gas and manufacturing synthetic gas from petroleum products. Both of these alternatives will require the investment of large sums by Public Service to build the needed facilities."

It took several years for the federal government to begin offering enough incentive to stimulate exploration.

In the meantime, PSE&G decided to build the nation's first synthetic natural gas (SNG) plant in Harrison, N.J. It went into service in March, 1973. Another SNG plant, with a capacity five times that of the Harrison plant, went into operation in Linden, N.J. late in 1974. This plant can produce 120 million cubic feet of gas daily and 10 per cent of it goes to Elizabethtown Gas Company.

This marked the return of manufacturing to a vital role in gas supply, though not in a form that gas veterans would find familiar. In the SNG unit, naphtha—a petroleum "feedstock" —reacted over a nickel catalyst with steam and hydrogen to yield a high-BTU gas that, like natural gas, consisted mainly of methane. The gas-maker observed the four-stage production and purification process on dials and charts in a control room, and from there he enriched the synthetic natural gas with a propane gas to bring it up from 985 BTU per cubic foot to the level of natural gas and sent it out into the distribution system.

As the natural gas difficulties worsened into a shortage,

with restrictions on, and even interruptions of, service to industrial and commercial customers, Public Service took other, more extreme measures to secure gas for its territory. For the first time, it bypassed the gas exploration and transmission companies and began to search for gas on its own.

PSE&G established the Energy Development Corporation, investing $7.5 million in this aggressive new corporate arm. The investment, admittedly, looked like a long shot at the time but it produced two successful wells within the record time—for a type of endeavor that rarely scores so fast—of a single year. Public Service delivered its own gas to the State for the first time on June 13, 1974. EDC has not always been successful in its search, of course. Recently, the PSE&G subsidiary and two partner corporations spent $350,000 drilling at an ideal site in the Gulf of Mexico. It came up dry. In fact, the industry average for striking gas or oil in exploratory wells is only 10 to 15 per cent. EDC's record is a respectable 29 per cent, through 1977. When development wells are included, EDC's average is well over 40 per cent.

In one of the other developments in gas supply, Public Service is today drilling for gas not just in the Gulf, but in a garbage landfill in South Jersey. At the site in Camden County and at other landfills, the garbage you threw out last year—steak bones, potato skins, barely-touched lima beans—is turning, via a process called anaerobic decomposition, into methane gas. In the past, this methane was merely a nuisance, migrating to neighboring properties, where it killed plants and created the threat of an explosion. But with the coming of the gas shortage, PSE&G engineers began to wonder if they could tap this troublesome gas supply and put it to profitable use. After much study with a gas chromatograph and other tools of the trade, it appears that they can. David Leich, a senior engineer in the gas planning department, says: "From the information we have now, if we got usable gas out of all the landfills in the company's territory, we could get enough gas to meet between three and five per cent of our annual requirements. And that's not bad. And at

20 cents a therm (a unit of heat measurement), let's say, we're figuring it could be worth between $10 and $18 million annually."

In 1972, Eascogas LNG, Incorporated, now a subsidiary of Public Service, filed an application with the Federal Power Commission for authorization to import LNG from Algeria over a 22-year period. The gas was to be delivered to tanks in Staten Island and resold to PSE&G, Elizabethtown Gas Company, New Jersey Natural Gas Company and South Jersey Gas Company. Today, almost six years later, not a drop of gas has yet been imported and the project is in limbo. The Arab oil embargo and the resultant dramatic increase in oil prices, plus a lack of prompt and decisive action by federal agencies, led the Algerians to withdraw their original proposal. An attempt is being made to restructure the project, but no progress can be made until a federal policy with regard to LNG importation, now under active consideration, is established.

On another front, Energy Development Corporation is going ahead with its participation in oil and gas drilling projects in the Atlantic Ocean.

James B. Randel, Jr., president of EDC, says that successful development of the potential oil and gas reserves off the East Coast could take a minimum of three to four years and as long as five to seven years. He notes that the time required will depend on how long it will take to secure drilling permits and on the availability of drilling rigs and platforms.

If the gas shortage has challenged PSE&G engineers and demanded innovation from them, it has caused some losses for the company and its territory.

One of the most lamented of these losses—albeit a minor one compared with the loss of profits and jobs—is the State-ordered shutdown, in PSE&G's 75th anniversary year of 1978, of all surviving gas streetlamps. The State Board of Public Utility Commissioners has labeled gas lights an economic misuse and ordered their elimination by June 30, 1978. Originally, the ruling affected 15 communities in PSE&G territory with 2,726 gas streetlamps—South Orange,

1,410; Glen Ridge, 666, East Orange, 319; West Orange, 103; Morris Township, 69; Riverton, 52; Trenton, 45; Palmyra, 18; Roseland, 15; Bloomfield, 11; Essex Fells, 5; Jersey City, 4; Verona, 4; Montclair, 3 and Morristown, 2. Statewide, the ruling could douse forever, in 36 municipalities, 4,700 lights.

Under the Board's ruling, however, exemptions to maintain a fragile umbilicus to the past will be available if a changeover to electricity would cause "a severe economic hardship."

As this is written, South Orange, East Orange, and Glen Ridge have already received exemptions and other towns have applied. One of the municipal applicants is West Orange where, ironically, one of the gas streetlights which could succumb stands in Llewellyn Park outside the home of the man who did more than anyone else to seal the fate of gaslight, Thomas Alva Edison.

At their zenith, in 1914, there had been 300,000 gas lights on streets across America, but as electricity began to overtake them they winked out one by one until now only the last few linger on. As far back as 1926, Newark had begun the handwriting on the wall that now dooms even those few by removing its street gas lights from service entirely.

Ultimately they will all go. Electricity will be cheaper, if less pleasant, and the gas thereby freed for other uses will be sufficient to heat about 300 homes a year. Thus will pass the gas department's last visible connection with its origins as a lighting company. And with it will go that "domestic radiance fit to eat by," that "old mild lustre" which Robert Lewis Stevenson so prized, and so many New Jerseyites have continued to prize ever since.

Post World War I Power

In the generating plants ... the superintendents ordered extra grain alcohol to clean their machines. "You mixed it with juniper berries, drank it, and breathed on the machines."
—Recollection of an engineer

For those who still doubted it, World War I had proved the advantages of electricity, particularly as generated by the large economical, and readily adaptable, central station. Public Service and other utilities in the heavily industrial east had delivered the power, according to *Electrical World*, despite "unprecedented obstacles like enormous increases in load, scarcity of good fuel, slow deliveries of new equipment, shortage of good labor and high operating expenses... "Now," McCarter reported in 1919, the company's enlarged generating capacity was being "absorbed by other industrial activities as rapidly as it was released from war work." The demand not only increased, he said, but it was now concentrated in a shorter workday, as plants cut back from round-the-clock operation to an eight or ten-hour day. At the same time, demand for electricity in the home increased enormously. Public Service that year installed 26,000 new meters, more than 90 per cent of them of the smallest size available. William Redshaw could remember the first electric appliances his company had powered back in the industry's pioneer days: Two light bulbs inside a cylinder of perforated tin to warm the feet, and a single bulb in a cocoa can for that aching back. But now such major appliances as the refrigerator, the washing machine, vacuum cleaners, radios and phonographs—all often purchased from the Electric Company's own commercial department—were becoming popular and taking their share of the company's generating capacity. Said *Electrical World:*

> "Power, in the form of electricity, has worked an economic revolution in this country. It has removed from the shoulders of our people a great burden of physical labor and by increasing production it has brought about a wider distribution of wealth, has released the services of thousands of workmen to new industries and has cut down necessary hours of human toil.
> "As a social force it has introduced a new standard of living in American homes, has turned what were once luxuries to be enjoyed only by the rich into necessities which it helps to put at the command of everyone and is constantly creating new luxuries that will, in time, become necessities.
> It has banished household drudgery and has given to our women a freedom which constitutional and legislative enactments were incapable of bestowing."

In the prosperous years following the war, the combined demands of home and business severely strained the facilities of the Electric Company. The coal situation, after a brief improvement in 1919, worsened drastically in 1920. A miners' strike the previous year had already depleted the utility's coal reserve, and with the combination in 1920 of a severe winter, a railroad strike, and a six-month-long shortage of coal cars, Public Service was very nearly unable to meet its day-to-day requirements. Again it bought coal on the open market, paying as much as $17.50 a ton. Even then McCarter reported, "It was only through appeals to the Interstate Commerce Commission, resulting in ordering assigned cars, that this and other public utilities were enabled to continue operations." Public Service subsequently purchased 600 railroad cars to guarantee delivery of coal in the future. But there were other, even more costly problems at home—problems that forced the utility to turn away would-be customers and, at times, to shut down industries that were already customers.

"The entire system cried out for relief in all its parts," wrote Rollin N. Conwell, in his in-house history of the Electric Company. "Requests for distribution reinforcement were coming in from every direction. Installation of generation in large amounts was an obvious necessity. Both programs required rearrangement and rebuilding of substations and an entirely new transmission development."

The 13,200-volt network was still the utility's main transmission system and it was not adequate. Company engineers had regarded this network, upon its completion, as the ultimate in transmission capacity, with the result, according to one company report, that they "put most of the engineering thought into the building of substations and stations, paying less attention to the relation of the transmission between . . . " Because of this emphasis, the report, which was published in 1916, concluded: "The rapid development of the territory, service, regulation and economy are suffering." Public Service had begun to correct this situation, establishing its first 26,000-volt circuit between Elizabeth and Metuchen in 1917. But the war had delayed needed development, so that only a few other such lines were now in operation. In the years after the Armistice, following much careful study, Public Service committed itself to improving its transmission and distribution networks along two lines. It would construct a 132,000-volt transmission system and convert all its circuits from one or two-phase to three-phase service. Both improvements would allow the company to send out significantly more power while minimizing expensive and unnecessary right-of-way problems. The three-phase conversion involved some changes in wiring and in substation set-up, as well as the installation of a third copper circuit on the armatures of the utility's generators. This was like adding extra cylinders to the engine of an automobile, according to one company engineer; it made possible the transmission of more power, more smoothly.

Of electrical developments during this period, *Public Service News* in 1922 reported:

"For several years past, and particularly during the war period, customers were added so rapidly to the distribution system that the lines as well as the transformers and voltage-regulating apparatus became heavily loaded. Financial conditions, and the difficulty of securing prompt delivery of apparatus, made it impossible to keep pace with the growth in load, with the result that the overloaded condition still obtains in many sections.

"An appropriation of over $400,000 is included in this year's budget for the purpose of relieving single-phase and two-phase lighting and power circuits.

"This circuit relief can in many cases be secured most economically through the change of the circuits from 2,400-volt, two-phase to 4,000-volt three-phase service, which gives approximately 50 per cent more capacity with the same amount of copper in the lines.

"Conduit work (underground wiring) in the various municipalities which was deferred because of the financial situation and the pressure of war work, has been practically resumed.

"Automatic (that is unmanned) railway substations which have been under development for several years past are now commercially practicable, and the company, in line with its usual progressive policy, has appropriated funds for the building of automatic substations at Newark, Leonia and Plainsboro."

Public Service also further expanded its larger central stations following the war, replacing what survived of the original installation at Marion with modern machinery, quadrupling the capacity of Essex, and enlarging Burlington to six times its 1914 output. It installed up-to-date coal-handling equipment at all three plants, and it applied modern methods to even the smallest details of operation. At this time, for instance, it pioneered development of a method for destroying algae in condenser tubes.

During the expansion of Essex, Darrow Sage had his first face-to-face encounter with McCarter, who was then taking considerable interest in the Electric Company:

"The one time I had to deal with him was when we were expanding Essex and building a brick wall for the number four, five, and six machines, and we were building the wall up high, 50 or 60 feet. I was out in the yard looking over the ash situation. The ashes would accumulate so fast I would have a terrible time getting rid of them. We would pile them up as high as we could, and then we would hire a contractor to come and haul them away, and that cost a lot of money. I was out estimating how long we could run before we would have to have a contractor to haul the ashes away, when I saw this limousine driven by a uniformed chauffeur fly by me. I looked a second time and there I saw that Tom McCarter was riding in it alone, and I said, 'Holy smoke, I got to follow him up and see that he doesn't get into trouble.' I was on foot, of course, and when I got down to him he was walking underneath that stone wall. And, you know, the masons when they get a cull, a short brick or something that isn't right, they just throw it over the wall. They don't pay any attention. And I had visions of one of the masons throwing a broken brick and hitting Tom McCarter in the head with it. And I rushed over alongside of him and said, 'My name's Sage, Mr. McCarter. I'm the superintendent here, and I don't think you ought to walk as close to the wall as that.' He said, 'In my stations I'll walk any place I feel like.' So I said, 'All right,' and I sung out, 'Look out overhead and don't throw any culls down, look out and don't throw any culls down.' And we walked the whole length of the wall. Then he said, 'What have you got to say about the station?' We talked a little bit about how I like how the machines were connected up, and the foundation, and all that sort of thing that the engineer must know about. Then he got in his car and drove home. That was the longest conversation I ever had with him. But he knew me after that. After he retired and I retired, we met down in Red Bank one day, accidentally. And he said, 'I know you. You're the fellow that didn't want me hit with a brick.' We sat down and talked for about ten minutes; it was a warm day like this, and we went into some bar for a cold beer. Then he got up and went home. But he did remember the incident."

Darrow Sage, reminiscing in front of the Essex Generating Station.

Though, at 97, Sage himself drinks nothing more potent than a good sherry, he often speaks of bars and of the occasional "jamboree booze" when he recalls the prosperous 1920s at Public Service. Few if any of the Electric Company's managers could have stood the headlong pace then had they been steady drinkers. And in the generating plants, where carelessness could be fatal, Sage and other superintendents insisted on sobriety. (As a superintendent, in fact, Sage, a former Navy man, was known for his strictness and, according to the Newark *Evening News*, for "his excellent powers of expression, having the ability to sum up a situation in a few colorful words and leave no question as to his meaning." "That means profanity," Sage notes happily. The "skipper," as Sage's colleagues called him, barked orders like a captain from his bridge, and once, finding his plant less than shipshape, directed all hands to turn to and "clean and sweep down fore and aft.") But once or twice a year, perhaps after they had fought it out with McCarter over the extent of the next year's expansion program, several of the Electric Company's leading engineers would head for a saloon. This now-and-again propensity to drink may have been a leftover from the electric industry's early years, when, as James Lawson later wrote,

> "A good handy man would trim lamps, help string wire and fire the boilers at night, except for the time he might be called on to shoot trouble or solicit business. He helped make out the bills and did the collecting and—the drinking. This last was an important duty, for he was expected to spend (money) over the bar when he collected from the saloonkeepers."

Saloons were big customers of the electric business then, and it must have been hard for a young man to maintain both the good will of the bartender and his own sobriety, especially in a place like Hoboken, the mile-square city, which in 1903 had 360 bars and beer gardens. One survivor of that period later recalled to *Public Service News:*

> "The writer was then employed as a collector and meter reader. Considerable interest and color were given to the work due to the fact that the company was just changing from a flat monthly rate to a meter rate. Customers had been accustomed to using lights all they wanted for a given fixed charge per lamp per month. When meters were installed, it took a little time for the customers to realize that each hour that a lamp burned cost them more money.
> "Collecting money from a saloonkeeper, who had burned current all day and most of the night on a flat rate and who found that on a meter basis his bills were doubled, offered a fine opportunity for one to exercise his utmost ability as a collector."

Saloons and later, presumably, speakeasies were still good customers after World War I. They did not use "liberal intensities of light," *Electrical World* noted, but they burned what lights they had an average of 19 hours a day. Public Service thus had good reason to oppose Prohibition. Moreover, many of the men who had started out by collecting bills from local saloons now ran the Electric Company. The utility's attitude toward the Eighteenth

Amendment came out in several ways. McCarter himself called Prohibition "a sham and a farce," and, though a lifelong Republican, supported Al Smith, the pro-Repeal Democrat, for president in 1928. In the generating plants, somewhat less publicly, the superintendents ordered extra grain alcohol to clean their machines. ("You mixed it with juniper berries, drank it, and breathed on the machines," one engineer recalls.) Finally, Darrow Sage tells this story about a happy collision between Public Service and the rumrunners:

"I always got into the station (Essex, that is) between eight and fifteen minutes past eight, driving down from Short Hills. One foggy morning I had just gotten to my office on the fifth floor when someone called me on the phone and said, 'There are a bunch of gangsters down here on the dock and they have driven us off with loaded guns and we can't operate the coal car.' I said, 'What do you mean, gangsters?' They said, 'Four or five men, they all have guns and they say no one must come on the (coal) barges and no one must come on that end of the dock.' So I went down to the dock and a fellow came over and said, 'Sorry, we are not going to let you on the dock or on the barges for about an hour.' This was during Prohibition. 'One of our rum-runners has crashed into one of your coal barges and is sinking,' he said, 'and we've got it full of Scotch and we are putting it on the barge now and we are having another motor boat come to take it off in about an hour. We are going to take possession of the dock and if you don't like it we'll kill you.'

"So I figured I could stop coal handling for an hour. It wouldn't bother anybody. I thought, *This is pretty serious, I'd better call my boss, Jake Barron.* And he said, 'What do you want to tell me that for? I don't want to know anything like that. Now that you've told me I've got to do something about it.' So in a few minutes the fire department arrived, the ambulances arrived, the reporters arrived, the Prohibitionists arrived, and a lot of other people. Seventy-five people were down there within a half hour and the chief of the fire department walks over and says, 'Shut everything down.' I said, 'Chief, there isn't anything wrong inside. I'm not going to shut anything down.' He said, 'When I give an order everything is going to be shut down, everything is going to be shut down.' And I said, 'As long as I've got a license and nothing is wrong, nothing is going to be shut down. Listen, chief, you didn't come down here to put out a fire. You came down to catch some firewater.' And everyone giggled and that saved the day. Otherwise, they would have had me in jail.

"Well, another motorboat came up. It was a very thick fog; that's why the first boat hit the barge. They transferred the booze and were all gone (with the gunmen) in less than an hour. They were all gone by the time the police got down there. We were all standing on the dock looking at one another when we heard the motorboat coming down, the rum-runner. And we all looked at each other and looked out. And God just gave us a hole in that fog and as the boat went by, the gunmen all thumbed their noses at us. They could travel faster than any boat on the river and they knew the river as no one else did.

"The next morning when we came in, sitting on the stringpiece of the dock was a case of Scotch with a note saying, 'Thanks for your cooperation.' I took one bottle and gave the rest to the yard gang."

At about this time, Sage, as superintendent of the largest Public Service generating plant, began "holding the speed" Statewide—that is, he held the output of all the utility's generators at almost exactly 60 cycles per minute. His memories of that onerous chore led Sage, by a roundabout route, to another story about drinking, this time involving McCarter himself.

Today, the generators of Public Service are designed to produce 60-cycle-per-second alternating current automatically, with so little variation that an electric clock is, if not on the second, very close. The North American Power Systems Interconnection Committee helps. When frequency variations have caused electric clocks to run four seconds slow or fast NAPSIC issues advisories to interconnections to change frequency by a two hundredths from 60 cycles per second for a specified time, to adjust the nation's and Eastern Canada's timepieces.

But at the start of the century, NAPSIC did not exist. And even as late as 1924, Sage recalls, "Our variation would be between 59-and-¾ and 61-and-½." In those days, he says, "that was damned little variation," but it was enough to cause him occasional trouble:

"I had a private phone in my office at Essex in case I wanted to call anyone. It stood on the shelf to one side of my desk, and one day it rang and the voice on the other side said, 'It this the superintendent of Essex Station?' I said, 'Yes.' 'Well,' he said, 'I want to get your hide. You ruined 800 yards of my blanket and I'm so doggone sick of it I'm going to build my own power plant.' 'Well,' I said, 'what happened?' He said, 'You let your speed move all over the State, all over the scale, and the shuttle going back and forth over the blanket changed its speed and it made wavy effects in the blanket and we didn't find out until we had run off 800 yards and it was all wasted and I think you people down there ought to have your tail fanned you are so darned careless about what you are doing.'

"Well, I remembered the fellow; he used about 300 kilowatts an hour. He was a good customer. I said, 'The next time you are going to run your blankets, let me know and I'll hold the speed. I'll go down myself personally to the throttles and hold the speed. 'Well,' he said, 'it's about time someone woke up.' He was as disagreeable and sore as he could be. So pretty soon, a couple of days later the phone rang and he said, 'I'm running my blankets tomorrow morning and if the speed changes I'm gonna build my own plant. Do you hear that? And I almost hope the speed does change.' He was just about as rotten as he could be. So I went down and I got the best cyclemeter, one that holds the number of cycles, and I set it up on the table right alongside of the throttle on the biggest machine, and the watch engineer and I stood right beside it and we were watching it. If we thought we saw the needle move a little bit, we opened the throttle. And if it were too far over, we'd shut the throttle. And we stayed there and stood with it. I had my noonday meal served right there. And he (the blanket-maker) never said a damned word. I never heard from him.

"At four o'clock I quit and I was thinking I had held the time so well the clock ran perfectly on time, and I thought, *Why can't we go to our customers and say we'll hold electric clocks on time for you?* They were very scarce in those days. I wrote a letter to Jake Barron, superintendent of generation, and I said, 'Why don't you buy me a Warren clock?' That's a clock that has a very good pendulum works on it and it has an electric clock too, and the two second hands, a red one and a black one, go around together. From the second hands you could tell immediately if your machines were running too fast or too slow. Jake called me up and said, 'That's another one of your damned fool ideas that you got, skipper. Where in the world do you get these ideas?' I said, 'All right, I just made a suggestion.' Two months later I got a letter, 'Buy yourself a Warren clock and hold the time.' We bought the Warren clock and held the time as best we could, so the two hands were off only about ten seconds an hour."

After that, the Electric Company's commercial departments sold many electric clocks. McCarter himself acquired several such clocks, but evidently had little confidence in them or in the whole concept of "holding the time." When the electric clocks disagreed with his own watch, he always assumed it was the clocks, and therefore Darrow Sage, that were wrong. He let Sage know of his doubts often, at all hours of the day and night.

"The funny thing about it," Sage recalls, "was that any time those boys in Newark got drunk and monkeyed with their watches, they'd call me up and say, 'Listen, Sage, your Warren clock is way off. You're not watching your Warren clock. You're all wrong.' I'd rush out and take a look at the Warren clock and see that it was within two or three seconds of the right time, and I'd never call them back. Tom McCarter himself called me up sometimes in the middle of the night, at two or three o'clock in the morning, at my home. And he'd say, 'Why don't you watch that thing?' He'd claim his watch was right and therefore the electric clock was wrong. Well, you can't say, 'You've had a few and your watch is wrong.' You can't tell the boss he's wrong."

A. Harry Moore, New Jersey's governor, and Thomas Alva Edison, New Jersey's resident inventor, get a tour at the dedication of the new Kearny Generating Station with Thomas N. McCarter as their guide, in 1926.

The Boom Twenties

"I called up Jake Barron, the southerner, and said, 'Boss, they didn't name that station (Kearny) after any Northern president, but they sure picked a damned good Northern general.'"
—Darrow Sage

By 1922, Public Service saw that its electric business was entering a period of great expansion—the rapid pick-up of demand after the recession of 1921 proved that—and it now took three important steps to meet the State's growing needs, forming the Public Service Production Company to handle design and construction throughout the system, establishing a load forecasting committee to predict where increasing demand would require that construction, and greatly expanding the role of the laboratory.

"The activities of the Electric Company are increasing at such a marvelous rate," said McCarter, in announcing the incorporation of the Production Company in 1922, "and its construction program is so large that it became altogether impracticable to have both construction and operation carried on by the same organization. They have, therefore, been entirely separated ... leaving the remaining electric organization free to devote its talents exclusively to the big problem of operating so large and varied a company."

This "marked a departure in the use of the company's engineering talent," according to R.N. Conwell. Thereafter, Public Service was able to maintain a large and innovative engineering staff for its own huge construction program and to keep that staff profitably occupied, when its own needs were low, with outside contracts designing and building highways, cement mills, office buildings, and industrial plants.

The load-forecasting committee, established in 1924, took on the somewhat dicier task of predicting exactly where Public Service would need new substations, bigger generators, or wires of greater capacity any time from six months to twenty years in the future. The utility did not want to get caught short of demand again, as it had after the war, and this committee, one of the first such in the industry, was to pioneer the development of accurate forecasting methods. Morris D. Hooven, Jr., an engineer in distribution, later, in 1929, gave an idea of the problems this committee faced:

> "For instance, in order to determine the effect of the Camden and Fort Lee bridges in their respective areas, studies were made of the effects of the erection of the Brooklyn Bridge and the building of the Hudson Tubes on population growth in Brooklyn and Jersey City. It was found that, in general, a population curve for such an area shows a sudden jump to the extent that an ordinary ten-year growth takes place in less than five years. After this period of rapid growth, the population curve again resumes its old trend at the higher level ...
>
> "In investigating the load of a small area such as that served by an individual substation or by small groups of substations, the general methods outlined above do not always apply, nor are there sufficient detailed statistics available to make such investigations. Consequently, it is necessary to study the load of each substation separately and to forecast its growth on the basis of past records. Neither should it be supposed that every substation has its peak at the same time as the system peak. For instance, Montclair for many years has experienced its peak around seven o'clock on Christmas Eve. A substation serving a purely industrial territory may have its peak at ten

o'clock on an autumn morning. Again local happenings may affect very materially the load in any community."

Hooven then detailed what must have been every forecaster's nightmare:

"It is interesting to speculate on what the load would be in Public Service territory if every light in every home were suddenly turned on, if at the same moment every electric household appliance were plugged in, if every factory from Hackensack to Gloucester were simultaneously set in motion, if every elevator in every office building were running, if every one of the nearly 2,000 street cars started at once. It is estimated that the load would then reach 1,900,000 kilowatts, or three and one-half times as much as all the generators running at full capacity could carry. Yet nearly every one of these lights, appliances, and motors is used for some length of time every day."

Hooven called the failure of this nightmare to materialize "a fortunate lack of coincidence." In the 1920s, the thinking of the load forecasting committee on this and more serious possibilities gave needed impetus to the development of the 132,000-volt transmission system, and led Public Service to an early realization of the advantages of interconnection with the electric systems of neighboring utilities—a realization which in due course led to the teamwork of the 11 companies whose cooperative arrangement today constitutes the PJM Interconnection.

Behind the scenes but making substantial contributions to the rapidly developing Public Service complex almost from the beginning was the testing laboratory. In charge there today is Joseph G. O'Grady, a genial man who flies light aircraft as a hobby. O'Grady says the facility's main job at its start in 1905-06, when it was located in a corner of the City Dock Station, was calibrating customer meters and, later, testing coal for the Electric Company's generating plants. But by 1926, the laboratory's work had increased some twenty-fold and involved all areas of utility operation, making it necessary to create four major work divisions—electrical, chemical, mechanical, and materials—and to relocate all four, plus a photography division, at the service building in Irvington. Later, when the walls of that building bulged, the laboratory would move to its own specially-built three-story building on a grassy stretch in Maplewood, where a separate structure now houses high-tension testing.

The consolidation of all testing within the company, at Irvington and then Maplewood, resulted in a steady upgrading of equipment performance as well as a number of important economies. It did away with duplication of testing devices and highly-trained personnel at the departmental level, and it made valuable information available system-wide and to customers. The lab performed a dizzying range of tasks from finding scientific ways to improve the quality of "cruddy water from Boiler No. 2" at Kearny or Essex or wherever, to determining honestly and exactly just how much money a company could save by switching to the utility's electric or gas service. Today, as in the 1920s, the lab calibrates and maintains much of the equipment used in generating stations and substations, tests all mechanical apparatus before the company buys it and during its lifetime of service, inspects everything Public Service buys before anybody uses it, determines whether materials somebody wants to buy are suitable for the job in question, runs extremely sophisticated tests on coal, oil, air and water—and, most recently, finds itself accountable for every conceivable aspect of generation of electricity by nuclear fission, down to the heat conductivity of coastal sands that would carry buried electric cables from an off-shore nuclear power station.

With an almost nostalgic undercurrent in his voice, Joe O'Grady pushes these subtle headaches aside for a moment and talks about the past: "Metering was the beginning, at any rate, and then other types of service came our way here at the testing lab as we went along. We are not sure what might have been the justification for some of the things that have been added over the years. We think we know how photography was added. We needed a photographer to take pictures for the reports we published. You know how it is. As long as the lab had a photographer and camera, other

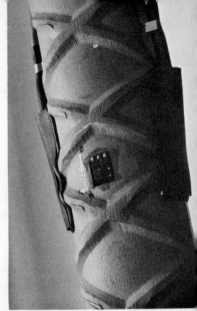

A photographer from PSE&G's Energy Laboratory zeros in on reinforcing bars in the Salem nuclear generating station, where tiny strain gauges installed by lab technicians on wrist-thick bars will measure stress after installation. Leo Miller is the photographer.

departments started calling up and saying, 'Would you mind taking this picture for us?' As time went on we developed an ability not only to take pictures of unusual situations, but also to do the same thing for other departments, just as an additional service."

One of the areas where the lab brought to bear its photographic and other kinds of expertise was in relation to appliances for use in the homes of Public Service customers. Throughout the 1920s, at an accelerating pace and as a perfectly logical business measure, Public Service sold household appliances to customers through its commercial department. With equal logic, to protect its customers from frying themselves and to guarantee that those customers plugged in their appliances and used them often, the utility called on its testing laboratory to check out the safety and reliability of appliances before placing any orders with manufacturers.

O'Grady says the lab turned down 75 per cent of all appliances submitted to it for testing. "A number of these small manufacturers who had to change over from war products to civilian products," says Joe, "found that one of the things they liked to make was the steam iron. As it happens, it takes a lot of know-how to make a good steam-iron. We had one iron come in that looked pretty good except that if you put a little too much water in it, it would boil over and squirt steam and water in all directions, so we turned it down on safety. A couple of weeks later, the president of the company that made it came in, a very pompous gentleman, and asked for a demonstration. We told him to stand back, because his iron would squirt. He refused to believe it. He just stood there, and it did go off and squirt him and he said, 'That sonofabitch is a booby trap,' and turned on his heel and walked out. We never saw him again."

O'Grady says the lab used to have high-powered salesmen come in and try to super-sell them into okaying an appliance. "One was Joe Grady of the Easy Washing Machine Company, an old-time salesman who would submit a new machine for testing and then have to come in and demonstrate it himself. We didn't care what he said or did, because we were going to make our own tests. This day he came in with one of their first automatics. It had a superior rinse cycle, Joe empha-sized, so we put our test clothes in and ran it. We had weighed them beforehand, and we knew how much moisture they contained and so on. As they were going through the test and had reached the second rinse, Joe Grady asked for a drinking glass, and proceeded to drink the rinse water to show how superior the rinse was. We told him, 'No, no! Don't do that, Joe! We urinated on the test clothes before we started!' He never did find out whether we did or we didn't."

Not getting people killed was a big part of the services the lab rendered to the company, from the peak of its involvement with appliances, around 1927, to as late as 1948, O'Grady recalls, "we were winding down."

Public Service was in what O'Grady calls "a rather unique position years ago. The company sold appliances, which as you know it doesn't do any more, and if someone wanted an electric iron, say, they would go to Public Service because they knew they would get the best iron there was—and, what's more, if there was something wrong with it, Public Service would take care of it. That was because our sales department insisted that everything they put up for sale first come to the lab for testing. We might get half a dozen irons, and we'd recommend which we thought was the best iron, and why, and since the company serviced the appliances it sold, we always took them apart and put them together again, to see if there was ease in servicing. Back then you didn't have these welded parts you have today that are hard to take apart.

"I think the philosophy the company went by was, if you sold an appliance to a customer and it wasn't really any good, then he was not consuming electricity with it, and that appliance in that house wasn't doing us any good at all. So if we were going to sell appliances, we wanted to be sure we sold and encouraged the sale of only those appliances which were relatively trouble-free, and for which we could have the reasonable expectation that the customer would use the energy we sell."

In an industry that turns out a product as fraught with potential danger as electricity, concern for safety is an understandable preoccupation. The mandatory checking out of the 7,100 pairs of rubber gloves the company buys each year to protect its linemen, for instance, obligates the lab to subject each and every glove, submerged in batches of 14 gloves at a clip in a tank of water, to far more powerful charges of electric current than the manufacturer designed the gloves to protect the wearer against. The gloves are black outside and red inside, and if a visual inspection lets the tester see the slightest suspicion of red during the electrically-charge submersion, nobody gets to wear that glove. A man's life, after all, hangs on its integrity.

So also with the appliances for Public Service customers. "One of the main things we stressed," says O'Grady, "was the safety, the shock hazard. We'd take these appliances and put them in a room which was 85 degrees Fahrenheit, 85 degrees relative humidity, and we'd soak them in there for 24 hours. Then we would perform the electric leakage test; we'd measure the leakage. We always tried to keep the leakage current down to two-tenths of a milliamp, whereas the manufacturers tried to hold out for one milliamp. So did the

Underwriters Laboratories in New York. We tested at 720 volts, and that's where the bulk of your appliances failed. The makers of appliances which failed tended to use insulating materials that were fibrous and would absorb moisture. They were actually blotters, and because of the conditions you could run into in summertime, they were dangerous. It was mainly electrical safety we were looking for, although we also took into account such things as sharp corners, space-heaters that could fall over, and so on. We'd put an appliance on what we call 'life test,' that is, we'd run them almost to destruction. We really weren't interested in recommending the appliances that would use the most energy, so much as in determining which were the safest and most reliable.

But this "educating of the public on the best buys from the standpoint of safety and reliability" had its cost for Public Service in other ways than the high profits O'Grady says the company was *not* making on the sale of the appliances its lab tested and approved. Retailers complained bitterly that Public Service was unfairly influencing the public to buy certain products, to the exclusion of others, "just because," O'Grady points out, "we wouldn't sell a product that could give a shock." Retailers felt this cut into their freedom to sell a wider range of products, many of which carried a higher mark-up, because when the word got around that a certain line had failed to win the Public Service seal of approval, educated consumers avoided that line.

O'Grady says the company declined to knuckle under to such commercially-oriented pressure. While the manufacturers took the position that a shock wouldn't kill you, and in general that was true, Public Service continued to refuse to sell appliances that could give a customer a shock because, as Grady points out, "what we were concerned about was the *secondary* reaction. The shock could make you fall off a chair or a ladder."

Public Service now felt, so Farley Osgood, the Electric Company's general manager, wrote in *Electrical World* in 1923, "that the industry is entering upon a phase of development in the use of electricity that is to be of

stupendous importance both to the people of the country
and to those within the industry itself, and that what is taking
place in New Jersey is indicative of a general movement." To
keep pace with this movement, Public Service that year broke
ground for a new power station, its first in almost a decade,
on a site in the meadowlands. This station would contain
what was, at its conception, the largest initial generating
capacity in the world—207,000 kilowatts. Darrow Sage, "the
skipper," tells this story about how the Kearny Generating
Station got its name:

"In 1923, the Public Service decided to build a new power
station, and the site that was picked was on the Hackensack
River, about 800 yards north of the old Plank Road. Now, the
old Plank Road had become part of the famous Lincoln
Highway between New York and San Francisco. And at that
time, the papers were full of advertisements of stores on the
Lincoln Highway in Illinois, on the Lincoln Highway in
Kansas, on the Lincoln Highway in Ohio, and so on. One
day, without any warning whatsoever, my good friend James
Lawson, who was the electrical engineer of maintenance for
the Newark office, came by and said, 'Get in the car. I'm
going to take you someplace.' I said I'd like to know where
first, and he said, 'None of your blankety-blank business!'"
That was his characteristic way. He was very rough, but in
times of trouble he'd take the shirt off his back to give you.

"We went down the Plank Road to a great big open field,
about 25 acres (actually closer to 100) on the Hackensack
River opposite Jersey City. He said, 'Now, you're down here
to look it over and suggest a name for the new power station,
and send your suggestion to Jake Barron, general superintendent of generation.' The idea came to me that it would be
a wonderful name if it were called the Lincoln Power Station
of the Public Service Electric and Gas Company on the
Lincoln Highway in Kearny, New Jersey. I made the
suggestion to my boss, Jake. He was a Southerner, very much
so. We used to fight the Civil War all over again among us. So
he called me up and said he wasn't going to name any power
station of his after a Northern president. And I said, 'Okay,
I've done my best,' And time went on.

"That much I know for fact. The rest is hearsay. When drawings of the new station were all finished they were taken to Tom McCarter for his final approval. Of course, not being an engineer, he didn't know what he was looking at, no more than if he'd been looking at a sheet of music. He looked over ten or twenty blueprints and pushed 'em to one side and said, 'What are you going to call the station?' Well, they had been quarreling among themselves and no one had a name. One said one name and one said another, and Tom McCarter said, 'Where is it?' They said, 'Why, it's on the east end of Kearny.' 'Well,' he said, 'call it the Kearny Station.'

"So ten or 15 days later I got a letter saying that the official name of the new station would be the Kearny power station. Well, I couldn't let that go by. We all know that Kearny was named after Phil Kearny, who was a general in the War between the States, and that he tore the South all to pieces with his cavalry riding down there. The Southerners hated him, hated the guts out of him. So I couldn't let that go by. And I called up Jake Barron, the southerner, and said, 'Boss, they didn't name that station after any Northern president, but they sure picked a damned good Northern general.' And Jake Barron was so mad he wouldn't talk to me for weeks."

Kearny was to be the first major project of the new Production Company, and it was a challenging one. Public Service had picked a site midway between Marion and Essex Stations that consisted of marsh land often partly submerged at high tide. There would never be a shortage of water at this plant, anyway. And coal barges would have easy access to the bunker house, too. But to form a sturdy foundation for its five big generators and 15 boilers, the builders had to drive 22,000 closely spaced piles into the shifting meadows. On top of the piles they placed 12,000 tons of steel, seven million bricks, and an immense quantity of concrete. The Kearny Station won praise from *Electrical World* in 1926, the plant's first year of operation, for its emphasis on economy and reliability. The journal noted the Public Service investment in "group arrangements, spare auxiliaries, duplicate buses and feeders, accurate and ample controls, vertical and horizontal isolation of conductors..."—all to guarantee continuous service. Within the company, according to R.N.Conwell's brief history, engineers saw Kearny as "an opportunity to develop an installation outstanding at the time in its use of new and modern design practices." The turbo-generators "embodied all the latest improvements in turbine design" and, in the boiler room, "the latest developments in auxiliary apparatus were installed." The plant, which Public Service intended to expand to 400,000 kilowatts over the next decade, was equipped, as the load forecasters had recommended, with a 132,000-volt substation and transmission capability. It could thus "be used readily for any future high-voltage interconnections." Kearny was also connected at 132,000 volts with Essex and Marion, and the three stations, operating in parallel with a combined generating capacity of 504,000 kilowatts, made up one of the largest and, said Public Service, most efficient generating units in the nation.

Sage, who was the first superintendent at Kearny, recalls that he was not so completely happy with the design of the new plant. He concedes that "I'm altogether too much on the advance side of things" and that he harbors the usual spirited distaste of a power-plant man for doings at the Newark office. Nonetheless, he relates: "Jake Barron held a meeting at his office and he said, "I want you all to write down what pressure you think Kearny should have in its turbines." Kearny was still in blueprints. So I put down 'boiler pressure 1,400 pounds, throttle pressure 1,200 pounds.' (There is normally some pressure loss between the boilers and the throttle of the turbine.) Jake said, 'I never heard such a lot of damned foolishness in my life.' But do you know that before Kearny was finished there were three plants in the State of New Jersey that had 1,400 pounds. Kearny should have been at 1,400 pounds, too, but it was only 385 pounds. They hadn't studied the situation as much as I had—that's a damned conceited thing to say—but I'd kept myself informed with mechanical and electrical engineering journals."

Electrical World also called the 385-pound pressure and 720-degree temperature of the steam at Kearny "a conservative starting point for good operating economy." It called the entire plant "conservative," in fact, but evidently did not consider that a pejorative, for it added that the plant "abundantly sustains the reputation of Public Service engineers for building soundly and well from the standpoint of giving reliable and economical service."

With the opening of Kearny—at ceremonies which Thomas A. Edison attended as guest of his friend McCarter—came the culmination of the utility's 25-year drive "to concentrate production in the larger and more efficient stations, to secure a wider and wider distribution of energy from the source of supply, and to eliminate waste that invariably follows duplication of plant and equipment." Public Service now abandoned the last of its original 20 plants, including Hoboken and Secaucus in 1925, Coal Street in 1928, and Cranford in 1929. This was a costly step to take. Dudley Farrand, with an engineer's characteristic affection for his machines, his "babies," had in 1922 listed no fewer than 48 generating stations "every one of which has been operated under my direction (with Public Service or its predecessors), and every one of which has been sold for scrap." Even earlier, he had commented:

> "In fact, in no other business involving large capital expenditures have the changes been so frequent or so extensive. The complete replacement of physical properties by the Public Service Company, or its predecessors in the same field from the early beginning of the industry to date, has required the expenditure of many millions of dollars, all of which amounts, although voluntarily expended by the financial interests supporting the properties, can justly be said to have been expended in the interest of either 'safe, adequate or reliable service' which recent legislation has approved by statute...
>
> "The average amount realized for sale of scrap equals about 2 per cent, so the remaining 98 per cent of the original investment is lost to the owners and should be allowed as one of the development costs in establishing the business. In addition to the item of power stations, the question of replacement applies to practically every part of the physical

apparatus employed in the business, so much as that excepting real estate and possibly some stray pieces of office furniture, there is not known to be in existence today any physical property owned or employed by the company for thirty years."

But the constant innovation and replacement were undoubtedly worth their high cost, in both economy and reliability thus achieved. Said McCarter in 1926:

"To take a few instances from the history of Public Service— the first central station in New Jersey, that of the Newark Electric Light Company, had a range of distribution reckoned in city blocks; the possible range of the new Kearny Station is at least statewide. At one time there were in the Public Service electric system no less than 26 (actually 32) generation stations; today ninety-six per cent of its output comes from its four most efficient stations (Essex, Marion, Kearny and Burlington). If transmission range had not been increased, the investment in generation plants necessary to provide the supply now required would be so great as to make necessary rates largely in excess of those now charged, while service could not possibly have reached present high standards."

At the same time as it was building Kearny, Public Service was seeking economy and reliability, plus additional power, in another, new direction. The same week it broke ground at the site on the Hackensack River, the utility put into service a cable beneath the Delaware River, tying together its southern system, which still operated independently, and the system of the Philadelphia Electric Company. With this first interconnection, the range of the New Jersey utility's generators passed for the first time beyond State borders. Actually, though, most of the power flowed the other way. "At the other end of the State," said McCarter, "we have tided over the present requirements by a physical connection with Philadelphia, taking surplus power that the Philadelphia Electric Company happened to have." On later interconnections, after Public Service had completed the expansion of its existing plants and the construction of Kearny, the power would, at different times, flow both ways. In 1927, Public Service agreed with Philadelphia Electric and the Pennsyl-

vania Power and Light Company to establish such an
interconnection. Walter H. Johnson, president of Philadelphia Electric, described the planned link-up this way:

> "No interconnection designed for the transmission of such
> large blocks of energy and involving companies operated by
> financially independent interests has ever before been
> attempted. It is estimated that there will be a saving in
> generating equipment of approximately 450,000 horsepower,
> resulting in a net saving of many millions of dollars ... "

The three companies would link themselves together via a
ring of 220,000-volt transmission lines—this only ten years
after Public Service had gone to 26,000-volt transmission.
Before constructing this ring, which McCarter later rightly
called "a pioneer achievement," the three utilities had to
perform a complex battery of tests in the "virgin field" of
applied mathematical-electrical theory, to determine the
possibility of high-frequency radio communications between
stations, and to learn the effect of lightning, wind, sleet and
snow on the transmission towers and lines. The planned
ring, more than 200 miles in circumference, was to be
shaped like a slightly lopsided baseball diamond, with
substations or switching stations where the bags would be.
Home plate was at Plymouth Meeting, Pa., near Philadelphia; first base at Roseland, N.J. (from which lines ran to
Essex, Marion, and Kearny); second base at Bushkill, Pa.,
across the Delaware River north of Stroudsville; and third
base at Siegfried, Pa., near Allentown. The transmission lines
between these points would join together an electric pool of
2,250,000 kilowatts in a complex and unprecedented financial agreement for the fair distribution among them of
construction and maintenance costs. This careful agreement
was designed to encourage accurate forecasting of load and
of generating capacity requirements, and to prevent one
company from depending unfairly on another.

To Public Service fell the task—for which the other
utilities, under the agreement, shared the cost—of building
the New Jersey links. This took more muscle and sweat than
one might, in this machine-coddled era, imagine. The men

To get supplies and equipment to sites where transmission towers were being constructed, plank roads and even narrow gauge railways had to be built.

hired to build the string of towers from Roseland to Bushkill were a tough and experienced lot, but that line took them through such a nightmarish array of swamp, mountain, rock and ravine, especially in Sussex County, that they called it "the cussed Sussex link." The crews had trucks to haul the heavy lengths of steel to a tower site, but the rough terrain was often passable only to dray teams—mules, horses, and even oxen—that were hired, together with wagons, from local farmers. At one point, the impassable swamps necessitated the building of a narrow-gauge railway to carry supplies. And at another site, in Morris County, the linemen were obliged to haul the steel themselves for the last 500 yards. Putting shoulders and backs to metal, they carried an entire 100-foot tower, weighing 12 tons, piece by piece, uphill. They built a tower every 1,100 feet, about five to a mile, along the 44-mile route, so there was plenty of occasion for this kind of rugged exercise.

A crew of about a dozen highly-skilled "topmen" worked on each tower, with "grunts" handing or tossing up light supplies from below. To raise the heaviest metal pieces, the crew set up a tall, wooden gin pole in the middle of the tower foundation, with a block and tackle fastened on top. Dray teams or trucks working with ropes would then supply the lifting power from the ground. It usually took a good crew a day and a half or two days to build a tower, but under the best conditions startled residents would see an entire tower rise in a day. A bad site could slow work to a week or more. In his 1934 novel *Slim* William Wister Haines described how a typical topman operated. (In a recent letter to the authors, Haines says he worked "as a lineman for the Public Service of New Jersey on a job near, or passing through, Boonton, N. J., in the summer and early fall of 1931." This could have been the transmission line built by Public Service between Roseland, N.J., and Bushkill, Pa.)

To set a crosspiece, Haines said, the men would shinny up the legs of a tower, moving too fast, even at great height, "to fool with a safety" belt. About halfway up his column, each topman would stop and insert a spud wrench—an open-ended wrench with a long, round bar for a handle—into a bolt hole. Throwing one leg around the protruding wrench and wrapping the other around the column, he would then call for a crosspiece. When this was swinging "idly" above his head, he would align its bolt holes with those on the tower leg—no easy task—hold it there with another spud wrench, then bolt it into place. Meanwhile, his partner on the other tower leg had affixed the far end of the crosspiece in the same way. Haines described two topmen named Red and Braithewaite:

> "As the boy watched, Red leaned far out to the left and pulled hard on the crosspiece. The tower leg around which his own long legs were firmly locked leaned slowly toward Braithewaite and, as Red extended himself with a gasp, crept slowly past the end of the crosspiece; now daylight appeared through the two (bolt) holes and, with a glinting stab of his spud wrench, Red caught them. He relaxed with a grunt of relief and bolted up. Braithewaite was already sitting astride

"Topmen" at work building a transmission tower. They called it "hanging" steel.

of the crosspiece; when Red finished bolting he swung one of
his legs over it and sat with his back to Braithewaite. On the
opposite side of the tower Frozear and a fourth lineman
(called Tom) had put on another crosspiece in the same way.
Now, as Braithewaite paired with Tom and Red with Frozear,
they put crosspieces on the two remaining open sides of the
tower."

The topmen were evidently careful, for there were no
serious accidents in the building of the Bushkill link. At
dangerous heights, the men worked intently, talking in
technical terms about "k pieces, X braces, strugs, legs, wing
sections, arms, and dropper plates." But there was also
evidently some horseplay. Haines showed Red, having
climbed the gin pole with spikes or "gaffs" attached to his
shoes and there affixed the pulley, ready to descend:

Red had taken a package of cigarettes from his pocket and
now he called again
"Dollar I beat 'em, Braithewaite."
"Dollar you don't," said Braithewaite.
With one motion Red tossed the package about ten feet
above his head, and before the cigarettes had begun to fall
was on his way down. No more was he using the short steps of
his ascent. His long left leg reached far below him, but before
it touched the pole his right knee broke outward and down,
freeing the gaff on his right hook, and he fell straight as a
plummet for about three feet; his left leg twitched, the gaff
went home with a thudding chunk, and he repeated the
process. As each gaff broke loose it left a long silver splinter
sticking out of the pole, and the boy perceived with a gasp
that these splinters were seven or eight feet apart. Each time
Red's hooks hit the pole it quivered beneath the impact of his
weight. The cigarettes had turned in their short parabola and
were falling, but only a little faster than Red himself was
dropping. He seemed to sense their approach and, extending
himself, he dropped the last nine feet sheer and sunk both
gaffs out of sight in the butt of the pole just an instant before
the package struck the ground.
"Dollar you win," said Braithewaite.

Another time, as he worked high in a tower, Red called
down to the ground for two one-and-a-half bolts. Before the

grunts could move, the watchful boss jumped to the bolt kegs:

"Comin' at you, Red," he shouted, and threw with a hard overhand drive. The bolt shot away on a speeding line for Red's face and disappeared with a thud into his waiting glove. Red turned back to his corner and shot the bolt into place. The boss, who was waiting with the other bolt, turned to the man who had been tying the steel.

"Watch me make him cuss, Charley!" He threw, and the second bolt soared away, but not so hard this time, and not so directly toward Red. Red watched it warily, his long legs tightened around the tower leg, and just as the bolt wobbled and turned to fall Red stretched like a striking snake, his whole body hanging out over empty space, and caught the bolt by his finger tips. As he snapped his body back to the tower, the boss's boast was realized in a tirade of profanity ...

"You make a lot of trouble about catchin' a little bolt, Red!"

"No trouble at all about catchin' it, but I did kind of want to get back to the tower after I had caught it! If I couldn't throw no better than that I'd get me a job throwin' out feed on a chicken farm!"

Many of the workers on the Bushkill line were, like Haines's drawling Braithewaite, Southerners away from home. But even Public Service linemen from Newark had to live in camps, at Stillwater and Millbrook, during construction—and that included the hard winter of 1928. The camps, called "rag cities" by the linemen, were in fact comparatively luxurious. The consisted of regulation Army four-man tents, erected on wooden floors and with wood siding, each containing a table and a coal stove in addition to the four cots. A watchman stoked the stoves throughout the night. Both camps also had kitchens and mess tents. At Stillwater, an added luxury was the bathroom equipped with a tub and a stove for heating water—but the nearest spring was a mile distant. Stillwater also enjoyed wildlife; during their stay there, the linemen killed no fewer than 27 rattlesnakes.

Despite such diversions, work on the Bushkill line progressed rapidly. When the topmen had finished "hang-ing' steel" for several miles, a follow-up crew would carefully lay out the wire and hoist it up. "Clipping-in" crews would then install insulators on the towers and fasten the wire to them. Finally, a mop-up crew would clean the site and inspect every tower and insulator assembly, before approving the line for service. Work on the other New Jersey leg of the interconnection, from Roseland to Plymouth Meeting, also went quickly after the company resolved some time-consuming right-of-way problems. When the two New Jersey links opened in 1930 and 1932, they, along with the two completed Pennsylvania links, formed a great ring that joined together one of the largest electric power pools in the world. This was the start of the Pennsylvania-New Jersey-Maryland Interconnection, now better known as PJM, in which Public Service, Pennsylvania Power and Light, and Philadelphia Electric are still members.

The benefits of interconnection were many, the most obvious being increased reliability of service to customers of all three companies. Where a power station failure or transmission difficulties might formerly have crippled an independent utility, neighboring companies could now keep the power flowing in almost any emergency via the transmission ring. Moreover, a utility could turn to the generators of neighboring utilities for power during routine overhauls of its own equipment. Though no utility could guarantee absolute freedom from blackouts, the greatly increased dependability afforded by interconnection was to be an important item in attracting industry to New Jersey.

The interconnection also enabled the three utilities to produce electricity more cheaply, by eliminating costly duplication of generating equipment. The system depended on what engineers call "load diversity." It worked like this. In the Public Service corridor, the peak demand for electricity occurred at 5 p.m. each day in winter, and at 8 p.m. in summer. (It's earlier these days.) Alone, Public Service would have had to maintain enough generating capacity to meet this demand, plus a reserve capacity for emergencies. But since demand in the mining districts of Eastern Pennsylvania peaked at 10 a.m. and fell off rapidly after 4 p.m., much of the Pennsylvania Power and Light generating capacity was available to help meet the New Jersey peak. Likewise, some Public Service generating capacity was available to meet the mid-morning-to-mid-afternoon peak demand in Pennsylvania. By thus pooling their resources, the three companies were able to serve their customers with significantly fewer generators—and therefore at lower cost—than would have been the case had they remained independent of one another.

Alexander E. Baughan, a Public Service interconnection engineer, wrote: "One (company) has a peak load of 100,000 kilowatts at five o'clock in the afternoon and a small load in the morning. The other company has a peak load of 100,000 kilowatts at 10 o'clock in the morning and a light load in the afternoon. Operating independently they must have available a total of 200,000 kilowatts of generating capacity. If they are interconnected by a transmission line, each company can assist the other in the carrying of its peak load, so that (together) they need have installed perhaps only 150,000 kilowatts of generating capacity. The difference, 50,000 kilowatts, is the load diversity saving."

By interconnecting, the utilities were also able to keep the most efficient existing plants running at capacity almost full-time. This not only made for more economical operation; it also enabled a plant to pay back the capital invested in it and earn a profit far sooner. Said McCarter:

> "Further large savings will accrue to the three companies, and hence to their customers, from the use of "economy flow" over the interconnection as provided for in the interconnection agreement. The companies are to operate their respective systems so that use will first be made of all hydro-electric energy (from the Philadelphia company's plant at Conowingo), and then steam stations will be brought on the line in the order of their respective economies. Thus, as a rule, only the more efficient plants will be operated, regardless of their ownership or location, less efficient plants being held in reserve."

Finally, the interconnected companies could coordinate their building programs. Instead of each company install-

A dispatcher keeps an eye on transmission conditions in the control room of the power pool to which PSE&G belongs—The Pennsylvania-New Jersey-Maryland Interconnection (PJM). The pool brings electric power to more than 21 million people in portions of five states and the District of Columbia, including the nation's capital.

ing a new generator each year, they were able to stagger this costly work among the three. The result: cheaper power.

To put what that meant into specific terms from an overall long-range standpoint, Baughan wrote:

> "It is estimated that the cost of this interconnecting ring when completed (with switching stations and substations in both States) will be about $26,000,000, and that it will save the installation of about $45,000,000 worth of generating capacity. Were it not for this interconnection, Public Service would be engaged in the installation of additional power plant facilities at this time."

The PJM power pool now consists of 11 utilities in portions of Pennsylvania, New Jersey, Maryland, Delaware, Virginia, and the District of Columbia, including the nation's capital. The pool serves more that 21 million people in this 50,000-square-mile area.

Only once in its more than half-century of service has the PJM power pool suffered a complete blackout. This occurred on June 5, 1967, when a line transmitting power to Philadelphia from generating stations along the Susquehanna River shorted out after becoming overloaded at 10:16 a.m. The result was a "cascading" effect which caused most generating facilities in the eastern portion of the power pool to shut down within six minutes. Power was restored to parts of downtown Philadelphia within an hour. Service to 90 per cent of the power pool area was restored by 5 p.m. and to the entire area by 7:55 p.m.

The failure occurred the day before PJM planned to energize a new 500-kilovolt East-West transmission interconnection extending from Pennsylvania into New Jersey and shortly before the start-up of the first 840-megawatt Keystone generating unit in western Pennsylvania, the largest portion of which is owned by PSE&G. "If these facilities had been in service, the interconnection utilities would have been able to withstand substantial disturbances without a widespread failure," the Federal Power Commission reported later.

The interconnection system has been further strengthened and devices to isolate generators and transmission systems have since been installed throughout the PJM system and it is highly unlikely that such a widespread loss of power can ever occur again.

Even as it was constructing the Pennsylvania interconnections, Public Service was achieving similar economies and a similar reliability by tying together its own northern and southern parts, based respectively around Newark and Camden. The 132,000-volt link between Metuchen and Trenton switching stations was to parallel the company's flat, seemingly convenient Fast Line route. But if mountains here posed no problem for the utility's work crews, swamps and quicksand easily made up for it, forcing Public Service to use heavier, taller towers and to place as many as 10 of them to the mile. The ground at one site was so unstable that it took a large gang of men working with 18 pumps 30 days to build a single tower. Still—by using cranes, tractors and other newly-developed machinery in place of muscle—Public Service was able to complete construction of the planned 295 towers within just six months, putting the 30-mile line in service before November 1, 1929. Meanwhile, it began construction of other transmission lines, including the so-called "inner ring" that was to encircle the company's northern zone. This 132,000-volt loop would back up and supplement the company's radial transmission system and, by making available huge quantities of power to industrial customers, was to play an important part in North Jersey's development as a manufacturing center.

During its first year of operation, the "inner ring" enabled Public Service to secure an important contract to supply large blocks of power to the Delaware, Lackawanna & Western Railroad in New Jersey. With this contract, Public Service had "established itself as a low-cost producer of electric energy."

Public Service built other high-tension lines at this time, mainly for emergency relief, tying its electric systems together with those of Jersey Central Power & Light, New Jersey Power and Light, Rockland Light and Power (now Rockland Electric), and Staten Island Edison. Such improvements, most of them unnoticed or at least unappreciated by the average customer, cost Public Service $151 million between 1923 and 1929.

Like virtually everyone else at Public Service, Darrow Sage recalls his company's early commitment to interconnection as a "darned good engineering move." But interconnection was also the final blow to the independence of the station superintendent. "After interconnection," says Sage, "if anything went wrong, they'd start up another machine maybe 50 miles away and it took all the romance out of running the station." Sage recalls the old feeling of being "essential" to the life of a community this way:

> "When I first went to Essex Generating Station, Essex was the only thing running north of New Brunswick after nine o'clock at night. I would go up on Chimney Rock, right above the Millburn Station of the Lackawanna Railroad. There is an old rock there. It bulges out and you can stand there and see a

colorful view all over North Jersey. I'd drive up there with my
wife at about nine or 10 o'clock at night and look at the whole
of Newark and way up as far as Edgewater. I could see trolley
cars running, neon lights, flood lights, and I'd think that
everything I can see is running under my throttles."

After interconnection, the superintendent could no longer
say for certain where the power under his throttles was
going, or exactly whose lives it was making more comfortable, and, as he was unable to see the results of his labor,
some of the satisfaction passed from the superintendent's
working life. Some abuses passed, as well. Not only had some
superintendents formerly been kings, but they had been
bigger kings the farther they got from Newark. In the nether
reaches of the southern zone, one superintendent had kept
his private motorboat at the coal dock, and another, at
Burlington, had built himself a tennis court on company
property, presumably with company money. As the Newark
office gained greater control over generation, it showed little
tolerance for such regal conduct, or for the common practice
of hiring and firing according to who your uncle was. Closer
management resulted, naturally, in a dollar savings. After
1929, for instance, Public Service saved $60,000 a year by
taking over from a contractor the chartering and dispatching
of barges supplying the waterside stations with coal. Because
of the economies, large and small, it introduced, and because
of interconnection and the quarter-century drive to centralize power production, Public Service was able to perform
some near-miracles in the generation of electricity, and in
bringing down the rates it charged for that electricity.

One measure of the utility's improved efficiency was the
rapid decline through the 1920s in its system "heat rate"—the
number of BTU its generating plants required to produce a
single killowatt-hour of electricity. In 1920, when the high
post-war demand for power forced operation of even the
most inefficient plants, Public Service had to endure a
system-wide heat rate of 33,161 BTU per kilowatt hour. But
thanks to the economies effected by centralization and
interconnection, and in other ways, the utility had by 1930

cut its system heat rate to 18,649 BTU. Put simply, it now needed only a little more than half as much coal to produce the same amount of power. This achievement enabled Public Service to cut its electric rates repeatedly throughout that decade.

For this difficult and often innovative work, Public Service in 1929 won the General Electric Company's prestigious Charles A. Coffin Award, the industry's highest honor. In reporting it, *Electrical World* cited the company's having distinguished itself

> "for outstanding achievement in creating a system comprehensive enough to meet present conditions, elastic enough to care for the future, plastic enough to assure high service reliability, economical enough to provide such service under rate schedules that stimulate use and provide reasonable and fair charges to all classes of customers—operated with full recognition to public, employees, and stockholders."

The Thirties

"The price of progress is trouble"
—Robert A. Baker

Even during the Depression, Public Service often led the industry in the development of new cost-cutting methods. The company was evidently not shy about taking up a challenge, for during this period it put into service, without fanfare, the largest transformer and the largest rotating turbine shaft in the world. Increasing the size of its equipment, particularly the turbines, was one important route to economy. Another example of the company's willingness to experiment, and of how far ahead of the times it could get, was its financing, more than 40 years ago, of the Madaras Rotor Power Plant, named after Julius Madaras, its Hungarian-born inventor, but now better known as the Burlington windmill. The proponents of the windmill promised "a new era in power generation" using the cheapest possible fuel: "the flowing ocean of air." With money from Public Service and five other utilities, they designed and built a pilot wind-power station in Burlington, New Jersey, that looked nothing short of futuristic. In contrast to the huge and bulky generating stations on the Hackensack meadowlands, it consisted of a single, cylindrical

tower, tall as an eight-story building and utterly unencum-
bered by great vanes, sails or supporting structures. This
neatly-capped tower, called a rotor, was to stand on an
oversized railroad car with a wheelbase 40 feet long and 30
feet wide. The rotor power plant was designed to operate on
the same principle a baseball pitcher uses to throw a curve.
As the ball leaves his hand, the pitcher twists it. The
consequent spinning of the ball through the air causes
pressure to build up on one side, suction on the other, and
this causes the ball to shoot in or out. A small motor on the
railroad car was to set the rotor spinning in the same way, as
fast as 200 revolutions per minute. As the wind wrapped
around the spinning rotor, pressure and suction would build
up, moving the entire railroad car forward on its circular
track at a speed of 20 miles an hour. The rolling wheels
would in turn drive an electric generator placed on the car.
Power thus manufactured would pass, via an electric line
paralleling the track, to a step-up transformer and substation, and thence out to Public Service customers.

A wind of as little as four miles an hour could supposedly
drive the 150-ton railroad car, but engineers believed
operation of the rotor plant would be economically justifiable
only when wind speed exceeded six miles an hour. Fortunately, they said, the winds at Burlington met or passed the
level 85 per cent of the time. Because the railroad track was
to be circular, it did not matter from which direction the
wind blew. It was, however, necessary for the tower—not the
railroad car—to reverse the direction of rotation twice on
each circuit. This was apparently a smaller problem for the
engineers than it might seem; they designed the tower to
reverse itself automatically and with only "negligible" loss of
power whenever the railroad car was parallel to the wind.

The utilities behind the Burlington windmill had planned
to follow up the pilot project with the construction of two
actual wind-power generating stations with a capacity of
20,000 and 30,000 kilowatts. The smaller plant, on the
Burlington site, was to consist of 20 rotors, each producing
1,000 kilowatts, joined together in a train. Each rotor-
carrying car would be 250 feet from its neighbors, so that it

A workman is dwarfed by the Madaras Wind Rotor, 90 feet high and 22 feet in diameter, in this 1932 photo. Designed as one of twenty rotors to catch the wind and spin it into power on a circular track, this first model proved unworkable, in a Public Service experiment at the Burlington generating station.

would have "undisturbed" air in which to operate. The entire plant would occupy about 200 acres and would—so its proponents claimed—produce power at only a fifth of the cost of steam power. But this happy prospect soon proved itself false. Company engineers made tests with a stationary rotor and concluded that the winds were too irregular and that the circular track would have to be too large to justify construction. The plant would cost too much and produce too little power. Even the larger plant would produce only slightly more power than the single, newest turbine at Kearny. Moreover, the Depression had slowed the electric utility's growth to the point that it did not need new generating capacity. And so the electric department shelved the wind-power project.

Another Public Service experiment, one that cost more money and caused far more trouble than the windmill, was the mercury boiler and turbine installed at Kearny Generating Station in 1933. The Kearny unit, manufactured by General Electric, was then only the second boiler/turbine in existence using mercury vapor instead of steam. The advantage of mercury over steam was simply that the superheated vapor could be used to produce electricity twice. As in a standard steam unit, an oil- or coal-fueled fire in the boiler heated an overhead rack of steel tubes. Within these tubes, the liquid mercury vaporized and then—at a temperature of 960 degrees and under 125 pounds pressure per square inch—passed through and turned a 20,000-kilowatt turbine. The hot vapor then entered the condenser, where its heat turned water to steam, 300,000 pounds of it per hour. This steam in turn drove a standard turbine producing 30,000 kilowatts. Meanwhile, the cooled-off mercury returned in a liquid state to its boiler, where the whole process began again. Getting more power from the same amount of fuel oil obviously saved money. But mercury had its disadvantages.

"The General Electric Company told us that the mercury would not attack the steel in the tubes of the boiler," recalls Darrow Sage, who was then superintendent at Kearny and a former General Electric employee. "In that they were correct. But they weren't correct in the fact that you could not get tubes that were completely homogeneous. Homogeneous means it contains nothing but iron, but you can't get that. There'd be little infinitesimal drops of zinc or silica or copper or something like that. And the mercury would find that and go through and in a few minutes punch a hole you could put your finger through. And that mercury would fall down into the fire. We had a great big pan underneath the mercury boiler tubes and what didn't go up the stack would fall into the pan, and we could filter it and use it over again. A flask of mercury held 37 pounds, and it was then worth about $25. Now, today, a flask holding 37 pounds is worth $250. So, because we could not contain the mercury without losing it, and losing it time and time again, and losing a lot of mercury every time you had a hole, the mercury boiler was given up. That's the truth of the matter.

"But when I could run the mercury boiler—as I said, Kearny could turn out a kilowatt for about 11,000 BTU—when I could run the mercury boiler I could get down to 9,000 BTU. And Public Service had to go to 2,300 pounds before they could equal that record. It took them till just about the time I retired, about 1950," Sage said.

Chief Engineer Robert A. Baker later commented on the many improvements in electric power production by Public Service during the 1930s and 1940s:

"The purpose of innovations in the design of electric generating equipment is to achieve three principal objectives: (1) low capital cost, (2) low operating cost, and (3) dependability. It is obvious that a successful plant is a happy compromise of these three objectives. The emphasis on each must be kept in balance, to the end that the customer may enjoy dependable service at reasonable cost. Our policy has been to take advantage of every technical advance in the art that was judged to be practical and dependable in operation. "More specifically, it has been to move continually toward higher steam temperatures and pressures for improvement in thermal efficiency and better utilization of fuel resources; to foster the development of heat resisting alloys, as well as techniques of joining them in power plant systems; to encourage the development of dependable high-speed equipment for power plant use; and to promote larger sizes of steam power plant components.

"As we look back on these developments, their worth, and the rightness of the decisions to undertake them, appear quite obvious. But I can assure you, at the time they were not quite so obvious. The ingredients for decisions such as these are experience, judgment, persuasiveness, and a certain amount of daring. I think it can be said that the advances, or extrapolations, from the then-current practice in many of our projects have been characterized by a long reach, rather than a short reach. These were stimulated by the anticipation of rising fuel costs. In retrospect, this has been a rewarding policy, because fuel costs have indeed risen since 1930..."

As examples of the troubles an innovative electrical engineer could face, Baker, who became an executive vice president before he retired, cited both the mercury unit at Kearny and an 18,000-kilowatt steam turbine capable of 3,600 revolutions per minute, installed at Burlington Generating Station in 1932. Of the latter, which advanced steam conditions to 650 pounds pressure and 850 degrees Fahrenheit, he said:

"Well, we did have trouble on this unit. The turbine seized when the dummies were being ground, and the jolt broke a cast-iron fitting in the turbine oil-supply system. The emergency oil pump functioned perfectly, pumping all the oil in the turbine reservoir onto the fire. The replacement turbine has been a fine machine, and is still giving good service.

"There followed a nationwide wave of replacement of cast iron fittings in turbine oil systems. The main steam piping for Burlington No. 4 is an all-welded system, and the field welds were made by a manual gas process. After the joints were completed, reinforcing straps were welded on. The boiler was designed to burn both pulverized coal through a bin system and Bunker C. fuel oil. Although we did not know it at the time, this No. 4 unit was, in many ways, the prototype of quite a few subsequent units.

"In contrast to Burlington No. 4, which was an extrapolation of current practice, and just about concurrently with its installation, we undertook another project that was a new departure—the mercury boiler/turbine installations at Kearny Generating Station. Although this could hardly be called an extrapolation from current practice, the decision to install was based on satisfactory operation of a prototype plant at Hartford. The capability of the mercury turbine-generator was 20,000 kilowatts, and its condenser-boilers furnished enough steam to produce an additional 30,000 kilowatts, with an overall design heat rate of 10,000 BTU per kilowatt hour. Again I say, please remember that this was in the early 30's, when fashionable system heat rates ran around 16,000 BTU per kilowatt-hour.

"The price of progress is trouble. Unfortunately, it can't be said that trouble is always an indicator of progress! There was plenty of trouble with the Kearny mercury unit—simply because know-how was lacking. In spite of this, it generated almost 4 billion kilowatt hours over its 20-year life, at a heat rate less than 11,000 BTU per kilowatt-hour. If a 15,000-BTU-per-kilowatt-hour machine had been installed, we would have had to buy about 600,000 tons of additional coal, or its equivalent, to produce the same output.

"These two installations—Burlington No. 4 and the Kearny mercury—had a profound influence on the design of subsequent units. Burlington No. 4 gave perspective as to what is a reasonable extrapolation. The Kearny mercury unit produced two items: (1) a healthy caution about large units of an experimental nature, and (2) confidence in the reliability of high-temperature power plant equipment. The throttle temperature of the mercury turbine was 950 degrees Fahrenheit.

"From this point on, we followed the course of long-reach extrapolation from current practice. Steam temperatures climbed from 850 Fahrenheit in 1932 to 950 Fahrenheit in 1938 (Essex No. 7) ... to 1,000 F in 1947 (Essex No. 1); to 1,050 F in 1948 (Sewaren); and to 1,100 F in 1953 (Kearny Nos. 7 and 8) and that is where we are now (1960). The 1,050 F and 1,100 F installations were first in the utility industry."

Disaster, in the form of wind, sleet, snow, or fire, has always been a part of utility work, and was especially so in the 1930s and 1940s, when two destructive hurricanes swept the State and a fire struck Essex Generating Station. Public Service had long concerned itself with accident prevention, implementing safer methods for dealing with gas and electricity; in the 1920s, for instance, it had substituted oil circuit breakers for the more hazardous bayonet switches, and it had developed a neon test stick to determine whether an appliance was still "live." It had also supported an expensive but life-saving safety program for its own employees and for school and civic groups around the State. But with so much equipment of all types spread throughout its territory, the utility was necessarily vulnerable.

The Essex fire began in a defective circuit breaker on the fifth floor of that station's switch house late on the afternoon of December 28, 1936, just as customer demand was reaching its daily peak system-wide. The fire quickly shut down the station's bank of 132,000-volt transformers. Trolleys stopped dead in the Streets of Newark, and light and power went off throughout most of Essex County.

Recalls Darrow Sage: "I was at Kearny. The fire came on about five or six at night, and they called me up and said, 'Keep all your machines running because there is a fire and Essex is shut down completely.' I said, 'We haven't got enough load. It will get too hot.' If Essex substation was shut down and the feeders that supply Essex County weren't running, Newark was pitch black and there wasn't enough load for the five machines at Kearny. 'Never mind,' they said. 'Don't shut anything down.' With a turbine, you know, unless you have enough steam going through the last stages, the steam condenses and there is nothing but a vacuum in there, and the wheels running round without the cooling of the steam get hot, and pretty soon the buckets (the spoke-like vanes of the rotor shaft) get to hitting each other, and pretty soon you'll have a chopped-up turbine. And I kicked about that, and they said, 'We'll take a chance.' We were producing the electricity with no place for it to go, and that causes the problem with the steam. But I was afraid to shut it down.

"At about half-past eight, I climbed the stack at Kearny so I could look over the top of the hill, the little knoll there, and looked up at Newark. And I could see the big, black swath extending from the Newark railroad depot in a great fan-shaped figure like this, way out as far as the East Orange border, absolutely black, pitch black. And light all around it, because Marion was serving the northeastern corner and Burlington Station was serving the southeast corner. But where Essex fire was, and all the Essex lines cut off, that was completely black.

"Well, I stood it as long as I could, and I said, 'I'm dead tired of this stuff here.' So along around nine o'clock I broke the rules and I left and went up to Essex to see what was going on at Essex. And there was everybody you could think of, the police department, the fire department, the safety department, the reporters, and everything you could think of—just crowded with cars and ropes and hoses. Just a mess, just a grand mess. And I ran into Irving Perry. He was a very good engineer who never got anywhere; he had no influence. But he said to me, 'Look, Skipper, come over here. If we saw off this bus here (a bus is a long copper bar connecting different circuits) and saw off that copper bus there, these lines here come in from Kearny and these lines here go up to Newark and light Newark; we can feed that part of Newark from Kearny'—which was my plant, which was running then chewing up its buckets. And I looked it over and I studied the thing. They had plenty of flood lights and flashlights and engine-driven generators on fire equipment, so there was lots of light all over the place, although there wasn't a wheel turning in Essex.

"And I said, 'We'll get Jimmy Lawson, the electrical engineer in charge here.' And Irving said, 'I've told Jimmy, but he said he was too busy with somebody else and he can't do it.' And I said, 'Well, you and I will go over and get him.' 'Well,' says Irving, 'he won't come.' 'If you pick him up, he'll come,' I said. Well, we went over in this massive crowd and pretty soon we saw Jimmy, and I said, 'Hey, Jimmy, I think we've got a scheme.' He said, 'Get outta here, I haven't got time to talk to you.' Irving got hold of him on the other side, and I got hold of 'im, and we picked him up off his feet. He cursed to beat the band, and said, 'I've just told this fellow to do something, and that fellow.' I said, 'You're going to look at what we want to do first. I don't give a damn what you say.' So we took him over and sat him down in front of the thing, and he looked and said, '*By God, you can do that.*' And in 20 minutes we had that power on. We got the load on our generators, so we didn't chew up our buckets, and we lit up Newark. Irving Perry's idea solved it. I don't want to take any credit for it at all, except I want to take credit for manhandling Jimmy Lawson."

Sitting in his 10-by-12-foot room at a home in Berkeley Heights, Darrow Sage recalls that the electric business often called for quick thinking and more—heroics—from the men it employed. One typical incident at Public Service stands out in his still-sharp mind:

"There was one fine fellow I had at the Kearny Station, Jimmy Nesmith. And underneath the mercury turbine was a room just about the size of this room, just covered with safety switches and electrical equipment, and one day that caught fire and pretty soon the whole wall was in flames. Jimmy Nesmith, he went in and sent for all the portable fire extinguishers in the building. Remember, the 'juice' was still on, he couldn't use water. We had the Station full of Pyrene extinguishers in those days. He stayed in that room with the fire going and pumped Pyrene with a hand-pump into that fire until he had it extinguished, risking his life. He was in there pretty close to an hour."

Some blackouts caused by natural disasters required more sweat and muscle than heroism. Arthur Horner, a retired distribution engineer, recalls that during the hurricanes of 1938 and 1944, service to some customers was out for as long as a week, even though emergency workmen were putting in 20-hour days, broken up only by brief naps on office cots. "Those were interesting times," says Horner. "You ate when you could, got a little rest, and after a while you ached so much you didn't mind it any more.

"We had some bad ones in the 1930s. I was in Elizabeth when a bad one hit us in about 1936 or 1938, and I guess Elizabeth and New Jersey were right in the center of the thing. I lived here in Westfield at the time, and I heard a tree go down and I thought, *Boy, if that's happening I'd better get in before I can't get in*—which was a dopey thing to do. But I got in the car and headed in, ducked a few streets and drove around fallen trees and got into the plant. Then it got worse and things were flying through the air. It was a real hurricane. I wouldn't let the men who had come to the plant go out. It was too dangerous.

"We waited until the wind calmed down, and got organized and then sent the men out. One of the places we looked was Edgar Road in Elizabeth, where Jake Barron lived. The whole street was shut down completely. The trees had come down and brought the whole pole line down right across the street. So the street was just one heaped-up mess of trees, poles, a couple of broken transformers. We couldn't get a truck in there. In fact, you could hardly walk in."

Thus Jake Barron and his neighbors had to wait a full seven days for their electricity to come on again, while Horner's work crews straightened out thousands of similarly-devastated—and less influential—blocks.

In addition to act-of-God disasters, Public Service occasionally suffered sabotage. In August, 1927, the utility began condemnation proceedings for permission to run the Roseland-Metuchen leg of its inner ring across the farm of John Crempa in Scotch Plains. Crempa, who did not want the wires over his land, asked for $100,000, spurning the $800 compensation set in court. He fought off Public Service work crews, and the company was able to set its towers and string wires from them only after obtaining an armed police escort. Over several years, Crempa repeatedly cut the wires, slinging a line over them with a slingshot. At least once, he succeeded in blacking out nearby towns briefly. He spent six months in jail for his efforts. His fight ended abruptly in 1935, when county sheriffs came around to deliver a contempt-of-court order. As had been their practice, Crempa, his family, and their neighbors belabored the sheriffs with brooms, stones, and pitchforks—and this time Crempa had a gun. In the resulting exchange, Crempa was wounded and his wife killed. None of the sheriffs was hit. Public Service eventually bought the property from Crempa's children for $27,500 in 1941.

A more typical protest occurred in 1934, when Public Service, with municipal approval, attempted to replace an old electric light pole in Camden. A Mrs. Barnebie, "who never did think (the) pole which stood in front of her house added to the sightliness of the landscape," stopped the Public Service work crew—to the cheering of her neighbors—by climbing into the hole the crew had just dug. Public Service wisely decided to leave her there, brandishing an American flag and being spelled intermittently by her husband. No corporation could please everyone.

"Public Service is a big concern," said McCarter, of such attacks on the company, "and it rubs against people in three different ways—when they ride in the cars, when they use gas service, and when they use electric service. It is a natural target for abuse and criticism but, on the whole, less so than it used to be."

Perhaps so, but the fact remains that there was no time, not even when families could hardly wait for the exciting new miracle of electric light to make its way into their homes, when people did not resent the presence of Public Service lines and towers in—or even near—their backyards or their streets, despite the conveniences which those lines brought them.

Today, a more image-conscious Public Service has adopted the mollifying tactic of "compensating" property-owners adjacent to a transmission route by leasing to them, for $1 a year, large swaths of its right-of-way. People now build pools or plant gardens on this practically-free land, and happily ignore the intrusive wires overhead. But from as early as 1904 through 1972, Public Service often unnecessarily aggravated the existing resentment by erecting poles and even high-tension transmission towers without first seeking the permission of municipal and other governing bodies involved. The first such incident occured in January, 1904, when the North Bergen Township Committee adopted an ordinance directing its road supervisor to cut down poles and wires of the Public Service Corporation "which had been put up without the authority of the township officials." The unauthorized construction was intended to improve trolley service, about which the same Committee was then over-wrought, but the politicians, in their anger at the utility's high-handed ways, chose to ignore any apparent contradiction. In North Bergen and other communities, Public Service was eventually able to prevent the dismantling of its equipment. But such after-the-fact settlements hurt the company's image with the public. The *Evening News* commented on one incident involving the railway company but typical of electric department methods, in 1915:

"Public utility companies profess not to understand the 'unreasoning criticism' sometimes leveled at them by the public and the newspapers. A recent incident before the Board of Freeholders ought to be enlightening, at least to the Public Service Railway Company. That corporation was sharply censured for what the committee regarded as its contemptuous treatment of the county board. Not only does the corporation refuse to move its tracks from the sides to the middle of Springfield Avenue, as ordered by the road committee, but it proceeds to tear up paving and put switches without waiting for the committee's permission or consent. This is a way that public utility corporations have, and to such high-handed methods is due no small measure of their unpopularity."

More recently, Public Service Electric and Gas Company attempted to erect transmission towers, without having sought municipal approval, in Roselle in 1956, in West Milford in 1965, and in Woodbridge in 1972, each time provoking community protest and a court fight. Responding to similar incidents within its jurisdiction, the New Jersey State House Commission felt compelled in 1971 to tighten up the granting of permission for electric lines to cross State property. Members of the Commission complained to the *Evening News* that it was common practice for a utility to "strip away the environmental cover along its proposed parkland routes, and often even install towers, before asking the State House Commission's approval." With the damage done, the Commission usually had little choice but to provide its "rubber stamp" consent. Commission members cited a Public Service line in Morris County as an example.

Richard O. Leinbach, the utility's manager of transmission projects, adds that, prior to 1970, "PS followed the understanding that full authority over transmission lines was held by the New Jersey Board of Public Utility Commissioners and, thus, that local ordinances were not operative in that respect." In 1971, the State Supreme Court ruled that transmission lines are subject to local ordinances. But even before that ruling, he says, Public Service had "established a procedure of full explanation of transmission line plans to local officials prior to construction..."

By obtaining permission beforehand, the utility could only ease public acceptance of its equipment; it could not, of course, guarantee that the equipment would be popular. "It should be noted," says Leinbach, "that local protest arises almost entirely by the fact of an overhead transmission line being planned and/or constructed."

Since at least 1930, those protesting the construction of transmission towers have urged the utility to put an end to problems of unsightliness, public resentment, and official consent by putting *all* its lines underground. But this has never been so simple a solution as it usually seems to outsiders. Public Service has been committed to underground construction in crowded areas for all of its 75 years, so that it now has about 18,000 miles of underground transmission and distribution lines. But to bury all of the utility's lines throughout its 1,400-square-mile territory would, according to one PSE&G estimate made in the early 1970s, cost about $3½ *billion*—a sum about equal to what the company had invested in all its generating stations, towers, poles, lines, trucks, equipment, offices, and land combined. Even installing all its *new* lines underground would be monumentally expensive for Public Service and its customers. In 1973 alone, when the company made its estimates, it would have cost $400 million more to install new lines underground, rather than overhead. The people who work out these projections figured further that, with increasing labor and materials costs, Public Service would be spending $800 million extra a year by 1980, if it acceded to the demands of environmentalists for an all-underground system.

As an example of cost-to-the-customer, PSE&G pointed out that to go along with the request of some residents of

Union and Middlesex Counties who wanted new transmission lines to go underground, would be to siphon off some $70 million more than it would cost to put the new lines above ground on existing PSE&G and railroad rights-of-way. If the approximately 127,000 customers in the 12 affected communities had to shoulder this extra cost alone, the tab per customer would run more than $500.

On the other side of the coin, PSE&G noted, was its compliance with a new regulation of the New Jersey Board of Public Utility Commissioners requiring installation of new residential lines underground on subdivisions of three or more homes—the cost of burying those lines being borne by the builders of the homes and, one may assume, being factored into the overall cost of construction.

The company conceded, in making these facts of underground installation known to the public, that while it might cost only twice as much to install such residential lines underground rather than on wood poles, it was also well to bear in mind "in most cases it (the cost) ranges as high as 20 times as much to install high-voltage lines underground instead of on steel towers, because of the need to use very expensive specially-insulated cables." There were other problems too that added to such costs: digging up and cosmetically replacing pavement in urban areas, for instance, a problem compounded by the longer time required to find, dig up, and repair the cause of any trouble that might develop in underground lines. Today's PSE&G took credit for having installed lines underground as a matter of policy "for years, wherever congestion of overhead facilities would result in operating difficulties, such as downtown streets," and for putting new high-voltage lines wherever possible in existing PSE&G or railroad rights-of-way, as well as for doing its best to see to it that trees suffered a minimum of clearance damage wherever towers had to be installed, and that those towers were sited to avoid their being silhouetted on high spots in the landscape.

The Forties

"There seems to be no peace for public utilities in this country"
—Tom McCarter

The start of World War II did not find Public Service unready or off guard. The industry, through the National Power Defense Committee, had noted the prospect of war as early as 1933, and had begun a number of studies to forecast wartime changes in load. Using its own estimates, Public Service began a program of expansion in 1939. Over the next four years, it added almost 400,000 kilowatts of generating capacity to its existing plants. It stepped up the output of many older machines and it installed three new 125,000-kilowatt cross-compound turbine generators, each supplied by two boilers, at Marion and Burlington. A shortage of materials delayed the second of the two Burlington installations for a year, but that unit went into service in time to meet the system's first million-kilowatt sendout. That peak came at 6:45 p.m. on December 16, 1943. Despite the chronic shortage of material, Public Service promptly met the energy needs of many large new customers; in one case, the company began tying in a 100,000-kilowatt aluminum war materials plant just two hours after receiving authorization from Washington, D.C. In the last year of the War, Public Service was able to meet such demands even as it deferred virtually all construction to conserve strategic materials. Finally, the utility continued to improve its efficiency, cutting the system heat rate from 16,800 BTU per kilowatt in 1937 to 14,700 in 1943.

If the War did not seriously hinder Public Service, a number of time-consuming challenges—McCarter considered them attacks—at about the same time from another source, the Federal government, easily made up for this. Public Service had joined the rest of the industry in opposing the Holding Company Act of 1935, which aimed to streamline the often multi-tiered structure of public utilities, and, when that law passed, the corporation had applied for an exemption from it. Fearing the Act would separate the company from its two largest stockholders, the United Gas Improvement Company and the affiliated United Corporation, with disastrous effects on the value of its stock, Public Service had asked for a ruling that it was not a subsidiary of either company. The Securities and Exchange Commission scheduled hearings on that application for 1941.

UGI had maintained a large interest in Public Service varying from a quarter to as much as a third of all common stock, since 1903, and had been involved in the development of New Jersey utilities long before that. According to one account, Bernard M. Shanley of Newark had introduced leading Philadelphia capitalists to the area during a tour in the 1880s that culminated at Eagle Rock in West Orange. Gesturing from that pinnacle at the rich territory between the Hudson River and the Watchung Mountains, Shanley had supposedly sold them on the value of an investment there. By 1903, UGI controlled most of the important gas properties of the State and some electric properties as well. When McCarter conceived his plan for a broad merger of gas, electric and traction companies in the State, it was necessary and, considering the Philadelphia company's long experience, wise to bring UGI into the deal. Of the initial issue by Public Service of $10 million in common stock, that company bought $2.5 million, or 25 per cent. In 1941, the SEC put UGI's interest in the New Jersey utility at 28.4 per cent.

PSE&G cadet engineers in 1946 before an early counterpart of the modern gas turbine; a 5000-kilowatt GE Curtis vertical turbine generator built in 1903 for Commonwealth Edison in Chicago, and installed as a monument at GE's Schenectady works. The late Herbert Wottrich, at left, supervised cadet training. Others, left to right, are Clarence M. Sanderson, Robert H. Shepherd, Francis H. Schiffer, Frank P. Librizzi, the late P. H. Nelson, Jack A. Casazza, Frank K. Faulkner, Richard C. Crockett, Thomas L. Wilson, Herbert H. Heller, Edward T. Francis, Arthur Teitelbaum, the late Clyde C. Ruffle and Clarence G. Troxell.

The United Corporation, controlling 13.9 per cent of all Public Service common stock, was a comparative newcomer. J. Pierpont Morgan and other banking interests had established the corporation early in 1929 in response to what one Public Service official called the "growing recognition in banking circles of the value of public utility securities as a field of investment," supplanting railroads in that respect. United acquired substantial (the SEC would say controlling) minority interests, not just in Public Service, but in UGI (of whose common stock it owned 18 per cent), and other important northeastern utilities. In addition to its main purpose of profitable investment, United Corporation announced that it also intended to foster cooperation, particulary in the form of high-tension interconnections, among the utilities.

At the hearing before the Securities and Exchange Commission, McCarter and other Public Service officials maintained that, while UGI had been "a very helpful influence" in the early years, neither UGI nor United Corporation had ever controlled the New Jersey utility. Testifying about a $55,000-a-year consulting contract with UGI during his company's first five years, McCarter said:

> "We had this new company upon our hands. I came to the head of it totally lacking in previous training and experience, such as public utility work, and felt the need of the best advice I could get, and the best people I knew in the business at the time were the United Gas and Improvement Company of Philadelphia."

> The Examiner: "They were also the largest stockholders, were they not?"
> McCarter: "One of the largest. And they were employed for a period of five years to advise and help in every way the operation of the new company. When July 1st, 1906, came about, the expiration time of that contract, I felt I knew my way around: I had learned quite a little of the business and saw no reason for renewing the contract and it was not renewed."
> An Attorney: "It was characterized as a sort of management contract, where they were to supply you with officers, wasn't it?"

McCarter: "Not at all. It was an advisory contract as to the details of operation of the company. It was not a management contract."
An Attorney: "Would you say that in earlier years they controlled Public Service Corporation?"
McCarter: "No, sir; never."

The Securities and Exchange Commission disagreed, denying the Public Service application and ruling that the utility was a subsidiary of both the United Gas Improvement Company and the United Corporation. "Indeed, if it were necessary," the SEC declared, "we would have no hesitancy in affirmatively finding that Public Service is controlled by UGI and United." Of the two companies' combined interest in Public Service it further stated:

"United and UGI are able affirmatively to pass any resolution or influence any course of conduct for applicant (Public Service) and they can thus defeat any resolution or action recommended by applicant's directors. They have the power to break a quorum at any Public Service meeting and they hold an absolute legal veto power over important corporate actions, such as mergers and consolidations, as to which the laws of New Jersey require a two-thirds vote of stockholders."

As an example of UGI control, the SEC cited the consolidation of the separate UGI and Public Service production companies into the co-owned United Engineers and Constructors. It said Public Service Production Company had been "by far the most profitable of the companies consolidated."

Public Service appealed the SEC decision up to the U. S. Supreme Court, but to no avail, and the company subsequently severed its connection with UGI and United under an SEC-approved plan. UGI distributed its Public Service securities among its own stockholders, accounting for most of the New Jersey company's 60,000 new stockholders in 1943. Public Service was now more and more a company owned not by corporations but by ordinary individuals, 150,000 of them, mostly women. The company's stockholding ranks did not quite consist entirely of "widows and children," but the idea was at least plausible now. Critics who had formerly jeered at the notion now were silent. Public Service had been promoting popular ownership of its stock since 1921, and, if the SEC decision benefited the company at all, it was in furthering this campaign. In justifying popular, and, in particular, customer ownership, McCarter had noted that "conservatism begins with ownership." It is possible that the gradual passing of the old "cordial hatred" toward Public Service—to be replaced be widespread public approval—began here.

The Federal Power Commission launched the second major government challenge to the utility in 1943, ordering Public Service to show why it should not cut almost $68 million out of the cost structure of the electric department. According to the Power Commission, the $68 million represented "write-up" or "water" in excess of the actual dollar investment in the electric plant. The valuation of electric properties was important because it determined just how much Public Service could legally earn (under the eight-per cent-profit standard) and therefore how much it could charge its customers. McCarter maintained that the company's books "today clearly represent the actual cost to it of its various properties, and that the value of such properties is largely in excess of the book costs, and so far as the electric property is concerned has been so determined to be by (the) Public Utility Commission."

McCarter seldom showed himself madder, or more mystified, than he was when he testified before the Power Commission in September, 1944, at age 77. He asked:

> "What in the world is this all about? Wouldn't it just as well in these troublous times to let a company go along with its business, serving the public as it has for the last 41 years, instead of trying to undermine and destroy it?"

Earlier he had said, "There seems to be no peace for public utilities in this country. The whole matter is beyond human understanding."

During questioning on his company's conduct of its business, McCarter shook his finger at the examiner and said:

"Young man, perhaps you can do better. In the years I have been associated with Public Service there has never been a breath of scandal. There has never been a reprehensible transaction. There has never been a shady deal."

McCarter denied, as he had been denying for 41 years, that there was "one drop of water" in Public Service, but the Federal Power Commission ruled otherwise. In October, 1945, the Power Commission and the New Jersey Board of Public Utility Commissioners jointly ordered Public Service to reduce by almost $58 million the valuation of its electric properties. Because of the $10-million drop in the cut as originally proposed and as finally ordered, and because of satisfactory compromise on other points of contention, Public Service decided not to appeal the order.

The final clash of this period between the New Jersey utility and the Federal government resulted, in 1948, in the dissolution of the Public Service Corporation and its replacement by the Public Service Electric and Gas Company. The Securities and Exchange Commission ordered the change, under the Holding Companies Act of 1935, to simplify the company's corporate structure. It made little visible difference to the company's customers or to its stockholders, and Public Service again accepted the government order. Its settlement with the SEC allowed Public Service Electric and Gas Company to inherit control of the Coordinated Transport Company, though the power and bus operations were not directly related—or "integrated," in SEC terminology.

So ended one major, decades-long phase of PSE&G's upwardly mobile but often seemingly star-crossed history. Almost without pause, another phase—destined to outstrip the achievements of the earlier phase, and to more than match its problems and challenges—was soon under way.

"Alvin, come quick! A new day has dawned!"

The Last Quarter-Century
and the Future

"Our job—indeed—our mandate, is to be there with the power when the
people need it and want it."
—Robert I. Smith

As Public Service Electric and Gas Company rounds out
three quarters of a century of often commendable—often
beleaguered—existence, it finds itself one of the nation's
largest utilities. Consider: It provides energy in two of its
most familiar forms—electricity and gas—to more than two-
thirds of the people in the nation's most densely populated
State. It gives gainful employment to nearly 14,000 highly
skilled men and women. In its 75th anniversary year it will
take in better than $2 billion and lay out in Federal, State and
local taxes more than the 17 cents out of every dollar it spent
that way the year before, when its tax bill ran in excess of
$216 million (up somewhat from the $836,928 it paid in taxes
for its first year of operation, 1903-04).

For its stockholders, there were some reassuring words in
1977 from McKinsey & Company, Inc., the management
consultant firm. Its report on management effectiveness had
some special words of praise for the company's financial
management. "Excellent" was the grade McKinsey gave it.

"PSE&G has developed and implemented a long-term
financial strategy that has enabled it to weather the period of

extreme difficulty between 1972 and 1975, and to substantially improve its current and future ability to raise needed external capital on favorable terms, even under 'worst case' assumptions," the report stated. "The essential element of this strategy was to strenghten the endangered AA bond rating—the most important measure of creditworthiness, and thus a determinant of interest cost and ability to raise money for construction."

Generally, the report noted, PSE&G has succeeded in obtaining financing at reasonable prices and had strengthened its credibility in the financial community.

Best of all, PSE&G is expanding its research activities. In 1977 the company formed PSE&G Research Corporation by combing its Research and Development Department and its Energy Laboratory.

Among other things, this group has launched a $447,000 effort to find out if solar energy can really produce in the Garden State. The Research Corporation has installed and has begun testing 11 solar water-heating, space-heating and pool-heating systems in customers' homes.

Harold Sonn, president of PSE&G Research Corporation, says his group will monitor these installations for three years to measure the real potential for solar energy in New Jersey. Four weather stations have been built throughout PSE&G's territory to record temperatures, sunshine intensity, cloud cover and other factors affecting the solar-heating systems.

Nuclear power will be the principal new means of generating electricity for the next two or three decades, but beyond that PSE&G may turn to two other promising methods. They are the fuel cell and fusion power.

Widespread use of fuel cells is closest to reality. It already has provided electricity for the capsules sent rocketing to the moon in the nation's space program. And on November 15, 1972, PSE&G researchers demonstrated that for the first time three 12.5-kilowatt fuel cells could produce power for an electric utility system. The tests were held in the downtown area of Newark, N.J., not far from the company's headquarters.

Edward R. Eberle, who was then PSE&G's president, said it was noteworthy that the testing was held in Newark because fuel cells could play an important part in supplying future energy needs of urban areas.

Along with eight other utilities PSE&G is continuing to support research to develop a 26,000-kilowatt fuel cell power plant for large-scale power applications. A major milestone was reached when a 1,000-kilowatt fuel cell pilot power plant was successfully tested by United Technologies Corporation in 1977. During the next phase, financed jointly by the U.S. Department of Energy and the Electric Power Research Institute, a 4,800-kilowatt fuel cell power plant will be installed and tested on an electric utility system. If additional research pays off—and experts feel it will—large fuel cells could be in use in the 1980s or 1990s.

The other likely power source of the future—fusion—got a boost from PSE&G in 1970 when the utility gave an initial grant of $50,000 to Princeton University's Plasma Physics Laboratory and agreed to take the initiative in encouraging other power companies to extend similar support. At Princeton, research is centering on a fusion process that uses hydrogen in water to produce power without smoke, carbon oxides, gases, ash, or radioactive waste.

It has been calculated that the energy that could be released from the deuterium in seven cubic miles of seawater would be equal to that of the entire initial supply of the earth's fossil fuels. On this basis, the world's oceans could supply 500,000 times this amount.

In addition to new sources of power, PSE&G Research Corporation is seeking ways to store power. It broke ground in 1977 for a $8.7 million Battery Energy Storage Test Facility. It will be used as a national test center for advanced battery systems. Development of these systems would permit generating stations to produce power during periods of low demand to be stored for use at times of peak requirements. PSE&G is providing $1.5 million of the cost of the project and the balance is being supplied by the U.S. Department of Energy and the Electric Power Research Institute.

The light buildings and ponds just left of center comprise the nucleus of PSE&G's aquaculture experiment at the Mercer Generating Station, near Trenton.

In addition to conducting research and development programs, the new subsidiary is exploring new ventures for its parent corporation.

One of these that is approaching the commercial stage is an aquaculture program at PSE&G's Mercer Generating Station in Hamilton Township, N.J. Here, trout, shrimp and eels are being raised in the warm water discharge from the generating station. This project has been financed by grants from the National Science Foundation totaling more than $1 million. If it proves economically feasible, PSE&G may soon find itself in the fish business.

All of this activity is designed to take New Jersey into the 21st century and to keep PSE&G in continuing good shape to meet the domestic and industrial light, heat and power needs of the State's growing economy.

All this would be reassuring at any other time but on the eve of PSE&G's 75th birthday there are other factors at work which tend to draw across this rosy picture streaks of gray. The climate for the utility industry in the Garden State today continues to worsen. This is true across the region and is on its way to becoming worldwide.

Even without the help of their increasingly vocal critics, utility executives, including those in charge at PSE&G,

recognize that that climate is already worse, in all probability, than it has ever been at any moment since kerosene lamps, one by one, doused the wicks in their carbon-blackened chimneys under the more gently glowing pressure of gaslight.

What Charles Dickens wrote more than a century ago in *A Tale of Two Cities* flickers today like some fatal omen over all the cities of mankind because they depend on this industry to provide them day and night the year 'round, with an unfailing supply of energy, "It was the best of times," Dickens began, "it was the worst of times, It was a time very much like the present."

Robert I. Smith, PSE&G's chairman of the board and chief executive officer, reflected somewhat the same view in speaking for his company, Jersey Central Power & Light Company, and Atlantic City Electric Company about electricity needs in the future at an all-day press information seminar in Jamesburg, N.J., on October 13, 1977.

"At the moment, I can tell you that we have ample power to take care of our needs," Smith said. "This past summer, as most of you know, new records were set in peak demands for power in all three of our electric systems and these demands were met, largely because of decisions made a decade ago, but also because of the Arab oil embargo in 1973, which had a drastic effect on the demand for—and the price of—electricity.

"That makes the picture bright enough for the moment, but when we look to the future, the picture is cloudy and from certain angles, it is downright dark.

"Possibilities for errors in judgment abound in projections for the next 10 or 20 years," Smith said. "Our crystal balls are very hazy. Much depends on the economic growth we experience. I am aware, as you are, that some people do not want to see any more growth in the conventional forms of electric-energy generation—fossil and nuclear. These people usually feel that various combinations of conservation, solar energy, the wind, cogeneration, geothermal power, tidal energy, and other alternatives can meet the demand of the future.

"The proponents of these alternatives enjoy a luxury that we in the utility business do not. They can make their propositions for the simpler life, and sit back and wait without much feeling of responsibility. If they turn out to be wrong and the lights go out, the politicians, the news media and the public will jump all over the utilities for failing to plan for the future.

"Our job—indeed—our mandate, is to be there with the power when the people need it and want it. And Americans—New Jerseyans—while they are conserving as power becomes more expensive, are giving no indication that they *want* to settle for the simpler life."

Smith told the story of the three drivers who filled three lanes of an interstate highway in the midwest, keeping a steady 55 miles an hour for many miles. They piled up hundreds of outraged drivers behind them, drivers who wanted to ignore the fact that they could save gasoline at 55 miles an hour and the fact that they were less likely to get into a serious accident.

"We live, as you may have noticed, in a democracy," Smith told the press.

"We in the utility business envision growth in New Jersey in the future," Smith said. "It will go on at a more modest pace than it has in the past, but it will go on. Indeed, if it does not, the unemployment problem this State faces today may get to the point where taxes will break the backs of the taxpayers, more industry will leave the State and class strife may well erupt. It will be the haves against the have-nots.

"We trust that will *not* happen, so we are going ahead, planning with the assumption that there will be modest growth and an increasing demand for electricity.

"The best way to meet that demand, we at PSE&G have concluded, is through the use of nuclear power. We have come to this conclusion after a hard look at the alternatives. While they offer potential help, we do not believe that they offer enough in time to meet the demands of the mid-80s and 90s," said Smith.

Smith talked about some of the alternatives at that seminar. He talked first about solar energy and made

Salem Generating Station on Artificial Island in Lower Alloways Creek, Salem County, New Jersey is PSE&G's first nuclear generating station within the state. It became operational in 1976.

reference to PSE&G's solar program to assess the year-round effectiveness of the sun in heating water and space in homes.

"More homeowners will install such systems," he said, "and I certainly would recommend that any *new* home builder investigate the feasibility of solar heating, but even if this use increased dramatically, it would have little effect in cutting down the demand for electricity. That is certainly so in Public Service Electric and Gas Company territory. Less than 2% of PSE&G customers use electricity for heating in their homes.

"There's a lot of wishful thinking," Smith added, "about using the sun's rays to produce electricity. It has been done in our space program and the government is soon to build a solar plant that, on a per-kilowatt-hour basis, will cost about 15 times what a nuclear power plant costs. That's a high price. In addition, you need an awful lot of land on which to place reflectors to catch the sun's rays, land that would be very hard to come by in New Jersey."

Smith also discussed cogeneration, which involves the production of electric power and other useful forms of energy from the same facility.

"It is a source of energy which Public Service has been utilizing for many years," Smith noted. "As a matter of fact, for the last 20 years Public Service has been conducting a large cogeneration project, the biggest of its kind in the world, with Exxon Corporation at PSE&G's Linden Generating Station. Public Service supplies Exxon's big Bayway refinery with 10 billion pounds of steam a year, plus half a billion kilowatts of electricity, while Exxon provides the generating station with millions of gallons of water and fuel oil.

"Recently," Smith told the press group, "the New Jersey Public Interest Research Group—virtually all of you know that's a Ralph Nader outfit—claimed that there was enough energy in industrial steam boilers throughout the state to warrant junking the plans for four nuclear power plants. What they did was make a list of the boilers licensed by the Department of Labor and Industry and they then made the mistake of assuming that every steam boiler on the list would be available and capable of the capacities listed. When we checked the list, we discovered that many companies on the list were out of business, had insufficient steam demand, or had to be disqualified for other reasons.

"For instance, the boilers at five oil gas manufacturing plants which Public Service operates were listed," Smith said. "These plants operate for a short time in the winter, when Public Service customers really don't need additional electricity, and not at all in the summer, when demand for electricity hits its peak.

"In 15 cases, the industries listed were out of business, their boilers had been removed or were about to shut down," Smith noted. "In one case, the company moved about 20 years ago. That gives you some idea of what kind of research the Public Interest Research Group did. When Public Service finished its investigation, it found only 18 industries with a potential of about 430 megawatts of generating capacity, about one-tenth the potential claimed by the Public Interest Research Group. Further, the installation of this 430 Mw of capacity would result in a present worth penalty to our customers of $400 million and a demand for 13 million barrels of high quality distillate oil over the next 20 years. Subsequently, only two industries expressed any serious interest in cogeneration."

In a talk given a year earlier at the Spring Business Conference of the Bergen County Chamber of Commerce, Smith had made reference to other alternatives espoused by opponents to nuclear power.

"It has been publicly suggested," said Smith, "that giant windmills be mounted on 150 to 500-foot towers out in the ocean, or that a string of them be placed along the Garden State Parkway.

"Now there is nothing new about big windmills. A number of them were tested in Europe between 1920 and 1950, and one was actually operated in Vermont during World War II," Smith told the group.

He then described the experience PSE&G had in the early 1930s with the windpower experiment at Burlington Generating Station, noting the two-part lesson that was learned—a lesson that awaits all windpower researchers in New Jersey: 1) the wind doesn't always blow and 2) even when it does, it can't generate enough electricity to achieve an acceptable unit cost.

Other alternate sources of energy don't offer much help either, according to Smith. Geothermal resources—heat trapped deep in the earth—are limited and located primarily in the western United States. Sites for hydroelectric power (falling water) just aren't available in New Jersey, and tidal energy cannot be counted on because only a few locations in the world have enough rises and falls of the tides for power generation to be practical. New Jersey is not one of them.

Among the conventional sources of energy, oil is the least attractive. It is too expensive and it puts America at the mercy of foreign nations that can shut off the flow without notice.

Smith therefore focused on the available alternatives that were for the moment anyway, really left: coal and nuclear power.

Smith made it plain that from his standpoint, and in the long run from the standpoint of everybody's pocketbook, in

The site for the Public Service Corporation headquarters on Park Place in Newark was a mix of modest homes and small shops in April, 1913, two years before ground was broken for the new building. Below, the company whose business is light observes an anniversary brightly. Opposite: The 26-story, glass-walled building that will become PSE&G's new corporate home, just east of its present headquarters, in 1980.

PUBLIC SERVICE

LIGHT'S GOLDEN JUBILEE 1879 1929

choosing nuclear-over coal-fired as the way to go in insuring
an uninterrupted supply of electric power, PSE&G had
pegged its decision to the one governing consideration of
fuel costs. There nuclear had it all over coal. When Smith
spoke, he cited a figure of 26¢ "to get a million British
Thermal Units of heat from nuclear fuel"—as against $2.10
for heavy oil and $1.75 for coal. He said all three costs would
rise substantially, beyond question, and that nuclear fuel
would go up "proportionately more than coal or oil." Even
admitting that, though, he declared that, according to sound
estimates about the way things would look 20 years from that
day, "coal and oil (would) still cost four to five times more
than nuclear fuel." And he said he was talking about the
cheapest coal available, high-sulphur stuff that "we assume
we would be able to use in New Jersey" if the company
equipped its coal plants with flue-gas desulfurizing units, or
"scrubbers," that would be required under the State's air
pollution code.

Then he struck a note, almost casually, about certain
assumptions that there is a tendency to make when people
think our immense resources in coal render nuclear-
powered generating plants, for whatever other reasons,
unnecessary. "We are also assuming," Smith said, "that the
coal will be available and that the railroads will have
sufficient capacity to ship the coal to New Jersey, something
that is not a certainty by any means." He said there was a real
possibility that, if such lack of certainty about available rail
transport increased, PSE&G would have to buy its own coal
mines and railroad cars, "and that could give nuclear even
more of an advantage."

"From an economic standpoint," Smith said, "it's easy to
see why we're going nuclear."

As examples of why that route was even then proving itself
a wise one, he noted that the State was already receiving
nuclear power from Peach Bottom Generating Station in
southeastern Pennsylvania, an installation of which PSE&G
owns 42 per cent. He said Peach Bottom had provided 15 per
cent of the company's electric output in 1975, and had saved
its customers $86 million "which we would otherwise have

had to spend on low-sulphur oil." He also pointed to the first unit of Salem Generating Station on the lower Delaware River in Salem County, New Jersey, which he said would go on line toward the end of the year, (It actually did go on line Christmas Day, 1976) with a second reactor slated to join it in 1979. PSE&G was involved with Salem Generating Station on the same basis as it shared in the cost and output of Peach Bottom, Smith said, with PSE&G and Philadelphia Electric Company each owning about 42 per cent, and Atlantic City Electric Company and Delmarva Power and Light Company each owning about 8 per cent. He spoke of having just broken ground for the twin-unit Hope Creek Generating Station, another nuclear-fired plant just north of the Salem installation. The first Hope Creek unit is scheduled for 1984 and the second unit for 1986.

As to the four projected floating nuclear power plants, the operating dates for these units have been pushed back three years since Smith spoke to the Bergen group, and they are now scheduled for 1988, 1990, 1993, and 1995.

The floating nuclear power plant concept originated at PSE&G in the mind of Richard Eckert, now a senior vice president with the company. He envisioned the marriage of two proven technologies—a nuclear power plant and a huge floating vessel. The design of floating nuclear power plants could be standardized and that, PSE&G reasoned, would keep the cost of construction down, not to mention the time required to build such a unit. Controversy has dogged the idea and at this point it is not clear that PSE&G will succeed in its plan to introduce the floating units to New Jersey waters.

Smith said that all the plants he'd been talking about would take New Jersey into the next century, and that sometime during that 100-year period, moreover, "we may be able to generate electricity by using fusion, a process in which two atoms are joined to create heat, rather than split, as in the current fission process." That was the point at which he speculated about how nuclear fusion would enable PSE&G and its sister utilities to "take the energy from a bucket of sea water and light up a whole city."

Contracts were signed for two floating nuclear power plants in September, 1972. The ceremony took place at sea, near the site of PSE&G's proposed Atlantic Generating Station, 2.8 miles out in the Atlantic Ocean, 12 miles northeast of Atlantic City. Seated, are Edward R. Eberle, then president of PSE&G, left, and Alexander P. Zechella, president of Offshore Power Systems. PSE&G executives looking on are, left to right: Edward J. Lenihan, Richard M. Eckert, Robert A. Baker, Robert I. Smith, John F. Betz, John F. McDonald, and Frederick W. Schneider. Below, an artist's concept of Atlantic Generating Station.

Until then, however, he said flatly that "we are relying on nuclear fission. We know it will do the job, providing the lifeblood that the economy of New Jersey ... will need." He said that without nuclear power the State's standard of living would fall, problems would increase, and people striving for a better life wouldn't have a prayer of achieving it. He ended with a plea that his audience do its part to keep that from happening.

Bergen County was a good place to make that plea since it was the site of one of the five steam-electric generating stations to which PSE&G had committed itself following World War II, and had built in rapid succession. Bergen Generating Station in Ridgefield, on a 110-acre site adjoining the New Jersey Turnpike, was at the time it began operation of its first unit in 1959 and another in 1960, the second largest in the PSE&G electric generating system, with an installed capacity from its twin turbine generators of 580,000 kilowatts. Over the next two years Mercer Generating Station, about four miles south of Trenton, would top Bergen with 640,000 kilowatts. But for Bergenites—especially residents of Ridgefield, who benefited from low residential taxes made possible by the enormous ratable that Bergen Station represented—the handsome blue-green complex sending power to their homes and industries from a site the company had foresightedly purchased 30 years earlier loomed as visible proof that PSE&G knew what it was doing, and that its president was a man to be listened to with confidence when he talked about the future.

Smith's predecessors—George H. Blake, Donald C. Luce, Watson F. Tait, Jr., Edwin H. Snyder, and Edward R. Eberle—had built and seen go on line in less than 20 years, between 1946 and 1964, more than 2,410,000 kilowatts in new generating capacity. First came Essex on the Passaic River. Second came Sewaren on the Arthur Kill three miles from Perth Amboy, the second salvo in PSE&G's post-World War II battle to keep up with the war-stimulated demand for energy. At the time, with its 480,000 kilowatts from an initial four units installed by 1951, Sewaren was the largest all-new PSE&G generating station since the War. Then came Linden

Generating Station, the trail-blazing "big swap" installation that exchanged process steam with Esso Oil (now Exxon) nextdoor for Esso's high-viscosity oil and water, and in the process added to the PSE&G system's output, with its two turbine-generators, another 520,000 kilowatts.

Linden went on line in 1957 at a cost of over $100 million, only four and a half miles north of Sewaren. A scant year later, however, projected load-growth studies indicated that ever greater generating capacity would be needed in that mushrooming central industrial area of PSE&G's territory. The company therefore decided to install a fifth unit at Sewaren and placed it in commercial operation in the fall of 1962, bringing the station's capacity up to 830,000 killowatts and making it the largest of the eight generating stations of its kind in the PSE&G system.

Two years earlier, the utility had brought on line the first of two 320,000-kilowatt units at its new Mercer Generating Station, and the second such unit in 1961. This was an especially historic move, because when Trenton's first electric generating station—the Peoples Electric Light Company, built at Chauncey Street in 1888—was leased to Public Service in 1903, it had an installed capacity of 1,808 kilowatts, consisting of "13 generating units: three 500-kilowatt, steam engine-driven, direct connected, alternating-current generators, ant 10 belt-driven, direct-current generators ranging in size from 15 to 60 kilowatts." This was quite a contrast with the spanking new Mercer installation because, as PSE&G noted with understandable pride, "the entire capability of the Trenton Generating Station in 1903 would, today, be just about adequate to drive the condensate pumps of one of the Mercer units. Such is the development of electric generating equipment in the twentieth century." Built to cope with the rising demand for electric power in South Jersey, Mercer's two 320,000-kilowatt units were larger than any of the 37 others in operation and brought the PSE&G system up to a capacity of 3,827,300 kilowatts.

The fifth of the post-World War II generating stations, Hudson, in turn topped Mercer, when its 400,000-kilowatt unit went into operation at the tail-end of 1964, as having the largest such unit at the time in the PSE&G system—and "the largest 3,600-rpm tandem-compound turbine-generator in service in the world." The Hudson unit increased the system capacity to 4,650,180 kilowatts. Hudson Generating Station, built on the Marion Generating Station property just north of that now defunct Station in Jersey City, had something else going for it. When the Marion site was originally developed to produce electric power and went into operation, in 1905, it was a model of its kind and the largest station Public Service had—even with a station capacity of only 13,000 kilowatts, and 5,000 kilowatts as its largest unit capacity. Those units, together with one 3,000-kilowatt unit that had gone into service, also in 1905, at the Coal Street Station in Newark, were the first turbine-generator units in the Public Service system, and had marked what the company called, the year it brought Hudson on line, "the beginning of a new era in the generation of electricity, and the close of the era of reciprocating engine-driven generators." Marion grew, of course, remaining the largest generating station in the Public Service system until 1924, when it had a total capacity of 98,750 kilowatts in eight turbine-generator units, the largest 22,500 kilowatts. "None of this equipment installed in the first quarter of the century is in service today," the company pointed out, "the last units having been retired in October, 1961, just before construction started on Hudson Generating Station."

One of the things which put Hudson out ahead of Marion is its design heat rate of 8,500 BTU per kilowatt hour—"less than three-quarters of a pound of coal per kilowatt hour," PSE&G observes, " ... a marked improvement over Marion Generating Station's early record of three pounds per kilowatt hour ... (and) a more than fourfold reduction in the amount of fuel required to produce electric energy..."

In the 1960s PSE&G took another step, system-wide, that might conceivably have reassured concerned critics of the utility industry that its executives and engineers do care about "emergency plans ... to make sure that even when separate crises combine ... the interruption of service remains small, localized, and short-lived." Starting with

Essex Station in 1963, the company began a program of equipping each of its steam-plant sites with a gas turbine generator unit. The purpose of doing this, as PSE&G's W.D. Bailey, a senior engineer in the electric engineering department, wrote in the May, 1968, issue of *Combustion* magazine, in the course of recounting the utility's experiences with two years of operating the gas turbine unit at Sewaren, was: "(a) to provide peaking power and (b) to provide power for blackout or "boot-strap" starting of the steam units at each site in the event we should have a system power failure."

Bailey noted that he and his associates had made it a practice to operate at what is normally regarded as the "peaking" rating whenever the unit was fired up—"close to takeoff power in aircraft use." In spite of treating the Sewaren unit—a 140-megawatt jet engine-powered unit, the largest in America, consisting of eight Pratt & Whitney Aircraft Division GG-4 jet engines supplying hot gases to four Worthington Corporation hot gas expanders —in that fashion to "shake the bugs out of it," the unit stood up so well, and with such relatively minor repair requirements, that Bailey reported all hands quite pleased with its "greater than 96 per cent" starting reliability. "It has proved," he wrote, "a dependable and valuable addition to our system."

The company obviously agreed, having gone ahead with units for Hudson, Mercer and Kearny Generating Stations. By the time the program of equipping its steam electric-generating plants with these powerful aircraft engines to insure "peaking power" was complete, Bailey said, the company would have 44 of these jet engines on line, ready to go in an emergency.

The Sewaren gas turbine unit went on line November 17, 1965, only eight days after Consolidated Edison and utilities in the rest of New York State and New England experienced their widespread blackout of November 9, 1965. It was there to help PSE&G recover relatively quickly from the June 5, 1967 blackout that hit New Jersey and other states. Like the other units in the standby reserve and "peaking power" system, the Sewaren gas turbine unit has been making PSE&G kilowatts when needed ever since.

Before gas turbines came on the scene, PSE&G had taken the first arduous steps in the direction of yet another accomplishment, called the Kittatinny Mountain Project. It projected for the 1970s a three-phase operation which, on completion, would provide an additional 1,630,000 kilowatts for New Jersey. The first stage of this undertaking, known as the Yards Creek Pumped-Storage Generating Station, was approved by the Federal Power Commission in 1963 and, with the dispatch that utilities can demonstrate once they get an official go-ahead, was in service by 1965. Its three combination pump/turbine motor/generator units provide full-load operation of a combined 330,000 kilowatts for about eight and one half hours of each generation period.

Yards Creek, located in two Warren County townships— Blairstown and Pahaquarry—is a joint venture of PSE&G and Jersey Central Power & Light Company. It exemplifies the only way there is to store electricity, in significant amounts, for future use. It does this by exploiting two things: 1) Surplus power available at night, when demand is low, to pump water from a lower reservoir to a higher one; and 2) gravity, to release the stored water down a tunnel to turn turbines which, as pumps, had sent it uphill the night before, and thus to generate peaking-power electricity for daytime needs.

The tremendous force to do this comes, at Yards Creek, from the 200-million-gallon differential between the upper reservoir, a body of water containing 1,560,000,000 gallons of water and situated on two small (310 acres) swampy tracts southeast of the Delaware River, and the lower reservoir, a 45-acre site a mile farther east on Paulins Kill containing 1,760,000,000 gallons. There is also an auxiliary reservoir of 45 acres containing another 163,000,000 gallons, a sort of insurance against dry spells. The hydro-pumps use surplus power to boost all that water 700 feet uphill by night to the upper reservoir, which is Yards Creek, and then, whenever required, the Station engineers open the gates and down a 20-foot-diameter tunnel and "penstock" comes thundering the 20-billion-gallon bore to set the turbines below spinning madly to meet the coming peak demand.

The tunnel is approximately 1,500 feet long, lined with concrete, and feeds into the penstock, also about that length, which narrows to intensify the roughly 24-feet-per-second downhill rush of the water. The lower 218 feet of the tunnel is lined with steel, and shrinks to a 19-foot diameter that the penstock further reduces to 18 feet. After an 1,860-foot trip through the narrower penstock, this tortured Niagara boils into three 250-foot-long penstock branches, each suddenly narrowing to 10 feet in diameter, to hit with the full force of its 700-foot downhill plunge the waiting spherical valves of the pump/turbine units. Once it has spun their shafts, out it goes, exhausted over a 145-foot tailrace channel or spillway into the lower reservoir, there to await nightfall and its return journey uphill, against the next day's need.

The remaining two segments of the Kittatinny Mountain Project—Tocks Island Dam and Sunfish Pond—apparently are dead, victims of environmental-protest entanglements and other thickets. Sunfish Pond has been given to the State and the Tocks project is, at least, in limbo. Meanwhile, unmanned, the fully-automatic Yards Creek Pumped-Storage Generating Station runs under remote control from the Jersey Central Power & Light Company's Systems Operation Center at Morristown, by microwave, to help keep North Jersey energized.

PSE&G engineers Harry Roman, Ron Venturi, Darwin Chang, Andrew Johnson and Alan Maltz at one of the 11 solar energy installations established in New Jersey homes for a three-year analysis of solar's potential in the state. PSE&G is underwriting the study at a cost of nearly $500,000.

Summing Up

"Everything is continually changing—not only the events themselves, but the very rules governing these events."
—Dr. Ralph Sui

To have accomplished what PSE&G has in 75 years obviously took not only know-how, drive, ingenuity and daring—it took a revolution in the way we live, and it sparked a dramatic uplift in our standard of living. It also took some extraordinary men, some of whom have already been mentioned here. Lest this book be found wanting, however, a brief profile of the leaders follows. As one observer put it, borrowing Emerson's phrase, "This company is more than the extended shadow of one man."

When Thomas N. McCarter, Sr., retired as chairman of the board of PSE&G on his 78th birthday, October 20, 1945, an era came to end. Edmund W. Wakelee, who had been serving as president of the company since 1939, predeceased him that year. McCarter had come to know and admire Wakelee when both served in the New Jersey State Assembly before the formation of the Public Service Corporation. Wakelee's indentification with Public Service went back to 1900 when he became counsel for the New Jersey & Hudson River Railway and Ferry Company. When the company was leased to Public Service Railway Company in 1911, Wakelee was retained as counsel of the latter.

Ten men have held the title of president and/or chairman of the board of PSE&G. Thomas N. McCarter was president from 1903 until 1939, when he became chairman of the board. He retired in 1945. In 1939, Edmund W. Wakelee assumed the presidency, but he died in 1945 and was succeeded by George H. Blake. When Blake retired in 1954, Lyle C. McDonald became chairman of the board and Donald C. Luce became president. McDonald retired in 1958 and Luce took over as chief executive officer, retaining the title of president. When Luce retired in 1965, Watson

WATSON F. TAIT JR.

EDWIN H. SNYDER

EDWARD R. EBERLE

ROBERT I. SMITH

JOHN F. BETZ

F. Tait, Jr., was named chairman of the board and Edwin H. Snyder became president. Tait retired in 1968, Snyder succeeded him as chairman, and Edward R. Eberle became president. Snyder retired in 1972 and Eberle succeeded him as chairman. At the same time, Robert I. Smith was named president. Eberle retired in 1975 and Smith succeeded him as chief executive officer, retaining the title of president. In 1977, Smith became chairman and John F. Betz was named president.

Edmund Wakelee, a New York University law graduate, had a personality that was pleasing, a mind that was keen, and a lively interest in public affairs. He was first elected to represent Bergen County in the State Assembly in 1899. Re-elected the following year, he was floor leader and on his way to becoming speaker of the Assembly when William M. Johnson, the Bergen County Senator, resigned to become Assistant Postmaster General of the United States. Mr. Wakelee was elected to fill the vacancy and served 10 years in the Senate. Within that period, he was chosen majority leader and president of the Senate and also served, at times, as acting Governor of the State.

In 1914, Tom McCarter asked Senator Wakelee to join Public Service as associate general solicitor. In 1917 he became a vice president and in 1923 he was named vice president in charge of law.

With all his other duties, Wakelee found time to promote a movement to save the Palisades along the Hudson River from encroachment by quarry men and others who sought to mar its scenic beauty. He was a leader in the creation of New York and New Jersey commissions to reserve the land as a public park and served years as a New Jersey Commissioner. When the two bodies were combined to form a single Interstate Commission in 1939, Wakelee was elected its president, directing the destiny of what is conceded to be one of the largest recreational areas in the East.

That same year—1939—Wakelee was also named president of Public Service, a post he held until he resigned shortly before his death in April, 1945, following a long illness.

George H. Blake, another attorney, and also a New York University graduate, was elected to succeed Wakelee and he took over the reins of the company when Tom McCarter retired. Blake started his Public Service career in 1910 as a trial attorney in Jersey City. He rose through the ranks of the law department, becoming a director of Public Service in 1934, vice president and general solicitor in 1937, and executive vice president in 1943.

The company marked its 50th anniversary during Blake's tenure and on that occasion in 1953 Blake foresaw a bright future for the company. During his tenure, an extensive construction program in electric and gas facilities went forward and in PSE&G's 1954 annual report, this paragraph, a portent of the future appeared:

"Since 1951 the Company has been actively engaged in studies for the use of atomic energy for the generation of electricity. It had contributed manpower and funds, along with 32 other companies, to the Atomic Power Development Associates, an organization concentrating on the actual design and eventual construction of an economical commercial power reactor. In addition, the Company is training some of its engineering personnel in this new field."

When Blake retired at age 70 in March of 1954, Lyle McDonald became chairman of the board and Donald C. Luce became president.

McDonald was also a graduate of New York University. He started with Public Service as an accountant in 1916. He became comptroller in 1937, was elected vice president and comptroller in 1944 and vice president in charge of finance in 1948. Finance was his primary area of expertise and he played a leading role in the utility's multimillion-dollar expansion program after World War II.

What could be construed as a stranglehold by New York University on the top spot at PSE&G was broken when McDonald retired in 1958 and Donald C. Luce took over.

Don Luce was one of many young engineers who came out of Lehigh University in the 1920s to join PSE&G. These engineers gravitated to the utility field because that's where the action was. Utility systems were growing at a tremendous rate and PSE&G was out in the forefront. Lehigh and its engineering graduates did not guess wrong, for many of the graduates rose to high positions in the utility .

Thus, in 1958, after 55 years under the guidance of lawyers and a financial expert, PSE&G had an engineer controlling its destiny.

Engineers flocked to the utility business in the 1920s and many of them rose to high levels at PSE&G in the last quarter-century. On the extreme right in the third row of this photo of cadet engineers is Donald C. Luce (No. 27). The photo was taken at Kearny Station, November 19, 1926. Luce took over as president of PSE&G 32 years later.

Luce spent years out in the field—at Marion Generating Station and Kearny Generating Station—before starting his climb to the top at PSE&G's General Office in Newark. He became general superintendent of generation in 1936, general manager of the Electric Department in 1942, vice president in charge of electric operations in 1948 and vice president in charge of combined operations in 1950. In the latter post, he became the first Electric Department man to take overall control of the Electric and Gas Departments within the company.

Growth in demand for electricity and gas continued unabated during Don Luce's term as president. Population growth was a factor. While the nation as a whole showed a population gain of 29 per cent from 1950 to 1965, the Middle Atlantic States gained 21 per cent and New Jersey outstripped both with a gain of 40 per cent. When Luce retired at age 65 in 1965, Watson F. Tait, Jr., was named chairman of the board and Edwin H. Snyder became president. Both were Lehigh men, moving wags to comment that you had to come from Lehigh to make it big at PSE&G. That proved to be untrue in the years following.

Watson (Buck) Tait had actually gone to Marietta College in Ohio, earning a bachelor of arts degree before he went to Lehigh to get a degree in electrical engineering. He came up through the ranks of the Electric Distribution Department, the group that gets electricity from the generating stations to an end use.

Tait had joined Public Service in 1922. By 1938, he had become assistant general superintendent of Electric Distribution. In 1948 he became general manager of the Electric Department and vice president of electric operation in 1950. During his years as chief operating officer of PSE&G, the company made its first application to the Atomic Energy Commission to build a nuclear generating station in Burlington City and Burlington Township. Later the site was changed to Lower Alloways Creek Township in Salem County.

There was a need for more generating stations and more gas facilities as New Jersey's economy continued to boom.

When Buck Tait retired in 1968, Ed Snyder succeeded him as chairman of the board and Edward R. Eberle became president.

Snyder had come out of Lehigh in 1923, a year after Buck Tait, and had joined Public Service the same year. During the Snyder years, PSE&G came to terms with pollution. A massive switch from coal to low-sulphur oil as a fuel in generating stations occurred. The switch began a year before New Jersey's stringent air pollution code was drawn up and it kept PSE&G in compliance well in advance as each of the code's steps was implemented. The first nuclear unit of Salem Generating Station began to take shape in those years and plans went ahead for more construction.

Ed Snyder had the distinction of serving as a member of President Lyndon Johnson's Electric Utility Industry Task Force on Environment, a 27-member blue-ribbon group which was part of President Johnson's Citizens Advisory Committee on Recreation and Natural Beauty. Both groups were chaired by Laurance S. Rockefeller. Subsequent to his service with this group, Snyder established a new Department of Environmental Affairs at PSE&G. He retired in 1972. Ed Eberle succeeded him as chairman at that time and Robert I. Smith was named president.

Eberle was a Yale man. Smith was from Brown. The Ivy League was back in business.

Ed Eberle's degree from Yale was in electrical engineering. He received it in 1931 in the heart of The Depression. He has often said that the real reason he went on to get a master's degree at Harvard School of Business Administration was that he couldn't get a job. He *did* get a job as a meter reader and collector with PSE&G in 1933 and for the next 24 years worked in the Commercial Department as service clerk, ledger clerk, special clerk, collection clerk, supervisor of collection and meter reading, assistant commercial manager, assistant to the general commercial manager, and finally manager of industrial relations. He was elected vice president in charge of services in 1962 and his promotions to president in 1968 and chairman of the board and chief executive officer in 1972 followed.

During the Eberle years, PSE&G became the first utility to put power into a transmission system from a fuel cell and the first utility in the United States to put a synthethic natural gas plant on stream.

Bob Smith, PSE&G's current chairman of the board and chief executive officer, succeeded Eberle as chief executive in 1975, having served as president from late 1972. After graduating from Brown University in 1940 with a degree in mechanical engineering, he joined PSE&G and rose through the ranks of the Electric Engineering Department after some service at Marion Generating Station in Jersey City. The stint at Marion was interrupted by service in the U.S. Navy during World War II.

Smith became chief engineer of the Electric Engineering Department in 1965. What followed was a series of rapid-fire promotions to general manager of engineering in 1967; vice president in charge of electric operations in 1968; executive vice president in 1971, and president in 1972. When Bob Smith became chairman in May, 1977, John F. Betz was elected president and became chief operating officer.

Betz is the first Rutgers man to become president of PSE&G. He received his degree at Rutgers in 1937 and joined PSE&G the same year. Like Smith, John Betz is an electrical engineer. Like Tait and Snyder, he came up through the Electric Distribution Department. In 1971, he was promoted to vice president in charge of electric operation, then senior vice president of planning and distribution in July, 1974. Three months later, Betz was named senior vice president of engineering and production. He rose to the level of executive vice president in 1975.

From 1903 until 1978, only these 10 men have achieved the presidency and/or chairmanship of PSE&G.

They have seen dramatic growth in the use of electricity. In 1945, the year Thomas N. McCarter, Sr., retired, a residential customer of PSE&G was using an average of 917 kilowatthours of electricity annually. A decade later, average annual use had more than doubled—the 1955 figure was 1,897. In 1965, average annual kilowatthour use per residential customer nearly doubled again, reaching 3,318 kilowatthours. By 1975, this figure stood at 5,348 kilowatthours, off somewhat from the peak that was reached in 1973—5,703 kilowatthours.

Nearly two dozen electric appliances had come into use in the first of those decades, and as the end of the 1970s hove in sight the number had soared to 35 or more. Refrigerators, TV sets, stereos, freezers, garbage disposals, washing machines, dryers, airconditioners, ranges, razors, dehumidifiers, toothbrushes, sonic sleep-inducers, can openers, frying pans, carving knives, ring cleaners, rock tumblers, yogurt makers, hot trays, egg coddlers, typewriters, power tools, heaters and other handy equipment for making life more pleasant did their part in increasing the demand for electricity.

The use of electricity in industry and business also grew dramatically. The first full year of operation—1904—saw

Kilowatt-hour Sales of Electricity 1903-1977

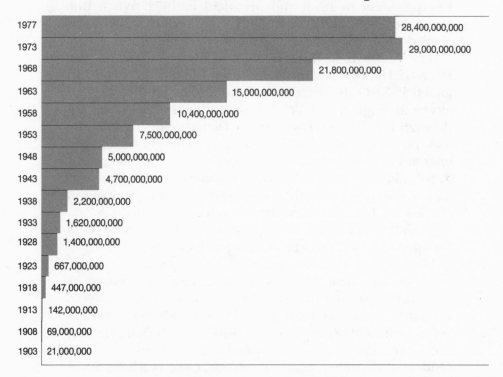

Year	Value
1977	28,400,000,000
1973	29,000,000,000
1968	21,800,000,000
1963	15,000,000,000
1958	10,400,000,000
1953	7,500,000,000
1948	5,000,000,000
1943	4,700,000,000
1938	2,200,000,000
1933	1,620,000,000
1928	1,400,000,000
1923	667,000,000
1918	447,000,000
1913	142,000,000
1908	69,000,000
1903	21,000,000

In the years between 1943 and 1973 PSE&G's sales of electricity grew six-fold and its sale of gas nearly did that in a twenty-year period, from 1943 to 1963. But several factors combined in the early Seventies to subdue that growth. An oil embargo pushed fuel oil prices up, resulting in conservation that brought consumption down. A recession, from which the state is still

approxiamtely 42.5 thousand kilowatthours of electricity sold. That included all sales-residential, commercial and industrial. By 1945, that total had increased more than 100,000 times to more than 4.3 billion kilowatthours and when 1977 drew to a close, the figure had hit 28.4 billion kilowatthours. This grand total was also off somewhat from the 1973 peak of more than 29 billion kilowatthours.

The use of gas also grew at a fast pace as use switched from gas lighting to cooking and heating. In the first 40 years, when records were kept in cubic feet, use increased more than six times, from 23 million cubic feet in 1903 to 168

Therm Sales of Gas 1903-1977

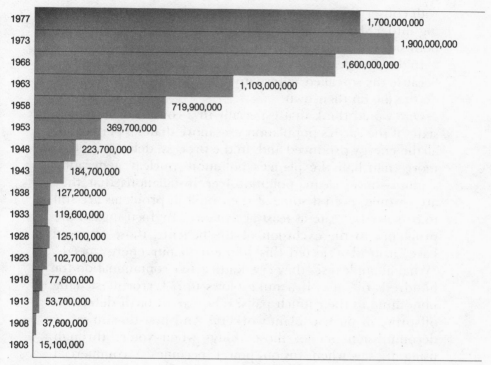

Year	Sales
1977	1,700,000,000
1973	1,900,000,000
1968	1,600,000,000
1963	1,103,000,000
1958	719,900,000
1953	369,700,000
1948	223,700,000
1943	184,700,000
1938	127,200,000
1933	119,600,000
1928	125,100,000
1923	102,700,000
1918	77,600,000
1913	53,700,000
1908	37,600,000
1903	15,100,000

emerging, slowed industrial and commercial use. And a moratorium on new gas installations imposed in 1973 held growth in that area in check. In 1977 low natural gas supplies caused the company to curtail service to some industrial and commercial customers for the first time in its history.

million cubic feet in 1942. Therm records show that by 1947, gas sold topped 220 million therms. This jumped to 624 million therms by 1957; 1 billion 510 million by 1967, and in 1977 stood at 1 billion, 742 million, down from the peak of 2 billion therms reached in 1972.

Throughout its 75 years, PSE&G has kept ahead of this growth despite the implacable determination of pressure groups. Individually, members of these groups were probably never prepared to yield an Angstrom unit in insisting on their right to the electrically-powered good life. As groups, they still are united in a matching determination not to let the utilities build new generating plant—especially if it is nuclear-fueled. The challenge of matching national need with conservationist perspective on ecology continues, moving into PSE&G's anniversary year, to engage and perplex both sides of a seemingly unresolvable tug-of-war.

In the decades ahead, it's either go nuclear or buy candles, because the so-called "alternatives" and conservation cannot do the job on their own.

One would think that especially in a country where one-sixth of the earth's population uses more than 35 per cent of all the energy produced and, in the process, delivers itself of more than half the planet's pollution, nuclear generating stations—nice, clean, pollution-free installations that they are—would, even if some of their built-in problems are still to be solved, create at least acceptance. By focusing on the problems, to the exclusion of the benefits, those opposed have, instead, rejected this solution to our energy needs. "What about leaks?" they cry. Radioactive contamination for hundreds of miles if a nuke blows up? Terrorists stealing plutonium in their lunch pails? The risk of birth defects in offspring of nuclear-plant workers? And how do you safely decommission one of those things when you're through using it, say when fusion power becomes a commercial reality?

Noting this opposition, John Betz, then a vice president, told an Energy-Environment Symposium in 1973:

"This is *not* a battle over environmental objectives—it is rather a question of survival—meeting customer demands—until considered objectives—placed in order of priority—can be met.

"We in the electric industry are not opposed to the aims of conservationists and environmentalists who would preserve the wetlands and return the ocean, the rivers and the air to the condition they were in before industrialization. No one in this room could be against this as an ultimate objective—so long as we don't do serious harm to our quality of life. I'm among those who believe that the people of New Jersey do not want to go back to the cold, the dark, and the horse.

"The preservation and enhancement of our environment can be achieved if all of us work together and compromise to reach solutions.

"The more zealous among conservationists and environmentalists must realize that in order to reach the objective—namely the good life, the preservation and enhancement of our environment—we must have electric power. Sewage treatment plants and air pollution control devices require electricity," Betz said.

"The more cost-conscious among those of us in electric utility management must realize that the days of cheap energy are gone and the cost of doing business is going up. To improve the environment we must pay the price and risk the wrath of the consumer, who ultimately pays for everything. At the same time, we must intensify our efforts to keep people from wasting electricity. And we must find new and better ways to generate ... ways that will hold the cost down.

"If we do not work together, the electric utilities of New Jersey will not be able to meet the demand for power in the future. Industry and business would not only stop coming to our state, but those firms we have would begin to leave. Jobs would be lost, vital services endangered, and the average citizen would find his whole way of life limited," said Betz.

Opposition to generating plants isn't all utilities face.

Other groups help utility brass go prematurely gray by campaigning vigorously for burial of those "unsightly" high-tension wires. It doesn't matter that high-tension transmission links are vital to the pooling of electricity and the computerized switching of it to areas as their needs fluctuate. Bury 'em. Nor does it have much apparent weight with those opposed to point out that, even if present technology and urban conditions permitted burial, it would raise everybody's electric bill phenomenally. Bury 'em.

The shortsightedness of this opposition had continued to be clear, but not to the opposers, for more than a decade.

The man who runs Consolidated Edison has summed up the problem neatly. "The realization is coming," said Con

Ed's chairman Charles F. Luce, "that if you oppose every site, eventually it will have an effect when you try to switch on the light."

PSE&G's Bob Smith put it another way in talking to a conference of Public Utilities Commissioners in 1973:

"Utility executives who conscientiously attempt to respond to the demands of consumers and environmentalists these days must certainly feel like the little man that people shoot at with an electric eye gun. I'm sure you've seen him wherever people gather for amusement," he said. "He purposefully plods across the marksman's field of view. The marksman squeezes the trigger, hits him in the shoulder with the electric eye beam, and the little man turns around and plods back in the other direction.

"If the marksman is good enough, the little man never gets anywhere. After a certain number of shots and a certain amount of time, the little man just stops dead and the lights go out."

Efforts to insure an adequate supply of gas in the future have also sparked opposition. Since 1972, PSE&G has been attempting to get approvals to import liquefied natural gas from Algeria, but to no avail. Opposition now exists to offshore drilling for oil and gas in the Atlantic Ocean.

To Tom McCarter, all this would undoubtedly have led to the conclusion that little has changed through the years. But it would make one wonder why he or anyone ever chose to do battle in this field.

During hearings before the SEC in 1941, McCarter testified about how the company got started. After they had settled on a $10-million capitalization to take care of debts of the combined companies and proposed expenditures of $3 million a year "we were on easy street," McCarter said. Then, somebody asked "Now that you have got this company, who is going to run it?"

The SEC examiner prompted gently, "Who was that somebody, Mr. McCarter?"

And McCarter answered, as if he still couldn't believe it himself even after 38 years in the saddle: "Somebody else at the meeting said, 'I think the man who invented the scheme ought to run it.'

"Well, if he had pulled out a pistol and fired it at me I couldn't have been more surprised. I had no conception of going into this business; I was a lawyer..."

Bob Smith, who like the engineer-presidents who succeeded McCarter, had the fullest intention a young man can have of going into "this business," and continues to cope with the problems, just as his storied predecessor did.

"My friend, Bob Gilkeson, of Philadelphia Electric Company, has often referred to the problems of the utility industry as 'opportunities'—and I don't have to tell anyone here today that we are up to our necks in opportunities," Smith told an American Power Conference in 1975. "Our critics are legion—and never before in history have they been so vocal. These are truly times of adversity—but adversity has its blessings. It was Homer who wrote, 'Adversity has the effect of eliciting talents which in prosperous circumstances would have lain dormant.'

"When times are bad—that's the time to do things—to make changes—to try something new. Many years ago, I heard the story of a chicken farmer who encountered a period of adversity every spring when the floods came and drowned many of his chickens. One year after a particularly bad flood, he came into the farmhouse and, in a voice filled with despair, told his wife, 'I've had it—I can't afford to buy another place—I don't know what to do.'—'I do,' said his wife, 'raise ducks!'" Smith said.

"I don't know of anybody in the power industry who is raising ducks, but Long Island Lighting Company is raising oysters in their discharge basin and Public Service Electric and Gas Company is raising fresh water shrimp in the summer and trout in the winter with an assist from the heat in the discharge water at Mercer Generating Station. Thermal pollution is one of the power-industry problems, and we must devise ingenious ways of utilizing this heat for social benefit—cooling towers are not the answer to the problem.

"While on the subject of water, I'm reminded of another story I read recently. It started to rain, and it rained steadily for thirty days and thirty nights. On the thirty-first day, a group of the world's foremost scientists met and decided that the biblical prophecy of rain for forty days and forty nights was about to be fulfilled, and that the whole world would be flooded. The scientists concluded that it would be appropriate to tell the leaders of the world's religions what was about to happen so that the people could be prepared. That day, the Catholic priests told their congregations to confess their sins and prepare for the day of judgment. The Protestant ministers told their congregations to search their consciences and prepare to meet their Maker. In the synagogues the rabbis told their people, 'You have exactly nine days to learn how to live under water.'

"We don't have to learn how to live under water—yet—but we do have to learn to live and operate in an environment which has changed radically in the last few years," said Smith.

Smith, a smart executive with a ready grin, tells another story to illustrate his point about change. It is about the interesting thesis of Dr. Sui.

"Dr. Ralph Sui," Smith recalls, "a consultant in the field of corporate strategy, has said that today's successful utility executive has to be proficient in the practice of a singularly important art which he calls Chinese Baseball. Now Chinese Baseball, the mastery of which is essential in dealing extensively with government and public groups, is played almost like American Baseball. There is one—and only one—difference, however. After the ball leaves the pitcher's hand, and as long as the ball is in the air, anyone can move any of the bases anywhere. 'In other words,' Dr. Sui says, 'everything is continually changing—not only the events themselves, but the very rules governing those events.' This kind of arena is alien to the technological tradition of fixed boundary conditions, clearly defined variables, non-subjective assessments and rational consistency within a closed system. In the new ball game—which must have been particularly frustrating for an engineer accustomed to having things stay where they're put—everything is in a state of flux.

"Furthermore," Smith went on, "there is no longer a social problem that can be solved for all time, like solving the mathematical problem of 'two-plus-two.' For instance, there is no such thing as an 'environmental problem.' There are only environmental issues never fully delineated, never solved, always changing."

For that American Power Conference he addressed in 1975, Smith had these concluding thoughts: "The rapid escalation of all of the costs involved in producing and distributing electricity has produced problems without precedent in the utility industry. Attempts to pass these costs on to the consumer who *must* pay them are met with frustration and delay in the regulatory process. Indeed, some states have legislated against the pass-through of increased fuel costs and one wonders about the adequacy of the legislative process in such a critical, albeit controversial, situation. True, the consumer is concerned about the increasing cost of what he considers to be a necessity of life— he has cut back his consumption, and this fact combined with reduced consumption because of the business recession has exacerbated the utility plight. Normal growth patterns have been altered and utilities have had to take drastic action to stay alive. As a result of the present situation, we are going to see changes in traditional utility rate designs. We are going to see a general flattening of rate schedules—we are going to see high peak demand rates, time-of-day metering, and winter/summer rate differentials. Although these rate changes will have a suppressing effect on utility growth, they will, in the long run, be of overall benefit. We should not waste energy or money, and these rate designs should have the effect of leveling our peaks and improving our load factor. This will result in more efficient utilization of our capital equipment and a reduction in capital expenditures. Don't think for a minute, however, that the demand for electricity is not going to grow—zero growth is just not realistic. As a matter of fact, the reduction in availability of petroleum and natural gas, which are finite resources, can do nothing but increase the demand for electric energy. As so many have advocated, we should be using petroleum and natural gas for petrochemicals and other necessities—not for heating homes or for other energy uses where electricity can be substituted. Every electric utility has always had the basic problem of raising the funds to provide new generating capacity when it is needed. This problem is compounded today by the difficulty of raising funds and the uncertainty as to when additional generating capacity is required.

"In closing," Smith said, "I'd like to recall my three-word energy crisis 'opportunity'— 'Cut Oil Imports.' We can accomplish this by generating electricity with coal and uranium and by utilizing other forms of generation which are not dependent on fossil fuels. We can do it by developing an acceptable electric vehicle. We can do it by substituting electric energy for fuel oil in heating our homes. We can do it by increasing our domestic supplies—by drilling off the Atlantic Coast, for example.

"What happens if we don't 'Cut Oil Imports?' Smith asked. "At the present time, $25 billion a year goes out of the country to pay for our oil purchases. If it keeps up, the Arabs and the other oil exporting countries are going to own us. In the long run, it may mean a reduction in our standard of living because there won't be as much money to spend at home. A bleak picture—but a time to use the 'I's' with which Americans have been traditionally endowed—the 'I's' of innovation, ingenuity, inventiveness, and initiative.

Use of that talent had resulted in a team effort at PSE&G. A sweeping reorganization of the Company, announced in May, 1977, saw the creation of the "office of the chief executive" in which Smith and Betz will function in directing the future affairs of the Company. Two other executives were named to join them—Edward G. Outlaw, who was named to the new post of executive vice president of corporate planning, and William E. Scott, who remains an executive vice president of finance. Outlaw had been serving as senior vice president of operations. He will coordinate all planning activities in the Company, with emphasis on strategic planning for the future.

When speaking to analysts, Smith usually gives a nod to Bill Scott, who came to PSE&G from Irving Trust in 1972 at the behest of Smith and Eberle, to share his fiscal know-how.

"We took Bill out of the grandstand and put him down on the playing field," Smith told New York Security Analysts at one of their meetings, "and when the events of 1974 hit us, I think Bill might have yearned to be back in the grandstand. The role of chief financial officer changed drastically in the '70s. Back in the '60s, the chief executive officers used to say to the chief financial officers, 'I'll run the business; you get the money.' But in 1974, the chief financial officer, of necessity, became deeply involved in operating decisions and, as a matter of fact, he called the shots."

Smith also makes it a point in talking to analysts to refer to the Monday morning meetings of the Management Council, and to talk about the Operating Committee, which consists of the Management Council plus the Company's vice presidents, two groups that comprise the executive management team. The entire team, says Smith, brings to bear a "wealth of talent with varied backgrounds and disciplines" in dealing with the problems and day-to-day running of the utility.

Managing a large utility is complicated and frustrating these days, but it is also challenging and, at times, even rewarding.

Bob Smith talks about a friend of his who once remarked, "If I wasn't in the utility business, I'd buy a ticket to get in."

Says Smith: "I'd buy one, too."

INDEX

Accidents, railroad, 65-7, 77, 88
Air pollution control, 369
Alcoholic Beverage Commission, 14-5, 19
Algerian liquified natural gas, 279, 376
Allen, John, 262, 272-3, 276
Alloys, 55
Alternating current, 56, 84, 289-91
Amusement parks, 91, 93-5
Anti-Saloon League, 16
Appliance selling
  electric, 298-300
  gas, 105, 252-5
Appliance testing (electric), 297-300
Aquaculture, 346, 377
Arc lamps, 33-4, 36, 40-3
Arlington Shuttle, 100
Atlantic City Electric Company, 347, 355
Atomic Power Development Associates,
  367
Atterburg, W.W., 208-9
Awards
  bus, 234
  C. A. Coffin Award, 318
Bailey, W.D., 360
Baird, David, 195-7, 203, 206
Baker, Robert A., 323-5
  photo 356
Bank of Manhattan Company, 73
Barrington, Patrick A., 99
Barron, Jake, 288, 301-3, 329
Battery Energy Storage Test Facility, 345
Battin, Joseph, 24-5
Baughan, Alexander E., 313
Bayonne Ferry Line, 102
Bedle, Joseph D., 68
Belleville Substation, 130
Bergen, Frank, 196-7, 201;
  photo 197
Bergen Generating Station, 357
Bergen Turnpike Company, 102-3
BEST, 345
Betz, John F., 371, 374, 380;
  photos 356, 365
Bicycles, 117-9
Big Hill Bull Ferry Road, 58
Bill collecting, 239, 242, 244-5, 254-5
Blackouts, 45-6, 315, 326-9, 360
Blake, George H., 357, 366-7;
  photo 364
Boiler firing, 128-9;
  photo 129
Boonton Power Plant, 127
Boss, The, McKean, 205
Boston Edison Company, 161
Boyd Street Railway Station, 46

Boylan, Matthew R., 229-31
  photo 189
Brady, Pete, 65
Brandle, Theodore, 209
Bunker oils, 256-7
Burleigh, John J., 196
Burlington Generating Station, 134-5,
  284, 305, 324-5, 327,
  335, 351
Burlington windmill, 319-22, 351;
  photo 321
Burns, Henry, photo 189
Bus companies, 205-8
  equipment, 222-3
  regulation, 215-6, 218-9
  ridership, 235
  subsidies, 235
  consolidation, 206
Bus engines
  diesel, 230-1, 233
  gas-electric, 222, 230-1, 233
Bus fares, 220, 233
Bus-trolleys see Jitneys; bus engines
Buses, 215, 234
  furnishings, 223
  photo 224
Bushkill line, 307-8, 311
By-products of gas making, 27-8, 108,
  257-8;
  photos 259
Cambridge Railroad, 62
Camden Coke Works, 269, 274
Camden, Gloucester and Woodbury Line,
  93
Carbon gas, 27
Carbureted water gas process, 29-32
Carey, Robert, 206
Carlyle, Floyd, 157-8
Casazza, Jack, A., photo 337
Catalytic reforming sets, 271
Central Avenue Car House, 97
Central Power Company Station, 46
Chang, Darwin, photo 362
Chase National Bank of New York, 155
Circuit breakers, 326
Citizens Advisory Committee on
  Recreation and Natural Beauty, 370
Citizens Gas Light Company, 25, 27, 36
City Dock Generating Station, 46
  photo 37
City Subway, 233
Clark, Harlow C., 40, 42, 53
Clark, John A., 117-20
Coal, 282, 351, 354
  transportation, 282, 354

Coal ash, 129
Coal gas, 26-7, 108'
Coal gas by-products, 27-8, 108, 257-8;
  photo 259
Coal railroad cars, 282, 354
Coal-stokers, 128-9;
  photo 129
Coal Street Generating Station, 54, 56,
  130, 359
Coal tar, 27-8
Coffin, C. A. Award, 318
Cogeneration of energy, 349-51
Coke, 27, 29-30, 108, 274
Coke plants, 247, 269, 274
Competition
  gas/electric lighting, 33-7
  railroad/bus, 213-21
  bus/auto, 233-4
Connors, Patrick, photo 189
Consolidated Edison Company, 157, 375
Consolidated Traction Company, 61, 63-4
Consumer surveys, 186-8
Contracts for electricity, 33, 41
Conway, Theodore M., 97-8
Conwell, Rollin N., 283, 294, 303
Corporate control, 338-9
Corporate symbol, 23, 190, 235
Cowcatchers, 87-8;
  photo 87
Crempa, John, 329
Crockett, Richard C., photo 337
Curtis, George W., 114
Czar of New Jersey, 9-11, 145-6
Daft, Leo, 48
Daft Electric Railway System, 48;
  photo 49
Davis, Frank, 146, 150
Daytime lighting, 42
Dear, Walter, 206-7
Delaware, Lackawanna & Western
  Railroad, 316
Delmarva Power and Light Company, 355
Diaphragms, gas meters, 272-4
Diesel engines (bus) 230-1, 233
Direct current, 42, 56, 84
Ditch diggers, 119-21
Dolan, Thomas, 195
Doubleday, Ellen, McCarter, 3-4, 14-5, 18,
  68-9, 73, 75-7, 140, 146, 152, 165-85;
  photo 103
Doubleday, Nelson, 69, 168, 171
Doyle, John, 98
Drip oil, 28
Drip-tank trucks, photo 111
Dryden, John F., 25, 72-3, 195
Dusenberry, James P., 24, 85
Eagle Rock Line, 95
Earnshaw, Edward, 110

Eascogas LNG, Inc. 279
Eberle, Edward R., 277, 345, 357, 369-70;
  photos 356, 365
Eckert, Richard, M., 355;
  photo 356
Edge, Walter E., 76, 199-201,
  203-4, 208
Edgewater Ferry Line, 102
Edison, Thomas A., 76, 304;
  photo 292
Edison, Thomas, chemical meter, 41
Edison Electric Illuminating Company,
  46-8
  Roselle Station, 47-8
Edison Electric Institute, 77, 159
Edison Park Commission, 76
Edwards, Edward I. 218
Eldorado Park, 58-9
Electric appliances, 297-300
Electric clocks, 289-91
Electric companies
  appliance selling, 297-300
  beginnings, 39-43
  competition with gas, 32-7, 40
  consolidations, 43, 50, 65, 125-7,
    131-2, 158-61
  cooperation, 306, 312-3, 345, 361
  early problems, 33-4
  energy research, 344-6
  finance, 134-5
  first N.J. company, 40
  founding, 40, 43
  investors, 40, 48
  management, 377-81
  securities, 336, 338
  subsidiaries, 336, 338-9
  war time operations, 136-7, 233, 269,
    335-6
Electric failures, 42, 45-6, 315, 326-9, 360
Electric light poles, 329-30
Electric lighting, 33-7, 39-41, 52, 106-7
  gas competition, 33-7, 40
Electric lines, 283
  environmental aspects, 330-3, 375
  installation, 306-12, 315-6
  overhead, 191, 329-32, 375
  regulation, 331-3
  towers, 306-11, 315-6
  underground, 131-2, 332-3, 375
Electric meters, 33-4, 41
Electric Park, 93
Electric power distribution, 42, 84, 125-6,
  283-4
  alternating current, 56, 84, 289-91
  direct current, 42, 56, 84
  reliability, 130-1
Electric power failures, 42, 45-6, 315,
  326-9, 360

Electric power forecasting, 293-5, 335,
347, 355
Electric power plants, 357-62
abandonment, 130-134, 304
capacity, 357-9
coal supply, 282
design and construction, 293-4,
301-4
early stations, 40-59
equipment, 50-6, 127-9, 135, 284-5,
323-5, 335, 360
fires, 45-6, 325-8
independent stations, 123-5, 127,
316-7
load, 312-3, 347
management, 317
pollution control, 369
power station crews, 50-3, 79, 123-5,
127, 316; photos, 122
safety measures, 326
water supply, 130
Electric power plants, Railroad, 48-9, 54,
59, 79, 81-2, 84, 124-5, 128
Electric Power Research Institute, 345
Electric power storage, 345, 361-2
Electric Railway Journal
on poor rail extension, 210
on public benefits of Public Service, 84
on view from Palisades, 95
Electric rates, 39, 41, 43
Electric street cars *see* Street railroads
Electric substations, 84, 127-8, 130-1, 134
Electric Utility Industry Task Force on
Environment, 369
Electric workers, 47
coal stokers, 128-9
lineman, 46-7, 299, 307-12
meter readers, 237-46
power station crews, 50-3, 123-5, 127,
316; photos, 122
topmen, 308-11
Electric World
on early electric company
consolidations, 43
on electric power, 282
on Kearny power plant, 302-3
on Public Service Electric Co., 282
on River Station fire, 45-6
on saloon electric usage, 287
on street railway service, 125-6
on World War I operations, 137
Electricity sales, 371-2
Elizabeth Journal
McCarter on railway complaints, 83
Elizabethtown Gas Company, 277, 279
Elmora Line, 229
Energy conservation, 348
Energy crisis, 347-51, 380

Energy Development Corporation, 278-9
Energy Laboratory, 295-300, 344
Energy research, 319-22, 344-5, 347-51
Energy storage, 345, 361-2
Environmental aspects
air pollution, 369
electric lines, 330-3, 375
nuclear power plants, 350-1, 374-6
Essex and Hudson Gas Company, 70, 154
Essex Club, 41
Essex County Electric Company, 43
Essex Generating Station, 134-7, 284-6,
288-90, 302-3, 305, 316,
325-7, 357, 360
Essex Passenger Railway Company, 63
Excelsior Electric Company of Harrison,
New Jersey, 43
Exxon Corporation, 350, 358
Fabulous 5000, photo 224
Fagan, Mark, 80, 208
Faraday, Michael, 56
Fares
bus, 233, 235
ferry, 94
trolley, 88, 93-4, 101, 210, 212,
215-6, 221
Fares, Please, Miller, 63, 222
Farrand, Dudley, 40-1, 55, 132, 304
Fast Line, 96, 233, 315;
photos 91, 224
Faulkner, Frank K.,
photo 337
Fenders (railway cars),
photo, 87
Ferry operations, 93-5, 101-2
fares, 94
Fidelity Union Trust Company, 9-10, 70,
72, 154-5
Finch, Charles V., 203-5
Fires, 45-6, 264-5, 325-8
Fitzgerald, F. Scott, 75, 156-7
Fleisch, A.J. 253
Floating nuclear power plants, 355;
illustration 356
Forecasting electric power, 293-5, 335,
347, 355
Fort Lee (ferry), photo 103
Fortune Magazine
on Public Service legislative influence, 3,
193
on streetcar accident, 65-6
on water gas making 29-30
Fox Film Corporation, 74-5, 147-8
Francis, Edward T., 45-6, 86-101, 128-29,
209, 228; photo 337
Fredonia Natural Gas Light Company,
268
Front Street Gas Works, 260

Fuel cell power plants, 345
Fuel cells, 344-5
Fuel research, 344-5, 347-51
Fusion power, 344-5, 355
Gannett News Service, 188
Garbage as fuel, 278-9
Garven, Pierre P., 203-4
Gas Age
  on gas asphyxiation, 260
Gas appliances, 27, 105-7, 252-5;
  photos 107-266
  advertisement, 104
  burner adjustments, 271-2
  gas ranges, photo 107
Gas companies
  appliance selling, 105, 252-5
  beginnings, 23-5
  by-product selling, 27-8
  competition with electricity, 32-7
  consolidation, 25, 65, 107
  early problems, 33-4
  first company, 268
  marketing, 105
  securities, 24-5
Gas cooking, 105-6
Gas distribution, 108, 110-11, 248, 271,
  274, 276
Gas-electric buses, 222, 230-1, 233
Gas exploration, 277-9
Gas explosions, 261-3
Gas heating, 269
Gas leaks, 258-65, 273
Gas lighting, 25-7, 32-7, 106-7, 279-80
  electric competition, 33-7
Gas mains *see* Gas pipes
Gas mantle, 34-5, 37
Gas manufacture, 26, 247, 256-7, 273-4,
  277-8
  by-products, 27-8, 257
  hazards, 258-65
  water gas, 29-32
Gas meters, 33-4, 36, 272-3
  diaphragms, 272-4
Gas oil, 256-7
Gas pipe laying, 111-2, 119-21, 248-51;
  photos 113, 249-51, 275
Gas pipelines, 270
Gas pipes, 108, 112, 119, 248, 272-4
  drippage, 111
  iron pipes, 256, 276
  joints, 112-3, 273
  maintenance, 121
  plastic pipes, 276
  steel pipes, 256, 276
Gas prices, 25, 33, 114
Gas ranges *see* Gas appliances
Gas sales, 25, 372-3
Gas sets *see* Water gas sets

Gas tips, 34-5
Gas workers, 114-21; photos 22, 113, 118
  hazards, 260-2
  transportation, 116-9
  wages, 119
Gas Works, 116, 247, 256-7, 268, 274,
  277; photo 24
  abandonment, 274
  automation, 112-4
  by-products, 27-8
  capacity, 269, 271
  equipment, 108-9, 256, 271
  first in New Jersey, 24
  interconnection, 108, 248
  load, 276-7
Gasoline tax, 226-7
General Electric Company, 318, 322
Generating stations *see* Electric power
  plants; Electric power plants,
  Railroad; Nuclear power plants
Geothermal energy, 351
Gilhooley, John J., 235
Gilkeson, Bob, 377
Gillen, Charles, P., 200-1
Gloucester line, 229
Gourley, William B., 198
Government ownership, 188
Grand View Park, 93
Gray, George R., 195
Great Gatsby, The, Fitzgerald, 75, 156
Grigat, William, 237-46; photo 236
Griggs, John W., 70
Grundy, J. Owen, 207
Guy, Elmer, 100-1
Hackensack (ferry), 102
Hackensack River gas main, 112
Hague, Frank, 9, 151, 199, 205-9
Haines, William Wister, 308-11
Harper, Herbert E., 234-5
Harris, Louis, and Associates, 187
Harrison Gas Works, 118, 255, 269, 274
Harrison Line, 61
Hart, William A., 267
Heat rate, 54, 317-8, 336
Heating by gas, 269
Heller, Herbert H., photo 337
Hoboken Generating Station, 128; photo,
  51
Hoboken substation, 124-5
Holding Company Act of 1935, 336, 341
Holland Tunnel, 76, 101
Honest John, 69, 71
Hooven, Morris D., Jr., 294-5
Hoover, Herbert Clark, 17, 148
Hope Creek Generating Station, 355
Horner, Arthur, 328-9
Horse-car operators, 58-9, 61
Horse cars, 57-63

Hot water heaters *see* Gas appliances
Hudson County Electric Company, 43
Hudson Generating Station, 129, 358-60
Hurricanes, 325, 328-9
Hydroelectric power, 351
Incandescent lights, 35, 41-3
Inclined elevators, 94-5, 101
Industrial power usage
    electric, 40-3, 136-7, 316, 335
    gas, 249, 251, 255, 269
Insulation (wiring), 47
Insull, Samuel, 159
Interconnected electric utility systems,
    123, 126-7, 130-1,
    289-90, 295, 305-7, 312-18,
    338
Interconnected gas systems, 248
Interstate Bridge and Tunnel Authority
Investors (electric utilities), 40, 48
Iron pipes, 256, 276
Jackson, Philip N. 45
Jersey Central Power & Light Company,
    316, 347, 361-2
Jersey City and Hoboken Gas Light
    Company, 26
Jersey City Daily Times,
    on 1865 street lighting, 26
Jersey City Electric Light Company, 43
Jersey City, Hoboken and Paterson Street
    Railway Company, 102
Jitneys, 213-20
Johnson, Andrew, photo 362
Johnson, Walter, H., 306
Jones, Mrs. H. A., 252
Kearny coke plant, 247
Kearny Electric Light and Power
    Company, 43
Kearny Generating Station, 301-05, 322-6,
    328, 360
Kelly, Carlos, 69
Kelly, Madeleine McCarter, 3-4, 69, 140,
    172, 176, 179-80; photo, 178
Kenilworth Line, 100
Killgore, James, N., 120-1, 260-1
King and Queen of England's visit, 143,
    182-3
Kittatinny Mountain Project, 361-2
Knight's Park (Collingswood), 94
Koppers Company, 27, 115, 274
Kreismer, Irwin F., 263-5
Kuser, Anthony, 73
Lafayette, Marquis de, 267
Lake Wales, Florida, 77, 185
Lamplighters, 117
Lane, Jim, 116
Lawrence, Frank, photo 189
Lawson, James T., 50, 52, 55,
    287, 301, 327-8

Lawyers Building, 70, 74, 154
Leasing of land, 330
Leich, David, 278
Leinbach, Richard O., 331-2
Lenehan, Arthur F., 2
Lenihan, Edward J., photo 356
Librizzi, Frank P., photo 337
Light tar, 28
Lightning, 47-8
Lightning arresters, 48
Lime, 27-8
Lincoln Avenue Substation, 130
Lincoln Park, photo 78
Linden Generating Station, 350, 357-8
Linemen, 46-7, 307-11
    camps, 311
    safety, 299
    wages, 46
Liquefied natural gas, 276-7, 279, 376,
    storage, 276
Liquefied petroleum gas, 269
Load (electric power), 312-3, 347
Load (gas), 276-7
Load Forecasting, 293-5, 335
Load Forecasting Committee 293-4
Lobbying, 193-207, 218, 225-8
Logo, 23, 190, 235
Long Island Lighting Company, 377
Lowe, Thaddeus, S. C., 29, 31-2
Luce, Charles F., 376
Luce, Donald C., 2, 357, 367-8; photos
    365, 368
Luke (Miss), 10
Lydecker, Frederick A., photo 264
McCarter, Eliza, 68-9, 75
McCarter, Fanny A., 68
McCarter, Isobel, 168
McCarter, Jane, E., 68
McCarter, John, 69-70
McCarter, John Pierson, 69
McCarter, Madeleine Barker, 134, 140-1,
    148, 172-3, 177, 180-2; photo 181
McCarter, Mary Louise Haggerty, 68
McCarter, Robert Harris, Sr., 68, 70, 152,
    156, 158, 165-7; photo 152
McCarter, Robert Harris, 9, 68, 146, 172
McCarter, Thomas Nesbitt, 68-9
McCarter, Thomas Nesbitt, Sr. photos 150,
    152, 164, 171, 178, 181,
    189, 224, 292, 363, cartoon 192
    administration of Public Service,
    5-10, 66, 132-6, 151-63
    chairmanships, 10
    compared to Rockefeller, 152-3
    death, 7, 18
    directorships, 70, 72, 74, 154-5
    distinctions, 76-7
    on early gas companies, 37

on education, 13-4
family background, 68-70, 155-6
family relations, 74-6, 140, 157-8, 163, 165-85
founding Public Service, 67-8, 72-3, 77, 79
on interconnection, 313
legislative influence, 3
on lobbying, 3, 201
obituary, 18-20
office staff relations, 10-2, 145-50, 163
on New Jersey, 174-5
personal finances, 73-5, 147-8, 152-4
personal politics, 9, 15-8, 70, 148-9, 151-3, 158
personality, 6-7, 10-3, 71, 174-5, 183-4
portrait, 11, 184
Princeton University relations, 75-7, 147, 151
Prohibition, 14-9
public offices, 67, 70, 151-2
on railway services, 83-4
recreation, 170-2, 175-6
retirement, 155, 160, 363
royal visit, 143, 182-3
Rumsonhill, 15, 73-4, 139-44, 156-7, 173
on security holding, 339
on utility regulation, 17, 158-62
writings, 12-4, 163, 182
McCarter, Thomas Nesbitt, Jr., 69, 141, 157-8, 167, 172
McCarter, Thomas Nesbitt, 3rd., 71-7, 151-63
McCarter, Thomas N. (ferry), 102
McCarter, Uzal Haggerty, 9, 25, 68, 72, 74, 152, 156, 165, 167-8, 174, 195; photo 152
McCarter, Uzal Haggerty, 2d, 69, 141, 146, 166-8, 172
McCarter Theatre at Princeton 75-6; photo 147
McDonald, John F., 3, photo 356
McDonald, Lyle, 149, 235, 367; photo 365
McDonald, Thomas, 206
McGregor, David, 232
McKean, Dayton D., 205, 227
McKinsey & Company, Inc., 343
McMenimen, Frank, 145-50
McMenimen, Vivian, 148
Madaras Rotor Power Plant, 319-22; photo 321
Malango, Salvatore, 120-1
Maltz, Alan, photo 362
Manhattan Trust Company, 195
Marion Generating Station, 54-55, 81, 84, 127-9, 135, 284, 303, 305, 327, 335, 359
Market Street Gas Works, 23, 112, 116, 118, 255, 274; photo 264
Mason, John, 62
Mechanic Street Power Plant, 40-2, 46
Medicine, patent, 28
Meeker Election Law, 158
Mellon, Andrew W., 209
Menlo Park, 76
Mercer Generating Station, 346, 357-8, 360, 377; photo 346
Mercury boiler/turbines, 322-5
Meter reading, 237-46
Methane, 277-9
Metropolitan Railway, 62
Metuchen Power Plant, 130
Metuchen shuttle, 99
Miles, Mary Hemschoot, 177
Military Park, 39-40; photo 78
Miller, John A., 63, 222
Miller, Leo, photo 297
Modern Battles of Trenton, Sackett, 80
Moke, E., 265
Montclair Light and Power Company, 43
Moore, A. Harry, 13-4; photo 292
Morgan, J. Pierpont, 338
Morgan, Randal, 25-6
Morris County Traction Company, 97
Morristown Gas and Light Company, 110
Morristown Power Plant, 127
Morrow, Dwight, 151
Mort, Paul R., 14
Mosquitoes, 92
Motor Coach Age
on bus equipment, 222
on bus/trolley competition, 219
on Public Service rail maintenance 209-10
on the trolley-bus, 230
Motormen *see* Railroad workers
Mountain Lake Club, 77
Mulberry Street Line, 99
Murdock, William, 34-5
Murphy, Franklin, 67, 70, 197
Naphtha, 277
National Science Foundation, 346
Natural gas, 267-74
storage 270-3
Natural gas supply, 277-9
Nelson, P. H., photo 337
Nesmith, Jimmy, 328
New Brunswick—Trenton Line, 96
New Jersey Alcoholic Beverage Commission, 14-5, 19
New Jersey & Hudson River Railway and Ferry Company, 363
New Jersey Governor's School Survey Commission, 13-4
New Jersey Natural Gas Company, 279

New Jersey Power & Light Company, 316
New Jersey Public Interest Research
    Group, 350
New Jersey Traction Company, 63-4
New Year's Day reception, 163, 185
New York Chemical Bank, 62
New York Times
    McCarter's obituary, 18-20
New York Tribune
    on the Kenilworth Line, 100
    on Newark Trolley Trust, 64
    on political influence, 195
Newark
    electric lighting (1881-6), 39-42
Newark and Bloomfield Street Railway
    Company, 63
Newark and South Orange Street Railway
    Company, 63, 232
Newark, Bloomfield & Montclair Horse
    Car Company, 63
Newark Consolidated Gas Company, 25
Newark Distribution Department, 121
Newark Electric Light and Power
    Company, 24, 40-3
Newark Electric Light Company, 305
Newark Evening News
    on bus company acquisitions, 220
    on Eagle Rock Line, 92, 95-6
    on Hague attacks of Public Service, 205
    on lobbying, 196-200
    on overhead lines, 331
    on paycar robbery, 97-8
    on political attacks on Public Service,
        194
    on Public Service unpopularity, 191
    on rail removal, 331
    on railroad cars, 216
    on D. Sage, 286
    on snowstorm of 1888, 99
    on South Orange last run, 231-2
    on Wise Law, 228
Newark Gas Company, 25, 36
Newark Gas Distribution Shop, photo 118
Newark Gas Light Company, 23-5, 109,
    255; photo 22
Newark Passenger Railway Company, 63-4
Newark Schuyler Electric Light Company,
    43, 48
Newark Trolley Trust, 64-5
Newport News (ferry), 102
Niagara Mohawk Corporation, 157
Nichols Electric Light & Power Company
    of Nutley, N. J., 43
Nicolson, Henry Whitcomb, 106-7, 111,
    115-6, 118-21, photo 264
North American Holding Company of
    Chicago, 159
North American Power Systems

    Interconnection Committee, 289-90
North Jersey Rapid Transit, 96
North Jersey Street Railway Company, 54,
    64-6, 85, 195
Nuclear fusion, 344-5, 355
Nuclear power, 344-57
    public opinion, 188
Nuclear power plants, 348-55, 369; photo
    349
    environmental aspects, 374-6
    floating plants, 355; illustration, 356
    opponents, 350-1, 373-6
Ocean City Electric Railway Line, 96
Odorizing gas, 273
O'Grady, Joseph G., 295-300
Oil gas, 30
Oliver, Jay, 265
Olympic Park, 93
One Phase of a Jerseyman's Activities,
    McCarter, 12-4
Opinion surveys, 186-8
Opponents of nuclear power plants,
    350-1, 373-6
Orange Common Council, 36
Orange Crosstown Line, 94
Orange Power Station, 130
Osborne, Edmund B., 201, 205
Osgood, Farley, 300
O'Toole, John L., 203, 227
Outlaw, Edward G., 380
Overhead electric lines, 191, 329-33, 375
Oyster shells, 27-8
PJM *see* Pennsylvania-New Jersey-
    Maryland Interconnection
Palisades, 94-5, 101, 233, 366
Palisades Park, 93
Passaic Gas and Electric Company, 50
Passaic River, 28, 108
Passaic Valley Sewerage Commission, 158
Patent medicine, 28
Paterson Gas and Electric Light Company,
    108
Paterson Gas Light Company, 23, 31-2,
    109, 115
Paterson Gas Works, 27-32, 108-10, 114;
    photo 109
Paterson-Newark Line, 96
Paterson Power Plant, 128
Paymaster's car, 97-8; photo 97
Peach Bottom Generating Station, 354-5
Peak load (electric), 312-3, 347-8
Peak shaving (gas), 276-7
Peale, Rembrandt, 32-3
Pennsylvania-New Jersey-Maryland
    Interconnection, 295, 312, 314-5;
    control room photo, 314
Pennsylvania-New Jersey Transmission
    Line, 306-12, 315-6

Pennsylvania Power and Light Company, 305-6, 312
Pennsylvania Railroad Station (Newark), 76
Peoples Electric Light Company, 50, 358
Peoples Light and Power Company, 36, 43, 45-6; photos 37, 44
Perils of Pauline, 94
Perry, Irving, 327-8
Perth Amboy Power Station, 130, 137
Philadelphia Electric Company, 305-6, 312, 355, 377
Photographic services, 296-7; photo 297
Plank Road Repair Shop, 85
Plastic gas pipes, 276
Poles, electric line, 191, 329-30
Political activities, 193-209, 225-8
Political contributions, 193, 199, 203-4, 207
Port Authority Bus Terminal, 234
Potato bugs, 92
Power failures, 45-6, 315, 326-9, 360
Power generating stations *see* Electric power plants
Power plants *see* Electric power plants
Power station crews, 52-3, 123-5, 128-9; photos 122
Presidents (Public Service), 357, 363-71; photos 364-5
Pressure groups, 350, 373
Pressures on the Legislature of New Jersey, McKean, 227
Princeton University
 1st McCarter as trustee, 68
 McCarter Theatre, 75-6, 147
 football games, 76-7
Princeton University Plasma Physics Laboratory, 345
Prohibition, 15-20, 287-9
Property owners compensation, 329-30
Protests of electric lines, 329-32
Prudential Insurance Company, 72-3, 154, 156, 195
Public Interest Research Group, 350
Public opinion
 electric lines, 330-3
 nuclear power, 188
 Public Service Corporation, 80, 189-91, 330-1
 Public Service Electric and Gas Company, 186-8
 Public Service Railway Company, 191, 218, 331
 railroad operations, 82-83
Public opinion surveys, 187-8
Public Service Coordinated Transport, 205, 208, 223-6, 231, 233-5, 341
 abandonment of routes, 234

auto competition, 233-4
awards, 234
equipment, 233-4
express service, 233-4
fares, 233, 235
finance, 225
interstate commuter service, 231, 233-4
ridership, 225, 233-5
Public Service Corporation Of New Jersey
 acquisitions & mergers, 50, 153, 160-1
 awards, 318
 bus operations, 205-9, 219-26, 230-1, 233-5
 capitalization, 67, 72-3, 80
 corporate symbol, 190
 directors (first), 195
 dissolution, 341
 electric business, 50, 123-37, 225, 281-90, 293-318, 323-9, 335, 340-1
 ferry operations, 93-4, 101-2
 finance, 134-6, 159, 205, 225
 founding, 23, 67-8, 72-3, 77, 79-83
 gas business, 105-21, 133, 136, 247-65, 268-9
 name, 8, 139
 office building, photos 164, 352
 officers, 357, 363-6; photos 364-5
 out of state operations, 131, 159-60, 305
 political activities, 193-209, 218, 225-8
 public opinion, 80, 189-91, 330-1
 railroad operations, 50, 64-6, 67, 79-96, 133, 136, 204-5, 209-14, 216-21, 225-6, 228-9231-3
 revenues, 68
 securities, 336-41
 size, 161, 190
 taxi operations, 103
 turnpike operations, 102-3
 valuation, 340-1
Public Service Electric and Gas Company, 343-62
 bus operations, 231, 233-5, 341
 corporate symbol, 23; cartoon 342
 electric business, 330-3, 354-5, 357-62
 energy research, 319-22, 344-5, 347-51
 environmental department, 370
 finance, 344
 financial management, 343-4
 founding, 341
 gas business, 269-80

management, 343-4, 380-1
office building, photos 352-3
officers, 357, 363-71
public opinion, 186-8
revenues, 225
securities, 343
subway operations, 233
switch to natural gas, 271-4
Public Service Electric & Gas Energy
   Laboratory, 295-300, 344
Public Service Electric & Gas Research
   Corporation, 344-5
Public Service Electric Company, 131-7,
   281-91, 293-318, 340-1
   equipment, 284-5
   founding, 131
   size, 161
   territory, 131
   World War I operations, 137, 281-3
Public Service Gas Company, 133
Public Service Hudson River Line, 96
Public Service News
   on electric bill collecting, 287
   on electric company pioneers, 40
   on gas leaks, 260
   on gas manufacturing, 114
   on gas work hazards, 261
   on paying railroad employees, 85
   on selling of coke, 27
Public Service Production Company, 293,
   302, 339
Public Service Railway Company, 101, 133,
   136, 213-7, 220-1, 331, 363
   abandonment, 225, 228-9, 231-3
   amusement parks, 93-5
   bus operations, 220-3
   competition, 213-21
   dissolution, 228, 233
   equipment, 86-7
   fares, 205, 210-2, 215-6, 221
   ferry operations, 93-5, 101-2
   finance, 204-5, 216-7, 225
   founding, 84
   maintenance, 85, 209-10; photo 211
   public opinion, 191, 215, 218
   rail extension, 209-12
   ridership, 86, 225
   service, 88-92
   strikes, 219-21
   track, 229, 233
   World War II operations, 233
Public Service Transport Company, 229
Public Utility Holding Company Act,
   159-61
Public utility regulations, 158-60, 188,
   195-7, 203
Pumped storage, 361-2
Queen of England's visit, 143, 182-3

Quick, Donald M., 124-5
Railroad companies, 62
   amusement parks, 91, 93-5
   consolidation, 63-5, 67, 77
   finance, 63-7, 77
   investors, 48
   securities, 64-5
Railroad workers, 81-2, 85-6, 97-101;
   photo 81
Railroads, Street *see* Street railroads
Rails (railroad), 79, 81, 92
Railway power stations, 48-9, 54, 59, 79,
   81-2, 84, 124-5, 128
Randel, James B., Jr., 279
Raritan Line, 96
Rate of return, 340
Rate regulations *see* Public utility
   regulations
Reciprocating engines, 50-5, 84
Record, George L., 9, 158, 207-8
Recreational trolley operations, 91, 93-5;
   photos 78
Redshaw, William, 46-8, 130, 281
Regulations of bus operations, 215-9
Regulations of railroad companies, 214-9,
   228
Retorts, 26-7, 29
Richards, Jack V., 31, 117-8, 256
Riker, Adrian, 70
Riker, Chandler W., 70
Right-of-way (electric lines), 329-33
River Station, 43, 45-6
Riverside Park (New Brunswick), 93
Road tar, 28
Robberies, 97-8
Rockefeller, John D., 152-3
Rockland Electric Company, 316
Rockland Light and Power Company, 316
Roman, Harry, photo 362
Roosevelt, Franklin D., 9, 17-9, 159-60
Roselle Station, 47-8
Rotor power plants *see* Wind power plants
Ruffle, Clyde C., photo 337
Rumson Country Club, 170-1
Rumsonhill, 15, 73-4, 139-44, 156-7, 173,
   177; photos 138, 142
Sabotage, 329
Sackett, William E., 80
Safety testing, 297-300
Sage, Darrow, 51-4, 123-4, 284-91, 301-3,
   316, 322-3,
   326-8; photo 286
Salem Generating Station, 349, 355, 369;
   photos 297, 349
Sanderson, Clarence M., photo 337
Schiffer, Francis H., photo 337
Schneider, Frederick W., photo 356
Schoellkopf family, 157-8

Schoonejongen, Cornelius, 31-2, 114-5
Schreiber, Martin, 82, 230-1
Schwernitz, Hugo, 98
Scott, Walter, Sir, 26-7
Scott, William E., 380-1
Secaucus Station, 130
Second National Bank of Red Bank, 154
Seglie, Paul, 206
Sentinel Of Freedom
   on Newark Gas Light Co., 25
Seven Sisters Act and Seven Brothers Act,
   9, 158-9
Sewaren Generating Station, 357-8, 360
Shanley, Bernard M., 25, 336
Shepherd, Robert H., photo 337
Shock, electric, 47
Shovels, 119-20
Silzer, George S., 205, photo 171
Singac Line, 93
Slim, Haines, W. W., 308-11
Smith, Alfred E., 15-7, photo 171
Smith, Robert I. 3, 11, 347-57-, 370-1,
   376-81; photos 356, 365
Smoke (coal gas), 26-7
Smythe, Charles W., 261-2
Snowstorms, 60, 98, 99; photo 217
Snyder, Edwin H., 357, 369-70; photo 364
Solar energy, 344, 348-9, 362
Sonn, Harold, 344
South Amboy, munitions explosion, 263-5
South Amboy Gas Plant, 110-1
South Jersey Gas Company, 279
South Jersey Gas, Electric and Traction
   Company, 50, 108
South Orange Avenue Line, 63, 93, 231-2
Speer, William, 228
Springfield Avenue Line, 93
Staten Island Edison Company, 316
Statue of Liberty, photo 38
Steam dummies, 62
Steel pipes, 256, 276
Stevenson, Robert Louis, 35-6
Straub, Louis, 57-60; photo 189
Street gangs *see* Gas workers
Street lighting *see* Electric lighting; Gas
   lighting
Street paving, 225-6
Street railroad companies *see* Railroad
   companies
Street Railroads
   abandonment, 225, 228-9, 231-3
   accidents, 65-7, 77, 88
   amusement parks, 91, 93-5
   bridge use, 228
   cars, 79-81, 84-92, 97
   electric powered, 57, 59, 62-5
   employees, 58-60, 81-2, 85-6, 97-101,
      221; photo 81

wages, 85
   equipment, 79-84
   fares, 88, 93-4, 101, 209-212, 215-6, 221
   first, 48
   final service, 231-2
   horse drawn, 57-63
   inclined elevators, 94-5, 101
   insect problems, 92
   maintenance, 79-80, 83-5; photo 211
   passenger traffic, 86
   power stations, 48-9, 54, 59, 79, 81-2,
      84, 124-5, 128
   public opinion, 80, 83
   rails, 79, 81, 92; photo 211
   recreational operations, 93-4
   regulations, 214-9, 228
   routes, 95-7, 100-1
   service, 79, 82-3, 86, 88, 97, 99-101
   street paving, 225-6
   street traffic, 90, 229-30
   strikes, 82, 219-21
   summer operations, 91-4
   trestles, photo 124
   unions, 81-2, 220
   winter operations, 60, 82, 97-9; photo
      217
Street traffic (trolleys), 90, 229-30; photos
   89, 229
Strikes
   bus, 205
   railroad, 82, 219-21
Submarine squadron, 193-207, 218, 225-8
Subsidiaries, 336, 338-9
Subsidies (bus), 235
Substations, 84, 127-8, 130-1, 134
Suburban Electric Light and Power
   Company, 43
Sui, Ralph, 378
Summit and Morristown Distribution
   Shop, 118
Sunday Call
   on Public Service founding, 80
   on Public Service and politicians, 199
Sunfish Pond, 362
Swamp Line, 100
Synthetic natural gas, 277
TNJ, 235
Tait, Watson F., Jr., 357, 369, photo 364
Tar, 27-8, 30
Taxi operations, 103
Teitelbaum, Arthur, photo 337
Tenafly (ferry), 102; photo 103
Tennessee Gas Transmission Company,
   270
Tennessee Valley Authority, 19
Testing Laboratory, 295-300, 344
Texas Eastern Transmission Corp., 270
Thermal pollution, 377

Thier, J. Ernest, 228
Thomson and Houston Electric Light
    Power and Heating Company of
    Newark, N.J., 43
Thorne log, 63
Tidal energy, 351
Tocks Island Dam, 362
Tomkins, Robert S., 85
Topmen, 308-11; photo 309
Tow boys, 57-8
Towers, Transmission *see* Transmission
    towers
Traction companies *see* Railroad
    companies
Trademark, 23, 190, 235
Transcontinental Gas Pipe Line Corp.,
    270, 276
Transformers, 56
Transit Journal
    on bus equipment, 222
Transmission lines *see* Electric lines
Transmission towers, 306-12, 315-6;
    photos 307, 309, 331
Transport of New Jersey, 235
Trenton Generating Station, 358
Triangle (corporate symbol), 23, 190
Trollye-bus *see* Bus engines; Jitneys
Trolley cars, 79-81, 83-92, 97, 216; photos
    78, 87, 89, 91, 217
Trolley companies *see* Railroad companies
Trolleys *see* Street railroads
Troxell, Clarence G., photo 337
Turbines, 53-5, 128, 324-5, 360-1; photo
    337
Turbo-generators, 53-6
Turnpike operations, 102-3
Underground electric lines, 131-2, 332-3
Union County Trust Company, 154
Union Line, 96
Unions, Railroad, 81-2, 220
United Corporation of New York, 160,
    209, 336, 338-9
United Electric Company, 50
United Engineers and Constructors, 339
United Gas Improvement Company of
    Philadelphia, 25-6, 73, 107, 114, 160-1,
    195,
    209, 336, 338-9
United Technologies Corp., 345
U.S. Department of Energy, 345
Valley Road Line, 229

Vanderpool, Beach, 25
Vanity Fair, Thackeray, 14
Venturi, Ron, photo 342
Violett, Atwood, 168
Voorhees, Daniel, 197
Wakelee, Edmund W., 197-8, 200, 216-8,
    363, 366; photos 197, 364
Ward, Leslie D., 195
Ward, Marcus L., 25
Washington Park, 93
Water gas, 29-32
Water gas sets, 29-32, 108-10, 112, 114,
    247, 256, 271
Water heaters, 105; photo 266
Water supply, 130
Waterbury, John I., 73, 195
Watered stock (railroads), 64-5, 80, 159
Way, Walter, 231
Welsbach (mantle) burner, 34-5, 37
Welsbach Street Illuminating Company,
    35, 117
West End Works, 112, 269
West Jersey Seashore Railroad, 96
Weston, Edward, 34, 39-40
Weston Electric Lighting Company, 39
Whitcomb, Henry D., 106-7, 115-6
Whitcomb, John G., 27, 108, 114
White Line, 94-5
Wilson, Thomas L., photo 337
Wilson, Woodrow, 9, 158
Wind power plants, 319-22, 351; photo
    321
Windmills, 319-22, 351; photo 321
Wise, Russell S., 228
Wise Law, 228
Wittpenn, Otto, 199-201
Woodlynne Park (Camden), 93
Working women, 20
World War I, 119, 136-7, 281-3
World War II, 233, 269, 335-6
Wort, Charles, photo 189
Wottrich, Herbert, photo 337
Yards Creek Pumped—Storage
    Generation Station, 361-2
Yellow Cab Company, 103
Young, E.F.C., 195
Young, Percy S., 85-6, 220-1
Zachary, Robert, 227
Zechella, Alexander P., photo 356
Zone fare system, 205, 215-6, 233